INTRODUCTION TO
MODERN THEOLOGY

Trajectories in the German Tradition

John E. Wilson

WJK WESTMINSTER
JOHN KNOX PRESS
LOUISVILLE · KENTUCKY

Book design by Sharon Adams
Cover design by Mark Abrams

First edition
Published by Westminster John Knox Press
Louisville, Kentucky

This book is printed on acid-free paper that meets the American National Standards Institute Z39.48 standard. ∞

07 08 09 10 11 12 13 14 15 16—10 9 8 7 6 5 4 3 2 1

Library of Congress Cataloging-in-Publication Data

Wilson, John Elbert
    Introduction to modern theology : trajectories in the German tradition.—1st ed.
        p. cm.
    Includes bibliographical references and index.
    ISBN-13: 978-0-664-22862-0 (alk. paper)
    ISBN-10: 0-664-22862-3 (alk. paper)
    1. Theology, Doctrinal—Germany—History—19th century. 2. Protestant churches—Germany—Doctrines—History—19th century. 3. Theology, Doctrinal—Germany—History—20th century. 4. Protestant churches—Germany—Doctrines—History—20th century. I. Title.

    BT30.G3W55   2007
    230'.0440943—dc22   2006053041

Contents

Preface

Karl Barth once justified confining a history of theology in the nineteenth century to a history of German Protestant theology by saying that German theology "was the signpost for theological endeavor elsewhere."[1] This is not entirely true, but it is true enough to warrant the concentration of the present work on the Protestant German-language tradition in the nineteenth century and, by extension of Barth's judgment, in most of the twentieth century, in which Barth himself was a major directional sign. In significant ways this tradition is also an American tradition, and in chapters 2, 4, and 7 major American figures are discussed.[2] I have sought to allow the theologians to speak for themselves, in their own words and concepts. Theological history is made up of words and concepts embedded in traditions of their use. A chief purpose of the present work is to demonstrate lines of continuity or trajectories in the traditions of German Protestant theology since Kant.[3] This should be of significant help in understanding

---

1. *The Humanity of God* (n.p.: John Knox Press, 1960), 11. Throughout most of this history there was little interaction of Protestant theology with Roman Catholic theology and hardly any with Eastern Orthodoxy. In fact, until after the Second World War, German Protestant theology was largely an "internal" affair. There were notable exceptions, but in the main German theologians read and conversed only with other German Protestant theologians.

2. I have not taken into account British theological developments. See, e.g., Reardon, *Religious Thought in the 19th Century*. See note 3.

3. Other histories of the period have to do with trajectories in a broad sense, whereas I have tried to demonstrate them more through their use of a relatively common language. In English, see Karl Barth, *Protestant Theology in the Nineteenth Century,* New Edition (Grand Rapids: Eerdmans, 2002); Stanley J. Grenz and Roger E. Olson, *Twentieth Century Theology* (Downers Grove, IL: InterVarsity, 1992); Alasdair Heron, *A Century of Protestant Theology* (Philadelphia: Westminster Press, 1980); F. Lichtenberger, *History of German Theology in the 19th Century,* trans. W. Hastie (Edinburgh: T. & T. Clark, 1889); James C. Livingston, *Modern Christian Thought,* 2nd ed., in 2 vols. (Upper Saddle River, NJ: Prentice-Hall, 1997); John Macquarrie, *Twentieth-Century Religious Thought* (London: SCM, 1963); J. D. Morell, *An Historical and Critical View of the Speculative Philosophy in Europe,* 2nd ed. (New York: Robert Carter, 1849) (this influential work was published in several editions); Jaroslav

the history both in its parts and as a whole. In the notes I have sought to provide access to the most important primary texts and an orientation to major secondary literature, including selected German sources.

"Modern theology" is a term that was apparently first formulated among the advocates of Ritschlian theology, but it is frequently used, and is used here, to designate the progressive stages of theological development since Kant. It includes both more conservative and more liberal theologies. Dietrich Bonhoeffer could use the term in reference to his theology.[4] Theologies that strove to be relatively timeless in their forms are not included in this history, since these forms were minimally affected by the developments considered.[5]

The first chapter is a historical overview of the political and social context of German theology for the period covered. The second chapter begins with Kant. His work marks both the culmination of the Enlightenment and, together with the French Revolution, the beginning of a new age, as those who followed him in philosophy and theology were aware.[6] Kant's critiques of reason and religion

---

Pelikan, *The Christian Tradition*, vol. 5, *Christian Doctrine and Modern Culture (since 1700)* (Chicago: University of Chicago Press, 1989); B. M. G. Reardon, *Religious Thought in the Nineteenth Century* (Cambridge: Cambridge University Press, 1966); Helmut Thielicke, *The Evangelical Faith*, trans. Geoffrey W. Bromiley, 2 vols. (Grand Rapids: Eerdmans, 1972, 1974); Thielicke, *Modern Faith and Thought*, trans. Geoffrey W. Bromiley (Grand Rapids: Eerdmans, 1990); Paul Tillich, *A History of Christian Thought* (New York: Simon & Schuster, 1968); Claude Welch, *Protestant Thought in the Nineteenth Century*, 2 vols. (New Haven, CT: Yale University Press, 1972, 1985); Heinz Zahrnt, *The Question of God*, trans. R. A. Wilson (London: Collins, 1969). In German: Carl Andresen, ed., *Handbuch der Dogmen- und Theologiegeschichte*, 3 vols. (Göttingen: Vandenhoeck & Ruprecht, 1988), vols. 2 and 3; Martin Greschat, ed., *Theologen des Protestantismus im 19. und 20. Jahrhundert*, 2 vols. (Stuttgart: Kohlhammer, 1978); Martin Greschat, ed., *Gestalten der Kirchengeschichte*, in 11 vols., volumes 8–10 (Stuttgart: Kohlhammer, 1984–86); Emanuel Hirsch, *Geschichte der neuern evangelischen Theologie*, vol. 5 (Gütersloh: Gerd Mohn, 1960); Friedrich Wilhelm Kantzenbach, *Programme der Theologie* (Munich: Claudius, 1978); Hans-Walter Krumwiede, *Geschichte des Christentums III: Neuzeit* (Stuttgart: Kohlhammer, 1977); Friedrich Mildenberger, *Geschichte der deutschen evangelischen Theologie im 19. und 20. Jahrhundert* (Stuttgart: Kohlhammer, 1981); Bernhard Pünjer, *Geschichte der christlichen Religionsphilosophie seit der Reformation*, vol. 2, *Von Kant his auf die Gegenwart*, 1st ed. 1883 (Brussels: Cultur et Civilization, 1969); Hans-Jörg Reese, *Bekenntnis und Bekennen. Vom 19. Jahrhundert zum Kirchenkampf der nationalsozialistischen Zeit* (Göttingen: Vandenhoeck & Ruprecht, 1974); Jan Rohls, *Protestantische Theologie der Neuzeit*, 2 vols. (Tübingen: Mohr Siebeck, 1997).

4. "I feel obliged to tackle these questions as one who, although a 'modern theologian,' is still aware of the debt he owes to liberal theology." Bonhoeffer is speaking of moving away from dogmatic theology into "the open air of intellectual discussion with the world." Dietrich Bonhoeffer, *Letters and Papers from Prison*, ed. Eberhard Bethge (New York: Touchstone, 1997), 378.

5. Cf., e.g., Hengstenberg in chap. 1.2 below. The attempt to maintain unchanging forms of doctrine, practice, and thought applies also to philosophy that opposes the permanency of "classical" forms to historical development, as, e.g., in Leo Strauss, *Natural Right and History* (Chicago: University of Chicago Press, 1953), and *Spinoza's Critique of Religion* (New York: Schocken Books, 1965). See the discussion in Hans-Georg Gadamer, *Truth and Method* (New York: Seabury, 1975), 482–90.

6. See, e.g., Jürgen Habermas, *The Philosophical Discourse of Modernity*, trans. Frederick Lawrence (Cambridge: MIT Press, 1987), 1–50. The Enlightenment or "Age of Reason" characterizes most of the eighteenth century, but there are no firm boundaries and much overlapping with old and new movements. A broader history would include, e.g., discussion of the influence of Rousseau, Leibniz, and Lessing. In theology see Karl Barth, *Protestant Theology in the Nineteenth Century*, chaps. 2–4; Paul Tillich, *A History of Christian Thought*, part 2, chaps. 1–2; Jaroslav Pelikan, *Christian Doctrine and Modern Culture*; Bernhard Pünjer, *History of the Christian Philosophy of Religion: From the Reformation to Kant*, trans. W. Hastie (Edinburgh: T. & T. Clark, 1887).

should be understood relatively well in order to avoid confusion about his later influence, therefore I have taken the reader step by step through his most important concepts. Kant is the point of departure for philosophical Idealism, and since later theology also presupposes the basic thought of Idealism, I have attempted to move in (more or less simplified) steps also through this development. In fact the whole of chapter 2 is foundational for the remaining chapters of the book. In the interest of following a certain trajectory from Kant through Idealism to post-Idealist thought in the 1840s, I have chosen to discuss Schleiermacher's magnum opus, *The Christian Faith,* following the discussion of this trajectory. The present work concludes with a group of German theologians who came to prominence in the 1960s, a decade of epochal significance in many respects. In order to remain within the confines of history I have limited discussion of these theologians to works mainly from the 1960s and early 1970s, in which the basis for their later thought was established, but I have also indicated the directions of their later work.

There are persons in this history that previous histories have either omitted or given only brief summary treatment: Schelling, Franz Overbeck, and Karl Hase, who illustrates a certain kind of mediation theology. Schelling and his influence are deserving of more attention than they have usually received. Other kinds of history—denominational history, the history of biblical interpretation, the history of Reformation Theology in the modern period—include theologians, events, and subject matter not considered here.

Understanding theology is a matter of understanding the language of its concepts. In most cases discussed here the key concepts stem from the theological and philosophical tradition. However, some concepts and terms developed in Kant and in Idealism are both new and significant for subsequent theology. They are discussed in the historical contexts in which they first came to prominence, which means in chapter 2, and mainly in the first three sections of the chapter: Kant, Early Idealism, and Hegel. Terms that are important for later chapters are italicized for easier recognition. In Idealism and in history after Idealism, the German word *Wissenschaft,* which is translated as "science," broadly referred not only to the natural sciences but also to philosophy and theology as the disciplined knowledge (*Wissen*) of their subject areas. Another important term is *Kultur,* which in German has both the narrow English sense of "culture" (the arts) and a broader sense that approaches "civilization." Only the context indicates the meaning.

References to primary literature are in parentheses. Cross-references to sections of the present work stand in square brackets and refer to chapter and section numbers. Square brackets also designate my additions for clarification within quotations. Where published English translations of texts are not clearly identified, the translations are my own.

My thanks for motivating this work and making it possible go first to my students, especially those who asked for more. My indebtedness to teachers, colleagues, friends, and family encompasses a number too great to name. Perhaps it is not untoward also to thank the spirits who wrote the books that I have had the great privilege of reading. Special thanks are due to Pittsburgh Theological Seminary for a generous sabbatical leave. I also express my thankful appreciation for the seminary's very fine library and its devoted staff. Finally I thank my gracious editor at Westminster John Knox Press, Don McKim.

Chapter 1

Germany: Historical Overview

1.1 REVOLUTION AND CLASSICISM

At a time when the newly born United States was in the process of consolidating its republic, the French Revolution erupted in a mire of democratic idealism and terror. Across Europe the very news of it spread enthusiasm among the underprivileged and the forward-looking intellectuals and at the same time fear and loathing among those who saw the revolution as the destruction of Christian society and the divinely ordained order of princes and kings. From the beginning the revolution had to defend itself against military alliances of the surrounding countries, and eventually it found in Napoleon Bonaparte (1769–1821) the general who could guarantee its continuance. His military successes forced the old aristocratic regimes to either enter alliances with him or suffer occupation and replacement. The popular support the French cause initially enjoyed among much of the middle and laboring classes in Europe turned with time to resentment, as ever again French armies marched across or occupied this or that country in ceaseless effort to dominate their enemies and quell revolts. At times conquest and occupation were cruel and barbaric. After Napoleon's defeat at Waterloo in

1815, the dominant mood in the countries he had earlier conquered was generally conservative. Strong patriotic feelings had been stirred, and patriotism meant reaffirming tradition both in government and religion. In 1817 Protestant Germany celebrated the 300th anniversary of the beginning of the Reformation by lifting up Luther as a national hero in the cause of freedom. These events joined with and gave new impetus to a broad religious movement that had emerged originally from Pietist circles around 1780, the "Awakening," which rekindled the religious values of personal spiritual experience and belief in the facts of revelation history. The "restoration" of the old order after Napoleon, however, was limited, insofar as across Europe the rise of the middle class, having been freed from aristocratic domination and now growing with the beginnings of the nineteenth century's Industrial Revolution, prevented the simple return to the way things had been before. And yet for the time being there were no innovations in government that opened the way for the transition to a modern social and political order.

The decade from 1780 to 1790 was the period of *Sturm und Drang* in German literature in which Romantic impulses especially from prerevolutionary France sparked a new sense of vitality. It celebrated the beauty of nature and the natural, as especially expressed in the early literary work of Johann Wolfgang von Goethe (1749–1832). In the context of old Europe the thought of the young Goethe was revolutionary in opening new horizons in intellectual life and social thought. In theology Johann Gottfried Herder (1744–1803) envisioned religious history as dynamic and progressively evolving.[1]

All of these influences were factors in shaping the highly creative "classical period" of German philosophy and literature, the "age of Goethe"—an age of sharp contrasts: revolutionary in Napoleon's early years, conservative in his last years and afterward. Goethe himself supported the restoration of the old order. The most innovative work took place prior to the restoration, when the major figures—Kant, Fichte, Schelling, Hegel (whose traditions were Lutheran) and Schleiermacher (from the Reformed tradition)—developed new forms of reconciliation of Christianity and reason, and indeed so effectively that there is no Protestant theologian in nineteenth-century Germany who does not deal with them in one way or another. Especially Hegel developed the understanding of history as the evolving harmony of Christianity with science and knowledge, a thought he based on the conviction that Christianity contained the absolute truth. He also thought that the best political governance was by the educated elite. But controversy followed in the wake of these philosophers: in the churches, controversy that centered in the question about the relationship of tradition to the new thought.

---

1. See Helmut Thielicke, *Modern Faith and Thought*, trans. Geoffrey W. Bromiley (Grand Rapids: Eerdmans, 1990), 51–139, 255ff.; see also Wilhelm Dilthey, *Selected Writings*, trans. H. P. Rickman (Cambridge: Cambridge University Press, 1976), 46–67. The Awakening and *Sturm und Drang* are often inseparable in the leading Protestant theologians of the time, who were, besides Herder, Johann Kaspar Lavater (1741–1801), Heinrich Jung-Stilling (1740–1817), and Johann Georg Hamann (1730–88). On Herder and Hamann, see Frederick C. Beiser, *The Fate of Reason: German Philosophy from Kant to Fichte* (Cambridge: Harvard University Press, 1987), chap. 5.

This creative period was associated with and influenced by another development in German culture. Beginning in the late Enlightenment, German scholarship not only intensely explored but also in significant ways identified with classical Greek antiquity. Histories of the pre-Christian world during and after this period were typically of developments that led up to the dawn of Greek culture and dwelled on the Greeks before moving on to Rome. Schleiermacher's translation of Plato's works is representative of theological interest, as is the renewal of the study of Greek patristic theology. Classicism dominated both the universities and the Greek-named gymnasium, the preparatory school for university studies, until the late nineteenth century.[2] A century and more of great music composers, performers, and orchestras enhanced the sense of cultural elitism; instrumental music within the home became a sign of higher culture and discipline. The period marked by the dates 1780 to 1830 is also with regard to music the classical period in German cultural history.

In the eighteenth century new German universities were founded and old universities reformed, mainly for the purpose of training servants of the state and specialists in technical sciences.[3] All universities had theological faculties supported by the state. The Reformation had highly valued the theological education of ministers in the universities, a tradition born in the Middle Ages but that emerged in full bloom in the Renaissance and the Reformation itself. In the last half of the eighteenth century emphasis in theological education began to be placed more on freedom of research than on conformity to dogma, which favored the development of both criticism in theology and the concept of academic freedom generally. But academic freedom was never considered unlimited. During the age of Enlightenment the university theological faculties were still governed by their respective confessional heritages, and university professors of theology and pastors were—and still are—required to take an oath obligating them to their church's confessional standards.[4] Since these positions were under the authority of the state, control and enforcement of the oaths were ultimately in the hands of the state, although the first line of discipline was in the faculties themselves.

2. Manfred Landfester, *Humanismus und Gesellschaft im 19. Jahrhundert* (Darmstadt: Wissenschaftliche Buchgesellschaft, 1988). The cultural elite were from the middle class, but gifted children of poorer parents could be sponsored for advancement—as was Kant.

3. The policies of Frederick the Great, king of Prussia from 1740 until 1786, were instrumental in this development. The Christian confessions in Prussia and its territories—the Lutheran majority, the large Catholic minority, and the smaller Reformed minority—all enjoyed equal protection. Jewish communities were also protected but were required to pay a supplementary tax. Walther Hubatsch, "Friedrich II., der Grosse, von Preussen," in Martin Greschat, ed., *Gestalten der Kirchengeschichte*, 11 vols. (Stuttgart: Kohlhammer, 1983), 8:313–26; Frank Eyck, *Religion and Politics in German History: From the Beginnings to the French Revolution* (New York: St. Martin's, 1998), esp. 340–62; Nicholas Hope, *German and Scandinavian Protestantism, 1700–1918* (New York: Oxford University Press, 1995).

4. Hajo Holborn, *A History of Modern Germany*, 2 vols. (New York: Alfred A. Knopf, 1973), 1:274f. Academic freedom (and freedom in publishing) was therefore limited. Particularly in the restoration after Napoleon, writings considered subversive were prohibited. Some principalities were more liberal than others. See also Frank Eyck, *Religion and Politics in German History: From the Beginnings to the French Revolution*.

Germany was not a united nation until 1870. Prior to this it was a loose federation of principalities, each with its established church. Lutherans were in the majority. There was a large Roman Catholic minority, and a smaller Reformed minority was concentrated mainly in western principalities.[5] Switzerland was also a federation of states or cantons, each having its own government of state and church. The Reformed cantons were mainly German speaking and, with the exception of Geneva, were located in the north, bordering on or in proximity to Germany. Until World War I the border was open, and cultural and economic developments were largely the same on both sides. The cantonal governments were democratically elected (by restricted electorates). Although the Swiss Reformed churches had the form of synods in church government, they, like the German churches, remained under governmental supervision in Switzerland until the mid- or, in some cases, the late nineteenth century. Democratic government opened a path for liberal politics and appointments to the theological faculties that was possible in Germany only where liberal-minded princes ruled.[6]

1.2 THE RESTORATION

The Congress of Vienna at the end of the era of Napoleon directed the restoration of the old order. The ideal of the restoration was expressed by the Holy Alliance signed in Paris in 1815 by the monarchs of Russia, Austria, and Prussia. It was influenced by the Awakening and clearly religious in nature. It affirmed that these three countries, representing Eastern Orthodoxy, Roman Catholicism, and Protestantism, were parts of one Christian nation whose true ruler is Christ. Its purpose was to preserve and perpetuate peace, justice, and religion on the continent of Europe. It further affirmed the "principle of legitimacy," God's ordered

---

5. Germany did not have church movements of a national scale united by common interests, as in Britain and America. Traditional regional Pietist areas in western and southwestern Germany, in Prussia and in Switzerland continued as areas of Pietist strength throughout the nineteenth century, and in some cases there was important missionary work. The world-missionary efforts of Britain's churches in the eighteenth century stood in connection with its expanding colonial empire. It is hard to imagine a German cleric in this century proclaiming, "The world is my parish," as did John Wesley (including the missions-minded Pietist leader, A. H. Francke). In Germany home missions, while having always been actively engaged by Pietist groups, did not become a united effort until approximately 1850, and even so it was mainly Pietist. See Nicholas M. Railton, *No North Sea: The Anglo-German Evangelical Network in the Middle of the Nineteenth Century* (Leiden: Brill, 2000), 93ff. In the nineteenth century the missionary work of British and American evangelicals led to the formation of a new German word, *evangelikal*, based phonetically on the English word, that is still used to designate evangelical churches and movements. In the post-Napoleonic period, the old word *evangelisch* was used to designate the movement to unite the Lutheran and Reformed churches (see below). Prior to that, *evangelisch* had been used for the churches of the Reformation, but far more often in everyday language one made the distinction between Lutheran and Reformed. The term "Protestant" is not as common in German as it is in English.

6. See Rudolf Pfister, *Kirchengeschichte der Schweiz*, 3 vols. (Zurich: Zwingli Verlag, 1964–84); Lukas Vischer, Lukas Scheker, and Rudolf Dellsperger, eds., *Ökumenische Kirchengeschichte der Schweiz* (Basel: Friedrich Reinhardt, 1994).

rule of life under kings.[7] This centuries-old sacred tradition, shared by all the monarchies in Europe, dominated the church's understanding of the relationship between state and church ("throne and altar") in Germany until Bismarck and beyond. There was also an important connection between the monarchies of England and Germany, namely, the German line of kings and queens that has ruled Great Britain since 1714, a relationship that particularly Queen Victoria renewed.[8] It was of influence not only for military alliances but also, in the nineteenth century, for cooperative efforts among the churches.

The union of the Lutheran and Reformed churches of Germany became a prominent issue in patriotic sentiment after Napoleon, an issue in which the connection between the English and German monarchies played a role. Frederick Wilhelm III, king of Prussia from 1797 to 1840, had been impressed by the unity of traditions the Church of England represented. The Prussian royal family had long been of the Reformed confession, although its subjects were largely Lutheran. The king's wife was Lutheran and, because of still surviving orthodox restrictions, he could not worship with her. In 1817 he followed the union idea and took the step of proposing a United Church in Prussia, which found enough support to become a reality, although there was also strong dissention among the majority Lutherans. Since the Reformation the Reformed churches had been more open to the idea of union than the Lutherans. The most important theologian at the university in Berlin, Schleiermacher, who was Reformed, supported the union, as did other university theologians. Schleiermacher did not think it possible to reconcile the Lutheran and Reformed confessions with new doctrines. He rather thought that only Scripture and, for the Eucharist, the words of Christ alone could provide the basis for union, since they had priority before the disunity represented by the confessions. Schleiermacher's doctrine of the church was also of importance for the union. The church is primarily the community of faith and practice in Christ; hence Lutheran and Reformed are already in Christian unity.[9] There were other elements in the church that supported the union: the Pietist centers of the Awakening and the recently founded Bible and

7. Sheehan, *German History,* 391ff. The conflict between the ideal of the Holy Alliance (which Sheehan and many other historians describe as "medieval") and the realities of post-Napoleonic Europe is reflected in Metternich's saying that he had been born "too late or too early": too late to enjoy life in the old society, too early to build a new one (ibid., 392).

8. An example of Queen Victoria's many and various links with Germany was a popular work of meditations from which she selected sections for translation into English: Johann Heinrich Daniel Zchokke, *Stunden der Andacht,* published in eight volumes between 1809 and 1816. It is a good example of the fusion of rationalism with a poetic and mildly Pietist spirituality in meditation literature that one still sees in our time. The queen had the large one-volume English work published after the death of her husband, German-born Prince Albert, for whom it had been a favorite reading: *Meditations on Life, Death and Eternity,* trans. Frederica Rowan (Boston: Houghton, Mifflin & Co., 1883).

9. Martin Redeker, *Schleiermacher: Life and Thought,* trans. John Wallhausser (Philadelphia: Fortress, 1973), 188–93. Conflict arose when the king and his advisors proposed a liturgical order for the United Church that Schleiermacher opposed (ibid., 193–99). On the history of the union: Hans Walter Krumwiede, *Geschichte des Christentums III: Neuzeit* (Stuttgart: W. Kohlhammer, c. 1977), 120–27.

tract societies were Protestant-ecumenical in nature.[10] When the United Church became a reality in Prussia in 1817, several smaller German states followed Prussia's example and formed united churches. Soon, however, these unions were to experience serious opposition from a renewed Lutheran orthodoxy and, with it, political conservatism.

While the ideas of political freedom, equality, and religious tolerance found favor among evangelicals in England during the early Napoleonic era, with time and experience there arose the suspicion that political liberalism was godless and, if left unchecked, would end in the dissolution of society.[11] Political conservatives in Britain and America feared the same thing.[12] After Napoleon, the same fear was present in Germany both in the aristocracy and among the middle classes. Censorship of intellectuals was applied, as it had not been under Napoleon. Most importantly the conservative mood of the time combined support for the monarchy and the revival of the Lutheran confessional tradition. Within a relatively short period of time, there was in all of Protestant Germany a new and vital "New Lutheranism" strictly based on the Lutheran confessions, sacraments, and liturgy. Here it was resolutely asserted that the new liberalism, in preaching democracy and political equality, opened government and church to the unending vacillations of opinion among the masses. God's orderly rule of Christian life was rather through the legitimate ruler, the king, and through his ministers. By law the king of Prussia now embodied the unity of church and state: he was both ruler and highest bishop. "Old Lutherans," those in Prussia who refused the United Church, were initially persecuted. In 1841 they were allowed to form their own organization.[13]

---

10. These societies had come into existence in Germany initially through the outreach of the Religious Tract Society in England and the British and Foreign Bible Society. Their initial points of contact were Pietist centers such as Basel's Deutsche Christentumsgesellschaft. See William F. Mundt, *Sinners Directed to the Savior: The Religious Tract Society Movement in Germany (1811–1848)* (Zoetemeer, Netherlands: Uitgeverij Boekencentrum, 1996). Ulrich Gäbler, ed., *Der Pietismus im 19. und 20. Jahrhundert* (Göttingen: Vandenhoeck & Ruprecht, 2000), 30–35.

11. D. W. Bebbington, *Evangelicalism in Modern Britain: A History from the 1730s to the 1980s* (London: Unwin Hyman, 1988), 100. High circles in the Church of England were and remained deeply conservative, also in reacting against the new German philosophies. In *The State of the Protestant Religion in Germany; A Series of Discourses before the University of Cambridge* (Cambridge: Deighton & Sons, 1825), 101, Hugh James Rose summarizes: "Such, then, have been the effects of the naturalizing doctrines in Germany; indifference on the one hand, and violent mysticism on the other. Into their farther effects . . . we are the less concerned to inquire, as without any knowledge of what these proceedings have done, we can have no difficulty in judging what they are likely to do— no difficulty in rejecting every principle which they involve with disgust and detestation." See also Ieuan Ellis, *Seven against Christ: A Study of 'Essays and Reviews'* (Leiden: Brill, 1989).

12. Henry F. May, *The Enlightenment in America* (Oxford: Oxford University Press, 1976), 224ff., 252–76. The classical English work on this subject was written at the beginning of the Revolution by Edmund Burke: *The Revolution in France* (New York: Reinhart, 1959). For Burke, democratic forms need the stability of tradition, law, and political wisdom to prevent them from succumbing to mob rule. The same idea is reflected in the restriction of the voting franchise in the American republic. The famous Swiss historian Jakob Burkhardt was of the same mind, as expressed in his famous lectures of 1871/72, *Weltgeschichtliche Betrachtungen*, ET: *Force and Freedom: Reflections on History*, ed. James Hastings Nichols (New York: Pantheon, 1943).

13. They were prominent in the founding of Lutheran churches in the United States, especially the Missouri Synod. On the history of Lutheranism and Lutheran confessions in the United States,

The churches of the minority Reformed tradition did not develop a confessional movement comparable to New Lutheranism. Depending on the principality in which they were located, most were in the United Church, which they supported. Not until 1884 was a Reformierter Bund (Reformed Alliance) formed, to whose voluntary membership individuals, organizations, and local churches were invited.[14] The most notable work on Reformed orthodoxy in Germany, *Reformed Dogmatics* (a compendium from works of the previous three centuries) by Heinrich Heppe (1820–79), also appeared relatively late, in 1861.[15] There were moderate Lutheran groups that desired a presbyterial form of church government; they were usually also in favor of a constitutional monarchy and legislature. There was no support among church leaders for a republic.[16] Contentious convocations were held in the 1840s in the interest of reaching a consensus on church order in the United Church, including a new confession, but no consensus could be reached. For most churches in the United Church, Lutheran tradition was followed, under the influence both of the Lutheran majority and the New-Lutheran revival.[17] Not until 1973, in the Leuenberg Agreement, was clarity about shared communion among the churches of the Reformation achieved.[18] Nevertheless the influence of the union was considerable. Where it reduced the influence of strict confessionalism, it increased the freedom of theology.

The social and political unrest of 1830 and especially the revolutionary agitation of 1848 originated with events in France and drew support from disadvantaged groups among the lower classes and from intellectual liberals and radicals

---

see E. Clifford Nelson, ed., *The Lutherans in North America* (Philadelphia: Fortress, 1975); James W. Richard, *The Confessional History of the Lutheran Church* (Philadelphia: Lutheran Publishing Society, 1909); Heinrich Schmid, *The Doctrinal Theology of the Evangelical Lutheran Church*, 3rd ed. (Minneapolis: Augsburg, 1961).

14. Hans-Jörg Reese, *Bekenntnis und Bekennen, Vom 19. Jahrhundert zum Kirchenkampf der nationalsozialistischen Zeit* (Göttingen: Vandenhoeck & Ruprecht, 1974), 98–102.

15. Heinrich Heppe, *Reformed Dogmatics*, trans. G. T. Thornton (Grand Rapids: Baker, 1978). Heppe was a professor at Marburg and hence a member of the United Church. Although there were confessional movements in the Reformed church elsewhere in the nineteenth century, they were relatively insignificant in Germany itself, as noted by Reese, 101. Hermann Friedrich Kohlbrügge published work on the Heidelberg Catechism, but the area of his influence was limited. Barth, *Protestant Theology in the Nineteenth Century*, New Edition (Grand Rapids: Eerdmans, 2002), 620–28.

16. An important work in support of the union, presbyterial church government, and constitutional monarchy with a representative legislature was written by the Reformed theologian Karl Bernhard Hundeshagen (1810–70), *Der deutsche Protestantismus, seine Vergangenheit und seine heutigen Lebensfragen*, 1st ed. 1846 (Frankfurt: Heinrich Ludwig Brönner, 1850). He attributes the development of "anti-Christian" radicalism in the 1840s to the failure of the Congress of Vienna to establish representative government and instead creating an authoritarian "police state." See esp. 130–45, 191ff., 219–27. On Hundeshagen see Lichtenberger, *History of German Theology in the 19th Century*, trans. W. Hastie (Edinburgh: T. & T. Clark, 1889), 486f.

17. Reese, *Bekenntnis und Bekennen*, 69–103; cf. 175–77, 511–27. *Theologische Realenzyklopädie* (Berlin: W. de Gruyter, 1977ff.), II, 55–83.

18. The 1973 Leuenberg Agreement gave mutual affirmation to the Lutheran, Reformed, and United Churches and to communion with one another, but in recognition of confessional differences. See *Agreement between Reformation Churches in Europe* (Frankfurt: O. Lembeck, 1973); www.leuenberg.net.

at odds with state and church. Their main effect was to reinforce conservative fears and reaction against attempts to bring democratic reform.[19] (In 1848 Karl Marx published the *Communist Manifesto* in Germany.) The Awakening had spread among the Prussian aristocracy (as it had among aristocrats in England) in close association with political conservatism, and the aristocracy was an important element in the barrier against democratic progress in church and state.[20] The problems that were the real causes of the agitation of 1848—mainly the social consequences of the Industrial Revolution, exacerbated by authoritarian government—were not solved, and in 1848 an important opportunity for the development of democracy and the redress of social problems was missed.

Another element informed the new conservatism. The educated elite contrasted their identification with the culture of Greek antiquity with the "barbarism" of the French Revolution and Napoleon. Academic humanists concluded (in spite of America) that democracy worked only in small or limited communities like ancient Athens and the Swiss cantons and that large states needed a strong monarch, like the Greek Pericles, who could place the interest of the nation above special interests. Schleiermacher wrote that democracy is a primitive form of government and that "states of a higher order" should have a (Christian) monarchy.[21] Patriotic enthusiasm for the uniqueness of Germany is expressed by an early work of the theologian W. M. L. de Wette. *Theodore, or the Initiation of the Doubter,* published in 1822, is the story of a young theologian's spiritual and intellectual journey. In the night before a battle against the French, Theodore reasons that the term "Christian" applies concretely to a specific "folk" and its own particular tradition of government. Folk and government are "necessary boundaries and the means of educating humanity, because . . . the spirit of [Christian] love and justice are embodied in them." To attack them is criminal; to defend them is an act of love.[22] (One hears similar sentiments in Schleiermacher's sermons from the

19. Sheehan, *German History,* 604ff., 656ff.

20. See John Groh, *Nineteenth Century German Protestantism: The Church as Social Model* (Washington, DC: University Press of America, 1982); Robert M. Bigler, *The Politics of German Protestantism; The Rise of the Protestant Church Elite in Prussia, 1815–1848* (Berkeley: University of California, 1972); Marjorie Lamberti, "Lutheran Orthodoxy and the Beginning of Conservative Party Organization in Prussia," *Church History* 37 (1968):439–53. An important German source is Karl Kupisch, *Die deutschen Landeskirchen im 19. und 20. Jahrhundert,* 2nd ed. (Göttingen: Vandenhoeck & Ruprecht, 1975). A broad comparison of churches is given by Josef L. Altholz, *The Churches in the Nineteeth Century* (Indianapolis: Bobbs-Merrill, 1967).

21. Manfred Landfester, *Humanismus und Gesellschaft,* on Schleiermacher, 75. Landfester's reference is to Schleiermacher's "Über die Begriffe der verschiedenen Staatsformen," in F. Schleiermacher, *Sämtliche Werke,* part 3, vol. 2 (Berlin: Reimer, 1838), 246ff.; esp. 268, 271.

22. W. M. L. de Wette, *Theodor oder des Zweiflers Weihe. Bildungsgeschichte eines evangelischen Geistlichen,* 2 vols. (Berlin: Reimer, 1822), 1:385. In the book the character "Härtling" portrays an ideal of German communal life: "Farmer, citizen, academician and artist must be of one mind in directing all they do and produce to the common life; they must sacrifice or at least subordinate their own benefit to the common benefit." To this Theodor replies, "So love, enthusiasm for the fatherland, selflessness, sacrifice is the soul of the common spirit." Threatening this common spirit is "the mechanism of business," for which French influence is blamed (ibid., 153f.). Cf. Hundeshagen, *Der deutsche Protestantismus,* 124–36: "folk" is "the unity on whose basis all human-made and natural differences [in society] again become a common whole." It is "the deepest, most immediate basis on

end of the Napoleonic era.)[23] "Folk" is higher than government; it implies the "will of the people" associated with the French Revolution. But for Theodore "folk" is neither an ideal of reason nor a cosmopolitan concept. He demonstrates that it is becoming a matter of belief that Christianity is uniquely embodied in the culture of a particular folk, a thought that will have a profound historical effect in the German churches of later history.

The new realities in church and state brought new appointments to the university theological faculties.[24] Two of the more important were Friedrich August Tholuck (1799–1877), appointed to the faculty at Halle in 1826, and Ernst Wilhelm Hengstenberg (1802–69), appointed to Berlin in 1828. Tholuck was a theologian of the Awakening. One of his students, Martin Kähler, wrote that Tholuck was not only a great preacher and pastor, but that "wherever he went he drew oppressed and needy souls like a magnet draws iron."[25] He was Lutheran, did not favor strict confessionalism, and supported the union. His interest in the United Church is reflected in historical publications that included major work in Calvin. Tholuck was also a "mediation theologian."[26] The term designates theologies that to a greater or lesser degree tried to unite traditional faith, the new philosophical thought, and historical criticism; in a broad application of the term, it describes the effort in the nineteenth century to harmonize faith and modern science [chap. 3]. One of mediation theology's characteristic features was the attempt of many professors and pastor-theologians—and many long since forgotten—to mediate between traditional Christianity and historical criticism of the Bible. Among these the most prominent are those who wrote the nineteenth-century lives of Jesus famously documented by Albert Schweitzer's *Quest of the Historical Jesus.*[27]

Hengstenberg's interest lay far more in the defense of the orthodox tradition, although Martin Kähler includes his early publications in mediation theology.[28] English translations of his biblical works, which stridently opposed the then-

which the state rests." "Not armies marched against Napoleon, but folk [*Völker*]." "We are long since accustomed, rightly, to date our religious revival too from the wars of liberation."

23. Friedrich Schleiermacher, *Predigten*, 4 vols. (Berlin: Reimer, 1834ff.), 1:230; 4:75, both partially quoted by Reinhold Niebuhr, *The Nature and Destiny of Man*, 2 vols. (Louisville, KY: Westminster John Knox, 1996), 1:87, 89.

24. Philip Schaff, *Germany: Its Universities, Theology and Religion* (Philadelphia: Lindsay & Blakiston, 1857), 29–31, lists the faculties then in operation, most of which were quite small. On the theological parties and their scholarly journals until 1857, see Schaff, 248–54.

25. Kähler, *Geschichte der protestantischen Dogmatik im 19. Jahrhundert*, ed. Ernst Kähler (Berlin: Evangelische Verlagsanstalt, 1962), 132. See also *The Spirituality of the German Awakening*, trans. David Crowner and Gerald Christianson (New York: Paulist, 2003). The most prominent figure of the Awakening in Berlin was August Neander (1789–1850), a converted Jew, professor of church history, a friend of Schleiermacher, and the students' most beloved professor. He is famous for the words—often taken as the motto of the theological Awakening—"pectus est quod theologum facit" (it is the heart that makes the theologian). See F. Lichtenberger, *History of German Theology in the 19th Century*, 167–85.

26. Kähler, *Geschichte*, 152f.

27. See the sections below on Schweitzer, chap. 4.9, and D. F. Strauss, chap. 2.5.1.

28. Kähler, *Geschichte*, 84.

developing historical-critical method in biblical interpretation, probably influenced the development of American fundamentalism.[29] He came originally from the Reformed Church and the Awakening. In Berlin he had to join his increasingly New Lutheran convictions with his official obligation to support the Prussian United Church. He was also a firm supporter of absolute (nonconstitutional) monarchy. From 1827 until his death he was the editor of the *Evangelische Kirchenzeitung* (Evangelical Church Newspaper), in which he wrote a yearly report on theology and the church. He did not hesitate to attack any theologian or group in the church that he considered theologically or politically dangerous, which meant any deviation from (Lutheran) orthodoxy, above all through biblical criticism.[30] An important ally, Friedrich Julius Stahl, became a professor of law in Berlin in 1840. Stahl made the legal case for absolutism in monarchy and church.[31] As a biblical scholar Hengstenberg defended the inerrancy of the Old Testament, particularly with regard to authorship.[32] Nevertheless he made use of historical criticism, and to this use D. F. Strauss devoted a large part of a book written against theologies that are "half faith" and "half science."[33] Hengstenberg's view of the world is reflected in his interpretation of the thousand years and its aftermath in Revelation 20:1–10: it begins with the coronation of Charlemagne in 800 and ends a millennium later.[34]

New Lutheranism could also oppose the authority of the secular prince in the church, although not with the consequence of disestablishment (established churches may or may not be administered by the state).[35] An important exam-

29. Little information on this is available. See Brevard Childs, *Introduction to the Old Testament as Scripture* (Philadelphia: Fortress, 1979), 37; cf. 116, 118.

30. Groh, *Nineteenth Century,* 185–91. In German, see Johannes Bachmann and T. Schmalenbach, *E. W. Hengstenberg. Sein Leben und Wirken nach gedruckten und ungedruckten Quellen,* 3 vols. (Gütersloh: Bertelsmann, 1876, 1880, 1892).

31. F. J. Stahl's major work is *Die Philosophie des Rechts,* 1st ed. 1829 (reproduction of the 5th ed. of 1878, Hildesheim: Georg Olms, 1963). He writes, for example: "Our judgment of the relationship of the people to the state is most deeply anchored in the Christian view of the world. God wills the transfiguration of humanity. The saints should rule in Christ with God, and they rule by obeying. What the unity of God and humanity is in the eternal kingdom is [in the present world] . . . the outward temporal kingdom of the state, the unity of hierarchy and people. . . . The basic ethical relationships remain the same on all levels. Authority and free obedience, the individual as co-carrier and co-originator of the ethical order under which the individual stands: this is the basic law and the final end of the ethical world" (II/2, 540f.).

32. E.g., Hengstenberg, *Christology of the Old Testament and a Commentary on the Predictions of the Messiah by the Prophets,* trans. Reuel Keith, 3 vols. (Alexandria, VA: William M. Morrison, 1836–39). A 2nd ET is by T. Meyer and J. Martin (Edinburgh: T. & T. Clark, 1854–58; reprinted Grand Rapids: Kregel, 1956).

33. D.F. Strauss, *Die Halben und die Ganzen* (Berlin: Franz Duncker, 1865), 65–128.

34. Hengstenberg, *The Revelation of St. John,* trans. Patrick Fairbain, 2 vols. (New York: Carter & Brothers, 1852), 2:534. As Strauss reports, Hengstenberg, in the *Evangelische Kirchenzeitung,* called Strauss's *Life of Jesus* the "beast from the abyss" (in reference to the book of Revelation) (Strauss, *Die Halben und die Ganzen,* 67). See chap. 2.5.1 on Strauss.

35. By an "established church" is meant a church that is favored by the state and is the recipient of special benefits (e.g., support by taxation), while other religious organizations are not. These may be tolerated but are not the recipients of favor. The contrasting situation is religious liberty (as in the United States), which favors no church. Church establishment in Germany varies historically from a state-church form (the officers of the church are officers of the state) to forms in which church officers are independent of the state, a form that came into force for Protestant churches after World War I.

ple was August Vilmar (1800–68), professor of theology in Marburg, which at the time was ruled by the prince of the province of Hesse. The established church was the United Church; Vilmar was a convinced New Lutheran. For Vilmar there could be no questioning of the fact that "outside the church there is no salvation." He mistrusted democracy as much as Hengstenberg; in all talk of the prerogatives of the congregation he found the tendency to revolution and corruption of the church. And like Hengstenberg he interpreted the revolutionary democratic movements of the late 1840s as apocalyptic signs of the end times. His theology of the church derived the high authority of pastoral office from the authority of the apostles. Pastors were to be educated in orthodoxy and appointed with no say by the congregation (this was ordinarily the case in Germany at the time). The church was maintained "from above" by "the Holy Spirit, Christ and his Word, his sacrament and his office." Theology was understood as strictly biblical and confessional and should take place only in and for the church.[36] Theological education was to be carefully controlled, and the officers of the church were to rule the religious life of the citizenry. The effect was an institutionalizing of Christ and the Holy Spirit that bore similarities to Catholicism.

The theology of a group generally known as the "biblical realists" was, like Hengstenberg's, based almost entirely on biblical concepts.[37] They were, however, typically associated with the tradition of low-church Awakening piety, not with its high-church forms in New Lutheranism. In fact they were inclined to separatism, as were many of their Pietist forebears. They were typically not associated with universities but with traditional regional Pietist centers. Johann Tobias Beck (1804–78) was an exception. He was appointed to the theological faculty at Tübingen in 1843 as a counterbalance to the liberal theology of F. C. Baur [chap. 3.5]. His work is often placed in the conservative wing of mediation theology, insofar as in significant instances he combines speculation with biblical realism.[38] He is best known as a proponent of "pneumatic" or spiritual exegesis, which soon became a pejorative term for an exegesis, like Beck's, that ignores

36. Vilmar, *Theologie der Tatsachen wider die Theologie der Rhetorik*, 1st ed. 1856, reprint of 3rd ed. of 1857 (Stuttgart: S.G. Liesching, 1864), 49–69, 89–101; *Dogmatik*, ed. K.W. Pidert, 2 vols. (Gütersloh: Bertelsmann, 1874), 2:181–214. On Vilmar see Karl Barth, *Protestant Theology in the 19th Century*, 611–19, and F. W. Kantzenbach, *Programme der Theologie* (Munich: Claudius, 1978), 72–82. Another important New Lutheran high-church work on doctrine—one with considerable influence in America—is by Wilhelm Löhe (1808–72), *Three Books concerning the Church*, trans. Edward T. Horn (Reading: Pilger, 1908). See also Claude Welch, *Protestant Thought in the Nineteenth Century*, 2 vols. (New Haven, CT: Yale University Press, 1972, 1985), 1:190–94.

37. The more well known are Gottfried Menken (1768–1831), Hermann Friedrich Kohlbrügge (1803–75), and Johann Christoph Blumhardt (1805–1880) and his son Christoph (1842–1919). See Karl Barth, *Protestant Theology in the Nineteenth Century*.

38. This is most prominent in Beck's *Einleitung in das System der christlichen Lehre*, 1st ed. 1837 (Stuttgart: W. F. Steinkopf, 1870). The first chapter in part II has the title "Religion or Revelation and Faith in General," where Beck refers to Hegel for the concept that the "religious consciousness" begins with an indeterminate content (51). This two-point beginning, one in the religious mind and one in faith, is characteristic of mediation theology [chap. 3]. Karl Barth gives a synopsis of this work in *Protestant Thought in the Nineteenth Century*, 604–8. In another book, *Die Christliche Lehr-Wissenschaft nach den biblischen Urkunden. Erster Teil: Die Logik der christlichen Lehre* (Stuttgart: Christian Belser, 1841), 33, Beck calls his work a "scientific" presentation, the "system" of the truth revealed

historical criticism. He marshals a large amount of biblical evidence in support of spiritual (pneumatic) judgment, that is, that God's gift of the Spirit enables the recognition of spiritual truth in the Bible.[39]

In 1832 the moderate Roman Catholic theologian Johann Adam Möhler (1796–1838) published his famous *Symbolic,* one of the most important theological works of the century. With considerable historical knowledge and skill and without a harsh polemical tone, Möhler compares Catholicism, Lutheranism, and the Reformed tradition in their basic doctrines—the origin of evil, original sin, justification, good works, the sacraments, and the church—in each case setting out the superiority of Catholicism. The work is especially noteworthy in its exposition of the differences in the doctrine of the church and the role of Scripture. Möhler reflects the thinking of New Lutheranism—which also places church authority beside Scripture—when he asserts that when Scripture alone is made the highest authority in faith and life, there is no way to prevent the individual reader from being the actual authority.[40] In the discussion that Möhler's work evoked, some Protestants became interested in relating the Catholic and Protestant confessions to one another in a positive way.[41] Catholicism was mainly regional (it was dominant, for example, in Bavaria), and since the Thirty Years' War it had existed peacefully alongside the Protestant churches. The Evangelical Alliance, which originated in England before mid-century and was well received in America, never attained the popularity in Germany that it had in those countries, partly because its confessional statement was problematic, but also because of the Alliance's anti-Catholic platform. Only later, after Vatican I (1870), was there a sense among Protestants that Catholicism posed a threat, and even then it was relatively short-lived.

---

in the Bible or the "logic of Christian doctrine." He characterizes this logic, with terms that stem from Idealism, as "a universal concept-reality, a thought world" that accurately reflects the whole of revelation and the world under God's rule.

39. See esp. Beck, *Outlines of Biblical Psychology* (Edinburgh: T. & T. Clark, 1877), 33–77.

40. Johann Adam Möhler, *Symbolik oder Darstellung der dogmatischen Gegensätze der Katholiken und Protestanten nach ihren öffentlichen Bekenntnisschriften,* 8th unchanged original ed. (Mainz: Florian Kupferberg, 1872), 395ff. ET: *Symbolism: or Exposition of the Doctrinal Differences between Catholics and Protestants,* trans. James Burton Robertson (New York: Catholic Publication House, 1843). In the 1830s and 1840s the Anglo-Catholic Oxford or Tractarian movement in the Church of England, while being to a certain extent a parallel to high-church confessional New Lutheranism, held Möhler in high regard. Owen Chadwick, *From Bossuet to Newman,* 2nd ed. (Cambridge: Cambridge University Press, 1987), 102–10.

41. See, e.g., the late Schelling in chap. 2.4.2 below, whose idea of a "Petrine" and a "Pauline" church and their future combination in a "Johannine" church was widely discussed. See also Karl Hase, *Handbook to the Controversy with Rome,* trans. A.W. Streane, 2 vols. (London: Religious Tract Society, 1906), 1: xxxi–xxxii; cf. Hase's friendly remarks on Möhler, xxi–xxii [Hase, chap. 3.4]. The relatively small and mainly Protestant "Katholisch-Apostolische Gemeinschaft" ("Irvingites," begun in England in the 1830s to a certain degree in connection with the Oxford movement) understood itself as a prophetic "Johannine" community pointing to the unity, catholicity, holiness, and apostolicity of the end times, and as an ecumenical worshiping community in which Christians of all confessions could participate. See Columba Graham Flegg, *'Gathered under Apostles': A Study of the Catholic Apostolic Church* (Oxford: Clarendon, 1992). Its leading German theologian was Heinrich Thiersch. J. E. Wilson, *Heinrich W. J. Thiersch und sein Lehrer Schelling* (Bern: Peter Lang, 1985).

1.3 FROM THE UNIFICATION OF GERMANY
TO WORLD WAR I

The German principalities were unified in 1871 as one nation under the king of Prussia, although they remained semi-independent provinces, each with its distinctive characteristics and its own territorially governed churches. The king became "Kaiser" (the original Latin pronunciation of Caesar) and the new nation was called a "Reich," the German word for empire. The purpose was to give the impression that the old Holy Roman Empire under the Germanic kings was being reborn, in order to give the diverse principalities an inspirational idea to rally round. The birth of the nation was the indirect result of the Prussian victory over the French in the Franco-Prussian war. The same events made the Prussian chancellor, Otto von Bismarck (1815–98), the chancellor of the new nation, a post he held from 1871 until 1890. He was a convinced Christian, who had been confirmed in the church by Schleiermacher and influenced by the Awakening in the Prussian aristocracy, but did not attend church. He belongs, as one historian writes, "to the age of Protestant private religion, as did most of the great minds of the second half of the 19th century."[42] Through quickly won wars with Denmark and Austria about territorial claims in the 1860s, Bismarck had solidified and extended the power of Prussia; now he was to do the same for the new Reich. While the "principle of legitimacy" of the rule of kings continued to live among those who believed in "throne and altar," especially in the church, power interests now clearly dominated European politics. Bismarck's "iron fist" politics was but a part of what all the large nations, including the United States, were pursuing: expansion of power and with it a national egoism of legitimacy, exploration of options for empire, and a strong and proud military. Events driven by power interests spiraled almost blindly toward the First World War, especially after Bismarck, when an unwise militaristic kaiser with imperialist ambitions took the reins of power.

Earlier in the century under the weight of popular demand a legislature (under a restricted franchise) had been formed in Prussia, but it had little actual power. In reality the monarch and the ministries still ruled. Control of the ministries and their bureaucracies was the key to any political program. The supposed virtue of the system lay in its centralized management by expert university-educated civil servants. One contemporary historian remarks that most people at the time would have agreed with something a respected Prussian historian had said early in the century: "Liberty rests far more on administration than on constitution."[43] Paternalistic government both permitted and limited liberties, according to its view of what was needed; the support for and limitation of women's religious and

---

42. Heinrich Hermelink, *Das Christentum in der Menschheitsgeschichte*, 2 vols. (Tübingen and Stuttgart: J. B. Meltzer and R. Wunderlich, 1953), 2:602.
43. B. G. Niebuhr as quoted by Holborn, *History of Modern Germany*, 1:460. The southern German states Baden and Bavaria had maintained legislative governmental bodies since the Napoleonic era, but these too were under the rule of princes and had limited authority.

feminist movements provides a good example.[44] University professors, including the theological faculties, were officials of the state and a part of the structure of government authority. The same was true of church pastors.[45] The churches were governed primarily by officers appointed by the appropriate ministry, among whom university professors were usually included.

Through its annexations Prussia was huge by European standards, and its decisions in church affairs were broadly determinative for the new empire. Tensions soon arose with the Catholic Church. In 1864 Pope Pius IX had published a Syllabus of Errors that condemned all modern progress in church and state. In Germany liberal and conservative Catholics divided in their attitude toward it, and it made Protestants suspicious of the political intentions of the Catholic Church. The proclamation of the infallibility of the pope at the First Vatican Council brought open conflict. What followed is known as *Kulturkampf* (Culture Fight), the attempt of Bismarck's government to force the Catholic Church to conform to laws that placed education under the control of the state. The Catholic Church resisted until the laws were repealed.[46]

From Bismarck until World War I the state was essentially identified with Protestantism, and Protestant leaders supported it. National destiny, colonialism, and war were commonly understood as matters of providence. Parallels are found in all Western countries of the period: while the church weakened under the advance of secularism in industrial society, it strengthened its identification with the "Christian" state and national culture. Serious social problems emerging in connection with rapid industrialization were also common among the Western powers. Bismarck's government never tried to create a political base among wage earners to support its policies but counted instead on expert management to provide solutions to the workers' problems. Industrialization progressed at a remarkable rate, and with it swelled a proletarian underclass that looked increasingly to socialism and communism for help. Church organizations formed in support of the working classes were loyal to the government and its ministries.[47]

---

44. Catherine M. Prelinger, *Charity, Challenge and Change: Religious Dimensions of the Mid-Nineteenth-Century Women's Movement in Germany* (New York: Greenwood, 1987).

45. Hundeshagen's judgment in *Der deutsche Protestantismus*, 182, was that the church was a "stone house" in whose pulpit stood "an officer of the high police."

46. The first instance of trouble came in Bavaria, where liberal Catholic teachers refused to recognize the infallibility of the pope and an appeal was made by the liberal government to Bismarck, although Bavaria had the authority to govern its own religious affairs. The separation of the Old Catholics, those who did not accept the infallibility of the pope, from the Roman Catholic Church only temporarily affected the Roman Catholic Church negatively. Another result of Bismarck's policy was the increasing secularization of the Protestant churches, since the same laws, which effectively removed the church from education, also applied to them (Groh, *Nineteenth Century*, 389–421). Cf. E. E. Y. Hales, *The Catholic Church in the Modern World* (Garden City, NY: Image, 1960), 213–27; Kupisch, *Die deutschen Landeskirchen*, 72–78.

47. Kupisch, *Die deutschen Landeskirchen*, 79–84. The result was the growth of socialism in indifference and often in hostility toward the church. See Karl Kupisch, *Das Jahrhundert des Socialismus und die Kirche* (Berlin: Käthe Vogt, 1959).

Darwinism entered German science and philosophy almost as soon as the *Origin of Species* (1859) was published.[48] It did not have the impact in the churches that it had in the United States, probably because Hegelian philosophy had prepared the way for it several decades before. Schopenhauer's pessimistic and atheistic philosophy, which saw the origin of the world in a dark irrational will or force, was widely read among the middle classes after 1850.[49] In 1871 David Friedrich Strauss published *Der alte und der neue Glaube* (The Old and the New Faith), which declared Christianity to be outdated in the modern world and in its place celebrated an eclectic combination of natural science and modern philosophies as the "new faith" of German culture. The later works of the enigmatic Friedrich Nietzsche sharply attacked the culture and especially Christianity for being morally dishonest and opposed to real life. In none of these cases is the government questioned—something typical of German intellectuals in this period and beyond.[50] Soon the atheistic works of the psychologist Sigmund Freud (1856–1935) raised new anxieties about the collapse of traditional values.[51] The prototype of racial propaganda was given by an Englishman living and writing in Germany, Houston Stewart Chamberlain, in his work, *Die Grundlagen des neunzehnten Jahrhunderts* (The Foundations of the Nineteenth Century), published in 1871. Chamberlain combined racist imperialism with a religious veneration of Richard Wagner's romantic music and Nordic myths. The popularity of his work gave significant impetus to the myths of empire: origin, race, destiny.[52] More and more—across the whole Western world—empire and its myths, and the wealth it generated, appeared to be the answer to all problems.

Anti-Semitism, so easily attached to these myths and for centuries a cause of intolerance and violence, was also common, if usually more subtle, among both conservatives and liberals in the German churches. There was of course open racism, but religious anti-Semitism apart from racial prejudice was also prominent.[53] Luther himself had been a nonracist, religious anti-Semite, seeing in Jews

48. Alfred Kelly, *The Descent of Darwinism: The Promulgation of Darwinism in Germany, 1860–1914* (Chapel Hill: University of North Carolina Press, 1981).

49. Arthur Schopenhauer, *The World as Will and Representation*, trans. E. F. J. Payne, 2 vols. (New York: Dover, 1966). The work was originally published in 1817. Schopenhauer's core thoughts are largely dependent on the early Schelling and Hegel.

50. Holborn, 2:408–11, cites the examples of Max Weber and Thomas Mann.

51. All of these figures depend on ideas developed in Idealism, including Darwin, for whom evolution is a form of historical dialectic. Freud also has a dialectic: libido and superego have their synthesis in the ego. In *Totem and Tabu* Freud explained religion naturalistically based on the Oedipus complex.

52. On Chamberlain, see Geoffrey G. Field, *Evangelist of Race: The Germanic Vision of Houston Stewart Chamberlain* (New York: Columbia University Press, 1981).

53. Uriel Tal, *Christians and Jews in Germany: Religion, Politics and Ideology in the Second Reich, 1870–1914* (Ithaca, NY: Cornell University Press, 1975). Tal distinguishes between racial anti-Semitism, Christian anti-Semitism, and anti-Christian anti-Semitism, all of which fed into Nazism. See also Jacob Katz, *From Prejudice to Destruction: Anti-Semitism, 1700–1933* (Cambridge: Harvard University Press, 1980); Jonathan Sheehan, *The Enlightenment Bible* (Princeton, NJ: Princeton University Press, 2005), 234–40; Hope, *German and Scandinavian Protestantism*, 522f., 537f.

the representatives of all unbelief.[54] The French Revolution had given Jews full civil rights for the first time ever in Europe, while at the same time denying rights to their religious assemblies. In German areas dominated by the French, the same rights were extended and denied again later, but there was nevertheless slow progress throughout the nineteenth century as secularism in the society became stronger. Full civil rights were extended in Prussia in 1869 and in the new Reich in 1871. Earlier in the nineteenth century many Jews had either become secular or had converted to an established Christian church, which gave them the civil rights enjoyed by Catholics and Protestants. Traditionally nonconverted Jews had been excluded from owning land and, except for very few cases, from the guilds of skilled workers. Many were shopkeepers and artisans. They made up only a small portion of the population in Germany (in 1933 only 1½ percent) and were concentrated in the cities. During the nineteenth century significant numbers made use of the means of social advancement available, the universities, and many became medical doctors, lawyers, and journalists. There were traditional avenues open in banking and financing, which were important resources for industrialization. Nonconverted Jews were not admitted to government office and only gradually to positions in the universities. From the Bismarck era to World War I the great majority of Jews belonged to the middle class; some were poor, and a number were wealthy. Politically they typically supported political parties that advocated social and economic progress, and through journalism their criticisms were given voice. Rapid industrialization went hand in hand with the disruption of the traditional social order in Germany, and Jews were identified with the disruption, becoming targets of criticism that labeled them corruptors of traditional German culture.[55]

In the period from the foundation of the new nation to World War I, Protestant theology in the universities was increasingly dominated by a new and rather loosely defined group of theologians, the Ritschlians, named for Albrecht Ritschl [chap. 4.2], professor of theology at Göttingen. Their theology is often called "culture Protestantism," insofar as they held that Christian doctrine was inseparable from formation and improvement of society through Christian values, and they (as all theologians of the period) valued German culture as historically Christian.[56] The Ritschlians were responsible for the most important theological journal of the time, which had the characteristic title "Christian World" (*Die Christliche Welt,* published

---

54. In several late sermons Luther gave violent expression to his anti-Semitism. See, e.g., Heiko Oberman, *Luther, Man between God and the Devil,* trans. Eileen Walliser-Schwarzbart (New York: Doubleday, 1990), 292–97. Luther's anti-Semitism was by no means something new but followed long-established tradition.

55. Holborn, 2:277–81; Tal, 235–59; Sheehan, 268f., 438f., 684. Population statistics are from the *Atlas zur Weltgeschichte* (Munich, 1982), 62, as reported by Victoria Barnett, *For the Soul of the People,* 124; cf. 128 (see reference below). See Tal, 271f., on the anti-Semitism of Paul de Lagarde, highly respected and influential professor of Oriental (biblical) languages at Göttingen, teacher of Ernst Troeltsch and Wilhelm Bousset [chap. 4.6].

56. See esp. H. Richard Niebuhr, *Christ and Culture* (New York: Harper Brothers, 1951), on Ritschl, 94–101 (cf. the American forms); Karl Barth, *Protestant Theology,* 640–47.

1889–1941). In the idea of German culture as Christian, the philosophy and theology of the "classical period" of German history played a highly significant role. Adolf Harnack [chap. 4.4], the most famous of the Ritschlians and a personal advisor to the kaiser, in a public speech in 1907, lauded the "epoch of German Idealism" (he names Kant, Fichte, and Schleiermacher) as the period in which an "indissoluble union" of the Christian religion with German spiritual and national life was forged. "Just for this reason our politicians cannot be simply politicians, as in other nations." "We . . . must hold and promote the religious expressions of the life of the nation . . . in the most inner union with all spiritual and national functions."[57] Characteristic of the attitude of the Ritschlians toward the educated laity was their emphasis on the freedom of personal judgment, especially about the results of biblical criticism, but with the assumption that good judgment about sound Christian values would be the result. Low church attendance was a secondary concern in relationship to a culture imbued with Christian values.[58] This was challenged as being unrealistic, most effectively by the sociologist Max Weber (1864–1920), who argued that in depersonalized industrial society it is impossible to "influence prevailing conditions by religious or moral means."[59] Nevertheless, according to Julius Kaftan (1848–1926), Ritschlian professor of theology in Berlin, "If we cease to believe in Christ, our whole civilization must in process of time sink back from the stage attained by Christianity to that of heathenism. . . . He who cannot allow himself to despair of the highest ideals of humanity and of the reason in history will have to decide for faith in the revelation of God in Christ."[60]

Ritschlians were often involved in attempts to make the church's creeds more liberal, for example, by eliminating articles on the virgin birth. In several territorial churches, particularly in Switzerland, they were able to modify church order in such a way as to focus on the confession of Christ as witnessed by Scripture, leaving room for interpretation.[61] Some Ritschlians, among them Harnack, were

57. As reported by Harnack's biographer, his daughter, Agnes v. Zahn-Harnack, *Adolf Harnack*, 319 [see chap. 4.4].
58. Stefanie v. Schnurbein and Julius H. Ulbricht, eds., *Völkische Religion und Krisen der Moderne* (Würzburg: Königshausen & Neumann, 2001), 124–34, 168–75. *Ökumenische Kirchengeschichte der Schweiz*, 282. In Germany and Switzerland Sunday services drew an average of about 5 percent in towns and villages, significantly less in large cities. Attendance at funerals, which included preaching, was far greater; holiday services usually drew larger numbers. W. R. Ward, *Theology, Sociology and Politics: The German Protestant Social Conscience 1890–1933* (Bern: Peter Lang, 1979), 167, comments on low church attendance in Karl Barth's parish of Safenwil. There were no "city crusades" like those of Dwight L. Moody in America, but evangelism to address the situation in the cities was undertaken by both the established churches and the far smaller free churches, which received financial support from Britain and America. The YMCA was an important and relatively effective import. Groh, *Nineteenth Century*, 422–46; Kupisch, *Die deutschen Landeskirchen*, 84–87.
59. This is a summary by Rita Aldenhoff, "Max Weber and the Evangelical-Social Congress," in Wolfgang J. Mommsen and Jürgen Osterhammel, eds., *Max Weber and His Contemporaries* (London: Unwin Hyman, 1987), 199. Weber is a prime example of the sophistication and influence of the secular intellectual in this period. He has been compared to the American philosopher John Dewey.
60. *The Truth of the Christian Tradition*, trans. George Ferries, 2 vols. (Edinburgh: T. & T. Clark, 1894), 2:407.
61. See Harnack, chap. 4.4, and Bonhoeffer, chap. 6.5.5 (note 198). On Switzerland, see, e.g., Rudolf Dellsperger, *Kirchengemeinschaft und Gewissensfreiheit* (Bern: Peter Lang, 2001), 312–14.

seriously engaged in trying to improve the lot of the proletarian working class. Adolf Stöcker (1835–1909) and, after him, Friedrich Naumann (1860–1919) were moderate socialists but put national (and imperial) interests above concrete social reform, in the belief, shared with Harnack, that the power and security of the nation were a necessary precondition.[62] Related to the Ritschlians in their social concerns were the Swiss pastor-theologians Hermann Kutter (1863–1931) in Zurich and Leonhard Ragaz (1868–1948) in Basel, who represented radical religious-socialist theologies on behalf of the rapidly growing and poor industrial-worker class, which they said was closer to the kingdom of God than the bourgeois church.[63] At the beginning of the nineteenth century, governments everywhere in the Western world were only beginning to understand how to deal with mushrooming industrial problems. The administration of President Theodore Roosevelt (1901–9) was the first to address the problem effectively in the United States.

Prior to the entry of Ritschlian theology in the United States, Ralph Waldo Emerson and the Transcendentalists [chap. 2.9], and after them a wave of Hegelian philosophers, had been the main representatives of German thought in America. But it was the Ritschlians who had the biggest impact in theology. Walter Rauschenbusch [chap. 4.5] was a prominent and influential Ritschlian. The influential Methodist theologian Bordon Parker Bowne (1847–1910), professor of theology at Boston University, studied personally under the philosopher Hermann Lotze [chap. 4.1], who was a major influence on Ritschl. At New York's Union Theological Seminary William Adams Brown (1865–1943) was an important representative of Ritschlianism, as was Shailer Mathews (1863–1941) at the Divinity School of the University of Chicago. These are but a few among many.[64]

1.4 AFTER WORLD WAR I

Under the weight of defeat and economic crisis at the end of the First World War, that part of the population that had been effectively excluded from political power, the working class—which bore the burden of the war both on the battlefield and in

62. "Of what use to us is the best social policy, if the Cossacks come? The man who wishes to secure domestic policy must first secure the nation." The words of Naumann are quoted in W. R. Ward, "Max Weber and the Lutherans," in Mommsen and Osterhammel, eds., *Max Weber*, 211.

63. W. R. Ward discusses all these figures in *Theology, Sociology and Politics*. On Naumann, see also Karl Barth's essay in James M. Robinson, ed., *Beginnings of Dialectic Theology* (Richmond: John Knox Press, 1968), 35–40. On Kutter, see the section on Karl Barth in chap. 6.1 (note 8).

64. See Gary Dorrien, *The Making of American Liberal Theology: Idealism, Realism and Modernity, 1900–1950* (Louisville, KY: Westminster John Knox, 2003), chaps. 1–3. In *The Gospel and the Modern Man* (New York: Macmillan, 1910), 9, Shailer Mathews's four-point essence of Jesus' teaching is very nearly a paraphrase of Harnack's famous three points [chap. 4.4]. On the fundamentalist opposition, see George Marsden, *Fundamentalism and American Culture* (Oxford: Oxford University Press, 2006). Perhaps the most important theologian in the fundamentalist movement, J. Gresham Machen (1881–1937) had studied in Marburg under Ritschlians and members of the history of religions school, notably Wilhelm Bousset. Machen's *The Origin of Paul's Religion* (New York: Macmillan, 1925) was written largely as a rebuttal of Bousset's *Kyrios Christos*, trans. John E. Steely (Nashville: Abingdon Press, 1970).

the factories—protested against the government so effectively that it collapsed. The kaiser abdicated, the Reich dissolved, and a republic was established for the first time in German history. But support for the Weimar Republic was weak. Max Weber had wished for some combination in government of popular democracy and the tradition of professional expertise.[65] For most educated Germans this was probably the ideal. The expertise, it was assumed, came from the universities; what concrete form the ideal should take was another matter.[66] The political parties whose elected delegates shared responsibility for the government represented widely diverging viewpoints, making compromise difficult, and agitation by left- and right-wing radical groups, among which the reactionary National Socialist (Nazi) movement attracted the most support, was constant. The deeply resented terms of surrender to the Allies included acknowledgment of sole guilt for the war, prohibition of rearmament in the midst of an otherwise heavily armed Europe, and heavy monetary reparations (the war had not been fought on German soil). The financial burden of payment of war reparations coincided with a high rate of unemployment and a continual economic crisis that culminated in the Great Depression of 1933.

The Nazis came to power through elections as a minority government in the political and economic chaos of 1933. Adolf Hitler whipped up fear of communism, using it to declare a dictatorship with emergency powers to solve the economic and social crisis. He immediately began rebuilding the military and was eager for revenge. Promises were made to end payment of the war debt, restore health to the economy, end both the threat of communism and dependence on the money interests of capitalism (and its depressions), provide a strong central government, unite all social classes in one national purpose, restore morality, and support "positive Christianity."[67] Popularity came as those promises seemed on

---

65. *Karl Jaspers on Max Weber*, ed. John Dreijmanis, trans. Robert J. Whelan (New York: Paragon House, 1989), 32, 46f., 179; esp. Jaspers on Weber, 68–73. In a remarkable commentary on the times, Karl Jaspers's *Man in the Modern Age*, trans. Eden and Ceder Paul, 1st German ed. 1931 (London: Routledge & Kegan Paul, 1951), reflects the fear of democracy among many German intellectuals; see 18f., 40–44, 81, 191f. See further Otto Piper, *Recent Developments in German Protestantism* (London: SCM, 1934). Piper was a conservative Lutheran who was dismissed by the Nazi government from a theological professorship because his wife was Jewish. In this work he rejects democracy as based on a naive view of the goodness of human nature, although later as a Princeton professor he changed his mind. On Dietrich Bonhoeffer's elitist political ideas, see Larry L. Rasmussen, *Dietrich Bonhoeffer: Reality and Resistance* (Nashville: Abingdon, 1972), 174–211. Cf. Rudolf Bultmann, *What Is Theology?* trans. Roy A. Harrisville (Minneapolis: Fortress, 1997), 74.

66. J. R. C. Wright shows that church leaders were typically indifferent toward the republic, although in it they gained greater control of church affairs than ever before: *'Above Parties': The Political Attitudes of the German Protestant Church Leadership 1918–1933* (Oxford: Oxford University Press, 1974), 19–48. On the remainder of this paragraph, cf. ibid., 49–65, 143–47.

67. "Positive Christianity" had become a slogan of conservatives in opposition to "critical" theology, which was seen as having a detrimental, negative effect on the church. Support for "positive Christianity" (with an appeal to Luther) is stated in the official "Program" ("Guiding Principles") of the Nazi Party (National Socialist German Workers' Party), which was widely publicized in the Hitler period. The text is found in Arthur C. Cochrane, *The Church's Confession under Hitler* (Philadelphia: Westminster, 1962), 219ff. In radio broadcasts to the nation early in the Nazi period, Hitler appealed to God, as, e.g., in a 1933 broadcast that he concluded with the words, "May the Almighty God take our work into his grace." Klaus Scholder, *Churches and the Third Reich*, trans. John Bowden, 2 vols. (Philadelphia: Fortress, 1988), 1:42. In 1941 at the latest, the atheism of Hitler's government became clear to the churches.

the way to being fulfilled—especially economic recovery, which was forged through a close and enduring alliance of the government with major business and finance interests. Hitler was overwhelmingly confirmed in 1936 by a democratically held referendum on his military reoccupation of a western territory occupied by the French after the war. He was both feared and popular—the "strong man" who created and maintained economic prosperity even during the war years.[68] He knew how to evoke and manipulate patriotism in support of his war, especially by exploiting mistrust of the victorious Allies of World War I.

Early support for Nazism cut across all lines of division in the churches.[69] Support was typically based on the belief that Nazism provided hope and opportunity for both national and church renewal. Often one finds associated with it the hope of overcoming the alienating social effects of modern industrialism. A renaissance in Luther studies that had begun earlier in the century had become a major force in theology in the 1920s.[70] It exceeded all previous work in Luther in extent and depth, and for many young theologians it blended with the new "dialectic theology" initiated by Karl Barth. But for a significant number of conservative Lutheran theologians, the thrust toward renewal of church and theology was attached to a doctrine of nation and "folk" that was to have serious consequences. Nation and folk were interpreted in terms of Luther's two-kingdoms doctrine, namely, as "orders" of law and custom given by the Creator to the "kingdom of the world." The "kingdom of God" in the church was connected with these orders as the God-given historical context in which the church existed. The obverse side of folk theology was anti-Semitism; Jews were faulted for being a primary cause of secular alienation from Christianity and the good order of traditional culture. Typical charges were that they instigated the destruction of traditional values by spreading deistic reason and modernist economic theories, whether capitalist or communist.[71] Racism of course was also a factor; often it was virulent. In the uni-

---

68. An important new German work on the economic success of Nazi control of the German population is Götz Alys, *Hitlers Volksstaat* (Berlin: Fischer, 2005).

69. The only united religious opposition was that of the small group of Jehovah's Witnesses, many of whom were to be executed during the war because they refused conscription.

70. The major figure was Karl Holl (1866–1926) in Berlin. See Holl, *What Did Luther Understand by Religion?* trans. James Luther Adams and Walter R. Wietzke (Philadelphia: Fortress, 1977). The definitive edition of of Luther's works, the *Weimar Ausgabe*, begun in the previous century under Ritschlian influence, was strongly supported in this period: *D. Martin Luther's Werke: Kritische Gesammtausgabe*, 81 vols. (Weimar: Hermann Böhlau and successors, 1883ff.).

71. This is illustrated by a speech by Paul Althaus (1888–1966, professor of theology in Erlangen) from the year 1927, in which he speaks in favor of a church mission statement calling to action against the immoral effects and alienation from tradition and folk caused by Jewish influence in "business, journalism, art and literature." As Althaus explains, it is a matter neither of hatred of Jews nor of blood nor of religious belief, but of a "very definite corrupted and corrupting big-city mentality whose bearers are in the first instance Jewish." Althaus laments the effect of "mass culture." "Whole classes of our folk are almost completely inaccessible for the church." Paul Althaus, *Evangelium und Leben. Gesammelte Vorträge* (Gütersloh: C. Bertelsmann, 1927), 130f., 103; cf. 127ff., where according to Althaus "folk" is an order willed by God. On Althaus and his support for the "Aryan paragraph," which excluded from church office Christians of Jewish heritage and those married to such persons, see Wolfgang Gerlach, *And the Witnesses Were Silent*, trans. Victoria J. Barnett (Lincoln: University of Nebraska Press, 2000), 39ff.

versities and churches it was usually couched in ostensibly innocuous terms, including beliefs about racial characteristics that were considered scientific.[72] All these proved to be avenues of acceptance of Nazism and entrance into the "German Christian" movement that supported it.[73]

An instructive example of folk theology and its attitude toward the state is Friedrich Gogarten (1887–1967), professor of theology in Göttingen and an early advocate of "dialectic theology." Gogarten rejected Nazi racial theory and the racist theology of the German Christians, but he apparently thought such errors would be mitigated in the Nazi state by the realities of government and church life. His understanding of the state was derived from Luther's distinction between law and gospel: the state is God's means of preserving humanity from chaos; the law and authority of the state are ultimately grounded in God's (natural) law.[74] This law is particularized in the traditional mores of a folk. Democracy is a modernist perversion of this law. It subordinates the divine dignity of the state and its relationship to the folk mores (and with them the "honor" that binds state and folk) to social-egalitarian purposes that corrupt these mores and therefore the moral foundation of the nation. The "orders" of state and folk have the purpose of preventing sin and evil in the social sphere. Folk is a *Gemeinschaft* (community, commonality); where this breaks down there is only *Gesellschaft* (aggregate society without inner cohesion). A necessary relationship exists between folk and church, and the state must have a strong authoritarian hand in upholding it. Nationalism should however not dominate or stand above the state, because in this case it becomes its own religion

72. The popular and influential biblical theologian Adolf Schlatter (1852–1938, originally Swiss, professor in Tübingen) gives an important example. He begins *Das christliche Dogma* (Calw: Vereinsbuchhandlung, 1911), 11–20, with the thesis that through the revelation in Christ there can be a right knowledge of all things, that is, when they are perceived in the light of God's work and will. So also "national Christianity is indeed a right thought, because we place ourselves under Christ not without but with our national particularity and task" (438). Every church "has the calling" to be a "folk church" [*Volkskirche*] (647). The concept of "folk" is rooted genetically in "physical and psychical inheritance." In history "types arise that encompass large groups, races that are united through physical and psychical commonalities" (66). Types have to do with the way we conceptualize the world (57). "Localization forms our experience and gives us our law" (52). Church and "folkness" [*Volkstum*] should coincide (75, 77f.). In 1935 Schlatter published an anti-Semitic tract. See Gerlach, *And the Witnesses Were Silent*, 104f. Together with the Tübingen faculty Schlatter approved the Aryan paragraph (see previous note), as noted in *Zeitschrift für Theologie und Kirche*, Beiheft 4: *Tübinger Theologie im 20. Jahrhundert* (Tübingen: Mohr Siebeck, 1978), 72, 76; cf. 48. But he eventually came to oppose Nazism as anti-Christian: see Werner Neurer, *Adolf Schlatter: A Biography of Germany's Premier Biblical Theologian*, trans. Robert W. Yarbrough (Grand Rapids: Baker, 1995), which omits mentioning Schlatter's anti-Semitism.

73. According to the "Guiding Principles" of the German Christians, "race, folk and nation" are "orders of existence granted and entrusted to us by God." The German race is to be "kept pure." Jews who become Christian bring "alien blood into our body politic." Reprinted in Arthur Cochrane, *The Church's Confession under Hitler*, 222f.

74. According to Luther the Decalogue is "written in the heart" of all persons (Rom. 2:15) but obscured by sin. In his teaching on the natural "orders" and "two kingdoms"—both of which were under God's rule—the state is the kingdom of law and reason, as distinct from the kingdom of gospel and grace in the church. Wolfhart Pannenberg, *Ethics*, trans. Keith Crim (Philadelphia: Westminster, 1981), 112–31; Bernhard Lohse, *Martin Luther's Theology*, trans. Roy A. Harrisville (Minneapolis: Fortress, 1999), 245, 274, 314–24.

and the highest value.[75] With these convictions Gogarten initially favored Nazism, but in time he realized that he had badly misjudged Hitler.[76] He is but one illustration of a way of thought that swept many Christians into a catastrophic political current far beyond their control.

From this point developments move rapidly to the Barmen Declaration of 1934, the complex history of the Confessing Church, the war, the Holocaust, and beyond. The significance of this history is far too great to be limited to a summary. One should turn directly to the important works of Wolfgang Gerlach, *And the Witnesses Were Silent: The Confessing Church and the Persecution of the Jews*; Victoria Barnett, *For the Soul of the People: Protestant Protest against Hitler*; and Klaus Scholder, *Churches and the Third Reich*.[77] In the following we give only a skeletal sketch of this history.

The early popularity of the German Christian movement collapsed because the radicalism of its leadership was unacceptable in most of the churches (for example, the proposal that everything Jewish in the Bible, including Paul, be declared nonauthoritative), and because its attempt to unite the different regional churches, who had their own governments, into a Reich Church under a single bishop (appointed by Hitler) met stiff resistance. But the movement nevertheless continued, with far-reaching consequences. In its initial success it had enacted into church law the infamous "Aryan paragraph," which excluded from church office not only Christians of Jewish heritage but also those married to Jews or to Christians of Jewish heritage.[78] This and other offenses of the German Christians provoked a reaction by the Pastors Emergency League, which had been quickly formed under the leadership of the Berlin pastor, Martin Niemöller. The reaction also led to the Barmen Declaration of 1934, whose principal author was Karl Barth, and to the establishment of the Confessing Church movement throughout Germany. The declaration affirmed the lordship of Christ over all things and made clear that the state may not encroach on the right of the church to govern itself on the basis of its confessions.[79] The Confessing Church was considered by

75. Gogarten, *Politische Ethik* (Jena: Eugen Diederichs, 1932), 203–20. (The difference between *Gemeinschaft* and *Gesellschaft* was a feature of the developing science of sociology [see below].) Cf. Scholder, *Churches and the Third Reich*, 2:423f. On Gogarten and dialectic theology, see James M. Robinson, ed., *Beginnings of Dialectic Theology*; on Gogarten, see also the section on Bultmann, chap. 6.3 (note 98).

76. Gogarten's initial complicity hardly rises to the level of his colleague in theology at Göttingen, Emmanuel Hirsch (1888–1972), who joined the Nazi Party. See Robert Ericksen, *Theologians under Hitler* (New Haven, CT: Yale University Press, 1985); James Reimer, *The Emmanuel Hirsch and Paul Tillich Debate* (Lewiston, NY: Edwin Mellen, 1989).

77. Bibliographic information for Gerlach and Scholder is given in notes 71 and 67 respectively. The work by Barnett was published in 2000 by the University of Nebraska Press in Lincoln. Another important recent work is Robert P. Eriksen and Susannah Heschel, eds., *German Churches and the Holocaust Betrayal* (Minneapolis: Fortress, 1999). See also Arthur Cochrane, *The Church's Confession under Hitler*, and Karl Barth, The *German Church in Conflict* (Richmond: John Knox, 1965).

78. The university theological faculties were asked to take a position on the Aryan paragraph, and several accepted it; see Arthur Cochrane, *The Church's Confession under Hitler*, 107. Bultmann coauthored the Marburg faculty's rejection; see Bultmann in chap. 6.3 (note 96).

79. The all-important first article of the Barmen Declaration stated that according to the witness of Scripture, Jesus Christ is the only Word of God and only source of the church's proclamation; the

many in the churches to be theologically too conservative or problematic, for example, in not recognizing natural law, and there was a diverse group of pastors and churches associated neither with the German Christians nor with the Confessing Church. The Roman Catholic Church had similar problems of resistance and complicity.[80]

The Confessing Church soon splintered under the weight of disagreements concerning nonecclesial government policies, territorial church autonomy, confession and administration, and the problem of legality. The Confessing Church was not originally intended as a separate church but as a synod of the established churches.[81] The carrot-and-stick policy of the state was a catalyst in the splintering. The carrot was the creation of a new government ministry for church affairs to work with the churches to accommodate confessional concerns. Among the sticks was the threat of loss of income for pastors in the established churches. Eventually most churches in the Confessing Church movement found some accommodation with the government. For many the key to survival (as it would be later under Soviet communism) was confessional orthodoxy as a citadel of truth and protection, although this also allowed room for various levels of complicity with Nazi race and war policies.[82] The so-called "radicals" in the Confessing Church refused any accommodation, and even they were subject to splintering. By 1938 the "radicals" were a separatist organization struggling to maintain existence. It had depended on voluntary contributions to support both its pastors and the seminaries it had established (one under the leadership of Dietrich Bonhoeffer). But in 1937 the government prohibited all such voluntary contributions and closed these seminaries. When war began, across all the churches pastors and seminary students who were perceived as problematic were conscripted. Anyone refusing conscription was considered disloyal and unpatriotic, a deserter in the face of the enemy, and was executed. Protest in the churches was typically weak or nonexistent. Most young pastors in the "radical" wing of the Confessing Church were conscripted; of these most died at the front.

In reflecting on this history, it is to be remembered that the religious emphasis on traditional culture, nation, and folk was not new in German history. Sociologists

---

second affirmed the claim of Christ to the whole of human life. It did not criticize anti-Semitism or the Nazi state. As a "declaration" it was expressly intended to have no effect on the authority of the traditional church confessions. Nevertheless some Lutherans saw it as an encroachment and withdrew.

80. In 1933 a popular concordat between the Nazi government and Rome was concluded, which secured the government a certain compliance of the church. In 1937 the encyclical of Pope Pius XI, *Mit brennender Sorge* (With Burning Concern), affirmed that obedience to God encompasses all areas of life, rejected the actions of those who sow seeds of mistrust, hate, and defamation, and attacked "the myth of blood and race." Pius XI died in 1939. The new pope, Pius XII, who soon faced an Italian-German war alliance, kept silent, apparently with the intent not to provoke hostility toward the church. Quentin Adrianyi et al., *The Church in the Modern Age* (New York: Crossroad, 1981), 47–85. Scholder, *Churches and the Third Reich*, 2:89ff., gives the history of the concordat.

81. It was officially called the Reich Synod of the Confessing Community of the German Evangelical Church. The German Evangelical Church was a federation of the established territorial churches (*Landeskirchen*).

82. Bonhoeffer laments "conservative restoration" in the Confessing Church in *Letters and Papers from Prison,* ed. Eberhard Bethge (New York: Touchstone, 1997), 328.

have shown that the same or related phenomena are found in all cultures making the transition from traditional to modern technical society, although Nazi Germany demonstrates its most reactionary form, a form in which violence is accepted as the necessary means.[83] The United States had not only its own form of "culture Christianity" (as it still does), but also its own reactionary response to modernism and its own glorification of "folk." At the end of the nineteenth century one of its most representative churchmen, Josiah Strong, president of the Evangelical Alliance, argued with the assured ease of self-evidence the superiority of the Anglo-Saxon race and its role in spreading Christianity over the world. It is important "to mankind and to the coming Kingdom," he writes, to guard "against the deterioration of the Anglo-Saxon stock in the United States by immigration. There is now being injected into the veins of the nation a large amount of inferior blood."[84] In the 1920s, as the Ku Klux Klan was spreading reactionary racist and political views across the rural United States, Charles E. Jefferson, pastor of the Broadway Tabernacle in New York City, wrote that the work of the Klan was that of "making America more thoroughly American." "The majority of the members of the Ku Klux Klan are sensible and earnest men, honest and honorable, and have the welfare of the country at heart."[85] One could cite many other instances in and outside the churches. And yet America did not fall to fascism, no doubt for many reasons. Among them perhaps none is more important than that voiced by Reinhold Niebuhr: "Any modern community which establishes a tolerable justice is the beneficiary of the ironic triumph of the wisdom of common sense over the foolishness of its wise men."[86] As subsequent history in the United States and the history of postwar democratic Germany demonstrate, the test of wisdom has no end in modern democracy.

The churches in Germany—still established regional churches—emerged from World War II and the Holocaust sobered and repentant. But for many—very many—repentance was buried in silence.[87] The various levels of guilt or complicity with Nazism were typically cloaked with secrecy, because of simple opportunism

---

83. Sociologically the term "folk" itself has been associated with reaction against the collapse of traditional social order in rapidly changing modern society; one typical response is the fanciful construction of folk history found everywhere in modernity. A classical text on the subject is Ferdinand Tönnies, *Community and Society*, 1st German ed. 1887 (New Brunswick: Transaction Books, 1998). Sociology as the scientific study of group behavior was initiated in the late nineteenth century, largely through the work of Tönnies and Max Weber. See Derek L. Phillips, *Looking Backward; A Critical Appraisal of Commutarian Thought* (Princeton, NJ: Princeton University Press, 1993), esp. 161–67.

84. Josiah Strong, *The New Era* (New York: Baker & Taylor, 1893), 79f.; cf. 54–80. See also Strong, *Our Country*, 2nd ed. (New York: Baker & Taylor, 1891), 208–27. Strong associates the strength of American capitalism with Anglo-Saxon superiority and generally blends social Darwinism with God's purposes.

85. Charles E. Jefferson, *Five Present-Day Controversies* (New York: Fleming H. Revell, 1924), 146. See further John Moffatt Mecklin, *The Ku Klux Klan: A Study in the American Mind* (New York: Harcourt Brace, 1924), 127ff.; Preston William Slosson, *The Great Crusade and After, 1914–1928* (New York: Macmillan, 1930), 287ff.

86. *The Irony of American History* (New York: Charles Scribner's Sons, 1952), 106.

87. On the church in postwar Germany, see the final chapter of Barnett, *For the Soul of the People*, and Gerlach, *And the Witnesses Were Silent*.

and a need for denial in the face of revelations about the death camps, but certainly also because of fear of the Allies' program of "denazification," which could mean loss of employment.[88] In the 1960s the veil of silence and secrecy began to tear in a movement mainly among university students that demanded both truthfulness and a clean break with a past that had too easily made the transition to postwar economic prosperity. The issues were remarkably parallel to the sharp questioning of Christian tradition in the United States in the "death of God" theology—especially significant as theology "after Auschwitz"[89]—and in the social criticism generated by the civil rights movement and the violence against it.[90] In Germany and the United States the churches were stretched between maintaining parish life and coping with the new criticism and the turbulence that accompanied it.

In reviewing postwar German history from the point of view of the church, what appears perhaps most remarkable is the renewed strength of theology, both Catholic and Protestant, that became evident almost immediately after the war. The Second Vatican Council of the Roman Catholic Church, held in several sessions in the 1960s and early 1970s, not only modernized Catholic theology and practice but also opened an unprecedented dialogue between Catholic and Protestant theologians. Certainly, however, the Nazi period and the Holocaust were indelible facts that no theology of whatever stripe could ignore, facts that placed a large question mark between past and present and imposed a more stringent requirement of self-criticism than theologians had ever known before.

88. Apart from unrepentant Nazis, the idea that, no matter how wrong the Nazis were, it was wrong to oppose fighting the enemy, infected the postwar generation with a certain sympathy for the Hitler period. Germany's suffering and death became sacred, as also happened after World War I. After the union of East and West Germany in 1989, a virulent Neo-Nazism, anti-Semitism, and hatred of foreigners emerged among working-class youth in former East Germany.

89. Richard L. Rubenstein, *After Auschwitz* (Indianapolis: Bobbs-Merrill, 1966). See further Thomas J. J. Altizer and William Hamilton, *Radical Theology and the Death of God* (Indianapolis: Bobbs-Merrill, 1966). In the United States in the 1960s the "death of God" theology represented a broad questioning of Christian tradition and the church's embeddedness in American social behavior.

90. See the trilogy by Taylor Branch on "the King years" from 1954 to 1968: *Parting the Waters, Pillar of Fire*, and *At Canaan's Edge* (New York: Simon & Schuster, 1988, 1998, 2006).

Chapter 2

The Formative Period

2.1 KANT

2.1.1 *Critique of Pure Reason*

The most important work of Immanuel Kant (1724–1804), professor of philosophy at Königsberg, is the *Critique of Pure Reason,* first published in 1781.[1] Its starting point is the distinction between what Kant terms "dogmatic" philosophy and "critical" philosophy. What makes philosophy dogmatic is its tradition of reasoning metaphysically about God and the world without first critically examining the conditions and limitations of what we can know through reason. "The world is tired of metaphysical assertions" (P126). This had to do not only with

---

1. Kant, *Critique of Pure Reason,* trans. Norman Kemp Smith (New York: St. Martin's, 1965). References follow the convention of citing B as the pages in the 2nd edition of Kant's work, published in 1787. In the following there are also references to Kant, *Prolegomena to Any Future Metaphysics,* ed. Lewis White Beck (Indianapolis: Bobbs-Merrill, 1950), cited in the following text as P. See also the new *Cambridge Edition of the Works of Immanuel Kant,* Paul Guyer and Allen W. Wood, general editors (Cambridge: Cambridge University Press, 1992ff.). On Kant's life and work, see Helmut Thielicke, *Modern Faith and Thought,* 273–308.

philosophy but also with theology, which especially during the Enlightenment made rational-dogmatic assertions about God. Kant was moved to this criticism by the Scottish skeptic David Hume (1711–76), who argued that all ideas are derived from and limited to what we know by experience. In *An Enquiry concerning Human Understanding* (1748) Hume charged all metaphysics (especially in Christianity) with extending the limited ideas of human experience into what is beyond experience, that is, into theories about God and creation. In the earlier *Treatise on Human Nature* (1734–37) he had argued that the mind understands certain experiences in ways that cannot be demonstrated but that are apparently instinctive, such as in the idea that everything must have a cause. Only experience can deliver the proof that everything has a cause, but experience gives no absolute proof; it shows only that this has been the case and will probably be the case in the future.[2] Kant read Hume as a challenge to philosophy to enter into a critical examination of its entire course of thought. This he began in the first critique, first published in 1781, the *Critique of Pure Reason,* which is an analysis of human perception and reason as the foundation of science.

How do we perceive space and time? Kant notes that we imagine geometric objects in space, and we imagine arithmetic series, which as successive are temporal or in time. In fact, whatever the imagination imagines, its objects are in space and time. Also, in the experience of external things, space and time are constant forms of perception while the perceived things change. Kant drew the conclusion that space and time cannot be derived from experience. He thought they are in the mind as forms that precede anything we imagine, experience, or think about (B42, B49).

In analyzing experience he also concluded that in sense experience the mind is both receptive of influence from outside itself and active in organizing what it receives by means of "concepts of understanding." Some of these—the "pure concepts" or "categories"—are part of the mind's makeup prior to any experience (B102ff.). Categories are the most elemental concepts of understanding: causality, magnitude, substance, existence, and possibility. The mind "spontaneously" applies its concepts to each sense experience by means of "*schemata*" (B176ff.) and "imagination" [*Einbildungskraft,* power of imaging] (B152)—which medi-

---

2. David Hume, *An Enquiry concerning Human Understanding,* ed. Charles W. Hendel (Indianapolis: Bobbs-Merrill, 1955), on metaphysics, see 158–73 (section XII). This edition includes in an appendix, 177–80, a section from Hume's *Treatise on Human Nature* that states Hume's empirical theory of causation. In the *Enquiry* Hume said that Christianity, in accepting miracles, defies the understanding or reason, and hence requires a miracle in the believer to be believed (Ibid., 140f.). For a discussion of Hume's influence on Kant, see Norman Kemp Smith, *Commentary on Kant's "Critique of Pure Reason,"* 1st ed. 1919 (Atlantic Highlands, NJ: Humanities Press International, 1992), xxvff. Prior to reading Hume, Kant had agreed essentially with the theology of the German philosopher-theologian Christian Wolff (1679–1754), a student of Leibniz (1646–1716). Wolff advocated a rational "natural theology" that united Christian faith and natural science. For Wolff, God is omniscient, omnipresent, omnipotent, and benevolent, and worshiped by adoration and moral life. Revelation supplements the truths of reason without contradicting them. In this regard he was quite like his Enlightenment counterparts in England and America. Hans-Joachim Birkner, "Christian Wolff," in Martin Greschat, ed., *Gestalten der Kirchengeschichte* (Stuttgart: Kohlhammer, 1979ff.), 8:187–98. There were also advocates of John Locke's philosophy in eighteenth-century Germany. See Frederick Beiser, *The Fate of Reason,* 169 and chaps. 6 and 7.

ate between concepts and sense experience—to produce "*representations*" [*Vorstellungen*] (B125ff.), that is, meaningful objects, a tree, for example. What we know through sense experience is formed by space and time and made meaningful to the understanding through the schemata. Concepts that are present in the mind "prior" to experience are, like space and time, "*a priori*." Some concepts, however, such as the laws of nature, are learned through experience. These Kant calls "*a posteriori*" concepts (B2f., B163ff.).

We know only what we perceive, that is, we know nothing about the "*thing in itself*" [*Ding an sich*] or the "*noumenon*," which means that which is only thought, not perceived through the way our cognitive faculty (schemata and understanding) represents it. What we perceive is a *phenomenon* (Bxxvi, B310).[3] All a priori elements of the mind are "*transcendental*"; they "transcend" concrete experience but are involved in every possible experience (B25). "*Transcendent*" has a completely different meaning, namely, that of transcending the limits of experience altogether (B352f.). Kant does not know what the "thing in itself" is because it transcends experience. In a famous inconsistency Kant says that the (transcendent) "thing in itself" is the unknown nonsensible "cause" of an object (B522). The inconsistency is that he defines causality as a (transcendental) category or concept of the understanding, not applicable to the thing in itself.

The root of all the mind's activity is the unity of the "I," which in free spontaneity all at once unites all the aspects of experience into the understandable world around us. Kant calls this the "*transcendental unity of apperception*" or of "self-consciousness." (We return to this important concept in the section on Idealism in chap. 2.2.2 below.)

Kant's usual word for a perception of sense experience is the German verbal noun, *Anschauung*, which is commonly translated "*intuition*" (B126, B132). The word "intuition" can be misleading unless one knows the original Latin meaning of the verbal form, namely, "to look at," which is also the meaning of the German verb, *anschauen*. The primacy of vision or of seeing is apparent. Our experience is made up of intuitions, schemata, imagination, concepts of understanding, and finally also of *judgments*. By means of judgments the understanding sorts through and compares its experiences in the application of general concepts. Kant deals with different kinds of judgments in his three critiques. In the *Critique of Pure Reason* judgments of reason are either *analytic* or *synthetic* (B10ff.). An analytic judgment has to do with what belongs to a given concept and is part of what defines it. For example, a tree includes limbs and leaves in its concept. Synthetic judgments combine different concepts; for example, a warm stone, a windy day. Synthetic a priori judgments occur when the mind makes a priori connections that go beyond what experience itself warrants, such as in the statement "everything that happens has its cause" (B13). Here the mind makes a legitimate judgment, even though it has not and cannot experience "everything that happens."

---

3. The word "noumenon" is derived from a Greek word meaning to "think." Other forms are noumena (plural), noumen, noumenous, noumenal.

Kant defines reason as the transcendental concept "of the totality of conditions" for any given thing (B379). A *condition* of something has to do with what makes it possible, such as earth making a plant possible: it is the condition of the plant. "The transcendental concept of reason is directed always solely towards absolute totality in the synthesis of conditions, and never terminates save in what is absolutely, that is, in all relations, *unconditioned*" (B382).[4] The "totality" has to do with everything (all conditions) necessary to understand the world. Reason "terminates" only when it finds something that is not just another "condition" among others in a world in which everything conditions or is conditioned by something else. The "unconditioned" is higher than all conditions. It is the concept of God.

Reason naturally seeks to expand its empirical knowledge to complete universal knowledge. This can lead and has led reason astray into an illusion of knowledge, namely, when reason becomes "*transcendent*" (as opposed to "transcendental"), when it transcends the "*bounds*" and "*limits*" of experience in the search for what is absolutely unconditioned. For example, in its search for an absolute or unconditioned beginning of the world, in order to satisfy its natural need for completeness of knowledge, reason naturally moves from effects to their causes, which are the effects of other causes. It moves along this line (or in this series of conditions) with the intent to find completion in a first cause that has no cause or conditions. Such a first cause can only be a thing of purely intellectual thought; it cannot correspond to any experience whatsoever. In fact, however, reason is never able to think to the end of a regression of causes and effects (B536ff.). So, for example, if one were to say the big bang theory of the origin of the universe is a statement of the first cause of the existence of the world, another person could counter with the statement that the big bang itself must have had a cause, and so forth. (All natural sciences necessarily involve an infinite regression.) The same thought, Kant said, applies to God as first cause, for one must ask what caused God? With this question, Kant said, "*all sinks beneath us [hier sinkt alles unter uns]*" into an empty void, nothingness (B641).[5]

The supposed proof of God from the argument of design and purpose in the world, which Kant considers the most impressive of theoretical proofs (B649ff.), has the same defect.[6] From what appears in many ways to be purposive design in nature, one can reason that there may be an unknown "architect" of nature, but nature's imperfections do not allow the conclusion that there is an all-sufficient creator whose ideas rule nature absolutely. Nevertheless Kant says that the thought of a creator of purpose and order in nature is given "a priori" in reason and has a "regulative" use for science, insofar as it is helpful for science to assume a reasonable order in nature. But the conclusion that this cause is the absolutely unconditioned being (God) exceeds reason's limits (B717). If pure reason were

---

4. The German word for "condition" is *Bedingung,* and for "conditioned," *bedingt.* "Unconditioned" is *unbedingt.* These words or concepts are also discussed in chap. 2.2.1–2.

5. Norman Kemp Smith translates these words as "all support here fails us."

6. Kant allows this proof in teaching morality: Lewis White Beck, *A Commentary of Kant's Critique of Practical Reason* (Chicago: University of Chicago Press, 1960), 276.

to posit God in spite of this impossibility, it would have to do it by a "*leap*" beyond its limits, which, however, could produce nothing for science (B665). *Critical or negative theology* has therefore an important task, namely, to act as the "censor of reason" in keeping it mindful of its limitations (B668).

But the mind is hardly satisfied with this conclusion, and it is not the end of Kant's thought about God. Having established the negative *bounds* of thought, he begins work on the positive. There must be, he says, an "unconditioned necessity" (God) that is the "bearer of all things," but it is "for human reason the veritable abyss," that is, it utterly transcends reason (B641, cf. B650). However the critique of pure reason, in discovering the *bounds* of reason and experience, has led "to the spot where the occupied space (namely, experience) touches the void (that of which we can know nothing, namely, the noumena [things in themselves]). . . . For in all bounds there is something positive . . . [whereas] limits contain mere negations." These bounds or boundaries belong to experience (P102–5). Kant has arrived at a point where he himself makes his own kind of "leap" in acknowledging the reality of the noumena.

One of the contradictions—Kant calls them antinomies—that reason confronts within itself when it speculates about its "bounds" has to do with *freedom*. On the one hand it reasons that causality according to the laws of nature is not the only cause of appearances in the world, that there must be a cause which is free of the chain of causes and effects, namely, a first beginning as an act of God's freedom. (By analogy to human freedom, Kant also attributes to God understanding and will.) The contrary antinomy is, as we have seen above, that reason is never able to find a first beginning. In fact, according to this line of thought, there can be no freedom in the world at all, but only different series of causes and effects whose connections are necessary (B481f.). Now when Kant turns to his argument for freedom, he says that it is "noumenal," a characteristic of God, who is outside the sensible world of conditioned causes and effects. But he gives a proof of freedom not by reasoning about God (who transcends reason), but by reasoning about human beings. Everything in human life is conditioned or determined by the natural chain of causes, including all the motives of inner life, except for one: the "*ought*" of the question, "what ought I to do?" When we act in accord with the *moral* concept—which is also an a priori concept given in the mind—we act in freedom, not simply as a result of the chain of natural causes that determine us to act one way or another (B566ff.). With this thought, Kant makes the transition to his second critique, the *Critique of Practical Reason,* published in 1788.

2.1.2 *Critique of Practical Reason*

In the second *Critique*[7] Kant argues that it is our noumenal freedom in moral choice that leads us to realize that the space-time reality of the world of cause and

---

7. Kant, *Critique of Practical Reason,* trans. Louis White Beck (Indianapolis: Bobbs-Merrill, 1956). References in the following text are to page numbers in this translation.

effect that we perceive in experience is not the only reality. There is freedom—ours and God's. Without freedom, we would have to conclude that all events, including those of our emotional life, are fatalistically determined by the chain of causes and effects (e.g., we act as determined by our environment, our instincts, or our genes). Without freedom God too would have to be subject to space-time. If God were conceived as the first cause of the whole chain of being, God would be conceived in space and time. The result, Kant says, would be "Spinozism."

According to Benedict Spinoza (1632–77), there is one substance of all reality, in two forms, (material) extension and thought, and all things that exist are rational modifications of this one substance. Everything that happens is determined or caused by this original substance. Spinoza had argued that this "One," which he called God, was "unconditioned" and "infinite," but Kant showed that he contradicted the concept of the "unconditioned" with his theory of causes and effects, a causal chain that ended in the One as a first cause.[8]

According to Kant, when one reasons from the perspective of noumenal reality (reality beyond the bounds of our experience), one must conclude that the first cause, creation by God, cannot be in space-time, that only noumena or things in themselves are directly created by God, and that humanity is created with both freedom and the capacity for reason and for space-time experience of the things in themselves (104ff.). "Practical reason"—which is pure reason centered in the awareness of freedom and of the a priori concepts of morality—cannot know God directly. But it is in practical reason that Kant finds a proof of noumenal, transcendent reality.

There are, he says, three "postulates" of practical reason: *freedom, immortality of the soul, and God.* A postulate of "pure practical reason is not as such demonstrable, but an inseparable corollary of an a priori unconditionally valid practical law." If the law is valid, the postulates have to be valid. They are all noumenal; they transcend the bounds of experience. On the immortality of the soul, he writes: "Complete fitness of the will to the moral law is *holiness,* which is a perfection of which no rational being in the world of sense is at any time capable." However, because holiness is required by the moral law and therefore necessary, it can be found "only in an endless progress to that complete fitness," which, Kant says, is possible only through a continuation of human life after death. Without this, Kant says, the moral law is degraded to what is only possible in this life, that is, to the indulgence of human weakness (126f.). The moral law therefore requires the postulate of the immortality of the soul. The third postulate, God, must be concluded from the requirement that there must be an objective reality that cor-

---

8. Spinoza theorized both that God is infinite or unconditioned and that, as the cause of the world, God is *natura naturans,* active nature. For Kant the "modifications" of God that for Spinoza form the transition from the infinite to the finite, natural world do not allow a distinction between the infinite and time and finitude or between unconditioned and conditioned. See Spinoza's theory in book I, propositions 25–30, and book II, propositions 1f., in Spinoza's *Ethics,* in Benedict de Spinoza, *On the Improvement of the Understanding; The Ethics; Correspondence,* trans. R.H.M. Elwes (New York: Dover, 1955). See Henry E. Allison, "Kant's Critique of Spinoza," in *The Philosophy of Baruch Spinoza,* ed. Richard Kennington (Washington: Catholic University of America, 1980), 199–227.

responds to the free moral will. Our freedom for the "ought" and moral law itself require a "highest good" as their true purpose and end. Furthermore, a component of this highest good must be the happiness of those who attain it. Now, he says, there is only one cause of the highest good that is adequate to its concept: God, the free creator and the unconditioned bearer of all creation (128ff.).

Kant insists that the moral law, with its profound effect on conscience (it is itself not the conscience, which may be weak), does not depend for its validity on one's belief in either immortality or God, but is in and of itself a power in the mind that requires fulfillment. The "categorical imperative"—categorical because it is a pure a priori concept, imperative because it is the moral law—requires that in all instances we act in the conviction that our action follows universal moral law. Kant identifies morality as Christian morality and the highest good as the Christian kingdom of God (132f.). At the same time he refers again to the task of "negative theology," which is to reject the illegitimate metaphysical extension of the concepts of God and the highest good "through alleged experience" and "super-sensuous intuitions or feelings." Such experiences fall within the space-time chain of cause and effect and can therefore only be sources of superstition and obstacles to the practical use of pure reason (141). Yet God and the highest good, both of which are placed before us through the moral law, are matters of "faith and even pure rational faith" (130). In the preface to the 2nd edition of the *Critique of Pure Reason* (Bxxx) Kant writes: "I have found it necessary to deny knowledge, in order to make room for faith."

2.1.3 *Religion within the Limits of Reason Alone*

In *Religion within the Limits of Reason Alone,*[9] published in 1793, Kant interprets concrete or empirical religion, namely, Christianity. He begins by stating that, while the moral law is given a priori in the mind, the mind has, from its sensuous physical being, natural "predispositions" that develop in opposition to morality, such as sexual desire and the desire for equality. Culture profits from the rivalry that arises from the desire for equality, but immoral motives such as envy also arise from it (I/1). Such predispositions develop into opposition to morality by degrees: first weakness in holding to morality, then the mixing of moral and immoral motives, and finally the "wickedness" of adopting immoral "maxims." Maxims are the principles of the will that govern human behavior. All human beings are guilty of all three degrees ("all have sinned"), although most do not commit open vice: "outward" compliance with the law is coupled with an "*inner*" disposition that does not want to obey it. The key to morality is the *disposition* (in biblical imagery the "heart"), the ground for the choice of maxims. "*Ground*" means the condition or presupposition on the basis of which something comes

9. The text used here is the popular edition, *Religion within the Limits of Reason Alone,* trans. T. M. Greene and H. H. Hudson, 1st ed. 1934 (New York: Harper & Row, 1960). References are to parts/chapters/sections in Kant's text, so that other editions text may also be used.

to be. For example, on the ground of a moral disposition moral maxims are chosen as the principles of a person's behavioral motives. The problem is that in all human beings this ground is corrupted by the immoral development of the predispositions (desires) of sensuous being, and because the ground itself, the disposition, is corrupted, this evil is "radical" (from the Latin *radix*: root).

The reasons for the corruption are only relatively known, and each supposed cause leads to a regression of causes that is finally impenetrable, so that no clear reason can be given. In any case the radical corruption of the disposition must depend on a decision made in human freedom (I/2). Freedom is noumenal, outside of all cause-and-effect relationships and therefore outside of time itself. So also the original decision that resulted in corruption is noumenal, and therefore it is beyond memory, completely inscrutable. Grace, given by God, cannot help here, because the absolutely necessary moral imperative cannot be compromised by any sort of relief from what it requires. The moral imperative always requires only one thing: moral behavior, without excuse. The only way forward is the resolve of the will to reorient the disposition (whose depths remain inscrutable) to "the good" alone by the adoption of moral maxims that subordinate the sensuous predispositions to them—and, in the inevitable experience of failing these maxims, to resolve ever again to do better. No matter how great one's success may be, this process never reaches perfection in this life, but continues beyond it. Only in a continuation of life beyond death is there hope for a complete reformation of the disposition (from the ground up) and therefore for meeting the requirements of the moral law. The sign of a disposition successfully making the transition is optimism motivated by the love of what is good (including love of God as its author). For together with the moral disposition is given the concept of its divine origin, and this acts upon the mind, the human spirit, to strengthen it and give it confidence. But the way morally upward is fraught with inner conflict. There are no gradations or shadings of good and evil. Good and evil are absolutely different—as different as heaven and hell (II/1).

But Kant also has his interpretation of the Christian doctrine of justification. By "intellectual intuition" or the pure perception of God's mind, without human concepts, God immediately perceives the whole of everything that undergoes space-time development, without the spatial separation and the separate moments of time. At every moment of human time God perceives the whole world of space and time and of every human being in space and time. God therefore perceives the completed or total moral progress of a person and accepts as completely "well-pleasing" the good disposition of the person who has just begun the progression, in spite of the evil the person has not yet overcome (II/I, c; I/IV, Gen.Obs.).[10]

The moral law requires the moral community expressed by the concept of the kingdom of God, in which God alone is the moral ruler and in which each per-

---

10. Xavier Tilliette has a thorough discussion of Kant's "intellectual intuition" in *Recherches sur L'Intuition Intellectuelle de Kant à Hegel* (Paris: Librairie Philosophique J. Vrin, 1995), 13–37.

son works for the well-being of the other. Kant prefers to call it the "ethical commonwealth" (III). While the moral laws are purely "inward" in each person, the ethical commonwealth must organize visibly according to rules and ordinances that correspond to the moral laws. It extends universally to the whole of humanity and is a dominion of peace and justice without coercion. In an infinitely distant future it must replace the coercive "juridical state" so that "God is all in all." Progress on the way to the kingdom of God includes the concept of a "league of nations" in which reason prevails for the purpose of peace and justice. Kant finds in the Christian church, in spite of serious faults, an effective organization for the advancement of the ethical commonwealth. The source of its moral-religious teaching is Jesus, the "Teacher" [III/II].

Jesus' teaching has the significance of a revolution within Judaism, which in its purity is based on "outer" observances with "no relationship to religion."[11] Judaism has no belief in the future life; rewards and punishments all take place in this world. It is therefore a political commonwealth rather than a religious faith. At the time of Jesus it had been infused with Greek moral-religious ideas, and the influence of its priests had been reduced by Roman power. In this way, Kant says, the appearance of Jesus had been "prepared" [cf. Strauss, chap. 2.5.1]. Kant is ambiguous about revelation, which cannot be demonstrated by historical proofs (these demonstrate no more than probability) (III/IIf).[12] The "pure rationalist," that is, Kant himself, "recognizes revelation, but asserts that to know and accept it as real is not a necessary requisite to religion" (IV/1). Religion is grounded in the moral law. In any case the New Testament contains Jesus' teaching and provides the church everywhere with a single source of moral teaching (III/I/6). It is also true that humanity would not have come upon true religion so early or over such a wide geographic area without Jesus' teaching (IV/I). But historical Christianity falls into serious illusion by understanding literally what is meant symbolically in the New Testament. The truth can only be that of practical reason, that is, morality; all other forms of religious language are drawn from the physical-sensuous, space-time world of experience (IV/II). The prescientific world that fell into this misunderstanding had not yet understood the truth of practical reason; without this, the fall into superstition was inevitable.

Kant's usual word for the symbolic forms of the New Testament is *representation* [*Vorstellung*] (II, II/I, IV/II/1n) [chap. 2.1.1]. The truth is "represented" in

11. The "outward" character of Jewish law observance characterizes Judaism in German philosophy and theology throughout the nineteenth century and into the Nazi period. Here Kant evidently shows religious anti-Semitism.

12. Kant's contemporary G. E. Lessing made the famous statement that "historical truths" (anything that happened in history), unlike the truths of reason, cannot be demonstrated, hence they are impossible assertions for philosophy. In later theology Lessing's statement is associated with the axiom that historical-critical investigation achieves results that are only probable. *Lessing's Theological Writings*, ed. Henry Chadwick (Stanford: Stanford University, 1957), 53; cf. 31ff.; Thielicke, *Modern Faith and Thought*, 109–39.

symbolic or figurative language. For example, "Son of God" represents the "arche-type" of practical reason in the mind of each person, as something that has, figu-ratively speaking, "come down from heaven." It finds remarkably pure expression in Jesus. It suffers "humiliation" in its union with physical nature, and in purely moral action it suffers at the hands of the sinful world. Its suffering includes sac-rifice for the betterment of humanity (II/I/a). The "Spirit of God" is true religion that "guides us into all truth" (III/I/6; John 16:13). When the truth of the repre-sentation or symbol is understood by practical reason, its true content is lifted into the pure concept it represents (with this, Kant anticipates Hegel). Kant himself has no need of the representations, or rather he is interested in them only for their educational value as a means of moral instruction for the common mind. Moral religion is also represented (to a lesser degree) in historical faiths other than Chris-tianity. Kant thinks that all faiths will finally merge into the religion of practical reason as conceptual truth, freed from the "shell" of historical representation (III/I/5; III/I) [cf. Harnack, chap. 4.4].

As long as the church is dependent not only on the truth of reason in Scrip-ture, but also on the historical forms of New Testament language, it must depend on scriptural scholarship and therefore on an elite group of learned scholars and clergy.[13] Kant is ambivalent about them. Their work should be conducted with the right understanding of true religion, but many or most do not have this insight. Through knowledge of ancient history and languages they endeavor to help the church understand the historical accounts in the New Testament, to val-idate the credibility of these accounts (although at most only their possibility), and through a system of doctrines to give the historical faith permanence. "Under this system historical faith must finally become mere faith in scriptural scholars and their insight" (III/I/6). Their historical work is of such magnitude that it "brings down upon its head the whole of antiquity and buries itself under it" (IV/I/2). The present is the best time in the history of the church, insofar as rea-son has freed itself "from the weight of a faith forever dependent on the arbitrary will of the expositors" (III/II). It is arbitrary because decisions based on histori-cal evidence without adequate scientific investigation do not rise to the certainty ascribed to them by the expositors. Finally, Kant allows the possibility of the mir-acles that aided the early spread of Christianity. They are, however, beyond rea-son and are therefore irrelevant for moral life, except for one point: if we were morally perfect, "nature would have to heed our wishes" (IV/I/Gen.Obs.n).

Kant's understanding of the relationship between pure religion and its histor-ical expressions in Christianity is essentially Platonic. Whereas the religious ideas of practical reason are both pure and divine in origin, their historical representa-

---

13. See Kant's discussion of the relationship between the theological and philosophical faculties in the university in "The Conflict of the Faculties," in *Religion and Rational Theology,* trans. and ed. Allen W. Wood and George di Giovanni (Cambridge: Cambridge University Press, 1996), 252, 262–93.

tions are clouded by transitory forms from the empirical world, as Plato's ideas are imperfectly embodied in the material world.[14]

2.1.4 *Critique of Judgment*

The *Critique of Judgment*,[15] published in 1790, addresses an area of reason and experience not explored by the other two *Critiques,* namely, aesthetics (the theory of the beautiful and the sublime) and the purpose of design in nature. Here no certain knowledge is possible, but both aesthetics and design involve the use of "reflecting" judgment. Kant says that they lead eventually to the ideas of practical reason.

What is beautiful or sublime (awesome) in a great work of art (or in nature) can, for the reflecting judgment, have no sufficient explanation in concepts of reason. One can talk about it endlessly, but it always has a "more" about it that exceeds all definition and boundaries. It is as if it were an actual experience of the "unconditioned" within the natural framework of conditioned space-time experiences (§57f.). For Kant the beautiful is also a symbol of the practical reason and its ideal of the highest good. There is no mention of Christian symbols in the discussion of the beautiful or the sublime. Their significance seems limited to what practical reason makes of them.

The case is similar with the reflecting judgment's conclusion about the purpose of design in nature. Organisms seem to design themselves and to have their purpose only in themselves. Reflection on theories of evolution of organic life leads to the same conclusion (§81). In their natural environments organisms are evidently dependent on one another, but one can come to no final conclusion about an ultimate purpose of these relationships. For reason and reflection, they simply are. Scientifically one must always approach nature as if everything can be explained "mechanically," that is, by the laws of scientific reason. But science can give no explanation of the origin or purpose of design in organisms in themselves or of their dependence on one another. If for example one were to say that human life is the purpose of their interdependence, then one must explain why human life suffers as part of the chain of destruction in nature. Yet in its struggle within nature humanity develops culture (arts and sciences) and, at the highest, practical reason and the awareness of freedom from the natural order of things in the world (§§83f., 86). Hence reflecting judgment finds it reasonable, but cannot demonstrate, that nature is directed to the end of humanity's moral development and that God is its creator. Kant concludes the 3rd *Critique* with a discussion of the practically reasonable but not theoretically demonstrable faith that God is

---

14. E.g., *The Republic of Plato,* trans. Francis MacDonald Cornford (New York: Oxford University Press, 1945), 179–89.
15. Kant, *Critique of Judgment,* trans. J. H. Bernard (New York: Hafner, 1951). References to the text follow the convention of citing section numbers.

author of the world and directs all things to the end of the highest good, which again includes human happiness (§§85–91).

2.2 EARLY IDEALISM

2.2.1 The "Unconditioned"

Accompanying and influencing the development of post-Kantian Idealism was reflective thought about art, literature, and religion in the movement that became known as Romanticism. Among its most important characteristics is its development of Kant's idea, in the *Critique of Judgment*, of the "unconditioned" in what is beautiful or sublime in nature and art. Realizing the impossibility of conceptualizing or defining the beautiful or the awesomely sublime, while at the same time responding to it with a flow of concepts, feelings, moods, or with silence—all this, so the Romanticists thought, in some sense brought the unconditioned, in itself ineffable, to expression. Philosophy or aesthetics reflected not only on modes of expression in art but also on artful expression in everyday language, especially metaphor. Certain concepts from Spinoza's philosophy, namely, that all things "conditioned" are derived from and contained within the unconditioned One, were interpreted in terms of the beautiful and the sublime. Building mainly on Kant and influenced strongly by the revolutionary political mood of the late eighteenth century, Romanticism held freedom in high regard and explored its meaning in philosophy and art. It initiated a new epoch with broad significance that continues to influence art, philosophy, and theology.[16]

The work of Spinoza had been largely ignored in the Enlightenment until a prominent German philosopher and literary figure, Gotthold Ephraim Lessing (1729–81), toward the end of his life claimed to be (to a certain degree) an adherent of Spinoza's philosophy, from which followed a philosophical discussion that also involved Kant. A significant figure in the discussion was Friedrich Heinrich Jacobi (1743–1819), who became convinced that Spinoza's philosophy was correct but led to atheism, while Christian faith had to do with an immediate consciousness of a personal God, a "feeling" of certainty that was prior to discursive reason.[17]

---

16. On Romanticism and its influence, see esp. Andrew Bowie, *Aesthetics and Subjectivity: From Kant to Nietzsche*, 2nd ed. (Manchester: Manchester University, 2003), and *From Romanticism to Critical Theory: The Philosophy of German Literary Theory* (London: Routledge, 1997). Bowie does not consider the problematic side of Romanticism: It produced bad art, philosophy, and theology as well as good, and in their disregard of conventions some Romantic spirits overstepped the boundary between good and evil. Romanticism was an important current in the social and intellectual thought that produced Nazism.

17. Jacobi was born into relative wealth and was from time to time an official of the state, but in the main he was a "man of letters" of broad learning and acquaintance. On Jacobi generally and the debate about Spinoza, see Frederick C. Beiser, *The Fate of Reason*, 44–91; Bernard Pünjer, *History of the Christian Philosophy of Religion*, trans. W. Hastie (Edinburgh: T. & T. Clark, 1887), 621–54; Hermann Timm, *Gott und die Freiheit, Studien zur Religionsphilosophie der Goethezeit*, vol. 1: *Die Spinozarenaissance* (Frankfurt: Vittorio Klostermann, 1974).

What was of particular interest for Jacobi and for the discussion about Spinoza was Spinoza's theory of the relationship between God—or what Spinoza called God—and the world. As we have seen [chap. 2.1.2], Kant exposed an inconsistency in Spinoza's argument that made his whole philosophy questionable. But this inconsistency itself—the problem of distinguishing between the "unconditioned" and the "conditioned"—posed a problem that required new reflection. In distinguishing between the one substance and the world of things, Spinoza used the Latin word *determinatio* to describe or define things. The usual English translation is not the derivative English word, "determined" (although it could be used), but "*conditioned.*" In German the common translation of Spinoza's word is *bedingt*, whereby the root word, *Ding*, means "thing," and *bedingt* literally means (to coin a word) "thinged." The common meaning of *bedingt* is "conditioned." Another German translation of Spinoza's word *determinatio* is *bestimmt*, and *unbestimmt* may also be translated "*unconditioned*" (nondetermined). *Bestimmen* is a common word meaning "to define" or "to condition." So both *unbestimmt* and *unbedingt* commonly mean "unconditioned." Kant had used these same words to distinguish between the world of perception on the one hand and the noumenal world of freedom on the other.

Jacobi agreed with Kant that human reason cannot escape the world of conditions, not even in thought, insofar as every thought is conditioned by another thought. Reason by itself cannot arrive at an "unconditioned." But, Jacobi said, the human mind does have within it the concept of the "unconditioned" beyond the world as the possibility of the world. Furthermore, by analogy with human freedom, the mind naturally conceives a free God as the first cause, which for Jacobi is the God of Christianity. But because neither the "unconditioned" nor its identification with the Christian God can be demonstrated by reason—or by Kant's practical reason—these must be believed through a "leap" of faith beyond reason.[18] Jacobi became known for this in the philosophical and theological tradition: the leap of faith based essentially on the subjective feeling of certainty. (He will later redefine his position as a kind of "reason," in agreement with the philosopher J. F. Fries [chap. 2.8].)

German Idealism, which holds that the world is made up of concepts or ideas of the mind, was a response to several important ideas in Spinoza, Jacobi, and above all Kant, who is himself a kind of Idealist, insofar as for him the world of representations is produced by concepts of the mind and not simply empirically given. But he is not a pure Idealist, because the representation of a thing is in some sense caused by the "thing in itself," which transcends all concepts. In early German Idealism one of the most important concepts is the "unconditioned," a

---

18. Friedrich Heinrich Jacobi, *Werke*, ed. Friedrich Roth and Friedrich Köppen, reprint of the edition of 1819 (Darmstadt: Wissenschaftliche Buchgesellschaft, 1968), IV, part I, 59; part II, 145–60 (Beilage 7); III, 405; on immediate consciousness as "feeling" (*Gefühl*) see IV, part I, 191ff. (Vol. IV of Jacobi's *Werke* is the 1789 edition of *Über die Lehre des Spinoza, in Briefen an Herrn Moses Mendelssohn* [1st ed. 1785]). Jacobi's "leap" earned his thought the name "fideist" (from the Latin word for faith).

concept with a long previous history. One finds it at the beginning of Western philosophy in Plato (see below). It is found in the tradition of "negative" theology (*docta ignorantia* or *via negativa*) in the Patristic period and the Middle Ages.[19] As a concept in religion it has been related to the indefinable nature (or ineffability) of God in Exodus 3:14, and to the God who "dwells in unapproachable light" in 1 Timothy 6:16. A concept with an almost identical meaning in Idealism is "*infinite*," whose Latin meaning is "without limits" or "without boundaries." In philosophy and theology the common German word *grundlos* (groundless) means without condition (possibility) for existence, *Grund* (ground) means the condition for something. *Abgrund* (an "abyss" in common German) means "groundlessness," which usually refers to the unconditioned or infinite. The unconditioned or infinite is also "no thing" or nothing, and yet it is not nothing in the sense of vacant space. It is rather pure (unlimited, unconditioned) power or possibility and is the condition or ground of actuality or existence. The "*Absolute*" has the sense of finality as the highest possible reality or thought; its root Latin meaning is "separated from" and can connote holiness. An illustration of the significance of the "unconditioned" (*das Unbedingte*) in nineteenth-century thought is Adolf Trendelenburg's extended discussion of the concept in his popular work on philosophy, *Logische Untersuchungen*, first published in 1840.[20] "The unceasing movement of the human spirit," he writes, "comes to rest only in the concept of the whole. . . . [P]hilosophical abstraction names this unconditioned, which carries the unity of the whole, the Absolute; faith, more alive, names it God."

There are other important terms in Idealism. "*Idea*" is a philosophical word taken from Ancient Greek. It implies something seen and is related to Kant's word *Anschauung* [chap. 2.1.1]. The related common German word *Idee* is the equivalent of "idea" in English. The Latin root of "*speculative*" is also a word for seeing. For Idealism it means thought beyond the boundaries of empirical knowledge that intellectually perceives higher reality.

2.2.2 Idealism in Fichte and Schelling

Two figures especially represent early post-Kantian Idealism: Johann Gottlieb Fichte (1762–1814), and Friedrich Wilhelm Joseph Schelling (1775–1854), who is also a figure of Romanticism.[21] Fichte began the Idealist response to Kant and was followed almost immediately by the youthful and precocious Schelling.

19. In the Middle Ages this concept was given expression particularly by Nicolas of Cusa (died 1464) and before him by Meister Eckhart (died 1327). See, e.g., Cusa, *The Vision of God* (New York: Frederick Ungar, 1960), 58–91; *Meister Eckhart,* trans. Raymond Blakney (New York: Harper & Brothers, 1941), 203–6, 227–32.

20. 2 vols. (Hildesheim: Georg Olms, 1964), 2:461–510. The following quotation is on 461.

21. Fichte, who came from humble origins, became professor of philosophy in Jena and later in Berlin. Schelling studied theology and philosophy in Tübingen, along with Hegel, who was several years older, and the poet Hölderlin. Schelling, the son of a Lutheran clergyman who led a preparatory school for the university, became professor of philosophy in Jena, Würzburg, Munich, and finally Berlin. English introductions include Andrew Bowie, *Schelling and Modern European Philosophy*

As we have seen [chap. 2.1.1], the unconditioned for Kant is that which is not derived from or conditioned by anything else, and as such it cannot be part of the space-time world in which everything is conditioned. No point of Kant's philosophy was immediately contested more than the supposedly unconditioned "thing in itself," because it cannot be even talked about without recourse to concepts, all of which are "conditions."[22] Kant says the "thing in itself" is (in some way) the "cause" of the objects of perception, and yet Kant also says it is beyond the bounds of all our concepts of understanding, among which is causation. Idealism draws the conclusion that Kant is wrong on this point, that there is no "thing in itself" involved in sense experience. But Idealism agrees entirely with Kant's concept of freedom: with both the moral freedom of the *Critique of Practical Reason* and the free "spontaneity" of human thinking in the *Critique of Pure Reason*. In fact, said Fichte, Kant's concept of the freedom of the ego (the "I," the self) is the key to a true philosophy that can correct Kant's mistakes.

How does one perceive one's own self? According to Kant's *Critique of Pure Reason*, the "I" or ego cannot be made into a object as if it were a thing in the world. If it thinks about itself, making itself objective to itself, its object is always only a past moment of the self, for the self is always actively thinking and in this sense never becomes its own object. Said in a different way, what it can "fix" of itself to think about is always a past moment, while thinking, so to speak, keeps on running. The thinking ego is always already prior to and the condition of whatever its object happens to be. While a certain thought itself can be an object (I remember thinking of a tree), thinking itself it is spontaneous activity and as such always already beyond any attempt to objectify itself to itself. This is the first and most important perception of Idealism.

A second important point is that the ego is the unity of all experience, as Kant had said. He calls this the "transcendental unity of apperception," that is, of self-consciousness (B132) [chap. 2.1.1].[23] We recall that for Kant an immediate perception of an object or thing is an "intuition." Kant names the ego's perception of its own spontaneous thinking an "indeterminate empirical intuition." But here again there is a problem. Kant says that "indeterminate" means the intuition is not of a sensible object, so that "empirical" in this case does not have to do with such an object (B422n, 429f.). But in every other instance in Kant's philosophy, "empirical" is a category (a priori concept) that is essential for the construction of representations of the objects of sensuous perception. But if it is not an empirical intuition, what kind of intuition is it?

(London: Routledge, 1993), and the introduction to *Idealism and the Endgame of Theory: Three Essays by F. W. J. Schelling*, trans. Thomas Pfau (Albany: State University of New York, 1994).

22. See *Between Kant and Hegel: Texts in the Development of Post-Kantian Idealism*, trans. George di Giovanni and H. S. Harris (Albany: State University of New York, 1983).

23. The unity of the "I" immediately unites all its functions and therefore its world. It is "transcendental" because prior to experience. *Critique of Pure Reason*, B131–35. Martin Heidegger's *Kant and the Problem of Metaphysics*, trans. James S. Churchill (Bloomington: Indiana University, 1962), is largely an analysis of the meaning of this concept.

Fichte and Schelling thought Kant should say the intuition is "intellectual," because it is not of a sensual or physical object but is perceived purely in the mind.[24] The term was drawn from Kant himself. Kant had said that if there were an intuition of the ego as spontaneous thinking, and if this spontaneous thinking were perceived apart from any and all concepts or representations, this intuition would be an "intellectual intuition." But Kant insists there is no intuition apart from concepts and representations (Bxl, B68, B307f). For Kant, human being perceives whatever it perceives only by means of concepts and representations.[25]

If Idealism no longer accepted the "thing in itself," then the first task of Idealism was to find a better explanation of perception. Fichte thought Kant was right in saying that the forms of space and time and the categories and concepts of the understanding were the means of construction of the given world. But he took a further step: the source of everything is the ego: the ego constructs everything in its world, so there is no need for a noumenal "thing in itself." Based also on Kant, Fichte said the ego is the "unity" of everything. It is utterly free, unconditioned spontaneity and the unity of all perception and reason. Therefore, he concluded, the first principle of everything, of all world-construction, must be the active ego.[26] We are not actually conscious of constructing the world, because this has always already spontaneously happened in the unity of the ego. Kant too had said that construction or representation of any object occurs prior to conscious thought, so that the ego always encounters the world as already given.

Although he does not use the exact terms, in Idealism Fichte is the originator of the *dialectic* triad found in different forms in all the post-Kantian Idealists: *thesis—antithesis—synthesis*. (1) The thesis is the unconditioned, spontaneous, free activity of the ego, or, as Fichte calls it, pure will. It is in itself unbounded. (2) The antithesis is the limiting of this activity by the categories and concepts of the ego in the construction of the objective world. The objective world sets boundaries to the free activity of the ego, the pure will. Without the antithesis, the activity of the ego would simply extend into infinity without any limit or boundary. (3) Synthesis occurs when the unbounded activity of the ego is reflected back on itself by the boundary of the objects it has created. The ego becomes aware of the object as object and of itself over against the object. Philosophy understands this

---

24. J. G. Fichte, *The Science of Knowledge*, ed. and trans. Peter Heath and John Lachs (Cambridge: Cambridge University Press, 1982), 38ff.; F. W. J. Schelling, *Werke*, ed. K. F. Schelling (Stuttgart and Augsburg: Cotta, 1856ff.), 1:215f., 401f. In the following, references to Schelling's *Werke* list the four volumes of the second division continually with those of the first division as vols. 11–14. On the relationship of Idealism and Romanticism to Kant, see especially Manfred Frank, *Eine Einführung in Schellings Philosophie* (Frankfurt: Suhrkamp, 1995), and *Einführung in die frühromantische Ästhetik* (Frankfurt: Suhrkamp, 1989).

25. As we have seen [chap. 2.1.3], Kant has his own special use for the term "intellectual intuition," namely, for God's perception of the world, which is outside of space-time and absolutely free and for this reason "intellectual" (in the sense of an immediate pure perception). It has nothing to do with the concepts of the human mind.

26. Fichte, *Science of Knowledge*, 94ff., 231ff.

as the unity of subject and object.[27] The true origin of the triad, however, lies in ancient Greek thought, as we shall see below.

F. W. J. Schelling disagreed with Fichte at a key point. The activity or act that creates a world in constant production both of nature in such enormous variety and of other human beings required an acting agent infinitely greater than the human ego, an agent of which the ego is only a kind of reflection or image. In defining the way of perceiving this "Absolute," Schelling uses the term he criticizes Kant for not using, "intellectual intuition." With this term Schelling names human being's immediate perception of the absolute unity (synthesis) of subject (infinite activity: thesis) and object (the bounding of this activity: antithesis) in the Absolute or God. It is the perception, the "intellectual intuition," of the unity of everything in God—a thought he shares with Spinoza, although he arrives at this thought in a different way. Schelling notes that philosophy has usually arrived at its concept of the Absolute by means of reasoning (which is also true of Spinoza's method): the Absolute is the final conclusion of a series of conclusions (for example, the world must have a cause). In contrast, Schelling's Absolute is not the final member of a series but the "center" of all that is, the "One," absolute unity. It is not the Absolute or the God of traditional metaphysics, because it is not perceived as an object (as is the case with God as a first cause). The thought of the "One" is hardly new; as a philosophical concept it may be traced back to Plato and beyond him to the philosopher Parmenides.[28] But Schelling's method of perceiving it in intellectual intuition is unique: the "One" is the "indifference" (non-difference) or "identity" of subject and object prior to separation into human subjective perception and things in the world. This is reflected in the human mind. Because of the original identity of subject and object, in every act of human perception there is, prior to objective reflection, a unity or identity of the two: the image of the object in the mind of the subject corresponds to or is the same as the object or thing perceived.[29]

The Absolute is directly perceived as absolute identity only in intellectual intuition, not by reasoning about God. But secondly, given the Absolute, Schelling speculates about the relationship between the Absolute and the existing world, using concepts from Greek philosophy. The Absolute is no thing or nothing, yet it is original power or "potence," the "possibility" of an existing world (a theory traditionally associated with Aristotle).[30] As the possibility of everything, the

---

27. Ibid., 275–78. This same pattern of thesis-antithesis-synthesis is already present in Kant as ego (subject), thing in itself (object), and cognition (unity); and in Spinoza as the unity (synthesis) of thought (subject) and material extension (object).

28. See Plato's dialogue *Parmenides*. On the same concept in Neoplatonism, see Gerard O'Daly, *Platonism Pagan and Christian* (Burlington: Ashgate, 2001), chap. 2. On "intellectual intuition," see Schelling, *Werke*, 1:367f. Cf. the contrast with "dogmatism," ibid., 6:157f.: "Dogmatism is a system that arises when the concepts of the finite world . . . are applied to the Infinite, the Absolute," e.g., when the Absolute is understood as first cause.

29. E.g., Schelling, *Werke*, 4:123ff., 137ff.

30. See Aristotle, *Metaphysics*, book IX on actuality, potency, and possibility.

Absolute is the "ground" of the world. But in order for a world to exist, there must be in the power of the Absolute some elemental principle or principles that account for the multiplicity of forms or beings in the world. Again in accord with Greek philosophy, but also like Fichte, he conceives a three-step process of the-sis-antithesis-synthesis. He argues that there can be no transition from "infinite" to "finite" unless the infinite acts to limit itself.[31] There is a first "potence" or power of unlimited, unconditioned expansion; it is countered by a second potence of limitation or condition. A third potence unites the first two potencies in the production of things that have duration in existence. It brings into exis-tence inorganic and organic stages of a world constantly in becoming and pass-ing away. The final formation of this synthesis is human self-awareness or self-consciousness of itself in its world. From the very beginning, in his days as a student, Schelling took the thought of these three potencies or "principles," as he also calls them, not from Fichte but from Plato: the endless, unlimited or uncon-ditioned, *apeíron*; limit or form, *péras*; and the concrete formations that arise from their interaction [cf. Kierkegaard, chap. 2.6].[32]

The first formations of the universe are, like Plato's ideas, archetypes of exis-tence. The interaction of the three potencies or principles produces space, time, and matter, the concepts or ideas of world-construction, and continues produc-tion through the evolution of organic nature, finally reaching its culmination in humanity and its history.[33] The German word for the self-conscious, reflective or thinking ego is *Geist,* which can be translated as "mind" but more appropriately as "*spirit.*"[34] In the evolutionary process it emerges as self-conscious spirit only at

31. Schelling, *Werke*, 7:143: "Not formlessness is the true infinite but what limits itself in itself and makes itself finite [*sich vollendet*]." The only finite model for such self-limitation is human spirit [*Geist*]: ibid., 1:313ff., 367ff. Nevertheless there remains for Schelling an infinite difference between the Absolute and its finite forms. Very probably Schelling conceived God from the beginning in rela-tionship to Plato's highest concept, "the Good." See *The Republic of Plato*, trans. Francis MacDonald Cornford, 211–20.

32. Plato, *Philebus*, 30a (27b); *F. W. J. Schelling, "Timaeus" (1794)*, ed. Hartmut Buchner (Stuttgart: Frommann-Holzboog, 1994), esp. 36, 47f. Cf. *The Collected Dialogues of Plato*, ed. Edith Hamilton and Huntington Cairns (Princeton, NJ: Princeton University Press), 1104 (*Philebus*, 27b): "The first . . . I call the unlimited, the second the limit, and the third the being that has come to be by the mixture of these two." Through all the stages of his work Schelling makes use of these Platonic principles, also in the traditional metaphysical form of material cause, efficient cause, and final cause: *Werke*, 12:112f.; see further, e.g., 1:356, 383; 11:388–95. On Schelling's early work on Plato's *Timaeus*, see Birgit Sandkaulen-Bock, *Ausgang vom Unbedingten* (Göttingen: Vandenhoeck & Ruprecht, 1990), 19ff.; Bowie, *Schelling*, chap. 1.

33. Schelling, *System of Transcendental Idealism (1800)*, trans. Peter Heath (Charlottesville: Univer-sity of Virginia Press, 1993); *Ideas for a Philosophy of Nature as Introduction to the Study of This Science, 1797*, trans. Errol E. Harris and Peter Heath (Cambridge: Cambridge University Press, 1988); *On Uni-versity Studies*, trans. E. S. Morgan (Athens: Ohio University Press, 1966); *Bruno, or, On the Natural and Divine Principle of Things*, trans. Michael G. Vater (Albany: State University of New York, 1984).

34. There is in German a long tradition of naming human spirit *Geist*, and Holy Spirit has always been *Heiliger Geist*. As a designation of human spirit *Geist* (which can also mean "ghost") means first rational personhood and then also what is characteristic of a person; one can also speak of the *Geist* of a group, such as a nation. In German Idealism *Seele* or soul is the equivalent of Aristotle's *psyche*; *Geist* is to a degree the equivalent of Aristotle's active *nous*. Spirit presupposes and is a development within soul (life).

the end the evolution of nature. Human being is nature that has developed into self-conscious awareness. It becomes self-conscious when it is aware of objects as objects: when, as Fichte had said, its activity is reflected back toward itself. In this way it "comes to itself." Schelling clearly takes the idea of this evolutionary process from Fichte. Spirit is its final product, and spirit can reconstruct the steps of the process in the science of the genesis and evolution of the natural world, humanity, and its history.

2.2.3 Religion in Fichte

In his later religious thought Fichte significantly modified his concept of the ego, evidently having been persuaded that there is a reality greater than the ego, but not Schelling's Absolute. In dependence on Kant's ideal of practical reason, he developed a theory of an absolute "moral world order" that makes itself known "inwardly" in every person. In a publication from the year 1798, *Über den Grund unseres Glaubens an eine göttliche Weltregierung* (On the Ground of Our Belief in a Divine World Order), he distinguishes between the physical world of the ego's sensuous experience and the ego's inner experience of freedom: "In my reason itself there are no . . . boundaries, I am free in all my expressions [and thought], and only I myself, by my will, can set myself a boundary." But in and with this power of the will one is aware of the morality of personal purpose in life, and from this arises awareness of what is greater than the ego: the determination or conditionedness [*Bestimmung*] for moral purpose of all human life, the "moral world order." Without this, personal life in its freedom would fall into "an unlimited ocean," chaos. Fichte is convinced that the moral world order is absolutely real and true; awareness of it is both "faith" and "revelation." "The moral order is the divine." "This is the only possible confession of faith: happily and simply to bring forth what duty commands, without doubt or care about the consequences."[35] Fichte joined with this a critique of traditional theism. "Personhood" and "consciousness" are qualities or conditions one finds in human being and therefore have to do with "limitation and finitude." If we conceive God as a conscious person, then we conceive God as finite, and a finite God cannot explain the moral world order.[36]

A consequence of this publication was a public charge of atheism, which led to Fichte's loss of his position in philosophy at Jena (he was later appointed to the same position at the new university in Berlin). He defended himself in publications in the year 1799. In the first, directed to the public, he equates the transcendent reality of the moral world order with Christianity's kingdom of God, a reality of which one is certain through inward "feeling" [*Gefühl*].[37] In the second, more extensive and more theoretical publication Fichte defends the view that God cannot be thought without finite concepts. Thought has to do with what is

---

35. *Fichtes Werke*, vol. 5, *Zur Religionsphilosophie* (Berlin: Walter de Gruyter, 1971), 181f., 185.
36. Ibid., 187.
37. "Appellation an das Publikum gegen die Anklage des Atheismus" (1799), in *Zur Religionsphilosophie*, 206f., 208, 212, 232. When Fichte speaks of "feeling," he refers to Jacobi [Chap. 2.2.1].

definite [*bestimmt*] or limited [*beschränkt*], while God must be infinite. For example, if God is thought "outside" the world, then a limit is given in the thought, insofar as an "outside" is limited by an "inside." Fichte supports his argument by referring to the biblical prohibition of making an image of God (also with reference to 1 Tim. 6:16).[38]

Fichte's most comprehensive statement of his faith is from the year 1806: *The Way towards the Blessed Life, or the Doctrine of Religion.*[39] The human ego, he says, is rooted in a ground that is also its ultimate goal, namely, transcendent or supersensuous moral reality as what is truly real. This moral reality is the divine itself, and it is attained by pure moral thought and the sacrifice of all self-interest of the ego to it. "Pure thought is itself Divine Existence"; that is, in pure thought the moral ideal comes into existence. But pure thought is rare, and Christ is its great example. His pure moral message is the true content of the New Testament, which is otherwise mixed with dispensable concepts from the time. Fichte is critical of biblical scholarship for not separating the historical from the moral truth of the New Testament. In this he essentially repeats Kant's critique of biblical theology [chap. 2.1.3].

2.2.4 The Early Schleiermacher: *On Religion: Speeches to Its Cultured Despisers*

Friedrich Ernst Daniel Schleiermacher (1768–1834) was a theologian at the new university in Berlin whose major work, *The Christian Faith,* was first published in 1821 [chap. 2.7.2].[40] His first book is very different in kind and has also been his most popular: *On Religion: Speeches to Its Cultured Despisers,* first published in 1799.[41] Later he revised it and added notes to bring it in accord with his mature thought and theology.[42] He was influenced by Kant, Spinoza, Jacobi, Schelling, and the new Romanticism, and he in turn influenced the religious thought of

---

38. "Gerichtliche Verantwortung gegen die Anklage des Atheismus," in *Zur Religionsphilosophie,* 265–67.

39. In *The Popular Works of Johann Gottlieb Fichte,* trans. William Smith, 4th ed., reprinted from the edition of 1899, 2 vols. (Bristol, England: Thoemmes, 1999), vol. 2. The quotation below is from 316.

40. On the early Schleiermacher, see Martin Redeker, *Schleiermacher: Life and Thought,* trans. John Wallhausser (Philadelphia: Fortress, 1973); Stephen Prickett, *Origins of Narrative: The Romantic Appropriation of the Bible* (Cambridge: Cambridge University Press, 1996), 180–203. Schleiermacher was the son of a Reformed clergyman in the service of the Prussian army. The family was strongly influenced by the pietism of the Moravians and had their children educated in Moravian schools. [See also chap. 1.2.]

41. Trans. Richard Crouter (Cambridge: Cambridge University Press, 1996). Page numbers in the following text refer to this edition. The "cultured despisers" are in the narrow sense a group of secular friends, in the larger sense the intellectuals of the time. The work Schleiermacher published in 1800 after the *Speeches,* the *Soliloquies,* ET Horace Leland Friess (Chicago: Open Court, 1957), is very close to the *Speeches* in spirit.

42. Trans. of the 3rd German ed. of 1830 by John Oman (New York: Harper & Row, 1958). The Oman translation, made in the nineteenth century, has been frequently reprinted with the same pagination. The 1st ed. of the *Speeches* was largely ignored until Rudolf Otto republished it in the early twentieth century [chap. 4.7].

Idealism. The *Speeches* were published in the year before Schelling's first significant publication on religion and in the same year as Fichte's second tract on religion. Here we consider only the first edition of the *Speeches*.

The two best known statements of the *Speeches* (they also stand in the final edition) declare that religion "springs necessarily and by itself from the interior of every better soul, it has its own province in the mind in which it reigns sovereign" (17, cf. 95). And "religion is the sensibility and taste for the infinite" (23). The relationship between the "infinite" or the "universe" and the "finite" underlies the whole discussion. "Everything finite exists only through the determination of its limits, which must, as it were, be 'cut out' of the infinite" (23f.). The language of limits is of course Kantian. In the "taste for the infinite" there is an immediacy of perception that unites subject and object, as in Schelling, but Schleiermacher's focus is only partly on this; it is mainly on the "feeling" ("taste") that accompanies religious perception.

In immediate consciousness all perception is a combination of "intuition" and "feeling," although in ordinary perception one is usually not aware of the component of feeling. Immediate consciousness is described as "that first mysterious moment that occurs in every sensory perception, before intuition [perception] and feeling have separated, where sense and its objects have, as it were, flowed into one another and become one. . . . How quickly it passes away. But I wish you were able to hold on to it and also to recognize it again in the higher and divine religious activity of the mind" (31). Religion is a unity of perception and a unique feeling of the unity of the universe. One cannot perceive the universe or infinite directly, but in perceptions of its manifestations, the starry sky, for example, one can feel the unity of the whole.[43] Religious experience is non or pre-objective; only secondarily is it objectified and does it become accessible for reflection and philosophical thought. Primarily it is intensely personal, and every person experiences it in a personal way (22–32, 100).

Throughout the *Speeches* Schleiermacher emphasizes personal freedom in religion in opposition to all forms of coercion. "Whether we have a God as part of our intuition depends on the direction of our imagination." In one direction the imagination may be atheistic; in another it concludes there must be a "free being," a "personification of the spirit of the universe" who is the origin of the activity of the whole (53). This is Schleiermacher's conclusion, as derived from his Christian experience. He quotes Matthew 11:27: "No one knows the Father except the Son and anyone to whom the Son chooses to reveal him" (120). The truth for Schleiermacher is Christian (115–23). But human being is religious and participates to some degree in truth prior to being Christian, assuming one is open to religious perceptions and feelings. The *Speeches* discuss religion, one could say, in "generic" terms. Religion in all its higher forms, where it is truly related to the

43. "But the Infinite, meaning not something unconditioned, but the infinity of existence generally, we cannot be conscious of immediately and through itself. It can only be through a finite object, by means of which our tendency to postulate and seek a world, leads us from detail and part to the All and the Whole" (*Speeches*, trans. Oman, 103).

infinite, gives human life some degree of its true meaning: the freedom from attachment to individual, finite things and so from "opinion and desire." What the Christian God is communicating to human being in the universe, the great message of the "infinite," is the love that embraces and joins all things in the unity of the universe (28, 34, 43, 72ff., 124). "To me everything is a miracle." Revelation is "every new intuition of the universe." Inspiration is "every restoration of a religious intuition." "What are operations of grace? All religious feelings are supernatural" (49). "Let the universe be intuited and worshipped in all ways. Innumerable forms of religion are possible" (123). Christ however is the "divine mediator" (119–21).

But the finite "strains against" the infinite; human life is morally corrupted and focused on particular things in such a way that "we do not perceive what is of the spirit of God." "The corruptibility of all that is great and divine in human and finite things is one half of the original intuition of Christianity" (122). It sees into the darkness of evil (117). The other half is the perception of redemption (115), the union of the finite "with the divine" (122).

Some interpreters of the first edition of the *Speeches* have understood the "universe" as God and have called the work pantheistic. In his later work Schleiermacher rejected this interpretation. In the notes to the final edition of the *Speeches,* he says that "universe" means "creation," according to Christian doctrine.[44] But God is omnipresent in creation and constantly communicates with every human being through creation.[45] It is plausible that, because the first edition was a work of apologetic theology, Schleiermacher sought not to be doctrinally correct but only to establish common ground with the "despisers" in order to lead them toward Christianity. The fourth speech could illustrate this: it asserts "once there is religion, it must necessarily be social" (73), which leads to a discussion of what the church should be and in truth is: a fellowship in freedom. Speaking to and hearing from others about religion are necessary for religious life (74). But the revisions and notes of the final edition of the *Speeches* are extensive, and in fact one has to do with two very different works. In the first edition Schleiermacher wrote that "it is not the person who believes in a holy writing who has religion, but only the one who needs none and probably could make one for himself" (50, cf. 121). This sentence was deleted in later editions. In another statement he equates true immortality with losing the "outlines of our personality" in the infinite (53), which later critics were to say was a good definition of death.[46]

44. *Speeches,* trans. Oman, 24; cf. 23. Schleiermacher refers to sections in *The Christian Faith* that have to do with the doctrine of creation (§§ 8.2; 36.1f.).

45. In *The Christian Faith,* §8, addition 2a, Schleiermacher says that in speaking of God one cannot, "strictly speaking," make a difference between "inside" and "outside" creation because this would "endanger divine omnipotence and omnipresence."

46. In the final edition Schleiermacher did not delete this, but added a note saying his intent had been misunderstood—it was only apologetic—and referring the reader to *The Christian Faith* [§158.2], which affirms personal immortality on the basis of teachings of Christ and the New Testament (*Speeches,* trans. Oman, 100f., 117).

2.2.5 Religion in the Early Schelling

Schelling began publishing his thoughts on religion in the year 1800, the most important being the *Vorlesungen über die Methode des akademischen Studiums* (Lectures on the Method of Academic Study) of 1803. For Schelling, the "identity" of subjective thought and the objective world means that in, under, and over the multiplicity of the world and thought there is a unity or oneness of all things and with this oneness a presence of the divine.[47] God is "absolute wisdom" and perceives all things.[48] God is also in constant communication with human being: creation is the "speaking" or word (Logos) of God [cf. Schleiermacher]. From this original "language" arises empirical human language.[49]

In the *Vorlesungen* Schelling divides all religion into "nature religion" and the religion of revelation, Christianity. Nature religion is a product of natural evolution that organically unfolds in pre-Christian religions through the work of the three principles or potencies. In nature religion the gods are essentially archetypes of nature and limited symbols of the Absolute. The highest nature religion is that of the ancient Greeks, whose remarkable culture in art, religion, and philosophy in harmony with nature still evokes admiration. Yet according to Schelling no natural religion can endure, for history evolves toward freedom from natural religion and a higher wisdom based on awareness of the distinction between the absolute God and the gods of natural religion.[50] The ultimate goal of evolution is reconciliation of the finite with God in the recognition of God as God. The "Son of God" is the finite itself "as it is in the eternal perception [*Anschauung*] of God," that is, in reconciliation with God. Prior to Christ the finite as the "Son" suffers the pain of history (in the nature religions) until he appears as Christ. Yet in Christ something new happens: the finite does not evolve into Christ but opens itself to receive God, who is now "born" into finitude; "the true infinite comes into the finite" in the person of Christ. In the resurrection, the boundaries

---

47. In a certain sense Schelling cannot avoid being called a pantheist, although not in the same way as Fichte. In his conception of God as *Geist*, God is self-conscious and separate from creation, and creation is not the same as God. The world is the finite appearance of God's powers or potencies.

48. Schelling, *Werke*, 5:216, 220. For finite understanding all consciousness, including God's, results from the triune structure of being, i.e., from the interaction of the three principles.

49. Ibid., 482–84. The thought is originally Platonic.

50. Natural human life is experienced as a conflict between necessity—the boundaries or limitations of fate—and inner freedom, a conflict expressed archetypally in Greek tragedy, whose only resolution is the ideal unity of necessity and freedom. Christ's fate is also tragic, but in this case the resolution is of a higher order, namely, providence, which joins freedom and necessity in (faith in) God. *Werke*, 5:310, 326; cf. 290 [cf. Karl Hase, chap. 3.4]. The "principles" or "potencies" [chap. 2.2.2] also play a role in natural life, however, mediated by the forms of evolution. The second or formative principle or potence (*perás*) has the significance of measure and reason. The first, the unconditioned (*apeíron*), can interrupt the order of human existence, exceeding all boundaries; in the dreadful and insane, it is destructive. E.g., Schelling, *Werke*, 1:336f. Cf. the beautiful and sublime in Kant's *Critique of Judgment* [chap. 2.1.4] and in Romanticism [introduction to the present chapter].

of the finite are ruptured and eternal life is revealed. The finite is reconciled with the infinite, and God becomes in truth an object for reflective thought.[51]

Christ identifies himself not with humanity at its highest but at its lowest— a sign of his relationship to the God above all distinctions of natural religion, the God who loves all creatures. After his death and resurrection ("he returns to the invisible"), he leaves in his place faith, the tradition about him, and the Spirit, who leads through time to final reconciliation of all creation with God. The unity or reconciliation with God in Christ cannot be directly expressed, because it has to do with what goes beyond the conditionedness of language. Therefore the forms of the church, including not only its dogmas but also its history and life, are poetic, symbols of God's transcendent reality. In the unity of reconciliation with God, the church is a "living work of art" as it moves through history.

Theology combines the historical testimony of Scripture with the idea of the world-encompassing, universal truth of Christianity. When, however, theology is too much focused on the letter of Scripture, it loses this universal significance; and in reverse, when it overly concentrates on its universal truth, it loses the concrete form that gives it permanence in time. Schelling finds that the "empirical" study of Scripture—objective historical analysis, including questions about authenticity—has been pursued to the detriment of Christianity's universal and higher significance and meaning. Christian truth, while expressed concretely in Scripture, transcends the empirical and lifts humanity into higher awareness of God and world. Schelling ends the discussion with the prediction of a new time when the universal significance of Christianity, which will overcome current "empiricism," will be poetically and philosophically reborn.[52]

2.2.6 Philosophy of Nature

Humanity is able to actualize its own potentialities in forming its cultural world, but according to Schelling, in doing so, it can and does misrepresent its relationship to God and therefore it also errs or sins. As the ground of the finite world or of nature, God is the source not only of all being but also of all meaning, and meaning can suffer diminution and loss.[53] Nature is unconscious spirit [Geist], in itself meaningful and intimately related to human life. Meaning is also mediated through art and religion, both of which are naturally related to nature and neither of which is objective like natural science. In art, music, and religion the world is experienced as (subject-object) unity. A great work of art is a visible illustration of "intellectual intuition," the unity of subjective and objective.[54] The

51. Werke, 5:292, 294, 298. On the resurrection of Christ: Schelling, Philosophie der Kunst, Werke, 5:425.

52. Ibid., 5:296f., 304ff. Schelling defines merely empirical history as collecting and reporting information and ordering it according to some "pragmatic" (e.g., political, didactic) purpose decided by the historian. Werke, 5:307f.

53. Schelling, Werke, 6:194–96; cf. 1:308; 5:219f.

54. Ibid., 3:625; cf. 627ff.; 5:344–52, 482ff., 634ff. See Bowie, Aesthetics and Subjectivity, 113–24.

same unity is experienced in living nature itself, as Schelling expressed especially in *Bruno,* published in 1802.[55] Modern humanity, however, has lost this experience, and with it nature too bears the consequence.

While Schelling anticipates a rebirth of Christianity that will include the rebirth of nature, Christianity has contributed to a general disregard for nature. Christianity is distinguished from nature religion both by its perception of God as other than and beyond nature and by its message that each person is in personal relationship with God. In modernity the cultural heritage of this tradition has become seriously problematic. The preachers of Christianity continue to require, as "the highest tribute of Christian piety," that God be "outside" of nature. The problem is that this tradition has become part of a culture that devaluates nature by "using" it, depriving nature of its life source, so that its meaning is lost and it simply exists. Nature has become a dead thing at the disposal of the "highest irreligiosity."[56] This also has consequences for human life: "the modern world begins with humanity tearing itself away from nature, but, since humanity knows no other home, it feels itself abandoned."[57] Schelling's emphasis on nature is expressed in his own designation of this phase in his philosophy, namely, *Naturphilosophie,* philosophy of nature.

In several of his works after 1800, Schelling so much concentrated on the "identity" of all in the Absolute that they earned his philosophy the name *Identitätsphilosophie,* philosophy of identity.[58] In 1807 Hegel, his friend, colleague, and ally in early Idealism (they had edited a philosophical journal together), who to this point had rather been in his shadow, published his first major work, the *Phenomenology of Spirit.* In the preface Hegel makes the famous statement—which was taken as a reference to Schelling—that "intellectual intuition" of the Absolute is the "night in which all cows are black." The life of the real historical world was so much darkened by the "identity" of all in the Absolute that one could no longer see its color, that is, its particular reality.

2.3 HEGEL

Georg Wilhelm Friedrich Hegel (1770–1831) had been the younger Schelling's friend and coworker, and prior to the publication of the *Phenomenology of Spirit,*

55. ET Michael Vater [see note 33]; cf. *Werke,* 5:320ff. Schelling's lectures on the "philosophy of art" are also important for the philosophy of nature. They were held at Jena in the early 1800s but published for the first time in the *Werke,* vol. 5.

56. Ibid., 109; 4:315; 5:221, 259f., 290. Fichte rather speaks of the domination and "use" of nature, for which Schelling criticized him: Schelling, *Werke,* 7:17; cf. Fichte, *The Vocation of Man,* trans. William Smith (reprint, La Salle: Open Court, 1946), 113–16. See Andrew Bowie, *Schelling and Modern European Philosophy,* 58. Cf. Schleiermacher, *Speeches,* trans. Crouter, 116: "The moral world order is progressing from bad to worse; being incapable of producing something in which the spirit of the universe really would live, it darkens the understanding; . . . it has extinguished the image of the infinite in every part of finite nature."

57. *Werke,* 5:427; 6:38ff.

58. Manfred Frank, *Einführung in Schellings Philosophie,* 112f.

Schelling had no reason to think Hegel was not in essential agreement with him.[59] In fact Hegel begins and ends his philosophy with the "Absolute" and employs the scheme of an evolution of mind or Spirit [Geist] coming to itself (to self-consciousness) through the dialectic movement from thesis to antithesis to synthesis. For Hegel, the Absolute is essentially reasonable or, better, it is reason itself. It makes no sense to say, as did Jacobi, that the Absolute is unconditioned and therefore beyond thought or too great to be thought. The unconditional is a thought that reason can think about.[60] With his particular understanding of reason Hegel moves in a different direction from Schelling, a direction that is far more scientific and far less poetic. In fact his philosophy is more like Fichte's than Schelling's.

In the *Phenomenology of Spirit* Hegel's procedure is to begin with self-consciousness and sense experience, not with the Absolute. For the sake of convenience, we begin with what the Absolute is prior to the appearance of a world. At this point it is eternal simple "being," "the indeterminate immediate" [*das unbestimmte Unmittelbare*] as "empty thought." Here being and thought or concept are the same, but there is nothing to be perceived or thought.[61] In the first act of creation this absolutely unconditioned being or thought produces out of itself an "other" than itself (how it does this, lacking any capacity for action, is not explained). This "other" is the natural world or what exists. Eternal simple being, prior to creation, is "in itself"; the "other" is something "for itself," but both are in essence identical: the "other" is simple being in another form. But this "other," existence, is in relation to eternal simple being mere appearance and "nonbeing." It is subject to time, so that it constantly passes in and out of existence.[62] This means that eternal "being in itself" and temporal "being for itself" are in a relationship of alienation or negation: they relate to each other as thesis and antithesis. Now enters the third term, the term of synthesis, "Spirit." Spirit

59. Terry Pinkard, *Hegel, a Biography* (Cambridge: Cambridge University Press, 2000). Hegel studied in Tübingen with Schelling and later coedited a journal with him. He eventually became professor of philosophy in Berlin. Writings by Hegel on religion prior to the *Phenomenology of Spirit* are found in *Early Theological Writings*, trans. T. M. Knox and Richard Kroner (Chicago: University of Chicago Press, 1948); *Three Essays, 1793–1795*, trans. Peter Fuss and John Dobbins (Notre Dame, IN: University of Notre Dame Press, 1984); and *Faith and Knowledge*, trans. Walter Cerf and H. S. Harris (Albany: State University of New York, 1977). *Early Theological Writings* give evidence that Hegel's thought originated as much with historical dialectic as it did with speculation. All these works are developments toward the *Phenomenology of Spirit*. See also G. W. F. Hegel, *Theologian of the Spirit*, ed. Peter C. Hodgson (Minneapolis: Fortress, 1997).

60. Cf. Hegel's critical discussion of Jacobi's concept of the unconditioned as beyond reason, in *Faith and Knowledge*, 97–152, and in *Lectures on the History of Philosophy*, trans. E. S. Haldane and F. H. Simson, 3 vols. (New York: Humanities Press, 1955), 3:410–23.

61. *Hegel's Science of Logic*, trans. A. V. Miller (New York: Humanities Press, 1969), 81f., hereafter cited as *Logic*. For the German text, we use Hegel, *Wissenschaft der Logik*, Jubiläumsausgabe, ed. Hermann Glockner (Stuttgart-Bad Cannstatt: Friedrich Frommann, 1965), cf. 87f. The *Logic* was published several years after the *Phenomenology of Spirit*. What follows in this paragraph is a summary, with references to pages in Hegel's *Phenomenology of Spirit*, trans. A. V. Miller with analysis by J. N. Findlay (Oxford: Clarendon, 1979), hereafter cited as *Phenomenology*. For the German text, we use *Phänomenologie des Geistes*, Jubiläumsausgabe, ed. Hermann Glockner (Stuttgart: Frommann Verlag, 1964). The preface to this work is the recognized best introduction to Hegel's thought.

62. *Phenomenology*, 87. On the remainder of this paragraph, see 11–23.

is the "mediation" or movement that unites thesis and antithesis. Its goal is the union or reconciliation of the whole, of eternal being "in itself" and temporal being "for itself." The uniting activity of Spirit takes place step by step in the process of historical development. (In all human experience, including religious experience, the "immediate" is the given that is "mediated" through the process into ever high levels of "synthesis.") The history of the world is the process by which Spirit gradually returns from "otherness" to itself, that is, when it recognizes and knows that it is one and the same Spirit both "in itself" and "for itself" [cf. thesis-antithesis-synthesis in chap. 2.2.2].

This synthesis, this knowledge of unity, occurs in human self-consciousness, in thinking Spirit. As self-consciousness emerges in human evolution, so does the awareness of its freedom, as it becomes certain of itself as an independently existing being in the world.[63] Spirit's means of progress is reason, first as reason in the process of inorganic and organic development, then as reasoning human being. With the freedom of its reason or its capacity to understand, human consciousness penetrates and comprehends the alien otherness of everything outside itself, so that this otherness becomes familiar and known. Understanding the world is a lengthy historical process. Each new stage of understanding is a new synthesis of thesis and antithesis in Spirit's progressive return to itself. The complete and final synthesis occurs when Spirit achieves complete understanding of who and what it is. When this happens it recognizes all that exists is what it itself has produced out of itself.[64] This Hegel calls "absolute knowledge," in which Spirit knows itself as the unity of the Absolute, and this is where the Absolute becomes truly Absolute. As both the eternal origin and as the recognition of itself in all temporal otherness, the Absolute is "in and for itself."[65] History is the "work" of the Spirit: in and through the struggles of human life, Spirit is driven to find solutions to the problems of alienation, of "otherness." Its suffering of history's real contradictions forces it to hard, difficult work.[66]

In the *Phenomenology of Spirit,* the Spirit's alienation from itself in early human history is characterized in human consciousness by the antithetical relationship of God and humanity, as symbolized by the biblical story of the loss of paradise. Alienation from God means that humanity is evil. Humanity behaves and vaguely perceives itself as evil; the first characteristic of human life is egotism, the affirmation of self as the negation of the other. Alienation or evil—"otherness"—is both the cause of suffering in human life and a necessary part of the process of Spirit. For suffering moves history forward in work for the elimination of suffering. Especially prominent in the history of Spirit is the "unhappy consciousness,"

---

63. Ibid., 119ff., 290, 355f.

64. Hegel's *Philosophy of Nature,* trans. A. V. Miller (Oxford: Clarendon, 1970), is an attempt to construct rationally the evolution of nature in a way that is related to such attempts in the early Schelling (as several friendly references to Schelling show), but it has nothing of Schelling's romantic sense: no opening of nature into the unconditioned, no limitation of reason in understanding how nature is generated.

65. *Phenomenology,* 479–93.

66. On the significance of work, see, e.g., *Phenomenology,* 118; cf. 266, 294, 359.

which is openly and intensely aware of its alienation and separation from truth. But its frustration moves Spirit forward to a new synthesis: the incarnation of God, the truth, in an individual human being, Christ, who represents and reveals the unity of God and the "other" in "the form of self-consciousness."

In Hegel's interpretation of the Trinity, the "Son" is the "other" as world, the whole of creation. The "Father" is the origin of all. "Spirit" is the upward development of creation toward ever-higher synthesis or unity. In the person of Christ, Spirit comes to the self-conscious recognition of itself in the "other": the moment of reconciliation of "Son" and "Father." Christ lives and teaches love for God and all humanity.[67] Love is synthesis, union.

But this new synthesis is not complete until the God-human, Christ, dies. That "God Himself is dead" would mean the extreme form of the "unhappy consciousness," insofar as death is the negation of life and ultimate alienation. But when it is God that suffers death, death itself is negated in God, and Spirit emerges triumphant and immortal, conquering the final "other," death, and returning to itself from its most extreme alienation from itself. The return of Spirit to itself is "resurrection," the realization of absolute truth. "Death . . . is of all things the most dreadful. . . . But the life of Spirit is not the life that shrinks from death and keeps itself untouched by devastation, but rather the life that endures it and maintains itself in it. It wins its truth only when, in utter dismemberment, it finds itself. . . . Spirit is power only by looking the negative in the face and tarrying with it. This tarrying with the negative is the magical power that converts it into being."[68]

This is of course not the New Testament's account of Christ's death and resurrection and the founding of the church, and it is not meant to replace the New Testament's account. But according to Hegel it is the true meaning of that account. The true meaning is the "concept" [Begriff] implicit in the historical account. The New Testament's historical account is "Vorstellung," a verbal noun that comes from a common verb that literally means "to place before" [vorstellen]. As a verb of mental activity, it means to think of or imagine something and is often translated as "to represent" or "to picture" something.[69] In the Phenomenology of Spirit Hegel defines religious Vorstellung as the synthetic union of "sensuous immediacy" (e.g., the person of Christ) with reflective thought about its meaning. In the New Testament's witness to Christ, we receive both his his-

67. Phenomenology, 458–60. See also Hegel's Philosophy of History, trans. J. Sibree (New York: Dover, 1956), 323f.

68. Phenomenology, 19, 475f. At the conclusion of his earlier work Faith and Knowledge, 190f. (cf. 112), Hegel speaks of the pure concept (the Absolute) as the Abgrund or abyss of nothingness in which all being is "engulfed" or according to the original German word in which all being "sinks" [versinkt]. This sinking into nothingness is, he says, the "speculative Good Friday," the "death of God," from which all being or Spirit is again resurrected. The "sinking" is most likely an image taken from Kant's statement that, with the question about what causes God, thought sinks into nothingness [see chap. 2.1.1].

69. In common usage it would be used, for example, as the equivalent of "think" in the sentence "How do you think you will be able to do that?"

torical person and his significance or concept in one *Vorstellung*. For Hegel, not only the New Testament witness to Christ but also Christian teachings and dogmas about Christ are *Vorstellung*.[70] At the highest level of religious development—the religious history of Spirit—stands the *Vorstellung* of the God-human unity revealed in Christ, his death, and his resurrection.

Spirit realizes the unity represented in Christ's resurrection in "the community" of Spirit. Only the community of Spirit knows the truth, a knowledge it has through faith in Christ. In history the community suffers the evil antitheses of historical life, but it knows that reconciliation and not alienation is the ultimate meaning of life. Hegel's use of words—he says not "church" but "community"—is indicative of his understanding of the relationship of the Christian community to the universal meaning of Christ. The word for "the community" is *die Gemeinde*. In Christ's resurrection the meaning of reconciliation has become *allgemein*, "general or universal."[71] The term common to both words, *gemein*, means "common or shared." The Christian *Gemeinde* is implicitly *das Allgemeine* (*All-Gemeine*), the universal. In fact Hegel names the Christian "community" "the divine universal Man [sc. Human]."[72] The Christian community is implicitly the divine Spirit incarnated in humanity that unites all humanity.

But the Christian religion is not the highest level of Spirit. Christian *Vorstellung* contains a remaining element of alienation of Spirit from itself: God and Christ are still thought of as "other," for example, as "Father in heaven" and "Christ in heaven" above and separate from the earth and humanity.[73] In "absolute knowledge," the title of the final chapter of the *Phenomenology*, Spirit comes to complete self-recognition now also in the otherness of God and Christ. Spirit knows it is the all in all. It knows that it itself is the whole process of being first "in itself," then being the "other," and finally recognizing itself in the other.[74] For absolute knowledge, history is no longer the memory of particular historical events: these are only *Vorstellungen*. It is rather all the concepts in Spirit's stages of development, or, as one could also say, the meaning of each stage: from alienation to the "unhappy consciousness" to reconciliation. The concept or meaning of each stage in history is now known. The stages are subsets or subdivisions of the one highest concept or meaning, the Spirit itself, the Absolute. The truth of religious *Vorstellung* has now been "lifted" into absolute knowledge [cf. Kant's use of this word in chap. 2.1.3].

Here one has to do with another important word: *Aufhebung*, from the common verb, *aufheben* (past participle: *aufgehoben*), which literally and in common

---

70. *Phenomenology*, 463. There is a tradition, stemming from the nineteenth century, of translating Hegel's important term *Begriff* with the in present usage unclear term "notion." *Begriff* is more clearly translated as "concept." (In the vernacular *Begriff* is a common word related to the verb *begreifen*, "to understand" something.)

71. Ibid., 462ff.

72. Ibid., 478.

73. Ibid., 465f., 477f.

74. Ibid., 485–93. "What in religion was *content* or a form for presenting an *other*, is here the Self's own *act*" (Ibid., 17). "For Spirit is the knowledge of oneself in the externalization of oneself; the being that is the movement of retaining its self-identity in its otherness" (Ibid., 459).

usage means to "lift up" something. But it can also mean to "keep" something and to "cancel" something (as to "lift" a curfew).[75] Hegel uses all these meanings at once in his word *Aufhebung*: when a religious *Vorstellung* (e.g., the historical Jesus of the Gospels) is "lifted" into absolute knowledge, it is canceled as *Vorstellung*, but its essential meaning is kept or preserved as the conceptual content of the *Vorstellung*. For example, the "concept" of the New Testament's *Vorstellung* of Christ is the God-human unity.[76] The concept is the truth of the *Vorstellung*. Hence, for Hegel, exegesis or interpretation has the task of understanding the conceptual or essential truth of the New Testament. In the *Phenomenology* Hegel faults Christianity for being fixed on the particular historical events, dogmas, and persons of the New Testament. It is fixed on the "outer" (past) history instead of its (present) conceptual truth.[77] In the absolute self-recognition of Spirit, absolute knowledge "lifts" the *Vorstellung* out of its particularity in Christian history and dogma into its universal concept.[78]

After the *Phenomenology*, Hegel's most important work is the *Science of Logic*, originally published in three volumes between 1812 and 1816. It bears a certain similarity to Kant's *Critique of Pure Reason* [chap. 2.1.1], insofar as it determines the categories, concepts, and judgments of reason as the possibility of all knowledge. Generally speaking, the method of the *Logic* is familiar: the concept is first "in itself," then as the "other," and finally as self-recognition in absolute knowledge. But the process in the *Logic* develops only in conceptual thought, nonhistorically. One commentator calls it "the ghostlike reflection of events of flesh and blood."[79] Hegel does not mention Christianity.

As in the *Phenomenology*, there is in the *Logic* no clear difference between finite or human self-consciousness and Spirit. Now, however, Hegel speaks of Spirit also as of the self-conscious "person" of the Absolute. Self-consciousness or personhood can only be the result of the process of Spirit first as the finite other and then as returning from this other to itself. In fact Hegel says that the personhood of the Absolute is the result of the process of Spirit coming to itself in human self-consciousness. He does not mean that the self-consciousness of the Absolute is the same as the human self-consciousness. What he rather means is that the Absolute or Spirit comes to its own absolute self-consciousness through the finite development of human being. It must therefore be inseparable from finite human being. But as absolute and self-conscious person, it knows itself in and as the whole of everything that is. Hegel designates it with another term: the "absolute Idea." The Idea is "the unity of the theoretical and the practical," or, as he says

75. Ibid., 68, where *Aufhebung* is translated as "supersession." "Sublate" is a more frequent translation but also problematic, insofar as its (Latin) meaning is not immediately understood. In translating *Aufhebung* and its verbal forms, we follow those who use the word "lift" and include the German word in brackets. Hegel explains his use of *Aufhebung* in the *Logic*, 106f.

76. *Phenomenology*, 477f.

77. Ibid., 463.

78. Ibid., 479.

79. Clark Butler, *Hegel's Logic: Between Dialectic and History* (Evanston, IL: Northwestern University, 1996), 279.

in another place, "the absolute unity of the concept and objectivity."[80] The absolute Idea unites all finite things with their concepts and these with the Absolute. It is, however, difficult to understand how the Idea or absolute self-consciousness can be located anywhere but in Hegel's own mind—and perhaps this is what he means.

After his appointment in 1818 as professor of philosophy in Berlin, Hegel extended his work into lectures on the philosophy of individual sciences. One series of lectures, begun in 1821 and repeated at different times over almost a decade, is on the philosophy of religion.[81] In these lectures philosophy and faith are intimately joined together, very nearly as two forms that have the same content. Hegel includes a detailed history of pre-Christian religions and of the life of faith, but the basic concepts are still those of the *Phenomenology*. The history of Spirit arrives at the synthesis or reconciliation of God and humanity in Christianity, the strength of which is true *Vorstellung*, which is then philosophically understood in the knowledge of the Absolute. The true content of Christian *Vorstellung* is the universal concept.[82] The cognitive distinctions human being naturally makes between things, other human beings, and itself are signs of separation and alienation (i.e., of finitude). Human being labors within the reality of alienation to make itself a life, although it longs for harmony and unity.

"God is love." In love the difference (otherness) between two persons is "lifted" [*aufgehoben*] into unity, yet without erasing the distinct personhood of each—just as the Idea preserves the individual things while "lifting" them into concepts. Hegel himself makes this association: the "lifting" of difference in love "is the simple, eternal Idea." Of love of another person he writes: "The consciousness or feeling of the identity of the two—to be outside myself and in the other—this is love. . . . I am satisfied and have peace with myself only in this other—and I am only because I have peace with myself; if I did not have it then

80. *Logic*, 824; Hegel, *Encyclopedia of the Philosophical Sciences in Outline, and Critical Writings*, ed. Ernst Behler (New York: Continuum, 1990), 127ff.; cf. Butler, *Hegel's Logic*, 279ff. In the *Encyclopedia*, 11, Hegel writes: "The True is the whole. But the whole is nothing other than the essence consummating itself through its development. Of the Absolute it must be said that it is essentially result, that only in the end is it what it truly is; and that precisely in this consists its nature, viz., to be actual, subject, the spontaneous becoming of itself." Cf. *Phenomenology*, 7. Hegel's word "Idea" is not to be confused with the common German cognate, *Idee*, which is translated as "idea" in the sense of "concept." It is also not to be confused with *Vorstellung*. In *Vorstellung* thought is not aware of the concept as a philosophical concept belonging to absolute knowledge. Rather the concept is integrated with and inseparable from the historical phenomenon, e.g., Christ in a theological doctrine of Christ.

81. The most convenient critical edition in English is *Lectures on the Philosophy of Religion. One-Volume Edition. The Lectures of 1827*, trans. R. F. Brown, P. C. Hodgson, and J. M. Stewart with the assistance of H. S. Harris (Berkeley: University of California Press, 1988). In this chapter we cite this edition. See also the more extensive three-volume set: *Lectures on the Philosophy of Religion*, trans. R. F. Brown, P. C. Hodgson, and J. M. Stewart with the assistance of J. P. Fitzer and H. S. Harris (Berkeley: University of California Press, 1984–1987). See also Hegel's late and posthumously published lectures on The *Philosophy of History*, 318–36; and P. Hodgson, ed., *G. W. F. Hegel, Theologian of the Spirit*. The original German edition is important for knowing how the lectures on philosophy of religion were read prior to the critical editions: *Vorlesungen über die Philosophie der Religion*, Jubiläumsausgabe, ed. Hermann Glockner, 2 vols. (Stuttgart: Friedrich Frommann, 1965).

82. *Philosophy of Religion*, 399–404; cf. *Encyclopedia*, 260–64.

I would be a contradiction that falls to pieces." The community of love is essential to human being, although this truth is ever again obscured by finite alienation. Love characterizes the relationship between Jesus and God. It is also the essential if hidden characteristic of the whole process of Spirit.[83] Evil is human being "for itself" within its finite limitations, alienated from God, nature, and other human beings.[84]

Jesus' proclamation of the kingdom of God and the love commandment, especially in the Sermon on the Mount, stands in radical opposition to the ethics of the alienated world. The kingdom that Jesus proclaims is an immediately present truth, "an intellectual, spiritual world" to which "humanity ought to belong." Of Christ's death he writes: "'God himself is dead,' it says in a Lutheran hymn, expressing an awareness that the human, the finite, the weak, the negative are themselves a moment of the divine, that they are within God himself, that finitude, negativity, otherness are not outside God." In death "the human, the negative" is stripped away so that the glory of the eternal Spirit appears.[85] This is the meaning of all immortality.[86] The *Philosophy of Religion* closes with the Idea as the "rational cognition of religion" and names the philosophy that has this cognition "theology."[87]

In the *Philosophy of Religion* the emphasis is placed on the unity of "the concept and reality" in the Idea. In his discussions of religion in *The Philosophy of Right*, Hegel emphasizes only the truth of the concept. The content of the Christian religion is absolute truth, but in religion itself this content is believed only on the basis of "authority," "faith" and "feeling." "Brought within its [sc. religion's] all-embracing circumference, everything becomes only accidental and transient."[88] According to one interpreter, in the last decade of his life—the decade both of his lectures on the philosophy of religion and of political-religious restoration in Prussia [chap. 1]—Hegel intentionally "pushed the 'negative moment' of the dialectical relationship between faith and knowledge into the background

---

83. *Philosophy of Religion*, 418, 418ff., 434f.

84. Ibid., 440–52.

85. Ibid., 452–70 (on Christ's death, 468). Cf. Hegel, *Philosophy of History*, 326–28.

86. *Philosophy of Religion*, 445f. "Human being as a single living thing, its singular life, its natural life, must die. . . . The fact of the matter is that humanity is immortal only through cognitive knowledge, for only in the activity of thinking is the soul pure and free. . . . Cognition and thought are the root of human life." Here "pure and free" probably refers to the pure thought of "being in itself," which is in Spirit the Absolute thinking itself.

87. Ibid., 488f. Here Hegel does not actually use the word "Idea," but this is evidently what he means. See ibid., 406–16, esp. 411; cf. 417–32.

88. *Hegel's Philosophy of Right*, trans. T. M. Knox (London: Oxford University Press, 1967), 166, 179 (the whole of §270 is relevant); cf. 127: the truth is the concept. Hegel repeats this evaluation of religion in the introduction to his *Encyclopedia*, §5. According to the *Logic*, 443, finitude necessarily consists in contradiction, "the finite is the inherently self-contradictory opposition." Cf. *Logic*, 389–443, 824. Contrasting views of the relationship between religion and philosophy are represented, on the one hand, by Clark Butler in *Hegel: The Letters*, trans. Clark Butler and Christiane Seiler, with a commentary by Clark Butler (Bloomington: Indiana University Press, 1984), 537ff., who favors the "Idea" as reconciling religion and philosophy; and on the other hand in Wolfhart Pannenberg's essay on Hegel in *The Idea of God and Human Freedom*, trans. R. A. Wilson (Philadelphia: Westminster, 1973), 162, 175f. According to Pannenberg, the "Idea" is unable to reconcile religion and philosophy.

and emphasized the 'positive moment' of their reconciliation."[89] Nevertheless in the same period he was accused of atheism and pantheism by certain theologians.[90] One hears the same claim being made in the twentieth century by the philosophical "left," which prefers Hegel without Christianity.[91] Among Hegel's advocates in the late 1820s two lines of theological interpretation emerged. The "right wing" held that Christian faith is not superseded but only interpreted or understood in the philosophy of the Absolute. The "left wing" said that any historical moment loses its significance as soon as it is "lifted" into its conceptual meaning, its concept. What does not pass away is true, and no phenomena escape the finitude of time. Both possibilities—the right wing and the left wing—reside in the ambivalence of Hegel's "Idea."

Hegel was not a Romantic; there is no mystery in his concept of God.[92] The movement of Spirit is that of reason, and reason is its end and purpose. At the conclusion of his *Lectures on the History of Philosophy* Hegel writes: "In scientific knowledge alone it [sc. Spirit] knows itself as absolute Spirit; and this knowledge . . . is its only true existence."[93] At the end of the second preface to his *Logic*, written shortly before his death in 1831, Hegel doubts "whether the noisy clamor of current affairs and the deafening chatter of conceit which prides itself on confining itself to such matters leave any room for participation in the passionless calm of a knowledge which is in the element of pure thought alone."[94] Oppositions and conflicts in religion too were part of that "deafening chatter." Pure thought alone is the business of pure reason, and this is the "true existence" of Spirit.[95]

A significant and influential aspect of Hegel's *Philosophy of History* is its description of the "dialectical" process of history driven by oppositions and conflicts: the real theses and antitheses of history.[96] As important as these antitheses are, Hegel's interest rather lies in the "lifting" of the concrete into the concepts that give the true meaning of the process. The last paragraph of the work states

89. John Edward Toews, *Hegelianism, the Path toward Dialectical Humanism, 1805–1841* (Cambridge: Cambridge University Press, 1980), 273; cf. 95ff., 141ff.

90. Hegel attempts a refutation in his 1827 lectures: *Lectures on the Philosophy of Religion. One-Volume Edition*, 21f., 118ff.; cf. *Encyclopedia*, §573. The most notable of the critics was August Tholuck [chap. 1, chap. 3.1]. See Wolfhart Pannenberg, *The Idea of God and Human Freedom*, 160–77.

91. Georg Lukács, *The Young Hegel: Studies in the Relations between Dialectics and Economics*, trans. Rodney Livingstone (Cambridge: MIT, 1966), 528. Karl Löwith, *Die Hegelische Linke* (Stuttgart: Friedrich Frommann, 1962), e.g., 171–73, strongly argues not only that Hegel's thought is essentially atheistic but also that Hegel is far more revolutionary than the "Young Hegelians" who follow him, insofar as he undermines both the belief of the church and the principles of the state.

92. On Hegel as a rational Idealist, see, e.g., Ernst Behler's introduction to Hegel's *Encyclopedia*.

93. *Lectures on the History of Philosophy*, 3:552.

94. *Logic*, 42. Cf. Löwith, *From Hegel to Nietzsche*, 28.

95. Cf. Aristotle, *Nicomachean Ethics*, bk. X, chap. 8, 1178[b]: true happiness is accorded to the life most like that of the gods, the life of contemplation. Aristotle, *Metaphysics*, bk. XII, chap. 9, 1074[b]: "It must be the act of thinking itself that the divine thought thinks . . . , and its thinking is a thinking on thinking."

96. See Theodor W. Adorno, *Hegel: Three Studies*, trans. Shierry Weber Nicholsen (Cambridge: MIT, 1993). Oddly Hegel's lectures on the history of religions in the *Philosophy of Religion* present the subject matter not as a dialectic but rather as individual stages of development.

that the history of the world is the realization of Spirit (the meaning of the process), which is the "justification of God in history," and that "what has happened, and what is happening every day, is not only not 'without God,' but is essentially his work." In the *Philosophy of Right* one finds essentially the same thought in Hegel's sentence: "what is actual [real] is rational and what is rational is actual." "To recognize reason as the rose in the cross of the present and thereby to enjoy the present, this is the rational insight which reconciles us to the actual, the reconciliation which philosophy affords."[97] Society and the state are appearances of progressive reason, and true freedom and happiness lie in one's ethical identification with and work for the good of the rational society (§123ff., §142ff.).[98] General recognition of Christianity, as the religion through which citizens are related to absolute truth, belongs to the rational state (§270). Hegel makes an important exception: "subjective" religion, that is, pietism, must be opposed because it relegates the "ethical world" outside of the religious community to godlessness, for "truth lies outside it [sc. the ethical world]."[99]

All the sciences search, discover, and comprehend the reason of things, whether in nature or in human social development. With any given problem, at first incomprehension and alienation is suffered, but finally understanding is won in Spirit's eternal return to itself. Present social conflicts will continue and may worsen; the evil forms of egotism will ever again arise; new enigmas will emerge; times of decay and renewal will come and go (although for Hegel there was greater reason to see in history overall progress than decay). In any case Spirit knows absolutely that it will not only suffer these but also deal with them rationally and finally emerge in the reconciliation of a new synthesis. This is the ultimate meaning of the Idea, the unity of all things in the Absolute.[100] In absolute knowledge—which has now been attained once and for all in Hegel—the present is the moment of the Absolute, of Spirit's eternally present knowledge of itself.

2.4 THE LATER SCHELLING

2.4.1 Human Freedom and the Origin of Evil

Schelling's answer to Hegel's *Phenomenology of Spirit* came in a publication of the year 1809, *On the Nature of Human Freedom* (*Über das Wesen der menschlichen*

---

97. *Philosophy of Right*, 10, 12. The last sentence of the preface contains Hegel's famous saying, "The owl of Minerva flies at twilight." The following references are to Hegel's numbered sections of the work.

98. "The state is the divine idea as it exists on earth. Only that which obeys the law is free; for it obeys itself . . ." *Philosophy of History*, 39. See Allen W. Wood, *Hegel's Ethical Thought* (Cambridge: Cambridge University Press, 1990), 21–30, 36ff., 69–71.

99. *Philosophy of Right*, 4, 166f. See Pannenberg, *The Idea of God and Human Freedom*, 156ff.

100. See esp. Hegel's "Preface to the System of Philosophy," in *Encyclopedia*, 1–43, esp. 7. On the relationship between the finite and the Absolute, see Hegel's *Logic*, 740–54, 818ff., 837–44; *Philosophy of Religion*, 394, 411f.; *Encyclopedia*, 257–64.

Freiheit).[101] (We refer to this work later as *On Human Freedom*.) Reflection on Hegel's work, but also a deepening personal existential experience, caused Schelling to develop his philosophy in a new way. The opening discussion concerns the problem of freedom in Spinoza, although the target of criticism is as much Hegel as Spinoza. Spinoza's philosophy does not allow for freedom because it conceives of God and the world as "abstract concepts," and in the system of concepts every concept is the "condition" of another in final dependence on the first concept, God [cf. Kant, chap. 2.1.2]. The system is lifeless and mechanistic. The world must be "torn away from abstraction" and "given life." Idealism has no place for freedom, for it has to do only with the general or universal [*das Allgemeine*] and therefore with what is only a "formal concept" of human freedom. The "specific" character and "real and living" concept of human freedom is the potential for good and evil, which is "the point of deepest difficulty" in the understanding of freedom. No previous philosophy has successfully solved the problem, least of all Idealism. "God is more real than simply a moral world order [as in Fichte] and has wholly other and more living powers of movement than those attributed to God by the needy subtlety of abstract Idealists [as in Hegel]."[102] "Were God for us only a logical abstraction, then everything would follow from God with logical necessity."[103]

Human freedom, and creation itself, can only follow from a real creative will. "Will is original being [*Ursein*]," to which belong "groundlessness [*Grundlosigkeit*], eternity, and independence from time." What is not in time is, like Kant's "thing in itself," free, and this freedom is "spread throughout the universe."[104] For Kant, noumenal reality and its freedom are present everywhere in the finite world. So also for Schelling, God is utterly free. God exists as "eternal Spirit [*Geist*]" who "dwells in pure light." God is eternally not only in absolute freedom above creation but also completely God, not dependent on historical process. However, as in the earlier Schelling [chap. 2.2.2], in God are elements that are the principles, potencies, or possibilities of creation. Now they are given new definitions, or more correctly, the former definitions are extended. The "ground" of God's existence is will, and in the will of the ground is "darkness." This element, equivalent to the "unconditioned" (*apeiron*) in Schelling's earlier work, is pure energy and utter possibility in the formlessness of chaos. The second principle is also will, but of an opposite kind: the "understanding," "light."

101. I use my own translation from the text of this work in Schelling, *Werke*, 7:333–416. However, there are available English translations that include the page numbers of the same German text: *Schelling: Of Human Freedom*, trans. James Gutmann (Chicago: Open Court, 1936); *Philosophical Investigatons into the Essence of Human Freedom*, trans. J. Lake and J. Schmidt (Albany: State University of New York Press, 2005). On interpretation, see Martin Heidegger, *Schelling's Treatise on the Essence of Human Freedom*, trans. John Stambaugh (Athens: Ohio University Press); Alan White, *Schelling: Introduction to the System of Freedom* (New Haven and London: Yale University Press, 1983).
102. *Werke*, 7:352ff., 356. Hegel ignores this work by Schelling, e.g., in his *Lectures on the History of Philosophy*, 3:512–45.
103. *Werke*, 7:394.
104. Ibid., 349–52.

This does not mean a dualism of total opposites, insofar as understanding is implicit in the dark chaos of the first principle, but as completely undeveloped and hidden in deepest mystery. The two principles are in truth an identity. God, who is "wisdom" and "eternal love," is eternally the unity or identity of the two principles in "eternal light."

In creation, the dark element is the material principle, the ground of the world. The understanding is the "Word" of God that brings the inner possibilities of the first principle to form and order. The ground is blind will without form or order. It is always present underneath all things, so to speak, "as if it could again break through" and destroy the ordered world. It remains the "incomprehensible basis of reality." Schelling describes it as gravity or heaviness, that which drags downward. The awareness of "the deep night" out of which it arose drives humanity "to strive toward the light with all its might." "All birth is birth from darkness into the light."[105] The first principle is not evil, but it is the potentiality for evil, and yet in its deep mystery it is also the potential for good. When it is ruled by the higher second principle, the Word of God, it is or becomes good. Only when it resists the Word and "tears itself away" from it, does the first principle become evil.[106] But the understanding or the Word is "actually the will in [all] will."[107] It is the will to good hidden in the mystery of the first principle. It is what God wills to be victorious over evil in creation, namely, love.

In an evolutionary history that is essentially repeated anew in every human life, human being in its origin is blind will without clear direction, searching desire, chaotic thoughts. Through the work of the second principle, the Word, understanding is gradually brought forth, and out of the interaction of the principles, the "soul" emerges as their unity, the "center." It is the basis of the higher development of human intelligence or spirit [Geist]. But it is an uncertain unity and center. The principle of understanding leads the human spirit upward toward the light of the wisdom and goodness of God, but in the human spirit the powers or principles are not in harmony. In Schelling's image, human spirit finds itself on a high and jagged peak, where an irresistible voice urges it to fall, where it is overcome with a kind of vertigo or "dizziness" [Schwindel]. The experience of being torn between the self's chaotic desires and the will to move toward the good is the "anxiety of life" that "drives the human spirit out of the center in which it was created." As it now falls away from the center, the self seeks to assert itself still as the center, as the unity of the powers of the principles of creation. It thinks it can rule over them as over its own possibilities in life, but it is doomed to find only "sin and death." The result is not only broken human being but also a bro-

---

105. Ibid., 358–61. While the new terms in Schelling's philosophical understanding of the principles remain essentially the same as earlier [chap. 2.2.2], Schelling here formulates them in concepts taken from the works of the seventeenth-century mystic Jacob Böhme (1575–1624). See Robert Brown, *The Later Philosophy of Schelling; The Influence of Böhme on the Works of 1809–1815* (Lewisburg: Bucknell University Press, 1977).

106. *Werke*, 7:400.

107. Ibid., 359.

kenness of the world, a "melancholia" spread over all of life, for nature too depends on humanity for its meaning.[108]

In spite of the "dizziness" the fall is ultimately an act of human freedom. Schelling refers again to Kant: an act of freedom is, as Kant says, outside of time and the network of causes and effects. In unstated reference to Kant's theory of radical evil [chap. 2.1.3], Schelling says that human being is from the beginning disposed to fall into evil, the corrupted disposition of human life. Therefore, although human being is free, its acts are necessarily determined by its disposition to evil. "Human being always needs help." This help and with it true freedom, the freedom from evil, comes from the Word, the second principle, which is also the principle of love. Love is revealed in its opposite, in evil's hatred, by changing it to love. Love's purpose is not to annihilate the corrupted first principle. It rather sacrifices itself, gives itself over to it, in order to heal it. This occurs in the incarnation of the Word in Christ. Christ is a human being without sin. In his person the first principle, the "will of the ground," does not fall into evil but is joined with the Word and is thus true "center," true human being. The "highest peak" of revelation is "the original [urbildliche] and divine human who was in the beginning with God and in whom all things and humanity itself were made." Through Christ sinful human being comes to trust and have confidence in God in an act of faith that is both free and "excludes all choice," for faith is the necessity of its reborn self.[109] Healing and reconciliation become real, while evil is revealed as unreality and "nonbeing." Truth is now recognized in God, the "living unity of the powers" and real "personhood," not "a merely logical abstraction." Natural humanity continues to suffer "vertigo" and fall into evil.[110] Evil however is now openly and powerfully opposed by the healing truth of Word and Spirit. Through the work of the Word evil will finally be no more, and ground and the Word will be joined in complete identity of truth and goodness in the life of all humanity and the world. Above will be God as "the love that is all in all" ("this is the secret of love, that it unites those that could be each for themselves and yet are not and cannot be without the other").[111]

After On Human Freedom and for years to come, Schelling published relatively little, although he constantly wrote and revised manuscripts. The most important of his later writings first appeared posthumously in the collected works, which his son edited and published much later, between 1856 and 1861. An indication of

108. Ibid., 361–64, 381, 399f.
109. Ibid., 377–80, 382–96. Schelling reflects the tradition of Augustine (and the New Testament) that only true freedom chooses the good, and only Christian freedom is true freedom. See, e.g., *The Essential Augustine*, ed. Vernon J. Bourke (Indianapolis: Hackett Publishing, 1974), 181f.
110. Schelling gives a famous exposition of eruptions of the fallen ground into human life, e.g., in insanity, in posthumously published lectures (*Stuttgarter Privatvorlesungen*) from the period following the publication of *On Human Freedom*: *Werke*, 7:468ff.; ET *Idealism and the Endgame of Theory: Three Essays by F. W. J. Schelling*, 233. The opposite direction, toward higher spirituality, is represented by another posthumously published work of the same period: *Clara or, On Nature's Connection to the Spirit World*, trans. Fiona Steinkamp (Albany: State University of New York Press, 2002).
111. *Werke*, 7:404–8.

the direction in which his later thought was moving may be taken from a lecture given at the University of Erlangen in 1821: "Here . . . everything that is a being must be abandoned, the last dependence disappear; here one must leave everything—not only, as is said, wife and child, but all that Is, even God, for God too is at this point only a being. . . . So God too must be abandoned by those who wish to place themselves at the point where a truly free philosophy begins. Here the words apply: 'Whoever will save his life will lose it, and whoever loses it will find it.'"[112]

2.4.2 The Philosophy of Mythology and Revelation

When Schelling became professor of philosophy in Munich in 1827 (where he probably read the major Catholic theologians, if he had not done so before), he initiated a rotation of lectures in introduction to philosophy and in the philosophy of mythology and revelation. When he was called to Berlin in 1841, in his first two semesters he lectured on the final and most important part of the rotation, the philosophy of revelation. Notes from these two semesters were published without his authorization and against his will.[113] To the end of his life Schelling revised the lectures. What we present here is mainly from their final version in Schelling's *Werke*.

The key feature is the "positive" philosophy of the priority of reality before reason; "negative" philosophy reverses the order, placing reason before reality. According to Schelling the priority of reality must lead to the conclusion that only an original free act that utterly transcends all that is—not just the world but reason and thought itself—can account for the existence of anything at all. Reason is able conceptually to comprehend itself and the world ("what" they are) and to determine the a priori relationship of the possibility of what exists to its actual existence (anything that exists must be possible). But reason is at a loss to explain not only why or how either the world or its possibility exists, but also why thought itself exists. It can explain *what* they are, but not *that* they are. Existence (the "that") is *unvordenklich*: reason cannot "think before" existence.[114] Schelling can say, "*die*

---

112. *Werke*, 9:217. Cf. *Meister Eckhart*, trans. Blakney, 231: "I pray that God may quit [sc. rid] me of god, for (his) unconditioned being is above god and all distinctions." The distinction in spelling between "God" and "god" is the translator's, not Eckhart's. The phrase in the quotation from Schelling having to do with "dependence" is perhaps meant as a reference to the use of the word by Schleiermacher, who in the same year 1821 published the first edition of *The Christian Faith* [see chap. 2.7 below]. Schelling certainly read this work, although he does not discuss it. He had no personal relationship with Schleiermacher.

113. The work, commonly known as the "*Paulus-Nachschrift*," has been reissued without the extensive derogatory additions of the original editor, who was not the (unknown) person who took the notes but a Professor Paulus, an enemy of Schelling: Manfred Frank, ed., *F. W. J. Schelling, Philosophie der Offenbarung 1841/1842* (Frankfurt: Suhrkamp, 1977).

114. See Schelling, *Werke*, 13:55–62, 562–66. Cf. ibid., 13:7: "Why does anything at all exist?" Cf. ibid., 256: "Perfect Spirit [*Geist*] is for us only the absolutely free Spirit. . . . The perfect Spirit is over all kinds of being, is beyond every, even the highest being. Therein consists this Spirit's absolute transcendence." It is with this original freedom that God acts not only to create but also to reveal

Zeit gab . . ." (time gave . . ."), which also indicates the priority of existence before thought. In another place he says time is the "bad conscience of all empty metaphysics, the point it gladly avoided."[115] When reason thinks that its concepts sufficiently "contain" reality—as in Hegel—it lives in its own "ether."[116]

Schelling's thought of an utterly transcendent act as the origin of all exceeds previous metaphysics in including thought itself in what is derived from this act.[117] For Schelling the act is related to revelation, but isolated for itself it only points to the mysterious fact of origin, about which nothing can be said other than that it happens. If God is the utterly free act of origin, there is no access to any thought of God, unless God acts to disclose or reveal God within the reality that human being can perceive.

It is at this point that Schelling's new thought on revelation, faith, and reason is to be understood. Science has to do with what applies universally for reason (*das Allgemeine*), as in Hegel's concepts. In contrast, Schelling writes, "faith remains something entirely by itself, independent of all science [*Wissenschaft*], even free from every contact with it, because it is—unmixed with all generality [*allem Allgemeinen*]—the most personal." For Schelling, faith relates "positively" to what it perceives as the reality of Christ described or put forth in Scripture. The only convincing proof of the Scripture's truth is the testimony of the Holy Spirit that works the faith that the testimony of Scripture is true (a subject-object unity). Yet human being is also reasoning being who must think and engage in science. Faith must be comprehensible for reason. Comprehension of the subject matter of faith is the work of theology, "the scientific mind of the church." Good theology is sorely needed in the church. Through it believers should have their reasoning perception of what is believed extended "by a system of Christian insights" and hence be truly "edified." In fact revelation is the true source for the knowledge of all reality. Schelling refers to a New Testament text: "the treasures of wisdom and knowledge hidden in Christ" (Col. 2:3).[118]

God's self. See also M. Frank, ed., *Philosophie der Offenbarung 1841/1842*, 250. See the discussion in Andrew Bowie, *Schelling and Modern European Philosophy*, 162–8. Aristotle conceived God as pure act, but Aristotle's "prime mover" is both the object of philosophical thought and not free: it cannot change and is eternally and necessarily part of the universe it enacts (*Metaphysics*, book 12, chaps. 6–7). Plato's concept of the Good is beyond being and is godlike, but it is thought (*Republic*, trans. Cornford, 211–20, 255, 262). What Schelling means is also not his earlier thought of absolute identity.

115. *Werke*, 12:589; 14:108.

116. According to Schelling, for Hegel "God only does what God has done; God's life is in the circle of forms in which God forever externalizes himself and forever takes himself back again." M. Frank, ed., *Philosophie der Offenbarung 1841/42*, 133. Hegel's God "cannot create anything new." *Werke*, 10:160. See Andrew Bowie, *Schelling and Modern European Philosophy*, 168–72.

117. Schelling acknowledges a certain similarity to Kant's idea of God as what transcends and limits reason and as the "unconditioned necessity" that is the "bearer of all things." *Werke*, 13:163. Cf. Kant, *Critique of Pure Reason*, B641.

118. *Werke*, 10:404–7 (from Schelling's 1846 foreword to the published works of Heinrich Steffens). Christianity (whose "true content" is Christ) contains within itself the key to its being understood: 14:235f.; cf. 234f., cf. 238, 227, 307, 32. The Gospels contain poetic legends about Christ that glorify Christ's divinity (Ibid., 14:232). In the same place Schelling reproaches those theologians who are led into doubt by mythical interpretation (i.e., by Strauss) as having little faith. That Christ

In another place he remarks about the relationship of faith and knowledge: "True belief would . . . prove itself by the fact that no effort was spared to discover the mediations via which that *in which* belief believes was also made plausible to reason and the strictest science."[119] The sentence seems paradoxical: the faith that seeks understanding has, from the beginning, a content that from the beginning was made plausible to science. In the same place Schelling says faith means both "will" and "act." It belongs to faith to be "courageously willed," for revelation transcends "our usual concepts."[120] But it is for Schelling always also "plausible to reason and the strictest science."

"Positive" philosophy corrects the basic fault of Idealism, that is, the thought that concepts or ideas contain reality. Such a thought must be "destroyed" for the sake of what is "more than the idea." A "turn" is required, a turn also motivated by existential reality: the "despair" in the experience of the emptiness of existence apart from truth, an experience deepened by the first "taste" of the perception of God. Already with this first dawning perception, the gap between oneself and God, a fissure that runs through all existence, is now perceived. The one who perceives this finally comes to "will" God as the "Lord of Being."[121]

The "true content" of Christianity is the historical person of Christ. "God is by no means the opposite of finitude . . . , one who only wants to dwell in infinity. . . . God does not rest, so to speak, until all is brought into the most comprehensible, most finite form. The limitation [historical form] of Christianity of which many speak is purpose, intention." Schelling contrasts a rationalized Christianity of general concepts to Christianity "in its complete concreteness" or "conditionedness" [*in seiner ganzen Bestimmtheit*] as expressed in the New Testament.[122] His method in the "philosophy of revelation" is to proceed from this concreteness to the general understanding of the truth of the world and to this truth as the center of all the sciences: Christ is the key to understanding the truth of all things, and so also of history.

---

is the source of all true knowledge (also with reference to Col. 2:3) had been said by the medieval theologian Bonaventura (1217–1274).

119. From Andrew Bowie's translation of *On the History of Modern Philosophy,* 178 (= *Werke,* 10:183). The original sentence is as follows: "Glaube hätte sich hier dadurch bewähren müssen, dass keine Anstrengung gescheut würde, um jene Vermittlungen zu entdecken, durch welche das *woran* der Glaube glaubt, auch der Vernunft und der strengsten Wissenschaft einleuchtend gemacht wurde."

120. *Werke,* 14:16. It is Christian tradition that faith involves all aspects of personal being, also the will. But here it is noticeably characterized as courageous will, and the "usual concepts" are not supportive of faith. Both are symptoms of modernity [cf. Heidegger in chap. 8.4.1].

121. 10:566, cf. 13:352, 363ff. In saying that existence without faith ends in despair, Schelling stands within a long tradition in Christian thought that has its most famous expression in Augustine's depiction of the human condition apart from faith: *Confessions,* bk. 8, chap. 7f.; bk. 12, chap. 11. ("The heart is restless until it rests in God" [ibid., bk. 1, chap. 1].) See also Tholuck in chap. 3.1 below. One also finds in Schelling certain concepts that later become current in existentialist philosophy, e.g., that of the human experience of being "thrown" into existence: a foreshadowing of the concept of *Geworfenheit* (thrown-ness): Werke, 13:202.

122. *Werke,* 14:35, 25f., 323.

The historical part of the philosophy of mythology and revelation is integral to Schelling's interpretation of Christianity; it is also the first revival of patristic Logos theology in modern German theology. In the main it is a revision and extension of the earlier writing, *On Human Freedom*. As Schelling now clearly says, God in God's freedom is always above time and history, while God also historically discloses God's triune being and the involvement of this being in human history. The disclosure occurs through revelation in Christ and, seen from the vantage point of revelation, in creation and in pre-Christian mythology. In creation God makes God's triune potencies or principles (1) the ground, (2) Logos (Word), and (3) the concrete formations in the whole of human history.[123] Humanity, in its sinful "fallenness" from the harmonious unity of created life, makes itself the lord of the potencies or possibilities of life. It thinks it can do as it wills and continue to be the master of its possibilities, but, unable to extricate itself from the consequences of its choices, it deceives itself. In humanity's fall, the triune potencies or principles in creation necessarily fall with it, so that nature, which depends on humanity, also becomes the victim of the fall.[124] The ground of human existence is now no longer the potential for human godliness, but the potential for evil. The central motif of mythological history is the interaction of the corrupted chaotic ground and the Logos, which leads it through suffering upward toward the good, until the "fullness of time" when the Logos is incarnated in Christ.[125] In the form of a completely human servant taken by the Logos, the full truth or glory (John 1:14) of the second person of the Trinity, his selfless love of God and humanity, is revealed. The prayer of Jesus in John 17 affirms his being in the Father and the Father in him. He is wholly obedient to the will of the Father, and his miracles are not by a divine power of his own but by the will of the Father.[126] Schelling devotes an extended discussion to Philippians 2:6–8, which speaks of Christ's "emptying" of himself in becoming human and obedient to God.[127]

123. Ibid., 12:89f.; 13:280f.; with reference to Prov. 8:23ff.:13:302f. The one God of the immanent Trinity (God in God's self) sets the economic Trinity, i.e., the work of the triune principles or potencies in the history of creation, mythology, and revelation.

124. Ibid., 13:350ff. The first two Platonic cosmic principles: the unconditioned or infinite and limit, are the structural elements in Schelling's mythology. The ancient gods have the characteristic of the all-consuming unconditional that annihilates progress at its nascent beginning (the unconditional limits human development). The historically developed Greek gods, however, are defined individuals with definite personalities and are patrons of culture. However, these gods evolve from the fall of human being and cannot transcend their fallen, evil ground. See J. E. Wilson, *Schellings Mythologie* (Stuttgart: Frommann-Holzboog, 1993), part II.

125. Cf. the meaning of "coming to itself" in the early Schelling and in Hegel [chaps. 2.2.3 and 2.3]. In the late Schelling the truth of history comes to itself in Christ.

126. *Werke*, 14:117, 185–88.

127. Schelling's exposition of this text makes him the first significant representative of "kenotic" theology. On Phil. 2:6–8: *Philosophie der Offenbarung, 1841/42*, 287–99; *Werke*, 14:37ff. Later in the century Isaak Dorner referred to Schelling the "chief representative or at least patron" of this theology. *Briefwechsel zwischen H. L. Martensen und I. A. Dorner, 1839–1881*, 2 vols. (Berlin: Reimer, 1881), 1:310. See also Dorner in chap. 3.3 below. On kenotic theology, see Wolfhart Pannenberg, *Jesus—God and Man*, 2nd ed., trans. Lewis L. Wilkens and Duane A. Priebe (Philadelphia: Westminster, 1977), 307–11; Claude Welch, ed. and trans., *God and Incarnation in Mid-nineteenth Century German Theology* (New York: Oxford University Press, 1965).

As fallen existence, sin is characterized not only by egotism but also by the world-forming conditions and possibilities of fallen existence, that is, belief systems or mythologies. In pre-Christian mythologies the work of the Logos or second principle is personified as a suffering but liberating hero-god who opens new horizons of meaning in conflict with the old gods, a conflict in which in some dark mythologies the hero-god is killed.[128] There are deeply evil mythologies and higher, humane mythologies, but all arise from the evil ground, which only the death and resurrection of Christ overcomes. Where the work of the Logos in mythological history is seen retrospectively in the light of Christ, the hero-gods are recognized as mythological analogies to the truth that is revealed in Christ. In the "philosophy of revelation" Schelling attempts to demonstrate in New Testament texts the relationship of prerevelation language, which is mythologically formed, to revelation.[129] The essentially prophetic language of the Old Testament is also formed in the context of the mythological world but, by the revelatory work of the Logos, in the Old Testament myth is transformed into prophecy that points to the coming of Christ. In Christ's death and resurrection the mythological gods cease to exist, because the corrupted ground of their being is conquered by Christ.[130]

After Christ, humanity continues to suffer the fall by willing itself to be the lord of its possibilities. Now, however, this fall can no longer corrupt the world-ground. Satan has fallen from heaven (Luke 10:18). Evil's place is now only earthly life, the secular sphere of human history.[131] But the conquest of the ground by Christ has an absolute consequence: if Christ has conquered the ground, all reality is finally in Christ. "Revelation perceives nothing outside of itself, and especially not its opposite."[132] Faith knows this and perceives all reality in the light of Christ. As in *On Human Freedom,* evil lacks true reality. Natural sinful history continues to unfold in forms of existence that can be disclosed as false belief systems and therefore as essentially mythological. These false belief systems, in which the Logos is always operative as the forward-leading principle (although its influence for the good can be rejected), also find their final meaning in Christ. The church is tempted by and suffers sin not only in the evil of the world but also in itself.[133] But through the power of the Holy Spirit it recognizes the sinful belief systems in itself and the world and knows the truth of their being overcome in Christ. There-

128. Schelling anticipates Joseph Campbell, *The Hero with a Thousand Faces* (New York: Pantheon Books, 1949). A symptom of a dark mythology is human sacrifice, a sign of pervasive fear, the gravity of the corrupted ground.
129. "Language is faded [*verblichene*] mythology" whose origin is poetic. Schelling, *Werke,* 11:52f.; cf. 56, 60. Cf. the early Schelling on religious language [chap. 2.2.5].
130. Ibid., 10:425f.; 11:52f., 241, 248; 14:88, 143ff., 152, 167ff. An example of a pagan god that dies is Pan: *Werke,* 14:240. When the pagan gods vanish, the natural world is desacralized.
131. Ibid., 14:263, 269ff.
132. Ibid., 13:530. "Christianity must be everything for us, therefore it must also explain the world and not leave this only to philosophy" (13:180). Justification is the objective act of God's acceptance of humanity in Christ (14:217).
133. One "falls again into the process," i.e., of mythology, false belief systems: 13:336, 455; cf. 11:245.

fore according to Schelling the only viable apologetic of Christianity is the philosophy of mythology: the analysis and disclosure of sin.[134]

Schelling's understanding of the history of church is Trinitarian. Like the medieval Franciscan Joachim of Floris, he envisions a future spiritual "Johannine" church as the church of the imminent second coming of Christ. This church, which like Christ is already in process of coming, is the unification (synthesis) of "Petrine" and "Pauline" churches. Petrine is the principle of stable tradition, while the Pauline principle, essentially already operative in Old Testament prophecy, breaks down antiquated and repressive aspects of Petrine authority and leads into the future. Both have typical errors: legalism on the one hand, libertinism and Gnosticism on the other, both of which follow mythological patterns of thought and behavior.[135]

Those who heard Schelling's Berlin lectures in 1841 included most of the academic community of the city and Søren Kierkegaard, who traveled to Berlin to hear them. The first part of the lectures, on questions of recent philosophy and especially on Hegel, enjoyed considerable success. The later part, which presented in abbreviated form the philosophy of mythology and revelation, saw the audience dwindle, with Kierkegaard too withdrawing in disappointment. The leading theologian of the Awakening in Berlin, Prof. August Neander, had warmly greeted Schelling as the "savior" of philosophy. In his first lecture Schelling said he had come to "heal the wounds" caused by recent philosophy.[136] The turmoil apparent already at the beginning of the 1840s must have made the need of savior seem rather urgent [chap. 1.2].

2.5 "YOUNG HEGELIANS"

The July Revolution in Paris in 1830, directed against an increasingly repressive establishment, signaled a surge of socialist and anticlericalist thought not seen since the French Revolution. Agitation in Germany built steadily into the 1840s, reaching a peak in the revolution year 1848 [chap. 1.2]. Hegel's students divided into a conservative right wing and the revolutionary left wing or "Young Hegelians" who departed from the system at several key points, especially from its Christian character. The right-wing "Old Hegelians," the dominant Hegelian group in the 1820s, held Christianity and Hegel's absolute philosophy in harmony; they were the same truth in two forms [see chap. 2.3].[137] The first point in the Young

134. Ibid., 11:52, 245–47; 12:122; 13:336, 339.
135. Ibid., 14:311–32. Karl Löwith gives a partial account of this in *Meaning in History* (Chicago: University of Chicago Press, 1949), 209f.
136. See M. Frank, ed., *Schelling, Philosophie der Offenbarung 1841/1842.* At the end of the book Frank includes texts in response to Schelling's lectures from the early 1840s written by philosophical figures, including Kierkegaard and Feuerbach.
137. On the Hegelianism of both the right (Old Hegelians, especially Philip Marheineke, 1780–1846, and Karl Daub, 1765–1836) and the left, see John Edward Toews, *Hegelianism*; Karl Löwith, *From Hegel to Nietzsche*, 53–136; William J. Brazill, *The Young Hegelians* (New Haven and

Hegelian program involved the recognition that Hegel's *Aufhebung* or "lifting" of religion into knowledge was implicitly revolutionary, because it negated what was "lifted." World history is progress, and progress is a matter of negation. Philosophy has to act progressively and negatively to change the world for the better. The second point revived the claim made by some of Hegel's earlier critics that the "Absolute" can only have its existence as "Son" not in a particular human being, Christ, but in all humanity. Hegel's universal [*allgemeine*] "Spirit" [*Geist*] that comes to itself in the process of history is nothing other than the "spirit" of humanity.[138] Feuerbach and Marx, who focused on human experience and history, agreed with the later Schelling's critique that Hegel wrongly made the concept prior to existence and, just as wrongly, thought existence was contained in the concept or evolved out of the concept. And the Young Hegelians generally had a high regard for the early Schelling's philosophy of nature.[139] But they entirely rejected the late Schelling's "philosophy of revelation," and they considered Hegel, however much he needed correcting, superior to all previous philosophers.

2.5.1 D. F. Strauss

David Friedrich Strauss (1808–71) spent his life as a private scholar and author. He was by education a theologian, and throughout his academic life he was a sharp critic of attempts to mediate faith and historical criticism in New Testament interpretation.[140] His most important work, *The Life of Jesus Critically Examined*, first published in 1835, demonstrated the thesis that the Gospel history was formed around the belief that Jesus was the promised Messiah of the Old Testament— something that at first seems not to be something new in the history of exegesis. But for Strauss the Gospel stories about Jesus were constructed almost entirely by means of the Old Testament sayings about the Messiah, so that from them little could be known about Jesus' life itself. They were "myths." Mythical interpretation was not new; it had arisen at the end of the previous century in Old Testament interpretation and had increasingly been applied to the New.

London: Yale University Press, 1970); Helmut Thielicke, *Modern Faith and Thought*, 420–89; Jürgen Habermas, *The Philosophical Discourse of Modernity*, 51–74. See also Isaak Dorner's discussion of the Christology of the right-wing Hegelians, *History of the Development of the Doctrine of the Person of Christ*, II/3:122–31, 161–73; cf. 140ff., 149ff. [see Dorner, chap. 3.3]. From 1838 to 1842 Arnold Ruge edited what quickly became a Young Hegelian journal, the *Hallesche Jahrbücher*, until it was banned by the government of Prussia.

138. Karl Löwith, *Die Hegelische Linke*, 14f. In the *Phenomenology of Spirit*, 478, Hegel had spoken of "the divine universal Man [sc. Human]" not as Christ but as the "community" [chap. 2.3]. Cf. Fichte's philosophy of the ego [chap. 2.2.2].

139. See esp. Manfred Frank, *Der unendliche Mangel an Sein. Schellings Hegelkritik und die Anfänge der Marxischen Dialektik*, 2nd ed. (Munich: Wilhelm Fink, 1992). Even before Schelling's 1841 lectures, Feuerbach knew the later Schelling's work from hand-copied notes, and, as Frank says, with obvious great respect sent Schelling his dissertation for review. Another Young Hegelian, Arnold Ruge, offered Schelling his services as editor of his lectures (Frank, 30).

140. On his life and work, see Toews, *Hegelianism*, 255–87; Horton Harris, *David Friedrich Strauss and His Theology* (Cambridge: Cambridge University Press, 1973).

A key question in mythical interpretation was whether or not biblical accounts were fabricated stories. The "pious lie" (*fraus pia*) had been known in the early centuries of the church, as for example in fictions about the lives of certain saints. Strauss said the Gospels were made up not of intentional but of unintentional fabrications, so they were not actually lies. He explained it this way: The Jews at the time of Jesus were not at the height of cultivated life enjoyed by the Greeks and Romans but were akin mentally to more primitive and credulous stages of cultural development. Their minds were formed by their traditions of direct divine intervention in worldly affairs and above all by stories of the coming Messiah. Under the impression of Jesus' person and teaching and especially after his death and resurrection, which Strauss interprets psychologically as a hallucinatory vision, they enthusiastically interpreted all he said and did in connection with Old Testament traditions about the Messiah. This happened in the form of stories that later came into written form in the Gospels. The authors of the Gospels knowingly made some fictional additions to the stories, for example, to make connections between them, but these are insignificant.[141]

In the "Concluding Dissertation" of the *Life of Jesus,* Strauss draws a series of conclusions, partly based on Hegelian philosophy. The Gospels, he says, can no longer be believed as historical sources for comprehending the historical Jesus. What he thinks he can see of Jesus through the myths is a religiously genial person, perhaps the greatest among those who have founded or ever will found a religion. But Spirit in its great wealth of meaning cannot possibly be embodied in a single individual; it can only be the unity of God and all of humanity, a world history of individuals with many gifts who "reciprocally complete one another." He also says his mythical interpretation, in making impossible a faith based on the Gospel histories, serves the truth. "The object of faith is completely changed; instead of a sensible, empirical fact, it has become a spiritual and divine idea ["*Idee,*" sc. concept], which has its confirmation no longer in history but in philosophy."

Finally Strauss argues for the progressive raising of the popular mind to philosophical enlightenment, and for this the church is still indispensable. His concluding section (§152) gives advice to the enlightened clergy for educating the laity: there is "a mode of reconciling the two extremes," faith and philosophical knowledge. "In [the cleric's] discourses to the church, he will indeed adhere to the forms of popular conception, but at every opportunity he will exhibit their spiritual [i.e., philosophical] significance, which for him constitutes their sole truth, and thus prepare—though such a result is only to be thought of as an unending

---

141. Strauss, *The Life of Jesus Critically Examined,* trans. from the 4th German ed. of 1840 by George Eliot (Ramsey: Sigler, 1994), 69–92. At the end of his introduction Strauss gives an extended discussion of how to judge whether or not a New Testament text is mythical. He classifies the criteria into two groups, "negative" and "positive," which may be summarized as follows. Negative: contradiction of the laws of nature, improbable sequence of events, improbable actions, and contradiction of other texts. Positive: speech in poetic or unusually elevated style and narratives that more likely express preconceived ideas than what happened in actual events.

progress—the resolution of those forms into their original concepts also in the consciousness of the church."[142]

In his next work, *Die christliche Glaubenslehre* (The Doctrine of the Christian Faith), which is a history of Christian doctrine, Strauss rejects any thought of coming to terms with the faith of the church.[143] The word that repeatedly occurs in the chapter titles on each doctrine is *Auflösung*, the "dissolution" of the doctrine. Strauss's thesis is that since the New Testament period a gradual but definite historical development of scientific thought has taken place within Christianity that has led to the freedom of modern humanity from faith, that is, from its way of thinking about truth in "representations" [*Vorstellungen*]. Now it knows the concepts themselves. At an earlier time in modernity attempts were made to mediate between faith and science, but now one must demonstrate the "deception and lie" in all attempts to mediate between faith and science. Agreeing with Feuerbach, Strauss writes that religion is essentially otherworldly fantasy based on subjective human needs, and many still find these needs to some degree met in religious faith. The enlightened philosopher comprehends the needs and understands their deceptive religious productions.

Strauss also agrees with Feuerbach in saying that those Hegelians are wrong that think that in the move from faith to philosophical knowledge only the form changes, while the content stays the same. The truth is that in the shift from faith to philosophy the content changes with the form. Faith and science (*Glaube und Wissen*) can only be distinctly different, and theology is in an impossible situation when it tries to mediate them.[144] The "Christian world view," as a metaphysics of the "other world," stands in opposition to the modern philosophical worldview, in which the finite and infinite are reconciled not in the beyond but in this world.[145] The New Testament's history of the life, death, and resurrection of Jesus is irrelevant for the modern world and can be given over to historical criticism.[146] The modern mind is free from the constraints that bind faith to its deceptive perceptions, and the expression of this freedom is historical and philosophical criticism. In the final chapters Strauss advocates a theory of ultimate reality in which the universe as a whole maintains its absoluteness only in an eternal

---

142. Ibid., 777–84. An "original" concept is the true concept.

143. *Die christliche Glaubenslehre in ihrer geschichtlichen Entwicklung und im Kampfe mit der modernen Wissenschaft dargestellt* (Doctrine of the Christian Faith in Its Historical Development and in Opposition to Modern Science), 2 vols. (Tübingen: Osiander, 1840–41). In the late 1830s Strauss had the misfortune of being appointed a professor of theology by a liberal government in Zurich that, because of the appointment, was turned out. The new conservative government refused him the appointment but honored the contract made with the previous government, paying him half-salary, which he contributed to charity. Perhaps it was this experience that caused him to turn against the church.

144. Strauss, *Die christliche Glaubenslehre*, 1:1–24. Feuerbach's *Essence of Christianity* appeared in 1841, the same year the 2nd volume of Strauss's *Glaubenslehre* was published. Here Strauss's references to Feuerbach are to earlier works, especially *Pierre Bayle*.

145. Ibid., 1:25ff.

146. Ibid., 2:336.

circle of origin and decay. To become united with this "One" in thought is all that modern science can say about immortality.[147]

Strauss's later so-called "second life of Jesus," *The Life of Jesus Presented for the German People,* published in 1864, attempts to explain Jesus' religious mind based on information that he now thinks can be gleaned from the sparse historical material among the myths of the Synoptic Gospels. Jesus, he says, gives offense to modern consciousness through the messianic arrogance (*Selbstüberhebung*) of claiming he is coming again to judge the world. But the core of his message still rings true, namely, the Sermon on the Mount, which gives expression to the "inner truth" of the human conscience. Here Jesus shows a serene unity with God more characteristic of Greek than Jewish thought, which teaches the absolute difference between humanity and God.[148] In this work too Strauss mainly expounds his mythical interpretation. In a famous metaphor he compares the New Testament myths that obscure the life of Jesus to a parasitic vine that grows up around a tree, sapping its life, so that the tree's own leaves fall away, its limbs decay, and all that is visible is the vine, as if it were the tree. In conclusion Strauss affirms again that modern progress requires a clear distinction between the historical Christ and the ideal of human being. "Christ-religion must be transformed into the religion of humanity."[149]

In his last work, *The Old Faith and the New,* the "old faith" is Christianity, whose antiquated major doctrines are contrasted with the reality of the "new faith" of the modern Darwinian worldview and modern culture. The resurrection of Christ is "world-historical humbug."[150] Strauss compares the "religious domain" in the modern human soul to the constantly shrinking lands of the Native Americans in the United States.[151] What is permanent in Jesus' moral teaching are the universal truths of humanitarianism. Religion is a "weakness" that should now be outgrown.[152] The only necessary being in the universe is the "One," the substance of all things; the accidents or appearances of the substance

---

147. Ibid., 667, 738f. In the last chapter Strauss quotes words from Schleiermacher's *Speeches* [chap. 2.2.4] that have to do with being one with the infinite, but Strauss's interpretation of these quotations is his own, not Schleiermacher's. He returns to this concept in his last work (see later in this chapter).

148. Strauss, *Das Leben Jesu für das deutsche Volk bearbeitet* (Leipzig: Brockhaus, 1864), 204–9 (cf. 180f.), 242. Strauss's appreciation of the Sermon on the Mount is perhaps dependent on F. C. Baur's work on the teaching of Jesus; see Baur, chap. 3.5 below.

149. Ibid., 621, 625. Strauss's image of the tree covered by vines is encountered in later theology, e.g., in Karl Hase's *Kirchengeschichte auf der Grundlage akademischer Vorlesungen,* 2:508 [see chap. 3.4]. With reference to Strauss he writes: "what . . . remains of history after the tearing down of the mythical vines is indeed a rather bare trunk, but it is still the cross."

150. *Der alte und der neue Glaube, ein Bekenntnis* (4th ed. Bonn, 1873), 73 (§27); ET by Mathilde Blind, *The Old Faith and the New, a Confession* (New York: Holt, 1874), 1:161. This translation, whose quality is considerably below that of George Eliot's translation of Strauss's *Life of Jesus,* has recently been reprinted without Strauss's important conclusion (New York: Prometheus, 1997).

151. Ibid., 141f. (§43). Another illustration of Strauss's talent for metaphor: Schleiermacher's Christ of faith is "only a reminiscence of bygone times, as it were the light of a distant star that we still see although the star died years ago" (*Der Christus des Glaubens und der Jesus der Geschichte,* 220).

152. *Der alte und der neue Glanbe,* 59–61 (§23), 83–85 (§31), 139 (§43).

are the world-things, which appear and disappear in an eternal cycle, among them Spirit itself.[153] The last chapters are devoted to the great German poets and music composers as the artistic expressions of the "new faith." In his conclusion Strauss returns to his scientific conception of the universe, a cause-and-effect machine in which one can be crushed to death. Each individual must find happiness within herself or himself.[154]

2.5.2 Ludwig Feuerbach

Ludwig Feuerbach (1804–72) studied under Hegel in Berlin in the 1820s and was for a short time lecturer at the University of Erlangen, but spent most of his life as a private scholar and author. For Feuerbach, Hegel's "Spirit" is simply human spirit projected onto infinity. He is famous for his statement that "theology is anthropology." Theology is "the deified and objective mind or spirit [*Geist*] of man, and in the last analysis theology is therefore nothing other than anthropology."[155] "Religion, expressed generally, is consciousness of the infinite; thus it is and can be nothing else than the consciousness which man has of his own—not limited and finite, but infinite nature."[156] This "infinite" is only a metaphor for the freedom of human thinking or imagination. All religious images and dogmas are imagined ideal projections of human nature into the "other" of the transcendent world. The antithesis of finite and infinite is the antithesis between human unhappiness in real life and its "infinite" wishes, its religious images of happy perfection. This antithesis, which in religion remains unresolved, is overcome for Feuerbach by rational enlightenment.[157] As in Hegel, religious representation or *Vorstellung* is "lifted" [*aufgehoben*] from its symbolic form to the form of philosophical knowing, but Feuerbach rejects Hegel's idea that the same truth has two forms, religious and philosophical. Rather, with the form the content changes, and therefore, through the "lifting" to philosophical knowing, religion is eliminated.[158] What is true in Christianity is love that joins all human life and nature; it is community in affirmation of nature and bodily life. It must be freed from faith in order to have real benefit for humanity, for faith is "the opposite of love." Faith restricts love by separating God from human being in making God a particular being defined by dogmas of right and wrong, and it extends no love to the "enemies of God."[159]

---

153. Ibid., 116–23, 129ff. (§§38–40). As in the previous work, *Die christliche Glaubenslehre*, Strauss quotes Schleiermacher (as, e.g., in §42: "the feeling of utter dependence" on the universe), but his interpretation of these quotations is philosophical and has nothing to do with Schleiermacher's religious meaning.

154. Ibid., 371–73 (§112). [On leaving final resolution to the individual, cf. F. C. Baur in chap. 3.5.]

155. Ludwig Feuerbach, *Lectures on the Essence of Religion*, trans. Ralph Manheim (New York: Harper & Row, 1967), 21.

156. Feuerbach, *The Essence of Christianity*, trans. George Eliot, foreword by Karl Barth (New York: Harper & Brothers, 1957), 2.

157. Ibid., 12f.

158. *Lectures on the Essence of Religion*, 12.

159. See the last chapter of *Essence of Christianity*, esp. 247, 276f.

Because of Feuerbach's emphasis on nature in contrast to the otherworldliness of religion, Karl Marx called him "Schelling in reverse," that is, without Schelling's direction toward the Absolute or his late philosophy of revelation.[160] Feuerbach also, true to his rationalism, did not share Schelling's (or Kant's) theory of the evil dispostion in humanity. Like Schelling he criticizes "abstract, negative" concepts of God, a criticism also directed against Hegel.[161] But Feuerbach too has his abstractions. The main subject of his philosophy is "humanity" or "the human spirit," which is his appropriation of Hegel's *Allgemeine,* the concept of the universal. Another Young Hegelian, Max Stirner, rejected Feuerbach's "humanity" as just another abstraction; for Stirner there is no universal "humanity," but only the individual ego, which should devote itself to its own interests.[162]

2.5.3 Karl Marx

Karl Marx (1818–83) considered Strauss and especially Feuerbach immediate forerunners who prepared the way for his philosophy. Religious distress is, he writes, "the expression of real distress and also the protest against real distress." "Religion is the sigh of the oppressed creature, the heart of a heartless world. . . . It is the opium of the people. To abolish religion as the illusory happiness of the people is to demand their real happiness." Religion has been produced by humanity's misunderstanding of its true situation in life. "Man makes religion"—this is what humanity must now understand.[163] If Marx in these statements shows he has learned from Feuerbach, he also faults Feuerbach (and Strauss) for thinking that criticism has finished its business with the critique of religion.[164] For Marx, "the criticism of religion is the premise of all criticism."[165] To stop with the premise would be to accomplish nothing. The social problems that cause human being's unhappiness, which in turn causes it to project a "heaven," must be removed by action. Human social circumstances have been produced by human being, and they can be changed by human being.

160. Marx's letter to Feuerbach, October 1843, in *Karl Marx, Frederick Engels: Collected Works* (New York: International Publishers, 1975), 3:350. (All following references to the *Collected Works* are to works by Marx unless otherwise noted.)

161. Feuerbach, *Essence of Christianity,* 35. See Manfred Frank, *Der unendliche Mangel an Sein,* 273–92.

162. Max Stirner, *The Ego and Its Own,* ed. John Carroll (New York: Harper & Row, 1971), 51–56 (on Feuerbach). The original title is *Der Einzige und sein Eigentum* (1845). *Eigentum* means "property." Hegel had identified property as the "existence of the personality," e.g., in the *Encyclopedia of the Philosophical Sciences,* 242. On Stirner's critique, see also Karl Barth's introductory essay to Feuerbach's *Essence of Christianity,* xxviii. In effect Stirner returns to Fichte's theory that all reality is the product of the ego, although Fichte never interpreted this, as does Stirner, in terms of self-interest.

163. *Collected Works,* 3:175f. The quotations are from the introduction to Marx's "Contribution to the Critique of Hegel's Philosophy of Law." There are several collections of his statements on religion, e.g., Karl Marx, *On Religion,* ed. Saul K. Padover (New York: McGraw-Hill, 1974). Padover's introduction also provides a biography. See also Denys Turner, "Religion: Illusions and Liberation," in *The Cambridge Companion to Marx,* ed. Terrell Carver (Cambridge: Cambridge University Press, 1991), 320–37.

164. *Collected Works,* 5:29 (from the section on Feuerbach in Marx's "German Ideology").

165. Ibid., 3:175.

The point now is to "change the world," not to keep on reinterpreting it, as philosophy has done in the past.[166] Not only religion but also philosophy has typically dealt with reality through the fantasy of imagination. It has produced "ideologies" (idea systems) that, as Marx says, turn the relationship between ideas and reality "upside down." The dominant social group, which is the beneficiary of the social environment, creates—or finds already given—support for this environment in a dominant religious and/or philosophical ideology. "The ideas of the ruling class are in every epoch the ruling ideas: i.e., the class which is the ruling material force of society is at the same time its ruling intellectual force. The class which has the means of material production at its disposal, consequently also controls the means of mental production. The ruling ideas are nothing more than the ideal expression of the dominant material relations."[167] Now this relationship must be reversed: "reality must itself strive toward thought," that is, the truth of reality exposed by criticism must produce a new way of thinking.[168] "The criticism of religion ends with the teaching that man is the highest being for man, hence with the categorical imperative to overthrow all relations in which man is a debased, enslaved, forsaken, despicable being."[169]

According to Marx, all humanity, including the ruling class, is "alienated," "estranged" from its true self. In modern society individual humanity is defined essentially by its market value—it must market itself like a commodity—and by the accumulation of wealth, through which one becomes a market consumer. Whether an individual is one of the few who are rich or one of the many who are poor, essentially the same alienation applies. The proletariat, as the suffering poor with the greatest interest in correcting the situation, are to lead the communist revolution, not simply for their own benefit but for that of the whole society. They in turn are led by the social analyses and planning of intellectuals, who possess the educational requirements necessary for the overview of the political, social, and economic situation. Marx finally has no absolute vision of a nonalienated communist society. The *Communist Manifesto* (1848) is rather typical in that it contains only criticism of existing conditions and political parties. The nonalienated society is apparently to be planned and replanned in view of the concrete situations but always with utopian ideals of what human life should be.

When the early Marx explains what nonestrangement is, he shows dependence on the Schelling of the philosophy of nature [chap. 2.2.6], which he interprets in his own way. He describes a pristine state of humanity in harmony with nature, in which its work is in direct relationship to human need and integrated into the life of nature. Estrangement follows from a kind of "fall" from this state,

166. Ibid., 5:7f. (from Marx's "Theses on Feuerbach").
167. Ibid., 36f., 59 (from the "German Ideology"). Every idea of the "ruling class" is swept up in this judgment.
168. Ibid., 3:183. To a certain degree ideologies are related to what is real for Marx just as Schelling's mythologies are related to the reality revealed by Christ. Both realities are truths distorted by erroneous systems of ideas (mythologies too have their ruling classes).
169. Ibid., 3:182 (introduction to "Contribution to the Critique of Hegel's Philosophy of Law").

in which nature suffers devaluation by becoming owned property. But instead of human being ruling over this devalued nature, the reverse happens. Human being's labor is now in servitude to something external to its own intrinsic nature. Property estranges human being both from itself and from all other human beings. Persons do their work and go home, because they are no longer at home in their work.[170] According to Schelling's philosophy of nature, nature in the modern world is dead or dying because "its principle of life has been withdrawn from it," which has resulted in a "highest irreligiosity" that uses the natural world "according to the meanest understanding."[171] For Schelling too the devaluation of nature means the dehumanizing of humanity. In a way that is reminiscent of Schelling's words, Marx speaks of the "dominion of dead [*"totgeschlagene,"* killed] matter over humanity."[172] Marx's goal in history includes the "resurrection of nature" as a component in the rebirth of the humane world.[173] Marx also shows dependence on the later Schelling in faulting Hegel for giving abstract concepts priority before the reality of concrete existence.[174]

This discussion has considered only the early works of Marx, works from the 1840s. In his later publications he rather forgets his interest in the philosophy of nature and concentrates entirely on political economics. His most famous work, *Capital,* is intended to be an objective science with a high degree of certitude. The "dialectical materialism" presumably authored by Marx's coworker, Friedrich Engels, makes political economics the key to universal history, and in doing so falls into speculative constructions typical of histories that organize the totality of everything for the purpose of arriving at the desired outcome. Especially "dialectical materialism" forms the transition to the systems of Soviet communism, systems in which Marx's original humanitarian ideals were completely obscured.[175]

170. Ibid., 273–77 (from "Estranged Labor" in the "Economic and Philosophic Manuscripts of 1844"). Hegel had described (industrial) labor as the temporary surrender of self to another, which, if it were the surrender of all one's time, would mean one had become the property of the other: *Philosophy of Right,* §67. See Karl Löwith, *From Hegel to Nietzsche,* 152f. In Hegel's *Encyclopedia,* §403ff., property is simply a "thing" without further significance.

171. Schelling, *Werke,* 5:109. [Cf. chap. 2.2.6.]

172. *Collected Works,* 3:267; cf. Marx, *Frühe Schriften,* ed. H.-J. Lieber and P. Furth (Stuttgart: Cotta, 1962), 1:555. See the "death of nature" in Marx's doctoral dissertation of 1841: *Collected Works,* 1:62.

173. *Collected Works,* 3:298. Cf. Andrew Bowie, *Schelling and Modern European Philosophy,* 58, 148, 177.

174. See Marx, "Contribution to the Critique of Hegel's Philosophy of Law," in *Collected Works,* 3:3–129. Hegel "everywhere makes the idea the subject. . . . The point of departure is the abstract idea" (11f.); "the rationale of the constitution [of the state] is thus abstract logic" (19). See also Marx's "Critique of the Hegelian Dialectic and Philosophy as a Whole," ibid., 3:326–46. Marx never admits dependence on Schelling, probably because he does not wish to be associated with Schelling's Christianity, but scholarship has demonstrated the influence. See Manfred Frank, *Der unendliche Mangel an Sein,* 44–46; Jürgen Habermas, *Theorie und Praxis* (Berlin: Luchterhand, 1969), 152f. See Friedrich Engel's attacks on Schelling's first lectures in Berlin (1841/42), in Marx and Engels, *Collected Works,* 2:181–264.

175. See, e.g., Frederic L. Bender, ed., *The Betrayal of Marx* (New York: Harper & Row, 1975); G. H. R. Parkinson, ed., *Marx and Marxisms* (Cambridge: Cambridge University Press, 1982). See further Ernst Bloch's revival of the early Marx in opposition to Soviet communism, in *The Principle of Hope* [chap. 8 below].

2.6 KIERKEGAARD

Søren Kierkegaard (1813–55) also published his major works in the 1840s. He was a theologian licensed to preach in the (Lutheran) Church of Denmark. Although he occasionally delivered sermons and seriously considered becoming a pastor, he never held such a position. As an author he enjoyed success in Denmark, but in spite of the fact that his works were soon translated into German, his works were not to see significant wider popularity until the early twentieth century. He knew German philosophy—which in his time meant Kant and the Idealists—and like the German intellectuals of the time he was well educated in Greek philosophy. He wrote his doctoral dissertation on *The Concept of Irony, with Continual Reference to Socrates*.[176] During his university study he read Hegel, and Hegel was significant for his dissertation and for his later work.[177] His stay in Berlin in late 1841 and early 1842 to hear Schelling was apparently a seminal period in the development of his central ideas; his most important books appear afterward in relatively rapid succession. What he shares with the later Schelling is, most obviously, a very similar criticism of Hegel, which may have been germinal before but after the Berlin period is at the core of Kierkegaard's thought. Hegel represents the superficial rationalism of the age.[178] Kierkegaard's reaction to the revolutionary movements of the 1840s was negative. He aimed not at all at the "crowd," as he could write, but at the individual, or rather the educated individual who had the time and interest to read and reflect.

Kierkegaard's most important works are written under a series of pseudonyms. The later pseudonymous works are written as expositions of faith by faith, while the pseudonymous earlier writings are identified mainly with the perspectives of certain idealized "observers." These pseudonymous authors lead the reader toward faith through their expositions of the dialectics of common life experiences or of intellectual endeavor. For Kierkegaard, who said that he himself was

176. *The Concept of Irony,* trans. Howard V. Hong and Edna H. Hong (Princeton, NJ: Princeton University Press, 1989). A brief guide to Kierkegaard is Reidar Thomte's *Kierkegaard's Philosophy of Religion* (Princeton, NJ: Princeton University Press, 1948). See also Johannes Sløk, *Kierkegaard's Universe; A New Guide to the Genius,* trans. Kenneth Tindall (Copenhagen: Danish Cultural Institute, 1994); Walter Lowrie, *Kierkegaard* (London: Oxford University Press, 1938); Julia Watkin, *Kierkegaard* (New York: Continuum, 1997); Joachim Garff, *Søren Kierkegaard,* trans. Bruce H. Kirmmse (Princeton, NJ: Princeton University Press, 2005).

177. Kierkegaard read Schleiermacher but has little to say about him. Henning Schröter, "Wie verstand Kierkegaard Schleiermacher?" *Internationaler Schleiermacher Kongress Berlin 1984,* ed. Kurt-Victor Selge (Berlin and New York: Walter de Gruyter, 1985), 1147–55.

178. Kierkegaard's notes from Schelling's lectures are translated and published by Hong and Hong in the volume with *The Concept of Irony* (see note 176). On Hegel as a symptom of the age, see esp. Kierkegaard, *Fear and Trembling; Repetition,* trans. Hong and Hong (Princeton, NJ: Princeton University Press, 1983), 54f., 68–70. Wolfgang Struve argues convincingly that the treatment of anxiety and human existence in Schelling's work of 1809, *On Human Freedom* [chap. 2.4.1], which Kierkegaard had in his possession, is the "background" to Kierkegaard's *Concept of Anxiety,* which we discuss later in this chapter. Kierkegaard rejected Schelling's speculation about God. W. Struve, "Kierkegaard und Schelling," in Steffen Steffensen and Hans Sörensen, eds., *Kierkegaard Symposion* (Copenhagen: Munksgaard, 1955), 252–58.

led forward by these writings, the method is related to what he believed was God's method of personal teaching: in or through each person himself or herself.[179] But therein also lay a problem that caused Kierkegaard a great deal of inner conflict: the problem of the difference between "indirect" pseudonymous and philosophical-poetic communication on the one hand, and on the other hand "direct communication" of Christian proclamation, the work of the church preacher. His inner conflict also had to do with his view of the church. As it actually existed the church was, he said, "secularly prudent," thoroughly accommodated to a Christianity everyone comfortably believed but no one understood. With an "indirect" method the "religious poet" must "help people out into the current" so that in the future the direct witness could again be effective.[180]

Kierkegaard's constant theme is the problem of the unity or rather disunity of existence as expressed subjectively in the existing self, the human spirit. Existence and the self are a "synthesis" of "infinite" and "finite," "eternal" and "temporal," "freedom" and "necessity," "unconditioned" and "conditioned" (or "limited"), or, in Plato's Greek, apeíron and péras.[181] These terms—each set is essentially identical to the others—are key to Kierkegaard's analysis of human existence. They are obviously taken from the platonic language of Idealism [chap. 2.2.2], but Kierkegaard uses them only for his analysis of human existence. He does not extend their use into theories about God whose "infinite qualitative difference" from human being makes such speculation impossible [cf. Schelling, chap. 2.4.2]. For Kierkegaard the oppositions in human existence meant by the terms are in synthesis but not harmony. Representative is the unstable synthesis of freedom and necessity. Echoing Schelling's analysis of human existence in On Human Freedom [chap. 2.4.1], Kierkegaard says that (unconditioned) freedom and (limiting) necessity are in such conflict that they cause spiritual "dizziness."[182] The symptoms or consequences of the conflict are anxiety and passion in the quest for meaning; without resolution the result is despair, the "sickness

179. "When God speaks he uses the person to whom he is speaking, he speaks to the person through the person. . . . But if it were so that God had once for all spoken, for example in Scripture, then, far from being the most powerful, God would be in the tightest squeeze, for a person can easily argue with something like this if he is allowed to use himself against it." *Stages on Life's Way*, trans. Hong and Hong (Princeton, NJ: Princeton University Press, 1988), 315f. Cf. Thomte, 82.

180. *Kierkegaard's Journals and Papers*, trans. Hong and Hong, 7 vols. (Bloomington: Indiana University Press, 1967–78), 6:241 (§6521), 180 (§6445); cf. 234 (§6511). The journal notes from 1848/49 and thereafter regularly reflect the ongoing conflict. See also Kierkegaard's late publications concerning his authorship, collected in the volume *The Point of View*, ed. and trans. Hong and Hong (Princeton, NJ: Princeton University Press, 1998). See further Kierkegaard, *Practice in Christianity*, trans. Hong and Hong (Princeton, NJ: Princeton University Press, 1991), 133–44. On the pseudonymous works, see Thomte, 190–203, and Mark C. Taylor, *Kierkegaard's Pseudonymous Authorship* (Princeton, NJ: Princeton University Press, 1975).

181. E.g., Kierkegaard, *The Sickness unto Death*, trans. Hong and Hong (Princeton, NJ: Princeton University Press, 1980), 13f., 35; Kierkegaard, *Concluding Unscientific Postscript*, trans. Hong and Hong (Princeton, NJ: Princeton University Press, 1992), 1:92; cf. 579. For the following discussion I am indebted to Walter Schulz, *Fichte; Kierkegaard* (Pfullingen: Gunther Neske, 1977), 35–69.

182. *Sickness unto Death*, 16, 144–48. Cf. Kierkegaard, *The Concept of Anxiety*, trans. Reidar Thomte (Princeton, NJ: Princeton University Press, 1980), 61, 130, 158.

unto death" of sin.[183] Every human life consists of this unstable, conflicted synthesis, and every person must make choices that determine the course of her or his life. In *The Sickness unto Death* one finds the following depiction of the elemental choice: "every moment in which a human existence has become or wants to be infinite, is despair. For the self is the synthesis of which the finite is the limiting and the infinite the extending constituent. Infinitude's despair, therefore, is the fantastic, the unlimited, for the self is healthy and free from despair only when, precisely by having despaired, it rests transparently in God."[184] This "transparency in God," in which the self understands itself in relationship to God, is the salvation toward which Kierkegaaard drives in the writings of the pseudonymous pre-Christian authors.

He presents the conflicts bound up in the synthesis as a series of idealized steps or stages in life. His literary gift lies in his ability to present these convincingly, in depth and with keen insight into human behavior. The first stage is the "aesthetic," in which attention is focused on the individual's fulfillment of desire, especially sexually. The person is intoxicated with its (infinite) possibilities, but it cannot make important decisions; it is passively and ironically self-observant, often despondent, and probably considers itself a genius. The aesthetic person ends in despair; life is essentially unfree and unstable, without real meaning. The second stage is the "ethical" or "ethical-universal." In *Either/Or,* which has to do with the dialectic of the "aesthetic" and the "ethical," a representative of the ethical stage writes to the person of the aesthetic stage that he should openly concede his concealed despair. In so doing he will discover and be challenged to choose another self, the "absolute," "infinite," "universal" self above the vacillating moods of desire. For this self personal freedom becomes real and good and evil become real choices. Despair seems to be overcome as personal life becomes an instance of the universal—a unity similar to that in Hegel's "Idea" [chap. 2.3]. "He does not become someone other than he was before, but he becomes himself. The consciousness integrates [in a new synthesis], and he is himself."[185] The "integration" of consciousness—the bringing of the infinite and finite into right relationship in the choice of the "absolute" self— is "salvation."[186] The ethical is the "universal and thus the abstract," therefore it is "outside" the individual until the universal "interpenetrates" the individual's concrete, finite life and gives it good order. This individual is the "universal human being."[187] The "author" of *Either/Or* is evidently a Hegelian.

183. Ibid., 13ff., 77ff. We have noted earlier in the section on the later Schelling (note 109) that the relationship between existential despair and faith is a significant theme in Augustine's *Confessions.* It recurs in nineteenth-century mediation theology [chap. 3] and in twentieth-century theology [chap. 6.2.1].

184. *Sickness unto Death,* 30. The sin of despair may also mean the loss of self in the external forms of existence, in limitation (33ff.).

185. *Either/Or,* trans. Hong and Hong (Princeton, NJ: Princeton University Press, 1987), 2:177, 214–24. This becoming of self is parallel in form to spirit's coming to itself in Idealism. On Hegel's Idea, see *Either/Or,* 1:53–57; cf. 616; 2:474, 489. In *Concluding Unscientific Postscript* Kierkegaard accuses Hegel of dissolving the concrete ethical in the abstraction of pure thought. For Kierkegaard it is always concrete existence that is emphasized.

186. Ibid., 216.

187. Ibid., 255ff.

The next stage reveals a problem in the ethical-universal stage. The good order created by the choice of the absolute self is undone by an overlooked "discrepancy," a "collision" between sinful existence and the ethical-universal.[188] Striking illustrations are provided by misfortunes, whether of an external or internal nature. Shakespeare's Richard III is an example: personal circumstances expel him from life in the universal and open him instead to terrible, demonic possibilities. Another example is Goethe's Faust, who conceals his all-encompassing doubt in a vain attempt to give the appearance that all is in order, "to save the universal."[189] The inevitable result of the collision is, once again, despair. "In despairing, I use myself to despair, and therefore I can indeed despair of everything by myself, but if I do this I cannot come back to myself. It is in this moment of decision that the individual needs divine assistance."[190] The impossibility of the return to self means there is no integration; no new synthesis is possible, nothing that brings unity to the human spirit. The only possibility of a higher stage, of salvation, must come from the divine help of the God who is not the ethical-universal absolute nor any form of the "infinity," "eternity," or "unconditionedness" that is always already present in the synthesis that is human being. God is "absolutely different" from human being; "divinity" cannot be grasped with reason. Here the "infinity," "eternity," and "absoluteness" of the human spirit encounters a "frontier," a boundary, that this spirit had not recognized before. So also it recognizes that what it had experienced in itself as unconditioned and free is not as unconditioned and free as it had thought.[191]

The difference between the ethical-universal and Christian faith is of crucial importance for Kierkegaard. In ethical-universal thinking, "God comes to be an invisible vanishing point," because God has no role to play other than the universal ethical itself.[192] The universal is always rationally open to complete disclosure of motives and ends, since in principle everyone can understand them, whereas the "discrepancy" or "collision" discloses communication as a problem: not everyone and perhaps no one understands the conflict that one is talking about. According to Kierkegaard language itself belongs to the universal, hence communication of what does not belong within the universal must always involve a contradiction at some level.[193] The problem reaches its greatest intensity in the religious relationship to God, which for Kierkegaard is so much a matter of individual discovery and so little a matter of the universal that one can speak of it

188. *Concluding Unscientific Postscript*, 1:257–59.

189. *Fear and Trembling*, 104–6, 107–8. In the "demonic," which to some degree is in everyone, the individual has sunk so deep into its sinful possibilities that it is anxious about the good in its environment rather than about evil. *Concept of Anxiety*, 118–154.

190. *Concluding Unscientific Postscript*, 1:258; cf. *Fear and Trembling*, 49.

191. *Philosophical Fragments*, trans. Hong and Hong (Princeton, NJ: Princeton University Press, 1985), 44–46. The thought is related to the limit of reason in Kant, beyond which is, for Kant, the thing-in-itself and God.

192. *Fear and Trembling*, 68.

193. Ibid., 60: "As soon as I speak, I express the universal, and if I do not do so, no one can understand me." Cf. *Philosophical Fragments*, 168, 255.

only in the language of paradox. Here there is no "mediation," whereas in the ethical-universal, "mediation" of any and all discrepancies is both possible and necessary. All particulars can and must be resolved into the universal (as Hegel had demonstrated). "Faith is namely this paradox that the single individual is higher than the universal."[194] The ethical is not invalidated, but it is placed beneath and reinterpreted by faith.[195]

In *The Concept of Anxiety* Kierkegaard returns to the problem of the synthesis in human spirit. "There is an old, respectable philosophical terminology: thesis, antithesis, synthesis. A more recent terminology has been chosen in which 'mediation' takes the third place. . . . Brilliance however demands more—one says 'reconciliation,' and what is the result? . . . the confusion of ethics and dogmatics."[196] By dogmatics Kierkegaard means the dimension of faith, which is the only possibility of a "reconciled" synthesis, and which is not to be confused with the ethical-universal. The natural imbalance and conflict of the components of the synthesis is the source of anxiety and despair, and yet also the source of the possibility of striving for the solution to every person's existential problem, of entering into the movement from aesthetic existence to ethical existence toward faith.[197]

In the *Concluding Unscientific Postscript,* another possible solution is given with the hypothesis that "subjectivity is truth." This possibility arises in response to an analysis that results in the insight that the human spirit can never come to truth on its own power. It is always caught in the conflicted synthesis of its being. And so it is able only to strive for truth, not to attain it. Therefore, the author concludes, the inward "passion for the infinite" or subjectivity itself is the only truth one can attain.[198] But he discovers a yet "more inward" expression for this, namely, "subjectivity is untruth." Human being is cut off from the transcendent infinite.[199] And yet human being does not and cannot realize that it is cut off from transcendence until God reveals this ultimate and final dialectic of human existence, and with it is revealed that to be in untruth is sin.[200] Kierkegaard iden-

---

194. *Fear and Trembling,* 54ff., 60.
195. Ibid., 70ff.; *Practice in Christianity,* 67f., 238–257.
196. *Concept of Anxiety,* 11f.
197. Ibid., 155ff. Anxiety, as the effect of human being's synthesis of infinite and finite, is "freedom's possibility" (155). It is human being's "being able" (44f., 49) to envision and enact its infinite possibilities in finite, bodily life. The fall into sin is succumbing to "dizziness" in looking into the "abyss" of possibility, but the succumbing itself is a "leap" of freedom that cannot be explained by reason (61) [cf. freedom in Kant and Schelling]. The result is sinfulness that perverts finite sensual life into desire and selfishness (40f., 77f.). Anxiously human being continues to envision and actualize its good and evil possibilities. Anxiety takes human life into its "school," driving it (assuming human being allows) to recognition of its distress and to despair, and finally to faith, with which freedom is found in God (155–162). Cf. "being able" [*seinkönnen*] in the later Schelling: for Schelling it is the unconditional first principle or "potence" in human being that falls into sinful existence (*Werke,* 13:209–16; *Paulus-Nachschrift,* 102ff. [see chap. 2.4.2]).
198. *Concluding Unscientific Postscript,* 1:199–203.
199. Ibid., 207f.
200. *Philosophical Fragments,* 13ff. What the universal-ethical thinker does not recognize is the "infinite qualitative difference" between human spirit and the true absolute, God. *Sickness unto Death,* 122, 126f.

tifies the ethical-universal in the state of "infinite, personal, impassioned, inter-estedness" (an "infinite passion of need") as "Religiousness A." It prepares the person for "Religiousness B," which is Christian faith.[201]

Salvation is given not by God's raising the human spirit to the true infinite, but by the paradoxical entry of God, the true absolute, into the finite world in the form of a servant, Christ, who discloses sinfulness as the despair of untruth and overcomes untruth and despair in the justification of the sinner. Justification returns the human spirit from its former brokenness to itself in a new unity or synthesis of its inherent opposite principles. It is also returned to its finite situation, which it now accepts, ending its anxious striving. In the infinite love of God it finds peace.[202] But because faith in Christ, when contrasted with the universal validity of the ethical and the reasoning of science, can only be paradoxical or "absurd," faith requires a courageous "leap" into trusting God.[203] But the leap of faith is not blind. It is the result of encountering God in Christ, which is its "condition." God is the "teacher" who gives the condition, which in this case makes faith real and therefore possible, so that the leap is actually God's work [cf. God in Schelling, chap. 2.4.2]. Now there is clarity for the human spirit. The definition of faith in *Sickness unto Death* expresses the culmination and end of the self's anxious striving: "in relating to itself and willing to be itself, the self rests transparently in the power that established it," that is, in God, its creator.[204] "Transparency" refers to the self's now clarified relation to itself; in God it has become unified.

To encounter Christ existentially is to be "contemporaneous" with him, which in no way depends on one's place in time, for he encounters persons, then as now, in the paradox of his reality as God and human being. Christ is the eternal and unconditioned in the form of lowliness, the suffering servant. His truth is the truth of life, and salvation means being drawn into his truth as the way and the life of love in obedience to God. To encounter him is to be faced with a choice for or against him, a choice that "discloses" the person in his or her recognition or refusal of personal sinfulness and of Christ's truthfulness. "Faith conquers the world by conquering . . . the enemy in one's own inner being. . . ." Because Christ exists in the form of the powerlessness and suffering of the lowly, the form of his self-communication is indirect: his divinity is concealed. (The miracles are ambiguous; they present problems of understanding.) Therefore his claim to be God always gives the "possibility of offence." The "church triumphant" is based on a mistaken interpretation of the triumph of Christ in the gospel story and of Christianity in "Christendom," which give false supports to faith. Every generation and

---

201. *Concluding Unscientific Postscript,* 1: esp. 202–6, 555–86.

202. This is the central idea, salvation, in the *Sickness unto Death* (see, e.g., 29ff., 126f.), and of Kierkegaard's *Philosophical Fragments.* See also *Practice in Christianity.*

203. F. H. Jacobi had argued that God must be believed by a "leap" beyond reason [chap. 2.2.1]. See *Concluding Unscientific Postscript,* 1:100–106.

204. *Sickness unto Death,* 131; cf. 46, 49, 82. In the *Fragments,* 61, Kierkegaard writes: "The paradox specifically unites the contradictories, the eternalizing of the historical and the historicizing of the eternal." Cf. *Fragments,* 9–36, 43, 47, 59.

every individual must begin anew, "in fear and trembling" with the real possibility of offence and of disclosure and with the choice for or against faith.[205]

There is no proof of God other than the recognition of eternal truth in Christ, since objective or demonstrative thought has no access—other than through paradox—to what is infinitely qualitatively different from the ethical-universal.[206] So also the search for some sort of historical proof of God in Christ is a vain quest. According to Kierkegaard, when a foolish faith feels it needs the support of evidence from historical research, it is simply confused about itself. The paradox of faith, which must be individually experienced, is completely withdrawn not only from objective science but also from an objective orthodox interpretation of Scripture, for both employ essentially the same objective method.[207]

In the *Philosophical Fragments* the paradox is contrasted with Socratic-Platonic "recollection," the way to knowledge based on the idea that all being is always already given for knowledge in the universal. One only has to reason step by step in order to arrive finally at universal metaphysical conclusions. Kierkegaard's point is that "recollection" represents the scientific thought of the modern age. It corresponds to the way Hegel thinks about humanity's access to truth, namely, through the complete correspondence of being to scientific thought. Scientific knowledge is not false knowledge, for it corresponds to universal features in the nature and composition of created being. But it can neither grasp who God is nor solve the riddle of human existence.[208] Here it encounters a boundary it cannot pass, beyond which is the "unconditioned," the God of the paradox. "All who serve the unconditioned have first received a blow that seems to crush them, yet without slaying them, a blow that infinitely elevates them again. . . . This blow is like a sunstroke directly to the brain. . . . It is the infinite concentrated intensively in one single blow and one single moment." The great servants of the unconditioned are the apostles, especially Paul and Luther. "The rest of us cannot bear to come this close to the unconditioned."[209] It has entered history in Christ. One's relationship to it is sui generis, of its own unique kind, incomparable. The apostolic proclamation is the only mode of communication suitable to it. To give reasons for it "would change the unconditioned into the conditioned."[210]

2.7 SCHLEIERMACHER: HIS MATURE THOUGHT

Schleiermacher served a long tenure as professor of theology in Berlin, a university he helped to found and in which he also taught philosophy. During his tenure

205. *Practice in Christianity,* 76–143, 202–224 and throughout.
206. *Philosophical Fragments,* 43; cf. *Sickness unto Death,* 129, 103.
207. *Concluding Unscientific Postscript,* 1:24–34, 570–84; *Philosophical Fragments* throughout; cf. additions, 200–205.
208. See especially the first two chapters in *Philosophical Fragments;* cf. *Concluding Unscientific Postscript,* 1:205f.
209. *Journals and Papers,* 4:516 (§4903).
210. Ibid., 511 (§4899), 513 (§4900). Cf. vol. 4 of the *Journals and Papers,* 508–27.

he served as pastor to a church in the city.[211] His mature work set a standard for theology in the nineteenth century. The most important concepts of the first edition of the *Speeches* [chap. 2.2.4], particularly "feeling" and God as the "infinite," are carried over into his mature theology, but with significant modifications.

2.7.1 Dialectics, Hermeneutics, Ethics

"What we seek . . . cannot at all be put adequately into thoughts, because thoughts, as conditioned [*ein Bedingtes*], are never able to represent the unconditioned [*das Unbedingte*]."[212] These words are from Schleiermacher's 1822 lecture on dialectics, a lecture on the nature of scientific and philosophical knowledge that he often repeated and revised. Its chief conclusions are that knowledge depends on an origin that transcends it, and that it moves within a totality, unity, or wholeness of thought and being that it only partly comprehends. Its thoughts are limited and finite, and for this reason knowledge always has to do with a "boundary" it cannot pass. Nevertheless Schleiermacher asserts that in the "transcendent ground," God, subject and object are united in absolute identity. Philosophy cannot demonstrate this unity; the "transcendent ground" is a mystery. But philosophy must conclude, from the mystery itself, that God is. In drawing this conclusion Schleiermacher refers to "religious feeling" as an immediate, nonobjective experience of unity in God [cf. chap. 2.2.4].[213] But feeling is not a theoretical solution to the problem of the knowledge of God.[214]

In a reversal of what Hegel thought about universal reason, Schleiermacher says that reason has no direct access to universal meanings of the whole of existence. He does not deny that there are such meanings, but says that we can at best only approximately perceive them. One demonstration of this is the interpretation of historical texts, in which one must deal with historical differences between the text and the interpreter. In this case the procedure of interpretation

211. See esp. Martin Redeker, *Schleiermacher: Life and Thought*, trans. John Wallhausser (Philadelphia: Fortress, 1973). A significant number of translations of Schleiermacher's works are currently being published in the series *Schleiermacher, Studies and Translations* (Lewiston, NY: Edwin Mellen). See further Richard R. Niebuhr, *Schleiermacher on Christ and Religion* (New York: Scribner's, 1964), and Helmut Thielicke, *Modern Faith and Thought*, 159–232.

212. Schleiermacher, *Vorlesungen über die Dialektik*, ed. Andreas Arndt (Berlin: Walter de Gruyter, 2002), 2:554 (= *Kritische Gesamtausgabe*, ed. Hans-Joachim Birkner (1980ff.), 2/10). Schleiermacher's first lectures on dialectics have been published in ET: *Dialectic, or the Art of Doing Philosophy: A Study Edition of the 1811 Notes*, trans. Terrence N. Tice (Atlanta: Scholars Press, 1996).

213. Schleiermacher, *Vorlesungen über die Dialektik*, 1:142–54 (from the lectures of 1814/15); 304–6 (lectures of 1828); 335f. (lectures of 1831). On p. 143 of this work Schleiermacher writes: "We know of the being of God in us and in the things but not at all of a being of God beyond the world or in God's self." Cf. *Dialectic, or the Art of Doing Philosophy*, 31: "The deity is just as surely incomprehensible as the knowledge of the deity [as incomprehensible] is the basis of all knowledge. Exactly the same is true also on the side of feeling."

214. The permanent incompleteness of knowledge of absolute unity bears a certain similarity to Kant's view that philosophy cannot comprehend what God always perceives from God's viewpoint outside of time, namely, the whole of everything in all time [chap. 2.1.3]. But Schleiermacher does not speculate about God's own perception of the world, because feeling provides no access to such a thought.

is to work toward a consensus about the meaning of texts within a community of scholarly discourse. For this discourse, reflection on hermeneutics is of crucial importance. Schleiermacher defines hermeneutics as "the art of understanding," which is necessary because we do not understand as much or as well as we ordinarily think we do.[215] All sorts of usually unrecognized problems prevent understanding, especially clear understanding, whether one is simply in conversation with another or engaged in understanding a historical text. There is no "universal language" in which all the meanings are the same. Languages arise historically in different cultural contexts; words are part of complex structures of meaning. Even in one language there are considerable variations in meaning, and meanings change over time. In simple conversation two persons may well associate different meanings with the same word. The tone of and accent on words affect their meaning, and even these can be understood in different ways. The problem is greatly magnified when one tries to understand a historical text and the style of an individual author.[216]

In his hermeneutics Schleiermacher attempts to establish scientific rules of understanding as guidelines, especially for work with ancient texts. The awareness of the difficulty of understanding leads him to say that there is no certain rule for the application of rules. There is always an open area in communication that cannot be scientifically fixed by rules, no matter, for example, how exhaustive the research of the situation and meaning of a text might be. It is in this context that he speaks of "divination" as the point where interpretation has no choice but to make conjectures, to try in some sense to place itself in the situation of the author, based on everything that can possibly be learned by historical analysis.[217] The historian, in conversation with other historians, must make judgments, and the historian can at best only approach universal meanings.[218] Schleiermacher holds to his presupposition that there is an ultimate unity of being and thought, and, even if it is always only approximate, science can make significant progress in understanding this unity.

215. Schleiermacher, *Hermeneutics and Criticism and Other Writings,* trans. Andrew Bowie (Cambridge: Cambridge University Press, 1998), 5.

216. Ibid., 5–29, 51f., 90–117, 271–80.

217. Bowie points out that Schleiermacher's "divination" has usually been misunderstood. Schleiermacher says that in the divinatory method one "transforms" oneself, "so to speak," into the other person "and tries to understand the individual element directly." The transformation is only a metaphor for an aspect of the "art" of understanding. *Hermeneutics and Criticism,* 92f.; cf. xi, 177–87, 195–98. See also the earlier work: Schleiermacher, *Hermeneutics: The Handwritten Manuscripts,* edited by Heinz Kimmerle, translated by James Duke and Jack Forstman (Missoula, MT: Scholars Press, 1977). Cf. Hans-Georg Gadamer, *Truth and Method* (New York: Seabury, 1975), 162–73.

218. Ibid., 271–80, where Bowie includes a section from Schleiermacher's dialectics lecture of 1822; the original German is in Schleiermacher, *Vorlesungen über Dialektik,* 2:626ff. Bowie's interest is not in theological but philosophical hermeneutics in discussion with contemporary philosophy of language. Besides his introduction to *Hermeneutics and Criticism,* see also his *Aesthetics and Subjectivity* and *From Romanticism to Critical Theory;* see further Manfred Frank, "The Text and Its Style: Schleiermacher's Theory of Language," in *The Subject and the Text: Essays on Literary Theory and Philosophy,* trans. Helen Atkins (Cambridge: Cambridge University Press, 1997).

Schleiermacher's philosophical ethics also presupposes an ultimate harmony or unity of purpose in nature and reason that is not realized in the here and now. It is the final goal of moral and ethical life, but it is realized only in the reality of God beyond this life. The point of reference for knowledge of this ultimate harmony is the person of Christ, and Schleiermacher's philosophical ethics presupposes his knowledge of this harmony in Christ. Philosophical ethics sets forth the structures or orders of ethical life in human community, beginning with the family and its virtues and duties. Christian ethics and the church, the community of faith and life, give these structures their true content or meaning. (Schleiermacher is the first theologian since the Reformation to have placed such emphasis on the church as community.) Hence the greatest approximation of human striving to the "highest good" in all ethical structures of human existence, including the state, depends on the Spirit of Christ in Christian faith and the church.[219] By the intent of original creation human "spirit" and the "Spirit of Christ" are in essence the same Spirit, an identity that was lost in human being's fall into sin. Through Christ the human spirit is raised to participation in the Spirit of Christ, but never in this life does human spirit become perfect.[220] Similarly theology and the church exist within the harmony or unity of being in God, yet the thought of theology and the real life of the church are always imperfect approximations to this unity.[221]

2.7.2 Theology

The first section (§1) of Schleiermacher's *Brief Outline on the Study of Theology*[222] states that "theology is a positive science whose parts join into a cohesive whole only through their common relation to a particular mode of faith, i.e., a particular way of being conscious of God." "Positive" means that the assemblage of information is "requisite for carrying out a practical task," namely, that of effective leadership in the Christian church. The *Brief Outline* divides theology into areas and gives rules for the practice of each. The divisions are philosophical theology (presuppositions and definitions), historical theology (biblical theology

219. Redeker, *Schleiermacher*, 122ff., 159–74; Schleiermacher, *Brouillon zur Ethik / Notes on Ethics (1805–1806)*, trans. John Wallhausser, and *Notes on the Theory of Virtue (1804/1805)*, trans. Terrence N. Tice, 2 vols. in one (Lewiston, NY: Edwin Mellen, 2003), 41–140, esp. 52, 121, 128, 131. (Art too is regulated rightly by its relation to faith or religion: ibid., 52; cf. 124f.) See also Schleiermacher, *Lectures on Philosophical Ethics*, trans. Louise Adey Huish (Cambridge: Cambridge University Press, 2002); *Introduction to Christian Ethics*, trans. John C. Shelley (Nashville: Abingdon, 1983).

220. Schleiermacher, *Sämmtliche Werke*, part 1, vol. 12, *Christliche Sitte* (Berlin: Reimer, 1843), 303. Cf. Redeker, *Schleiermacher*, 122, 158–74. Some particulars of Schleiermacher's ethics are worth noting. According to Redeker, 171, he thinks that with increasing moral conditioning the state will abolish the death penalty. In *The Christian Faith*, §70 (see note 223), he gives warning that the natural state may be so much subject to the "self love of the folk" that "all kinds of injustice" are possible toward a minority.

221. The fourth Speech in Schleiermacher's *Speeches* in the third edition (ET Oman)[chap. 2.2.4] is an important discussion of the characteristics of religious community. The whole of this work parallels Schleiermacher's ethics in relating the general in religion to the particular of Christian religion or faith.

222. Trans. Terrence N. Tice (Richmond: John Knox, 1966).

and exegesis, hermeneutics, and systematic or dogmatic theology), and practical theology (pastoral theology and church government), in which all theology culminates in its concrete task. While Schleiermacher's method in describing theology is scientific, he remarks that, as persons cannot be scientifically constructed, so also faith communities cannot be (§32). Since, however, the church, "like every historical phenomenon, is subject to change," it must be able to demonstrate that "the unity of its essence" or its confessional identity is not endangered by the change (§47). Change or historical development makes necessary a scientific hermeneutics of understanding and the interpretation of history and Scripture. As Schleiermacher also says in his hermeneutics, science is a matter of discourse about meaning. "The development of doctrine is determined by the whole state of science and especially by prevailing philosophical views" (§167).

Schleiermacher's main theological work is *The Christian Faith,* published first in 1821/1822 and then in an extensively revised second edition in 1830. The rules and guidelines of the *Brief Outline* are now applied in a work that covers both philosophical theology and systematic or dogmatic theology. It is intended as a theology for the unity of the Lutheran and Reformed communities as Christian faith communities [cf. Schleiermacher and church union in chap. 1.2].[223] Dogmatics, he says, takes its material from the church's actual expressions of faith or "piety." These have their origin in the communications of Jesus and the New Testament and are passed on through the community of faith (§15f.).[224] Emphasis is placed on faith itself, as the perception of Christ in the present historical time: "Doctrine is developed . . . through continual reflection upon Christian self-consciousness" (§177). This statement reflects Schleiermacher's theory of understanding in his hermeneutics, insofar as the center of hermeneutical-doctrinal reflection is what the Christian of the present perceives and understands of the communication of Christ and the New Testament.

The Christian perception of God is a matter of "feeling." Feeling is "immediate self-consciousness" of the unity of the whole in which humanity lives. We are aware or feel that we are "utterly dependent on" this unity. The unity is ultimately God, and our feeling of utter (or absolute) dependence is our "God-consciousness." The relationship of dependence is a "conditionedness [*Bestimmtheit*] of immedi-

---

223. Schleiermacher, *The Christian Faith,* trans. of the 2nd German edition, ed. H. R. Mackintosh and J. S. Stewart (Edinburgh: T. & T. Clark, 1928), §24 postscript. The translators (at times unavoidably) occasionally make a choice of words that does not well correspond to Schleiermacher's intended meaning. I have often used my translations from the currently standard German edition: *Der christliche Glaube,* ed. Martin Redeker, 2 vols. (Berlin: Walter de Gruyter, 1960). In the following text, references are given to sections (§), which are numbered continuously through both volumes.

224. Cf. *Brief Outline,* §90: "The history of doctrine is simply the development of the religious ideas of the community." According to Schleiermacher much of the Old Testament is not an expression of pious feeling. He encourages use by the church only of the prophets and the Psalms, and these with reservation, insofar as they contain elements that do not reflect the piety of the new covenant in Christ. Hence in his opinion the Old Testament should be ordered after the New (*Christian Faith,* §132). [Cf. Harnack, chap. 4.4.]

ate self-consciousness" (§4).[225] Whereas human existence is conditioned (§51.1), God is "absolutely undivided oneness [*Einheit*]," not a conditioned, particular being. If God were a particular being, this would place God along with other individual beings in the "world of oppositions" (§§32.2, 50). God's attributes are expressions of this unique oneness (§50.3).[226] God is "nonobjective" (§56.2), not like a thing either in the world or in thought. What for Schleiermacher is only sought in dialectics or philosophy is found in the immediate self-consciousness of utter dependence: absolute unity, the ground and end of all that is or will be. Only this absolute nonobjective transcendent unity is God, never its finite manifestations (it is not "pantheism": §8.2). Sin is turning away from and denying dependence on God through worship of what is not God (§8). It means being for oneself (self-love) that ignores or refuses the unity of the God-consciousness and hence misses true beneficial life (§§68, 74).

The God-consciousness of Christ (the "second Adam") and the founding of his community give form and content to human nature as it should be, in communion with God (§89). God-consciousness purely for itself has no definite content but is only an indefinite feeling or awareness. It is a structure of human being, a "religious capacity" (if it has not been "crushed out"), through which each person has the possibility of being in definite, Christian relationship to God.[227] But it is never merely indefinite: it always has definition through some religious community or tradition (§§3.1, 9.1, 6 addition). In an important passage in *The Christian Faith*, Schleiermacher says that the concept of the "feeling of utter dependence" is an abstraction from Christian piety or faith experience, which is a result of salvation in Christ who frees the God-consciousness from the sin of alienation from God (§62f., esp. §62.3).[228]

---

225. Cf. Redeker, *Schleiermacher,* 113f. The English word "utter" translates Schleiermacher's preferred word, *schlechthinnig,* although he allows the word "absolute" ("absolute dependence"). He discusses these words briefly in a note to §4. (In this historical period the word "absolute" is best used only in reference to "the Absolute.")

226. Schleiermacher's thesis in §50 states: "All qualities that we attribute to God do not designate something particular in God, but only something particular in the way we relate the feeling of utter dependence to God." In Christianity the knowledge of God is mediated by Christ through the Holy Spirit in the faith community. All knowledge of God comes only from this revelation (cf. Schleiermacher's dialectics). For the Christian, God is from eternity creator and sustainer of the world (§§36–41), and the lord of predestination who, while being "unconditioned" (*unbedingt*), "conditions" persons to rebirth (§120). Since God can only be one, Schleiermacher indicates his preference for Sabellianism. See also Redeker, *Schleiermacher,* 120–22.

227. See the final ed. of the *Speeches,* trans. Oman, 124.

228. The understanding of the "feeling of utter dependence" is a contested point in the interpretation of Schleiermacher. The generalized discussions of the character of religion in the beginning sections of *The Christian Faith* have an appearance of being "neutral" statements of a philosophy of religion; however, they are written from the point of view of Christian faith (see esp. §4). Important for the discussion is another text: In the *Brief Outline,* §32f., Schleiermacher states his intent to understand scientifically the "distinctive nature of Christianity" as a religion, which requires comparison with other religions, and this in turn requires "in the logical sense" a standpoint "above" or "outside" of faith itself. (The same point is repeated in §6 of the 1st but not the 2nd definitive ed. of *The Christian Faith*;

Human nature is receptive for revelation; if it were not, the alternative would be that receptivity itself would have to be given to human being, and for this, Schleiermacher says, there is no evidence "in the Gospels themselves."[229] However, for the receptivity to be actualized, an act of God is required; otherwise it remains lost in the error of sin. In conversion to Christian faith we are utterly dependent on the work of Word and grace, which are received without any work of human activity (§108.6; cf. §107). The feeling of utter dependence on God is communicated only in and through the community that is the Christian church, and such consciousness can exist only in affirmation of the community that is the church (§24.4). In Christ faith knows that God is love (§166f.) and rules the world with love, the will to unity (§165.1; cf. §§121–26). Sin pervades human being but does not efface its receptivity for grace (§70f.). Grace is the communion with God mediated by Christ and his Holy Spirit (§63).[230] Like grace and salvation, which are always related to life in community (§§115f., 121ff.), sin too is social, so that in sin individuals affect, and are affected by, all others in the community (§71.2). Sin is recognized for what it is only through conversion and being in Christ. In conversion, which is union with Christ or spiritual rebirth, justification is received. Schleiermacher distinguishes this from the Catholic doctrine that unites justification and sanctification. Justification is done "to" the person as acceptance and forgiveness of sins, while sanctification is the effect of God "in" the person. As converted persons we are active in willing good works, so that acts of love join utter dependence on God and human freedom (§112.1).

It is a "maxim" that the error of pre-Christian religions is understood only in the light of true religion, Christianity, to which they are always related by the element of truth in them (with reference to Romans 1:21 and Acts 17:27–30). Through this element they are in principle receptive of true religion (§7.3). In Christ, who is the truth, the being of pre- or non-Christian religions becomes untruth, "nonbeing" (§13.1). But they continue to exist, and they show different levels of comprehension of religious truth (§11ff.). Their degree of truth is measured solely by Christ, the *Urbild* or perfect manifestation of human God-consciousness (§93). His God-consciousness has universal-human, archetypical

---

see *Der christliche Glaube*, ed. Redeker, 500.) On the one hand this seems to be only a matter of drawing conclusions from comparisons and not to affect Schleiermacher's understanding of the faith itself. But the objection is that it determines his theological method. Against this objection, see Redeker, *Schleiermacher*, 118f., and Brian Gerrish, *Tradition and the Modern World* (Chicago: University of Chicago Press, 1978), 22–48. The opposite view is represented by Karl Barth, *Protestant Theology in the Nineteenth Century*, 425ff. According to Barth, Schleiermacher's philosophy of religion dominates his understanding of faith. (The same question is relevant for how he conceives the relationship of dialectics to faith and of philosophical ethics to Christian ethics.) On the title page of *The Christian Faith* Schleiermacher quotes Anselm's phrase, "Credo ut intelligam" (I believe that I may understand).

229. Kierkegaard advocates the alternative [chap. 2.6].

230. Schleiermacher also names "sin" in the lectures on dialectics, namely, where the scientist errs through improper subjective speculation due to vanity and lack of thoroughness, which means straying from the direction of true knowledge. *Vorlesungen über die Dialektik*, 1:163; *Dialectic, or the Art of Doing Philosophy*, 60.

(*urbildliche*) character, which, when made known, is intimately familiar to each individual person (§§93, 121–27). He is the only savior, not a superior one among inferior saviors (§92). He will lead the converted of the whole world into the kingdom of God. This goal of history is only approximately reached in history itself and ultimately in life after death (§§157–65).

Schleiermacher made significant contributions to New Testament scholarship throughout his career, beginning with the controversial demonstration that the New Testament letter, 1 Timothy, was not written by Paul.[231] His critical works on the New Testament, which strive to be scientific—there is no "special hermeneutics" for dealing with the New Testament (§130.2)—often show a mediation of historical-critical method and the dogmatics of *The Christian Faith,* so that one supports the other. One illustration involves Schleiermacher's judgment that John is the only Gospel written by an eyewitness, John the disciple, while the other three are compilations. His judgment has to do with his view that Jesus gives "direct" instructional teaching about himself and his mission in the Gospel of John. In *The Christian Faith* Schleiermacher states that what Jesus communicates to his disciples is his "self-proclamation" in "straightforward form" [*streng besonnener Form*], a form to which his prophetic and poetic speech (parables) are subordinate (§16.2).[232]

The most evident instances of the mediation of science and the dogmatics of *The Christian Faith* are given by Schleiermacher's interpretation of Jesus' miracles. He says that belief in the miracles comes only through the experience of the "Spirit and power" of the gospel (1 Cor. 2:4), not by any other means of persuasion, but without the miracles faith would be as unshakable as with them (§14 addition). Then he says that in the interpretation of miracles there is a relationship of "harmony" between "the interest of piety and that of science." Natural science cannot be so confronted with or related to the supernatural that it simply ends where miracle begins (§49 addition, cf. §54). One must understand, he says, that there are significant differences between the present and the time of the New Testament in comprehending what a miracle is, due to modern progress in natural science; and we should not confuse belief in Christ itself with belief in the scriptural account of a miracle (§103.4). Moreover, science today does not yet understand the causal relationship between spiritual and physical life, especially in the case of a person of such spirituality as Christ (§14 addition).

231. A general account of Schleiermacher's work in the New Testament is given in the recent reprint of Schleiermacher's *Luke: A Critical Study,* trans. Connop Thrilwal (Lewiston, NY: Edwin Mellen, 1993).

232. On John, see Schleiermacher, *The Life of Jesus,* trans. S. Maclean Gilmour (Philadelphia: Fortress, 1975), 240f., 245, 262, 265ff. Regarding the German phrase *in streng besonnener Form,* the English translation (p. 80) translates *besonnen* as "reflective," which misses Schleiermacher's meaning. The root of *besonnen* is the verb *besinnen,* which has to do with reflection, but *besonnen* has attained the independent meaning of one who is clear-headed, even cold sober. Schleiermacher means to contrast Jesus' speech with poetic speech, which can be too much influenced by imprecise imagery. As Schleiermacher's "addition" to §16 makes clear, it is theology's task so to work out, as much as possible, the exact meaning of poetic speech where it occurs in Jesus and elsewhere in the New Testament: §18; cf. §§16, 50.1, 52.1, 130, 131, 135.1.

In his lectures on the "Life of Jesus" Schleiermacher tries to show how explanations of the miracles that do not conflict with science are possible. Perhaps most significant is the understanding of the healing miracles: they occur through the power of Christ's spirituality and will, but they are analogous to acts of more ordinary human spirituality and will.[233] Schleiermacher has an additional motive for his critique of miracles: the avoidance of docetism, of a Jesus who is not human or not fully human.[234] In the interest of affirming the full humanity of Christ, he questions the virgin birth as a means of explaining Christ's sinlessness, attributing this instead to his unique spiritual development (§97.2). Schleiermacher's account of the resurrection of Christ in his "Life of Jesus" theorizes that Jesus did not actually die on the cross but was revived by the uniquely pure life-force within him.[235] In *The Christian Faith*, however, the New Testament accounts of the resurrection are defended, because the apostolic witnesses cannot be said to have been bad judges of what they witnessed. In any case, for Schleiermacher, belief in the New Testament resurrection stories (or those of the ascension and second coming) is not necessary for faith, for according to the Gospels Christ drew persons into faith prior to these events (§99). Only belief in Christ is necessary for faith, namely, being drawn into his unity with God. Christ is "the *one* miracle" (§47.1).

Schleiermacher's important answer to his critics, published late in life (1829), in two "public letters" to his friend and former student, G. C. F. Lücke, speaks of the future with foreboding. He foresees a coming separation of natural science and the science of historical work from theology. "Shall the tangle of history so unravel that Christianity becomes identified with barbarism and science with unbelief?" Freedom for scientific research is traditionally Protestant, the lack of it, Catholic.[236] He also warns that the difference between "esoteric and exoteric

233. Schleiermacher, *The Life of Jesus*, 190–229, esp. 204f.

234. In Schleiermacher's view the traditional doctrine of the Trinity, with its doctrine of the two natures of Christ, tends toward Docetism (§§170–72, 97.2). His theory of the incarnation places emphasis on the natural: "As a human person Christ was becoming with the world [itself]" i.e., involved in the world's own process of becoming (*Christian Faith*, §97.2). The incarnation is God's "eternal act" that emerges in the person of Christ; Christ is predestined to appear in history "in the fullness of time" (§§13.1, 97.2, 118.1). The miracle of his person is embedded, so to speak, in providential history.

235. *Life of Jesus*, 420–81, on Jesus' death, resurrection, and ascension. Cf. death in *The Christian Faith*, §158f.

236. Schleiermacher, *On the "Glaubenslehre." Two Letters to Dr. Lücke*, trans. James Duke and Francis Fiorenza (Atlanta: Scholars Press, 1981), 61. In a letter to F. H. Jacobi from the year 1818, Schleiermacher writes: "With the understanding I am a philosopher; for this is the original and autonomous activity of the understanding; and with feeling I am completely a person of piety, and indeed as such a Christian." Trying to maintain their equilibrium "is certainly nothing other than an alternate lifting of one and sinking of the other. But, my friend, why should we not accept this? The oscillation is the general form of all finite existence. . . . So my philosophy and my dogmatics are decided not to contradict one another. . . . Understanding and feeling remain apart for me too, but they make contact and spark an electrical current. The inmost life of the [human] spirit is only in this electrical operation, in the feeling of understanding and the understanding of feeling, whereby however both poles always remain turned away from each other." *Aus Schleiermachers Leben. In Briefen.* vol. 2, ed. W. Dilthey (Berlin: Reimer, 1860), 349–53. See R. R. Niebuhr, *Schleiermacher on Christ and Religion*, 165–71.

doctrine" violates Christ's teaching that "all should be taught of God" (John 6:45).[237] Here he is probably referring to the Hegelian distinction between philosophical knowing and the faith of the church.

One could object that he too, in effect if not intent, separates an "esoteric" theology from the "exoteric" faith of the existing church, namely, in his own use of philosophical language. But with these concepts theology only tries to understand the faith of the church, which is primary. As faith evolves in history, theology also works to preserve continuity with the church of all ages. In Schleiermacher's judgment, what is antiquated is the metaphysical worldview that requires objective thought about God and, as a consequence, an objective understanding of faith as belief in dogmas. The old metaphysics is not just antiquated; it missed something essential. "Pious feeling," Schleiermacher writes, is "the original expression of an existential relationship to God."[238] The experience of faith must be prior to and the source of objective thought, and this is the only way faith can know true certainty (Christian Faith, §14).

Among Schleiermacher's contemporaries Hegel was his sharpest critic. He strongly objected to Schleiermacher's assertion that immediate self-consciousness, feeling, was human being's most basic and essential relationship to God. In the Phenomenology he had written, "since the man of common sense makes his appeal to feeling, to an oracle within his breast, he is finished and done with anyone who does not agree." In contrast, he says, science brings minds together.[239] In another place Hegel says that in feeling "knowledge of absolute reality becomes a matter pertaining to the heart," but it is no more than "a product of culture" and makes "arbitrary will the principle of truth."[240] In yet another place he rejects both the appeal to feeling and—in probable reference to Schleiermacher's dialectics—the philosophy of "approximation," calling it a "half-philosophy."[241] And in a notorious published comment from the year 1822 Hegel wrote: "If the feeling of utter dependence is the essence of religion and of Christian faith, a dog would be the best Christian, since a dog . . . lives predominantly in this feeling. A dog also has feelings of salvation when its hunger is satisfied by a bone."[242] Hegel is defending the consistency of rational conceptual science in all areas of knowledge, including religion. D. F. Strauss continued this strident Hegelian critique in attacking not just Schleiermacher (especially his Life of Jesus) but also the

---

237. Letters to Lücke, 64.

238. Ibid., 40. In a given age (the best) theology represents a progression in the perception of truth: Christian Faith, §19 addition; cf. §§19.2, 28.1f. See also Brief Outline on the Study of Theology, §§9–11, 329ff.

239. Hegel, Phenomenology of Spirit, 43. In an early work he linked Schleiermacher and Jacobi: Hegel, Faith and Knowledge, 150f. See also Hegel, Lectures on the History of Philosophy, 3:508–10.

240. Hegel, History of Philosophy, 2:45; 3:419, 421, 509; cf. 1:40; cf. Encyclopedia, 4f.

241. Philosophy of Right, 12.

242. In Hegel's introduction to Hermann Hinrichs, Die Religion in ihrem Verhältniss zur Wissenschaft (Heidelberg, 1822), quoted by Redeker in his introduction to The Christian Faith, xxxv. See Eric von der Luft, trans., Hegel, Hinrichs and Schleiermacher on Feeling and Reason in Religion: The Texts of Their 1821–22 Debate (Lewiston and Queenstown: Edwin Mellen, 1987).

theology of his time for being "half-half": half Christian faith, half scientific, hence neither with integrity.[243]

2.8 FRIES AND DE WETTE

Schleiermacher's understanding of religion has at times been confused with that of the philosopher Jacob Friedrich Fries (1773–1843) and the theologian, Wilhelm Martin Leberecht de Wette (1780–1847), who derives his religious thought from Fries.[244] De Wette belongs in mediation theology [chap. 3], but since he was the principal religious interpreter of Fries, he is included here with Fries. For a time de Wette was a colleague of Schleiermacher's in Berlin, but most of his academic career was spent in Basel, where he made significant contributions to biblical criticism. Fries was professor of philosophy at Heidelberg, a Kantian influenced by F. H. Jacobi [chap. 2.2.1][245] and to a degree by the first edition Schleiermacher's *Speeches*.[246] For his part, Hegel hardly gives Fries notice, naming his philosophy and concept of reason subjective and irrational.[247]

According to Fries, Kant rightly distinguishes between phenomena and the noumenal world that lies beyond the phenomena. Kant is also right in saying that the "understanding" is limited by the bounds of physical sense to the comprehension of phenomena. But for Fries reason includes more than the experience and understanding of phenomena, a "more" that is something other than the rational speculations of Idealism. Reason has within it a receptive sense of noumenal reality itself. "Our belief in the eternal . . . comes originally and immediately

243. See esp. Strauss, *Der Christus des Glaubens und der Jesus der Geschichte. Eine Kritik des Schleiermacherschen Leben Jesu* (The Christ of Faith and the Jesus of History. A Criticism of Schleiermacher's Life of Jesus) (Berlin: Franz Duncker, 1865); *Die Halben und die Ganzen* (The Halves and the Wholes) (Berlin: Franz Duncker, 1865), which deals with the liberal theology of Daniel Schenkel and the conservative Ernst W. Hengstenberg [see chap. 1; see Strauss, chap. 2.5.1].

244. Rudolf Otto gives an introduction to Fries and de Wette in *The Philosophy of Religion, Based on Kant and Fries*, trans. E. B. Dicker (New York: Richard R. Smith, 1931); see also Leonard Nelson, *Progress and Regress in Philosophy*, trans. Humphrey Palmer, 2 vols. (Oxford: Basil Blackwell, 1970f.). On de Wette, see John W. Rogerson, *W. M. L. de Wette, Founder of Modern Biblical Criticism* (Sheffield: Sheffield Academic Press, 1992); Thomas Albert Howard, *Religion and the Rise of Historicism: W. M. L. de Wette, Jakob Burkhardt, and the Theological Origins of Nineteenth-Century Historical Consciousness* (Cambridge: Cambridge University, 2000).

245. Thomas McFarland, *Coleridge and the Pantheist Tradition* (Oxford: Clarendon, 1969), 289f., has a brief discussion of Fries and Jacobi.

246. In distinction from Fries and de Wette, Schleiermacher does not conceive of feeling as an immediate relationship to a noumenal reality that directly communicates true ideas. In the first edition of the *Speeches* [chap. 2.2.4], religious content is communicated through the medium of the "universe," which is not perceived immediately as a whole but only through particular parts or through individual things. Cf. Rudolf Otto's complaint against Schleiermacher [chap. 4.7]. In both his early and his later work Schleiermacher excludes reason from religious feeling.

247. Hegel, *Lectures on the Philosophy of History*, 3:510f., cf. 417f.; *Philosophy of Right*, 5f. Schelling's negative critique of the later Jacobi's concept of reason, which the older Jacobi takes from Fries, can also be considered as aimed at Fries: Schelling, *On the History of Modern Philosophy*, 164–85.

from the essence of our reason as a necessary addition to our knowledge of the finite."[248] "Belief" begins with the awareness that philosophical speculation cannot reach beyond Kant's boundaries. But it is aware that there are ideas that come to us through a unique "aesthetic sense" or "feeling" of noumenal reality. The idea of the unconditioned Absolute, and Kant's ideas of God, freedom, and the immortality of the soul, and the moral law itself are all true ideas communicated to us directly from noumenal reality. Fries says the same thing about Kant's aesthetic and teleological judgments in the *Critique of Judgment*: the "beautiful" and "sublime," and the "purpose" of all things are true in eternity.[249] Love, virtue, and "eternal justice" are truths which are the basis of human moral action. But only some ideas communicated from noumenal reality are relatively clear, particularly the moral ideas already named. "As soon as, in faith [belief], we go beyond the universal ideas of the perfect, the unlimited and the unconditioned, we have to employ finite representations in order to think the eternal. Our mode of knowledge of necessity becomes metaphorical, and its value is soon only figurative. . . . Our language must, therefore, make use of metaphor."[250] All religion speaks of the eternal mystery only in symbols and myths, and these have different forms in different cultures and times—they are "national" in character. Serious error arises when these symbols themselves are taken as absolute truth.[251] The religions of the world show progressive degrees of noumenal truth, with Christianity as the highest: it is "the world religion."[252] Human being responds to eternal mystery in a "holy mood" of devotion.[253] "Holy intuitive awareness raises us above all scientific language. And we, recognizing the rights of that intuitive awareness, will never seek to make it scientific."[254]

De Wette extends Fries's interpretation of Christian revelation into dogmatics. Religion has an "inner" mode of being, namely, the aesthetic sense of reason as Fries defines it, which perceives the "utterly unconditioned" and "the final unconditioned ground of reason." Religion also has an "outer" mode, the historical forms of religion and the religious community.[255] Outer revelation is above

248. J. F. Fries, *Knowledge, Belief and Aesthetic Sense,* trans. Kent Richter (Cologne: J. Dintner, 1989), 75f.; cf. Fries, *Dialogues on Morality and Religion,* trans. David Walford (Totowa, NJ: Barnes & Noble, 1982), 178ff.

249. Fries, *Knowledge,* 73–157; *Dialogues,* 209ff.; cf. Otto, 78f., 93; Nelson, 2:233f., 277–84. The "aesthetic sense" is "a necessary conviction from feeling alone" (Fries, *Knowledge,* 46, cf. Otto, 93).

250. *Dialogues,* 216.

251. Ibid., Dialogue VII, "Religious Practice," 98–124. According to Otto, 82, for Fries the last judgment and the end of the world are symbols of the Absolute as unconditioned power in relationship to the natural world.

252. Otto, 145–47; Fries, *Dialogues,* 105–8.

253. Fries, *Knowledge,* 122–26, 85–87; Fries, *Dialogues,* 178; Otto, 119.

254. Fries, *Dialogues,* 53; cf. Otto, 93. Otto, *Philosophy of Religion,* 99, summarizes Fries's view of faith: "what we believe is really true." See *Ahnung* below.

255. W. M. L. de Wette, *Theodor oder des Zweiflers Weihe. Bildungsgeschichte eines evangelischen Geistlichen,* 2 vols. (Berlin: Reimer, 1822), 1:116f. "What God is for the world, revelation is for the human spirit. Revelation is like an inner God that the human spirit believes and from which it draws light and life."

all the Christ of Scripture, the "mediator" of the highest truth.[256] The purpose of outer revelation—like Fries's aesthetic symbol—is to kindle awareness of the inner life of the aesthetic sense and to mediate its truth. "Religion lives in the Unconditioned, Infinite, Eternal."[257] "Faith in revelation is . . . the acknowledgement of the unconditional truth or the convergence of an [outward] religious appearance with the archetype of reason (of inner revelation)."[258] As for Fries so also for de Wette, all religious language is aesthetic or symbolic. It is "the presentation in visible imagery of an idea for feeling."[259] The internal witness of the Holy Spirit is the Christian form of the aesthetic sense: the truth of Christian symbols is validated by a spiritual feeling of certainty, so that inner and outer revelation confirm one another. Christ appears "in true exaltation and completion" when he is viewed "purely as the object of feeling or as aesthetic symbol." He is "the highest religious symbol."[260]

Some confusion can result from the English translation of a synonym that Fries employs for the "aesthetic sense," namely, the word *Ahndung* (in modern German, *Ahnung*). This comes from the common word *ahnen*, "to surmise or have a presentiment of" something. Especially in consideration of the way Fries uses the word, as the feeling or sense of some noumenal truth, one would normally translate *Ahndung* with the common English-American sense of the word "intuition." However this is the word used to translate Kant's, Fichte's, and Schelling's word *Anschauung* [chap. 2.1, chap. 2.2.2].[261]

2.9 EMERSON

Ralph Waldo Emerson (1803–82), the main founder of American Transcendentalism, was for a short while a Unitarian pastor in Boston but soon left the ministry for a life as an author and lecturer. In brief, Transcendentalism is the American form of nineteenth-century Romanticism. Its roots lie partially in the American religious awakenings of the nineteenth century and partially in early British and American Romantic literature. Philosophically the main influences were German, as mediated particularly by the British literary and philosophical figures Samuel Taylor Coleridge (1772–1834) and Thomas Carlyle (1795–1881). Coleridge's work was related to the Platonic tradition in English philosophy; it was this tradition that provided the initial opening for his appreciation of German Roman-

256. Ibid., 158; cf. Otto, 165f.
257. Ibid., 233; cf. Otto, 173.
258. W. M. L. de Wette, *Dogmatik der protestantischen Kirche,* 2 vols. (Berlin: Reimer, 1840), 2:37. In Christianity "the symbolic is given in and with the historical." De Wette, *Theodor,* 1:342f.; cf. Otto, 170.
259. de Wette, *Theodor,* 1:235.
260. Ibid., 342.
261. Fries makes a point of distinguishing his philosophy from Schelling's. See Fries, *Dialogues,* 42; cf. 10, xv (on the translation of *Ahndung*).

ticism and Idealism.[262] In the early 1830s the young group of Boston Transcendentalists eagerly turned to what was available of works and commentaries on Kant, Schleiermacher, Schelling, and figures associated with German Romanticism. They typically formed these influences, as did the British, according to their own paths of thought. Emerson was the most important forerunner of later liberal theology in the United States, but his influence was far broader. His name is inseparably bound to the whole Romantic movement, which sooner or later affected most American religious thought. It is not an exaggeration to say that for much of the nineteenth century he was known abroad as America's most important intellectual.[263]

Emerson's Divinity School Address of 1838 was given at the invitation of the small graduating class in theology at Harvard. It teaches that the world is the product of one will, mind, or spirit that is active everywhere and is love, to which the beauty of nature witnesses. The "law" of this spirit is goodness, and its perception awakens in the mind the "religious sentiment." In becoming aware of this sentiment, the soul becomes aware that it is "illimitable" and that in every person the soul is "an inlet into the deeps of Reason." The religious sentiment "creates all forms of worship"; its expressions are sacred "oracles of truth." Jesus gave it a pure expression. But the truth of the sentiment cannot be received from another; it is a purely personal "intuition." "I must find true in me" what another expresses from her or his religious sentiment. "There is no doctrine of the Reason which will bear to be taught by the understanding." The understanding, when it does not comprehend Reason's superiority, perverts Reason's truths, making them false authorities.[264] One sees rather clearly that these concepts in Emerson's Address are related to the thought of the early Schleiermacher but are far more similar to that of Fries.

In the following part of the Address, Emerson turns his attention to criticism of the church and conventional Christianity. He faults the church for two errors. First, it "has dwelt on the person of Jesus," whereas "the soul knows no persons." If Jesus' teaching is not heard as the expression of God's being in one's own soul, then it is false authority. The second error is that the church teaches revelation as a past event, "as if God were dead," instead of an ever-present reality of the life of the soul.[265] These errors must be corrected, or religious life will continue to degenerate, to the detriment not only of the church but also of society. Human

262. Coleridge, *Aids to Reflection*, ed. John Beer (Princeton, NJ: Princeton University Press, 1993), see cxvi ff.; *The Correspondence of Ralph Waldo Emerson and Thomas Carlyle* (Boston: James R. Osgood, 1889); Douglas Hedley, *Coleridge, Philosophy and Religion* (Cambridge: Cambridge University Press, 2000); Rosemary Ashton, *The German Idea* (Cambridge: Cambridge University Press, 1980); Thomas McFarland, *Coleridge and the Pantheist Tradition* (Oxford: Clarendon, 1969); Reardon, *Religious Thought in the 19th Century*, 239–53.

263. He is mentioned, e.g., in D. F. Strauss, *Der alte und der neue Glaube*, 190, 260, 286.

264. Emerson, "Divinity School Address," in *The Spiritual Emerson*, ed. David M. Robinson (Boston: Beacon Press, 2003), 67–70.

265. Ibid., 71–73.

being must be taught that it is "an infinite Soul," and that it "drinks forever" the "soul of God." As a correction to bad Christianity Emerson admonishes the person who hears him "to go it alone; to refuse the good models . . . and dare to love God without mediator or veil."[266] But he also advises the recognition of two advantages of Christianity: the Sabbath, the social institution that suggests to everyone the "dignity of spiritual being"; and preaching or speech, "the most flexible of all organs, all forms."[267] For Emerson all of this issues finally into a private form of philosophical faith, a church "of one," as he would later call it,[268] and becomes a part of his philosophy of benevolent "self-reliance."[269]

Other discussions in Emerson's early essays can remind one of the early Schelling [chap. 2.2.2]. In his essay "The Over-Soul" of 1841, one reads: "Within man is the soul of the whole . . . the universal One. . . . The act of seeing and the thing seen, the seer and the spectacle, the subject and the object, are one."[270] In the first essay, "Fate," in his most important philosophical work, *The Conduct of Life*, he makes use of a translation of Schelling's *On Human Freedom*.[271] In other essays in the book he demonstrates the interest in the practical affairs that characterizes his later thought, when the issue of slavery and its abolition focused the attention of the Transcendentalists on moral issues rather than philosophy and religion.[272]

In the wake of Transcendentalism Horace Bushnell (1802–76) appropriated Coleridge and elements of German "mediation theology" for a more conservative interpretation of Christianity.[273] Later Transcendentalism, with its interest in moral progress, was only a step away from the Hegelianism that spread among American university philosophers in the second half of the century, especially as the Civil War made Hegel's historical and Christian dialectic a viable way of looking at history.[274] Theologians too had begun to take a far greater interest in German philosophy and theology. Soon numbers of them were studying in Germany. D. F. Strauss's *Life of Jesus* quickly became required reading. John Williamson Nevin (1803–86) developed a high-church theology influenced by Schleierma-

266. Ibid., 73–79.
267. Ibid., 81f.
268. Ibid., 240, from an essay only recently published for the first time.
269. See his essay of this title, ibid., 83ff.
270. Ibid., 134.
271. *The Conduct of Life* (Boston: Belknap, 2003), see the notes to the work by Joseph Slater: 182, 189f.
272. See, e.g., the theologian Theodore Parker, whose religious thought is much like Emerson's and who was known as a fiery abolitionist preacher in Boston. John Edward Dirks, *The Critical Theology of Theodore Parker* (New York: Columbia University Press, 1948); Robert E. Collins, *Theodore Parker: American Transcendentalist* (Metuchen, NJ: Scarecrow, 1973).
273. See Bushnell, *God in Christ*, 1st ed. 1876 (New York: Charles Scribner's Sons, 1903), chap. 1; *Christ in Theology* (Hartford: Brown & Parsons, 1851), esp. 84. See James O. Duke, *Horace Bushnell* (Chico, CA: Scholars Press, 1984); John Muirhead, *The Platonic Tradition in Anglo-Saxon Philosophy* (New York: Macmillan, 1931), parts 2 and 3.
274. William H. Goetzmann, ed., *The American Hegelians* (New York: Alfred A. Knopf, 1973); John E. Smith, *America's Philosophical Vision* (Chicago: University of Chicago Press, 1992), 111ff., 121ff.; Reardon, *Religious Thought in the 19th Century*, 381–91; see also 352–73.

cher and German "mediation theology" at the German Reformed Seminary in Mercersburg, Pennsylvania. At about the same time a German theologian was hired at the same school, Philip Schaff, (1819–93), a Swiss of humble origins educated in Germany. In the middle of the century he was the single most important mediator of German theology in the United States.[275] We return to him in the following chapter.

---

275. Nevin's chief work, *The Mystical Presence* (Philadelphia: J. B. Lippincott, 1846), begins with an essay by the German mediation theologian Carl Ullmann [chap. 3, introduction], translated by Nevin. See further James Hastings Nichols, *Romanticism in American Theology: Nevin and Schaff at Mercersburg* (Chicago: University of Chicago Press, 1961); Sam Hamstra Jr. and Arie J. Griffioen, *Reformed Confessionalism in 19th Century America: Essays on the Thought of John Williamson Nevin* (Lanham, MD: Scarecrow, 1995). On Schaff's origins: Ulrich Gäbler, "Philip Schaff at Chur, 1819–1834," Elsie Anne McKee and Brian G. Armstrong, eds., *Probing the Reformed Tradition* (Louisville, KY: Westminster/John Knox, 1989), 408–23.

Chapter 3

Mediation Theology

"Mediation theology" broadly designates theologies in the nineteenth century whose basic method is stated by Schleiermacher in the *Brief Outline on the Study of Theology,* namely, that Scripture and tradition must be understood or interpreted in terms of the language of the time. The term covers a relatively wide and varied spectrum of more conservative and more liberal theologies. In individual instances liberal mediation theology could as easily blend with the Awakening and with aspects of more conservative mediation theology, as conservative mediation at the other end of the spectrum could blend with strict Lutheran orthodoxy. Martin Kähler's definition of mediation theology is that it mediates "between historical Christianity and the development of spiritual [*geistiger*] culture as it has developed" in the present, "especially this culture in its literary-scientific form and particularly as philosophy." He includes most theology in the nineteenth century.[1] Our interest here is in the main group of mediation theologians, the ones to whom the term most evidently applies. Most were Lutheran, advocates of the United Church, and

---

1. Kähler, *Geschichte der protestantischen Dogmatik,* 87; on mediation in orthodox theology, 153f. A work on the theological developments of the period is a landmark of liberal mediation theology: Karl Schwarz, *Zur Geschichte der neuesten Theologie* (Leipzig: Brockhaus, 1856). At the time Schwarz was associate professor of theology at Halle.

political moderates [chap. 1.2]. In the following sections we have chosen only a few important and representative mediation theologians for discussion.

Mediation theology believes in and works on the supposition of the ultimate unity of truth in Christian faith and science [*Wissenschaft*].[2] This conviction is due primarily to the impact of the concepts of science and reality expounded by the philosopher-theologians of the early part of the century: Kant, Fichte, Schelling, Hegel, Schleiermacher, Fries, and de Wette. (Schelling's late writings were not officially available until they were published in the collected works, 1856–61.) In all of these, reality and science were interpreted—in their view certainly—as Christian. The mediation theologians were eclectic in what they took from these philosophers. Hegel might be considered insightful about one thing but wrong about another. Selection was also practiced on the other side of the mediation, the faith tradition, insofar as it was necessary to adjust traditional doctrine to accommodate the new science. Whether they were more orthodox or more liberal, they often demonstrated a remarkable confidence and optimism in going about their projects and an impressive knowledge of theological history. And whether in agreement or disagreement, they were a community of discourse.

Historically the term "mediation theology" emerged first with reference to a group of theologians associated with the journal *Theologische Studien und Kritiken*. One of the founders of the journal, Carl Ullmann (1796–1895), explained that "mediation reduces relative oppositions to their original unity; through mediation an inner reconciliation and higher standpoint is gained in which the oppositions are 'lifted' [*aufgehoben*]."[3] The "oppositions" were faith and science [*Wissenschaft*], which meant both philosophy and the now rapidly developing historical criticism of the Bible. The "original unity" of faith and science included the conception of an ontological connection between the self (the agent in *Wissenschaft*) and God (the ultimate end of *Wissenschaft*), as developed in Idealism and Schleiermacher. Rather as the finite was related to the infinite, the being of the self was related to God. But the true nature of God, the self, and their relationship could be defined only from the standpoint of Christian revelation, and the relationship itself could be realized or actualized only in Christian faith. In the theological histories of mediation theology, creation and fall were succeeded by Christian rebirth and regeneration, in such a way that the potential of created humanity for true spiritual life with God, broken by the fall, is restored by the act of God in the revelation of Christ.

2. Cf. Karl Barth, *The Humanity of God*, 15–27. (See the preface of this book on the meaning of *Wissenschaft*.)

3. Vol. 9 (1836), p. 41, as quoted in Carl Andresen, ed., *Handbuch der Dogmen- und Theologiegeschichte*, 3:166. Carl Ullmann was for a time professor in Halle, then chief *Oberkirchenrat* (akin to bishop) of the liberal state of Baden. In spite of the Hegelian appearance of the quotation, the theologians associated with the journal were generally students of Schleiermacher. The most prominent were Carl Immanuel Nitzsch (1787–1876, professor of theology in Bonn, later in Berlin), Friedrich Lücke (1791–1855, professor of New Testament in Göttingen), and August Twesten (1789–1876, Schleiermacher's successor in Berlin). Nitzsch failed in an attempt to write a new confession for the United Church (see Lichtenberger, *History of German Theology in the 19th Century*, 185–96). Lücke made significant contributions to New Testament research. Others connected with the journal were Richard Rothe and Isaak Dorner.

Philip Schaff gives a perceptive introduction to the state of German theology after Schleiermacher in his book *Germany, Its Universities, Theology and Religion,* published in 1857. The book is a kind of tour guide for Americans interested in studying in Germany. Schaff is appreciative of that "extraordinary genius," Schleiermacher, and his service to theology and the church in overcoming rationalism. But Schaff quickly leaves him behind in his discussion of important theological developments, and he notes approvingly that Schleiermacher's students are more orthodox than their teacher.[4] Perhaps this opinion is a reflection of the church of his time [chap. 1.2].

Schaff rejects as "infidels" David Friedrich Strauss [chap. 2.5.1] and the Tübingen School of F. C. Baur [chap. 3.5]. His judgment of the strict confessional Lutherans is that their concerns are understandable but their theology is wrong in not being open to the new advances in philosophy and theology.[5] Schaff identifies himself with the moderately orthodox and Pietist mediation theology associated with August Tholuck. In speaking of the reconciliation of the spirit of the times and Christianity in the "last thirty or forty years," he remarks: "The human sciences, too, which, superficially tasted, had led away from God, began to return, in some of their profoundest representatives, to the source of all truth and wisdom.... History was now treated . . . in a much better spirit, and from a far higher standpoint, as a theatre of the unfolding of the plans of divine wisdom and mercy. The prevailing tendency of the general literature of Germany for the last thirty or forty years . . . looks . . . towards a reconciliation of science with faith, reason with revelation, of modern culture with old and ever young Christianity, the unfailing source of truth and life." Yet, he says, there continues to be a "most powerful conflict between Christ and Anti-Christ, faith and infidelity, theism and pantheism." This conflict makes "the last period of German theology one of the most instructive and interesting chapters in the internal history of the church."[6] All of this is characteristic of mediation theology, including the statement about the continuing conflict, which at this time principally meant opposing D. F. Strauss's *Life of Jesus.* Strauss's book drew a large number of responses from the mediation theologians.

3.1 AUGUST THOLUCK AND JULIUS MÜLLER

August Tholuck is representative of the Awakening, for example, in emphasizing the personal experience of spiritual rebirth through the free personal acceptance of Christ. The work for which he is best known is, in its English translation, *Guido and Julius, or Sin and the Propitiator Exhibited in the True Consecration of*

---

4. Philip Schaff, *Germany: Its Universities, Theology and Religion,* 154f., 320ff. Karl Bernhard Hundeshagen, *Der deutsche Protestantismus,* 278f., cf. 525, also notes approvingly a conservative correction to Schleiermacher in the mediation theology. An example from among Schleiermacher's students is Carl Immanuel Nitzsch, *System of Christian Doctrine,* trans. Robert Montgomery and John Hennen (Edinburgh: T. & T. Clark, 1849).

5. Schaff, *Germany: Its Universities, Theology and Religion,* on Strauss and Baur: 159f.; on the strict Lutherans: chaps. 18–20; cf. Hengstenberg, 28.

6. Ibid., 157.

the Skeptic, first published in 1823 and followed by eight subsequent editions.[7] (The English translation does not include five important appendixes that Tholuck added in later editions, which also delete the first words, "Guido and Julius," from the title.) The form of the book is a series of letters between two friends, one of whom experiences religious doubt. Its central themes are the reality of sin, the necessity of redemption through Christ, and the deceit of the "pantheist" philosophies of the Absolute.[8] Pantheism meant a rationalism that could even make Satan the origin of God, a reference to Tholuck's interpretation of Schelling's theory of the "ground," the first power or principle in *On Human Freedom* [chap. 2.4.1]. Evil, said Tholuck, comes from the fact of human sin, and only the fact of redemption in Christ can overcome it. In the educated person the symptom of sin is radical skepticism, which is an endless descent into despair. Tholuck quotes the famous words of Augustine: "Descend that you may ascend."[9] In the descent into despair one discovers the sinful, selfish condition of the inner self and is thus made ready to accept Christ, just as the world had been prepared, through its sense of sin and guilt, for Christ's appearance on earth. Religion is not a matter of philosophical theories but the fulfillment of the subjective human "need" of it. The descent into despair is a natural feature of the human condition. The law given in the Old Testament is only a higher, clearer power of what the Gentiles also have; it brings about the need of the redeemer and the longing for his advent.[10] In the later additions to the book Tholuck adds that, with Schelling's Absolute, one is left with only "the infinite, the unconditioned" and the philosophy of nature that flows from it. God is not distinct from the world, and free human self-determination is made impossible (apparently by the disposition of the will in *On Human Freedom*). But the truth of God's separate being and personhood cannot be proved, nor can free will. Within the "boundary" of human perception we cannot perceive "the absolute being" of God. But faith, by means not only of "feeling" but also of reason, may believe that God is a free personality separate from nature. It is true that, given the limitation of our perception, freedom is "inconceivable," for philosophy demonstrates only determinism. But in faith we may assume free personal self-determination.[11]

In the last of the appendixes to *Guido and Julius* Tholuck develops his mediation theology. Nature, he says, is the sphere of constant change. The "ground" of

---

7. *Guido and Julius,* trans. Jonathan Edwards Ryland, first ET ed. 1836 (Boston: Gould & Lincoln, 1854). The book is written as a corrective answer to de Wette's *Theodor.* On Tholuck and Julius Müller, see also Schaff, *Germany,* 278–94, 340–46; Lichtenberger, *History of German Theology,* 473–77.

8. See Tholuck's charge against Hegel in chap. 2.3 above.

9. *Guido and Julius,* 78. The quotation is from Augustine's *Confessions,* chap. 12. [Cf. Augustine in chap. 2.4.2 (note 121).]

10. Ibid., esp. 43ff., 68ff., 80, 101, 133, 193f.

11. Tholuck, *Die Lehre von der Sünde und vom Versöhner, oder: Die wahre Weihe des Zweiflers,* 7th ed. (Hamburg: F. Perthes, 1851), 176–80, 207. Cf. Kierkegaard. (The later German editions, which include the five appendixes, delete "Guido and Julius" from the title.) This seventh German edition is the source for the following discussion, which mainly has to do with the fifth and last appendix, entitled "The Relationship of Reason to Revelation," 226–75.

this change is the "unity of infinite and finite" outside of time, in a transcendent "world." Reason is "actually infinite" but is "born into" changing nature. In its created being, human spirit is in immediate relationship to God through the whole of its perceptive activity, that is, through reason, which includes feeling as a "sense of the divine." Reason's true source is the unity of all in the transcendent world. In nature and natural life, however, reason is confused with "understanding," which has to do only with individual things and thoughts. Reason is the source from which reflective thought and motives for action arise.[12] The inner immediate relationship of reason to God and world is human being's original relationship to truth, a relationship that is corrupted but not destroyed by sin. It is a "disposition" that makes us "receptive" for the truth of Christianity.[13] It is an "inner language" of spiritual hunger and thirst, a longing for salvation, which Tholuck finds in Plato, the tragedies of Sophocles, and all religions. "The savior presupposes, as necessary for the acknowledgment of Christian truth, the disposition of the inner person for it, which consists in the life of the original truth in the person."[14] The orthodox-supernaturalist denial of "the life of God in the soul, the one root of perceiving and willing," is rejected.[15] Tholuck's concept of reason is evidently similar to if not the same as Fries's and de Wette's concept of reason, as has long been recognized.[16]

Tholuck applies these concepts in his criticism of the rapidly developing historical science of biblical studies. According to Tholuck scholarship is led into error by being "separated from immediate inspiration through the inner sense, that is, from the perception of God in the human spirit," and so it has sunken to a "dry and arbitrary understanding" of its subject matter. It places undue emphasis on historical knowledge, as opposed to the immediacy of religious feeling and reason.[17] According to Tholuck's interpretation of Old Testament prophecy in another work, *Die Propheten und ihre Weissagungen* (The Prophets and Their Predictions), there is a point of reception in natural humanity for the supernatural gift of the prophet, namely, an "inborn ability for divination" that has been obscured by the concentration on mere understanding in modern culture.[18] *Ahnung* and vision in religious history should be interpreted through the interpreter's own relationship to divine reality and only secondarily by the empirical evidence for prediction and fulfillment.[19]

---

12. Ibid., 208, 235f., 244f., 251f.

13. Ibid., 246–52. Tholuck's New Testament references are Acts 17:26–28; Rom. 1:18, 22; 2:14f.; John 1:4, 9f.; 3:21; 4:24; 6:45; 8:42f.

14. Ibid., 257f. In another work he discusses early Christian apologetic theology in relation to the preparation for Christianity in pre-Christian antiquity: *Die sittliche Charakter des Altertums* (*The Moral Character of Antiquity*), 3rd ed. (Gotha: Friedrich Andreas Perthes, 1867).

15. *Die Lehre von der Sünde,* 240; cf. 217–25.

16. Rudolf Otto, *The Philosophy of Religion, Based on Kant and Fries,* 216–21.

17. *Die Lehre von der Sünde,* 241f.

18. *Die Propheten und ihre Weissagungen. Eine apologetisch-hermeneutische Studie* (Gotha: Friedrich Andreas Perthes, 1860), 2f., 6, 13f.

19. Ibid., 45f., 56f., 76f. See further Tholuck, *Commentary on the Gospel of John,* trans. Charles P. Krauth (Philadelphia: Smith, English & Co., 1859), esp. 66, where the historical revelation of Christ corresponds to an archetype in the human soul.

Julius Müller (1801–78), professor of theology at Halle, was a friend of Tholuck's and like Tholuck a theologian of the Awakening. (The wise "Julius" of Tholuck's *Guido and Julius* is supposed to be Julius Müller.) As for Tholuck, so also for Müller the certainty of faith is based on personal experience. His most significant work, in its English translation, is *The Christian Doctrine of Sin*. It is regarded as a classic of theological scholarship in the nineteenth century, a reliable work to which theologians often returned. It comprehends the biblical doctrine, its history in the church, and its contemporary interpretation.[20] Like Tholuck, Müller opposes the "pantheism" of the philosophies of the Absolute because it erases the boundary between God and human being.[21] For Müller pantheism meant particularly Hegel, and he thought Feuerbach was the direct consequence of Hegel.

Mediation theology in Müller has to do with the understanding of sin and human freedom, and it is at the center of his thought on the doctrine of sin. Like Kant, Müller thinks that human freedom cannot be explained by the "conditioned" world of causes and effects. It must, he says, have an origin that is like itself, and this can only be God.[22] He has high regard for the understanding of sin and freedom in Schelling's *On Human Freedom*, although like Tholuck he does not accept the doctrine of God in this work. For Müller, as for Schelling and Kant, human freedom's will and its original act of sin are outside of time, beyond the "conditioned" world of determined causes and effects.[23] This means that sin in its origin, and the fall of human being it brings about, is beyond comprehension.[24] If sin had its origin in the conditioned world, it could be explained, insofar as science or reason has access to all things in the conditioned world. As it is, however, the "why" of sin can be neither explained philosophically nor mastered morally. Only the fact of the savior, Christ, and faith's acceptance of Christ can overcome it.

3.2 RICHARD ROTHE

Richard Rothe (1799–1867), professor of theology at Heidelberg, was a friend of Tholuck and Müller and known as a person of sincere piety.[25] He is one of the most remarkable figures in nineteenth-century theology. Among the mediation theologians his influence, along with that of Isaak Dorner, has been the most

---

20. *The Christian Doctrine of Sin,* trans. William Pulsford, 1st German ed. 1838, 2 vols. (Edinburgh: T. & T. Clark, 1852f.). See Karl Barth, *Church Dogmatics* III/3:312ff.; Christine Axt-Piscalar, *Ohnmächtige Freiheit* (Tübingen: Mohr Siebeck, 1996); Hans-Peter Willi, *Unbegreifliche Sünde* (Berlin: Walter de Gruyter, 2003).

21. E.g., Müller, 1:120f.

22. Ibid., 2:153ff., 199f.

23. Ibid., 103–18 [cf. Kant, chap. 2.1.3].

24. Ibid., 189f. [cf. Kierkegaard, chap. 2.6, note 197]

25. On Rothe: Helmut Thielicke, *Modern Faith and Thought,* 409–23; Lichtenberger, *History of German Theology,* 492–526; Schaff, *Germany,* 360–75; Hans-Joachim Birkner, *Spekulation und Heilsgeschichte* (Munich: Christian Kaiser, 1959); Heike Krötke, *Selbstbewusstsein und Spekulation* (Berlin: Walter de Gruyter, 1999).

enduring. In his work on biblical interpretation, *Zur Dogmatik* (Concerning Dogmatics), Rothe combines a belief in God's miraculous historical acts ("manifestations") with the internal testimony of the Holy Spirit (inspiration, prophecy). By means of manifestations and inspiration, which forms the mind to comprehend a manifestation, God leads biblical history to the revelation of God in Christ. Manifestation and inspiration "go into each other" so that they form a unity. In analogy to the light of the sun, in God's revelation in Christ (manifestation), the light of revelation (inspiration) falls on all else, revealing it in truth. Manifestation without inspiration would not be understood; inspiration without manifestation would be "a fantastic will-o'-the-wisp." Christ is the perfectly inspired perfect manifestation of God, so that he alone is the authentic interpreter of himself. Christ and the miracles of his life are "absolute" miracles, without any sort of natural mediation that could be "explained" in some way (here Rothe argues against Schleiermacher). For the Christian community revelation works the "purification" and "strengthening" of the "God-consciousness," which is otherwise clouded by sin. This is the work of the Holy Spirit, *fides divina* in contrast with *fides humana*, belief based on rational or moral proofs.[26]

Because Scripture has to do with revelation, the right relationship to it is *fides divina*. However, Rothe thinks that eventually, at the end of all historical development, science (*fides humana*) will understand what one now knows only by faith. The New Testament as a whole awakens the nonobjective or preobjective feeling of the certainty of its truth. However, in its particulars there are problems recognized by historical criticism that require objective determination, by the "laborious work" of the critic, of what does and does not belong "infallibly" to revelation.[27] The revelation of God is Christ himself, of whom a kind of "photograph" (photography was new in Rothe's time) is given in the minds of those close to him. This photograph is then transmitted to the writings of the New Testament. These writings render the photograph in the different perspectives and conditions of the authors and their traditions, and these include nonessential elements and in some cases mistakes. Historical criticism has the task of reproducing the photograph in its essential infallibility, a work that always only

26. Rothe, *Zur Dogmatik,* 2nd ed. (Gotha: Friedrich Andreas Perthes, 1862), 59–83, esp. 60f., 68–70, 76, 83; on absolute miracle: 96ff. (For the concepts "manifestation" and "inspiration," Rothe, p. 70, refers to Carl Immanuel Nitzsch, *System of Christian Doctrine,* 71.) The term *fides divina* originated in Lutheran orthodoxy as a formulation of the Reformation doctrine of the internal testimony of the Spirit (e.g., Calvin, *Institutes* 1.7.4f.; cf. Rom. 8:16) in opposition to the *fides humana* of Socinian rationalism. These terms were reintroduced into theological discussion in the nineteenth century by Karl Hase's *Hutterus Redivivus,* 1st ed. 1828 (11th ed. Leipzig: Breitkopf und Härtel, 1868), §37. Leonhard Hutter or Hutterus (1563–1616) was an orthodox Lutheran theologian. Hase's intent was to compare Hutter's orthodoxy with recent theology. In the nineteenth century *fides humana* possessed currency in discussions about the problematic nature of historical-critical science. *Fides divina* in distinction from *fides humana* is commonly cited especially by mediation theologians in Rothe's time. D. F. Strauss strongly rejects *fides divina* as irrational: *Die christliche Glaubenslehre:* 1:114–36 (esp. 136), 224f., 354f., and he comments on it in other places in this work. F. C. Baur rejects it as interfering with objective history: *Lehrbuch der christlichen Dogmengeschichte,* 3rd ed. (Leipzig: Fues, 1867), 300f., 364–67.

27. Rothe, *Zur Dogmatik,* 142ff., 312ff.

approximately succeeds. In opposition to the plenary inspiration of Scripture in orthodox theology, Rothe argues for the "illumination" (again in analogy to the sun) of the New Testament authors by Christ and the Holy Spirit. This illumination was not given only to them; it was rather the gift given all members of the early church. (All experienced the unity of "manifestation" and "inspiration" in Christ.) The truth of revelation includes the miraculous "facts" of the holy history, among them the resurrection, the miracles of Jesus, and the realization of the meaning of Jesus in the Gospel of John.[28] Rothe's interpretation of the life of Jesus shows the influence of D. F. Strauss, but with a completely different intent than Strauss [chap. 2.5.1]. In his unpublished 1854/55 lectures on the life of Jesus, Rothe, modifying Strauss's definition, defines myth in the Gospels as a "history-like clothing of early Christian ideas formed in unintentionally poeticizing legend." "[This] poetry however is not invention but poetic comprehension and presentation of the factually given." It gives what no objective biography could present. "Our Gospels do not intend to give an actual life-history but a religious character-picture of Jesus as the God-human and the savior." All that is needed to present him as the Christ is contained in them. "We perceive in him the pure and full revelation of God in God's historical appearance; without the clear view [Anschauung] of this appearance we do not have what is given us in Christ."[29]

The work for which Rothe is best known, Theologische Ethik, has also not been translated (only his book of aphorisms, Still Hours, a collection of sermons, and an excerpt from the beginning of the first edition of the Ethik are in translation).[30] The Ethik revives the concept of a world-transforming Christianity and foreshadows attempts in the twentieth century to understand Christianity's relationship to secularism in a positive way.[31] In the extensive introduction Rothe draws eclectically from Hegel, the earlier Schelling, and Schleiermacher to develop a speculative theology that begins with the unconditioned Absolute. "While in the experience of the world we find each individual thing conditioned by other things in the way of causality, this observation reflects, with logical-psychological necessity, the thought of . . . an utterly unconditioned being."[32] His presupposition is

---

28. Ibid., 118, 166f., 285–99, 308–11.

29. An account of this unpublished lecture, based on the lecture notes of Martin Kähler, is given by Hans-Georg Link, Geschichte Jesu und Bild Christi (Neukirchen: Neukirchner Verlag, 1975), 193ff.; the quotations from Rothe's lecture are from Link, 194f., 197f. On poetic form, see Schelling [chap. 2.2.5].

30. Rothe, Theologische Ethik, 2nd ed., 5 vols. (Wittenberg: Koelling, 1869–71) (1st ed., 3 vols. 1845–48). Rothe's Still Hours, trans. Jane T. Stoddart (New York: Funk & Wagnalls, n.d.), contains a long introductory essay on Rothe by John Macpherson. The original German edition, Stille Stunden, a book of aphorisms from periods in Rothe's life, was published posthumously in 1872. (On p. 225 Rothe speaks of faith as a confidence or trust in Christ that requires a "clear and lively historical image of his character.") The translated excerpt is in J. D. Morell, Philosophy of Religion (New York: D. Appleton, 1840), 340–59. See also Rothe, Sermons for the Christian Year (Edinburgh: T. & T. Clark, 1877).

31. See the discussion of Rothe in Helmut Thelicke, Modern Faith and Thought, 409–22.

32. Rothe, Ethik, 1:75; see also the following discussion, 75ff.

the Christian consciousness of the personal God. "Theological speculation" is "the expression of the immediately certain content of the immediate pious consciousness, that is, the content of its God-feeling, from which thought about God arises in its specific determinateness [*Bestimmtheit*] and conceptual form."[33] As for Schleiermacher, for Rothe pious Christian consciousness is received from Christ through the church.

The history of God's plan for humanity is actually two histories. The first is a "normal" history of humanity without sin ascending from material animal creation through progressive moral-religious domination of nature to the community of love in perfect communion with God.[34] Whereas in this history humanity in its freedom makes the right moral-religious choices, in "abnormal" history humanity makes the wrong choices, allowing its sensual nature to draw it into self-interest and hence falling into sin. In this history humanity's salvation from the destruction of sin and the development toward moral perfection is possible "only through Christ and in union with him."[35] Christ, whose person is a supernatural miracle, is the "mediator" who draws God and humanity together in himself, his life, his message, and the creation of the community of love. In the miracle of Christ's resurrection God bursts the limitations of Christ's physical nature in space and time so that Christ assumes a completely spiritual body (1 Cor. 15), the form of perfection to which humanity finally also attains. But evil and wickedness continue, and final victory over sin is won by the miraculous second coming of Christ, in which evil and those who are fully absorbed by it are cast out.[36]

The factual intervention of God in Christ, who is now lord of the world, corrects the course of sinful development enough for the two histories to move closer together, so that "normal" historical development becomes both visible and possible for the Christian and the church. "Normal" development is what the Christian and the church can see and do see as the right, good, and true course that should be followed in all areas of life, although the course is never perfectly followed or realized and it is usually distorted by sin.[37] An example is Rothe's treatment of "normal" political life: "theocracy" functioning through representative democracy and an elected head of government. The head of government is not elected for life and does not at death pass monarchic authority to an heir.[38] With regard to actual (abnormal) history, however, Rothe says that while there is an obvious need for representative government, large numbers of people are not capable of it. The tendency of the time is toward a constitutional "inherited

33. Ibid., 45.
34. Normal development is the content of the first part of the *Ethik* (1:411–552, and vol. 2). Schleiermacher thought original human life was darkly animal: *Christian Faith*, §5.
35. Abnormal history is the content of the second part of the *Ethik*, the history of sin and redemption (vols. 3–5). The quotation is from *Still Hours*, 199.
36. *Ethik*, 3:141–51, 189.
37. Ibid., 171ff.
38. Ibid., 2:438–60, esp. 453; 476. The states among themselves form a "world league of nations": 471 [cf. Kant, chap. 2.1.3].

monarchy."[39] Another example of the link between normal and abnormal history is Rothe's concept of "*the Christian outside the church.*" This person is in sin and yet believes to some degree in Christian truth. "Within the compass of Christendom there can be no absolutely pure 'natural' man. All persons develop from the first under the influence of the principle of redemption, which has to some degree become historical in every sphere of life. This is true even of those within its pale who do not acknowledge Christianity, and who have, perhaps, a creed in opposition to it."[40]

The vision of what should be, and through Christ can be, in the real world, and his reflection on the situation in which there are "Christians outside the church," lead Rothe to envision the progressive Christianizing of the state. This happens through the reduction of the distinction between church and state. Rothe understands the state as the whole moral community of a nation (as in Hegel). The state will become ever more theocratic, so that the church is largely but not entirely absorbed by it.[41] Christianity's mission is to convert the world. Rothe sees this more as the work of the Christian state than the work of the church. The state, the moral community in its full extent, communicates to other nations the broad meaning of sinful life morally and religiously transformed by Christianity, which is not a Christianity confined to church and doctrines.[42] Rothe thinks that sin and evil are not strong enough to deter Christian development throughout the world, although they present constant and often dangerous obstacles to be overcome until the second coming of Christ. The reason for his optimism is his belief in Christ's lordship. Because Christ is lord of the world, Christianity must exceed and has already exceeded the limits of the church in its moral influence on secular and political life.

The same conviction determines theology's relationship to science. Rothe recommends freedom in theology for rigorous scientific work [*Wissenschaft*], in the belief that rightly understood "Christianity cannot come into conflict with science." Indeed "science is essentially word of God and the scholar is essentially enlightened by God and is a prophet."[43] All things are moving progressively, if often imperceptibly, toward the kingdom of God.

39. Ibid., 5:358, 303ff., 422–29; cf. 2:456f. Schaff, *Germany,* 374, reports a conversation in 1854 in which Rothe saw in the United States an example of a state in which Christianity "had become, or promised to become, a truly national concern, the voluntary expression of the people's will, an inherent element of the general life, and that was the very thing he wanted." Karl Bernhard Hundeshagen, a colleague of Rothe's at Heidelberg, was also an advocate of representative government. In his main work, *Der deutsche Protestantismus,* 228–58, he evaluates the experience of an estimated six million German immigrants in the United States. On Hundeshagen, see Schaff, 399–402 [see also chap. 1.2 note 16].

40. *Still Hours,* 409, cf. 407–21. Rothe is known for the concept of the "unconscious Christian." See Birkner, *Spekulation und Heilsgeschichte,* 82. [Cf. Bonhoeffer, chap. 6.5.5, and chap. 8.4.4.]

41. *Ethik.,* 2:248f.; 3:171ff., 183; 5:307–9.

42. Ibid., 5:483–96. Cf. *Still Hours,* 406: "I am firmly convinced that the invention of steam engines and railroads has had a much more important positive influence on furthering the kingdom of Christ than the elaboration of the dogmas of Nicea and Chalcedon." "Islam was the first great historical interference on the part of divine providence to prevent the absorption of Christianity into a church."

43. Ibid., 5:175; 2:359. It was with this belief and in the interest of addressing the increasingly secular educated public that he became a cofounder of the *Protestantenverein* (Protestant League or Union), to which a large number of liberal theologians and pastors belonged.

Theology is, however, only in part free science, for it carries responsibility for the church and its confession. The attempt to revise the confessions in view of scientific progress is fruitless; no real agreement can be reached. The time of formulating confessions has passed. The church has reached the peak of its own separate development and is already in the long process of transition into the moral community of the state. The situation of the church in the world requires that the test for ordination to the ministry should be whether or not the candidate affirms the "fundamental pious feeling" of the truth of the "factual" revelation in Christ as the ground from which the historic confessions arose. Ministers should be pastors to their communities of faith, which requires Christian self-denial in not insisting on their progressive theological points of view but conforming to the faith expressions of the community.[44] The church has important work to do among the poor and uneducated. The form of the church that best suits the poor and uneducated is pietism, lay Christianity. Such work is directed not only to home missions but also to foreign missions as new churches are born, for these are populated with persons essentially like those addressed by home missions. "Methodists and Moravians are the true missionaries of the evangelical church."[45] The Christian mission of the state is the spreading of Christian "humanization and civilization," after which follows the missionary work of the church.[46]

3.3 I. A. DORNER

Isaak August Dorner (1808–84) was appointed professor of theology in Berlin in 1862. He was a friend of Rothe, Müller, and Tholuck. He is best known for two works, the *History of the Development of the Doctrine of the Person of Christ*, first published in 1839, followed by a much enlarged second edition, and *System of the Christian Doctrine of Faith*, whose first volume appeared relatively late for his generation of mediation theologians, in 1879, when the theological tide was turning to Ritschlianism.[47] Nevertheless he was a widely respected and influential theologian. Dorner's eclectic method takes certain key ideas from Schleiermacher, from Schelling, and to a lesser degree from Hegel, while maintaining

44. Ibid., 5:434–40, 449f.
45. Ibid., 493; 422–29.
46. Ibid., 483f. See Jürgen Moltmann's summary of Rothe's view of church, state, and mission in *The Coming of God*, trans. Margaret Kohl (Minneapolis: Fortress Press, 1996), 362f. [chap. 8.2].
47. I. A. Dorner, *History of the Development of the Doctrine of the Person of Christ*, trans. William Lindsay Alexander and D. W. Simon, 5 vols. (Edinburgh: T. & T. Clark, 1864–66); *History of Protestant Theology*, trans. George Robson and Sophia Taylor, 4 vols. (Edinburgh: T. & T. Clark, 1871); *A System of Christian Doctrine*, trans. Alfred Cave and J. S. Banks, 4 vols. (Edinburgh: T. & T. Clark, 1883–85); Claude Welch, ed., *God and Incarnation in Mid-Nineteenth Century German Theology* (New York: Oxford University Press, 1965), 103–294. See also discussions in Karl Barth, *Protestant Theology in the Nineteenth Century*, 563–73; Claude Welch, *Protestant Thought in the Nineteenth Century*, 1:273–82; Christine Axt-Piscalar, *Der Grund des Glaubens* (Tübingen: Mohr Siebeck, 1990); Thomas Koppehl, *Der wissenschaftliche Standpunkt der Theologie Isaak August Dorners* (Berlin: Walter de Gruyter, 1997); Jörg Rothermundt, *Personale Synthese* (Göttingen: Vandenhoeck & Ruprecht, 1968).

critical distance from all three, especially in the interest of representing a more orthodox position on traditional doctrines. In the second edition of the *History of the Development of the Doctrine of the Person of Christ*, he writes that Schelling's "undying service"—a "turning point" for both philosophy and theology—was to show that in perception subject and object are originally in subject-object unity. In interpreting this theologically, Dorner refers the reader to his previous discussion of Luther: certain sermons (with reference to biblical texts such as John 17:21ff. and 2 Pet. 1:4) emphasize the union of the believer with Christ.[48] In the first chapters of the *System*, this same unity, which Dorner also expresses with Schleiermacher's term "God-consciousness," is one of two main themes. The other is "certainty": first as the certainty of faith, then as the "scientific verification" of what faith believes. For Dorner, religion or faith is produced by the Word of God and the internal testimony of the Holy Spirit; in and of itself it has nothing to do with science. However, human being also has reason, the means of scientific understanding. What faith believes is true, and the science of Christian theology verifies this truth for the benefit of the church [cf. Schelling, chap. 2.4.2].[49]

Other ways of understanding the relationship between faith and science are for Dorner inadequate. For example, the merely objective belief in doctrines must lead to subjective skepticism. The same is true of the attempt objectively to validate the authenticity of Scripture by historical proofs; even where it is successful, *fides humana* can never demonstrate more than probability. *Fides divina* or the testimony of the Holy Spirit overcomes such problematic objectivity.[50] On the other hand, merely subjective religion—whether in feeling, the intellect, the will, or some combination of these—has the "idea" without the historical reality and is therefore also deficient and inadequate. Kant, Hegel, Jacobi, and Schleiermacher are Dorner's primary examples: Hegel tries but fails to arrive at certainty through eternal ideas. Kant fails at the same effort through the moral will. Jacobi and Schleiermacher try to find certainty through pious feeling, but this too fails. In all these the same thing is missing: the objective truth of faith.[51] Science or

48. Dorner, *History of the Doctrine of Christ*, on Schelling: 5:100; on Luther: 4:59ff.; cf. also *History of Protestant Theology*, 4:358f. Dorner is otherwise critical of the early Schelling : *History of the Doctrine of Christ*, 5:101ff.

49. Dorner, *System*, 1: esp. 58f., 72–76, 110, 154–56. The following notes are primarily references to vol. 1.

50. Ibid., 85f., 90–115.

51. Ibid., 115–19; on Schleiermacher: 171–73. Dorner applied the same criticism to some of his contemporaries. The conservative Lutheran theologians Johann Christian Konrad v. Hofmann (1810–77) and Franz Hermann Reinhard v. Frank (1827–94), both professors in Erlangen, were like Dorner concerned to validate scientifically the certainty of faith. For them however—in dependence on both the Awakening and Schleiermacher—only the experience of the living Christ in spiritual rebirth gives such certainty, especially in the face of historical criticism. "The knowledge and expression of Christianity must be . . . above all the self-knowledge and self-expression of the Christian." *Der Schriftbeweis; ein theologischer Versuch*, 2nd ed. (Nördlingen: C. H. Beck, 1857), 10. Faith contains a subjectively certain content that corresponds not only to what Scripture says about salvation and regeneration but also to the whole of salvation history in Scripture. Christian experience is so certain that it is placed confidently beside all other claims for scientific certainty. Dorner's critique is that this certainty is only subjective; where objective content is asserted, the certainty of it is always

philosophy by itself naturally seeks God, but vainly; it can show neither that God does exist or that God does not exist, and it is full of conflict and contradiction in what it thinks about God. But, Dorner says, all such conflict aids the work of theology by moving it forward.[52] The fulfillment of science's quest is found only in Christian faith.

Dorner now presents, in addressing the question of how religious certainty is attained, an extended account of the preparation of the individual to receive Christ. His presentation is much like Tholuck's. Intellectual and moral experience or awareness lead to doubt, which confronts the self with the practical need to maintain its harmony or unity with itself, for doubt divides the mind. Here the self should recognize, in the practical question about what benefits or is good for this harmony, that Christianity is united with what is good, namely, God. In this recognition the "religious impulse" latent in the self is fostered or developed. This religiousness eventually recognizes, however, that it is neither whole nor pure. The "natural" person desires the ideal but cannot realize it and must confess that he or she is "a guilty sinner." At this moment one begins "to stand in the world of truth," for the "high and pure image of God-likeness has entered" the human heart. Now one asks whether or not there is "a true religion, a religion of reconciliation, without which the awakened religious sense cannot live."[53] With the sorrow of the sinner "a faculty for the understanding and reception of the gospel message is disclosed," for the soul longs for "living communion with God." Now God's objective acts in history, and especially the "picture" of Christ painted everywhere in the New Testament, are "renewed for and within the subject." Dorner interpolates: "God's infinity would be straightway made finite, if the world stood over against Him as an insuperable limitation, so that He was unable to prove Himself living in the world." Subjectively and objectively God is involved in human being and the world.[54]

The history of recent biblical criticism shows that one may be led astray by "relatively unimportant matters"; the main thing is "to fix the eyes upon the core and center of Scripture, Jesus Christ. In this way faith is able to assert its independence of the wavering course of learned critical investigations." The religious community, the Scriptures, and the sacraments are "objective phenomena" that in their effect on the self unite the human and divine.[55] The truth works in the person, "the heavens open." The new believer "knows himself to be united with the center of truth in heaven and on earth, and has found the most precious

taken from subjective experience: Dorner, *System*, 1:52–58. On Hofmann, see Helmut Thielicke, *Modern Faith and Thought*, 233–47.

52. Dorner, *System*, 1:121–30. At the time Dorner wrote the *System*, the atheistic and pessimistic philosophies of Arthur Schopenhauer and Edward von Hartmann, as well as the last work of D. F. Strauss, were being widely read.

53. This is like the religious quest of the pre-Christian world. Ibid., 131–40.

54. [Cf. parallels in Schleiermacher's *Christian Faith*, cited in chap. 2.2.4, and in Schelling, chap. 2.4.2.]

55. Dorner, *System*, 1:140–51.

treasure, religious certainty of Christian salvation, fides divina." By virtue of the union of subject and object "our certainty knows itself to be grounded in objective Christian truth that makes itself evident and authoritative." "Both testimonies, that of the self-consciousness and the objective testimony perceived by the God-consciousness, must become one." The God-consciousness is also integrated with the consciousness of world, so that the divine Spirit is understood to be the source of life of the whole world.[56]

The religious certainty now attained is the presupposition of scientific certainty. Dorner quotes the text, Colossians 2:3: in Christ "all the treasures of wisdom and knowledge" are contained [cf. Schelling, chap. 2.4.2]. Faith, Dorner explains, must involve the rational nature of humanity, so that it too participates in divine illumination, the living truth of God in Christ. Faith's perception of God, together with the mind's ability to form ideas and judgments, reflects "real thoughts of God and of truths" that are then given to science for their verification. "Faith desires to become knowledge." It is the task of dogmatic theology to unfold the riches of the faith in reasoning objective thought, in order to complete and secure faith's certainty. It exhibits the Christian idea of God as scientifically true and necessary. Dorner again points to a presupposition in human nature: "There is an indissoluble association of the idea of God in general with the reasoning nature of man," an association that is "perfected and completed" in the Christian idea of God. Hence in dogmatics, Dorner says, one begins with the "natural" or universal consciousness of God "and proceeds according to the methods of universal rational thought" as this is "restored to a normal state" [cf. Rothe, chap. 3.2]. "Universal rational thought" finds its fulfillment, and Christianity appears as the conclusion "of the revelation of the divine Logos which began in the common reason of man."[57] This history of the Logos includes world history and the pre-Christian history of religions [cf. Schelling, chap. 2.4.2]. All that is "extra-Christian" is "in some way . . . a preparation for or prophecy of" the incarnation. Otherwise "not merely would Christianity figure as an abrupt phenomenon, but the universality of its destination for all men in the multiplicity of their modes of faith would be in danger." "The absolute religion must preserve the truth contained in them all, emancipate and satisfy the best longing in each and all of them."[58]

There is in faith no absolute knowledge of God. God is and remains unfathomable. But the knowledge of God that we have through revelation is nonetheless true.[59] This truth includes the doctrine of the "immutable" God who is both "unconditioned infinitude" and "in Himself objectively and eternally conditioned," that is, whose definite attributes are God's own, not invented by human reason. The attributes of God are essentially ethical (e.g., love), and they are made known only by revelation in Christ.[60] The idea of the ethical is the "highest thought" and there-

56. Ibid., 152–55. Cf. Karl Barth, *Protestant Theology in the Nineteenth Century,* 565ff.
57. Ibid., 159–71.
58. Ibid., 232–34.
59. Ibid., 211f.; cf. 200–213.
60. Ibid., 187, 212.

fore, Dorner says, it is opposed to the thought of God as pure or simple unconditionedness. In the idea of God, all is "subordinated to and regulated by" the idea of the ethical. For human being it is in the sphere of the ethical that "the question of the why of everything" must arise. "Schelling rightly says, in his Philosophy of Revelation, that this ultimate question must also be considered, if thought is to attain full content—[namely] the question of why thought itself exists" [chap. 2.4.2]. The answer, Dorner says, may be found only in the ethical God, for otherwise the ethical would be subordinate to some higher or more general concept of God.[61]

In defense of the doctrine of the immutability of God Dorner objects to distinguishing between the "immanent" Trinity as it is in itself and the "economic" Trinity as it manifests itself in the world by means of a "doubling" of the Trinity [cf. chap. 2.4.2, n. 123].[62] This would mean changes in the being of God. Furthermore, since God is immutable, the Logos does not empty itself to become the human being of Jesus, as in recent "kenotic" theology.[63] Rather, Jesus is the one who changes, namely, by growing in the process of his human life into perfect union with the Logos, the second person of the Trinity. Essentially the same union with God that takes place imperfectly in Christian faith takes place perfectly in Christ through "inspiration without measure." Christ is perfectly "receptive" of God, so that through his personal development he becomes the perfect image of God [cf. Schleiermacher, chap. 2.7.2].[64]

3.4 KARL HASE

Karl Hase (1800–90)—a grandfather of Dietrich Bonhoeffer—was professor at Jena, where he dominated the theological faculty for half a century. He is mainly known for his church histories, among which was a standard handbook covering all of church history.[65] His critique of Ferdinand Christian Baur and Baur's Tübingen School is considered the best criticism of Baur published during Baur's lifetime.[66] In 1828 he published the first significant nineteenth-century life of

61. Ibid., 308–11; *History of the Doctrine of Christ,* 5:209f. and elsewhere. Dorner opposes Schleiermacher's doctrine that there are no "distinctions" in God's own being: ibid., 1:401.

62. Dorner's three-part series on the doctrine of God, published 1856–61, is in English: *Divine Immutability,* trans. Robert R. Williams and Claude Welch (Minneapolis: Fortress, 1994); see esp. 156–60; cf. 71. See further Dorner's critique of the late Schelling's concept of God: *System,* 1:406f.; *History of Protestant Theology,* 5:362ff. The third part of Dorner's *Divine Immutability* was previously published, together with sections on Christology from Dorner's *System,* in Claude Welch, ed., *God and Incarnation.* See also Dorner, *History of the Doctrine of Christ,* 5:249ff. See further Robert F. Brown, "Schelling and Dorner on Divine Immutability," *Journal of the American Academy of Religion* 53 (1985): 237–49.

63. Dorner gives a history and critique of "kenotic" theology in *System,* 1:233–38, 264–68.

64. *System,* 2:207, cf. 194; 3:328ff.; *History of the Doctrine of Christ,* 5:249ff.; cf. 233f.

65. *A History of the Christian Church,* trans. Charles E. Blumenthal and Conway P. Wing (New York: D. Appleton, 1856). Hase's collected works were published after his death: *Gesammelte Werke* (Leipzig: Breitkopf und Härtel, 1890–92).

66. Hase, *Die Tübinger Schule.* See also Baur's chapter on Hase in P. Hodgson, ed., *Ferdinand Christian Baur on the Writing of Church History* (see note 73).

Jesus, a work that went though several editions. His dogmatic theology first appeared in 1826 and also went through several (greatly expanded) editions under the title, *Evangelische-Protestantische Dogmatik,* to which we turn in the text below.[67] The dominant theological influence is Schleiermacher, but Hase also has high regard for the early Schelling, taking his concept of freedom from *On Human Freedom* [chap. 2.4.1].

Hase's method in his dogmatics is to develop theologically the relationships among God, world, and humanity prior to turning to the concrete historical existence of Christianity. "Religion is objectively a relationship of humanity to the infinite, subjectively a being conditioned by the infinite." The infinite is also a "component and energy" of the human spirit from which religion springs "eternally young." Christian faith is "a believing as true, on the basis of religious life, certain ideas about our relationship to the infinite" (§§1–4). Dogmatics is the ordered knowledge of the Christian religion (§§7, 17). Pre-Christian religion develops in stages that are also the progressive stages of cultural development, each with its own aspect of religious truth (§5). "All the pious worship in many tongues the same God" (§111). Christ is the "perfect religious spirit," whose truth "corresponds to humanity in its highest development." In the community of Christ's Spirit human life moves toward its completion, and Christians are known by their love and piety (§6).

The Scriptures and Christian tradition contain both true history and myths that are not historical; the myths symbolize important religious ideas in early Christianity and were formed without intent to deceive (§7f.). For example, the story of the virgin birth symbolizes the truth that Jesus was born with a disposition to human perfection (§147). Faith is not based on the results of historical research (*fides humana*), which can attain only probable results (§24f.). Rather, faith is worked by God in revelation (§18) through the Holy Spirit (*fides divina,* §178). Historical criticism determines the authenticity of biblical writings but has no significance for the use of Scripture in the church, the divinity of which is confirmed by the Holy Spirit (§193). Hase opposes obligating modern pastors to strict adherence to the Lutheran confessions. They should preach the truth they perceive "according to Scripture" and that is "beneficial to their congregations" (§220).

Human freedom inherently strives toward the infinite, but it is ultimately finite and limited. Through Christ the infinite God gives human being the gift of love of the infinite God, creating a new freedom in the relationship to the infinite that exceeds all other experiences of freedom (§§45–50, 67, 146). "All in religious life is grace, and all is freedom, that is, freedom is itself the great gift of grace; grace is its continuous ground, and the greatest gift of love is Christ." All Christian dogma and ethics is derived from or produced by this love (§51ff.). Human beings are the "doers," but God is the first and continual cause of their

---

67. Karl Hase, *Evangelische-Protestantische Dogmatik,* 5th ed. (Leipzig: Breitkopf und Härtel, 1860). The following section numbers refer to this edition.

ability to act in love (§§79, 166). Justification is being in the love of God (§174). Blessedness and increasing holiness are the result of life lived in the love of God, in whom human life finds its completion (§§97, 178). Hase is ecumenical in his teaching on the sacrament of the Lord's Supper: each of the three doctrines, Catholic, Lutheran, and Calvinist, has equal claim to be the correct interpretation of Scripture, and none is absolute (§209).[68]

Human being is created in the image of God (§54ff.), which is perfectly present in Christ (§192). God is to be thought of according to this image in Christ.[69] "The freedom and all excellence of human being is comprehended in human personhood. Therefore absolute freedom must also be thought as personhood. Hence . . . the idea of humanity elevated over all limitation is the idea of God, insofar as it is and can be revealed to humanity. Revelation cannot be other than pure anthropomorphism" (§97). An expression in the first edition of the work, deleted in later editions, is *deus est humanissimus,* "God is the most human." If this were not the case, Hase says, the relationship between God and humanity would not be love. The concept of the "infinite" itself is a human, anthropological concept.[70] The healing miracles of Jesus, the perfect image of God, are the "intelligent mastery of nature by the soul." "The human soul, originally endowed with dominion over the earth, recovered this in the holy innocence of Jesus, conquering the unnatural power of sin and death. Therefore there was in the miracles no violation of the laws of nature but, on the contrary, here the disturbed world recovered its original harmony and truth" [cf. Schleiermacher, chap. 2.7.2]. "The universe rests in the love of God."[71] "From the love of God proceeds the faith in an eternal Kingdom of God" in which God's love of human beings remains unbroken (§§84, 87). In the awareness of freedom in God and in love of God, one is aware that eternity is already "in-breaking" in the present (§83).

In dialectical contrast to what otherwise seems to be an optimistic depiction of human freedom, Hase speaks of the effect of sin, from which in this life there is no final freedom (§67). In the world its rule is powerful, ever again reproducing itself through cause and effect (§69). Through sin and evil an entire historical epoch can go to ruin (§124). Hase wrote about the heroic lives of great figures and movements in Christian history who, although not free from error, envisioned the infinite God in ways that dramatically affected the course of events, but whose

68. Hase's work on Roman Catholicism is in the form of a friendly discussion of differences, particularly with Möhler [chap. 1.2]: *Handbook of the Controversy with Rome,* trans. A. W. Stearne, 2 vols. (London: Religious Tract Society, 1906).

69. Hase affirms in the *Dogmatik* the traditional attributes of God's perfection: omniscience, omnipresence, omnipotence, holiness, truthfulness, goodness, justice, blessedness (§110f.). God is always complete, pure perfection, and always to be loved and worshiped (§99). Cf. §§93ff.

70. *Lehrbuch der evangelischen Dogmatik* (Stuttgart: J. B. Metzler, 1826), 240f. In support of the concept of the humanity of God, Hase cites F. H. J. Jacobi, who wrote, with reference to the "image of God" in human being: "Creating human being, God 'theomorphised.' Therefore human being necessarily 'anthropomorphises.'" Jacobi, *Werke,* 3:418.

71. Hase, *Life of Jesus,* trans. James Freeman Clark (Boston: Walker & Wise, 1860), 98f.; cf. 96: the laws of nature are "the constant expressions of Divine will." According to Hase's *Dogmatics,* §118, the natural world is a "free revelation of God's love and lordship."

lives ended tragically. "Every genuine and great history ends tragically"[cf. Schelling, chap. 2.2.4 note].[72] In confirmation of this general rule but at its highest point of love, Christ dies a tragic death of sacrifice on behalf of humanity. In dying to sin with him we find salvation in the infinite love of God (§153).

3.5 F. C. BAUR

Ferdinand Christian Baur (1792–1860), professor of theology in Tübingen, belongs to the left wing of mediation theology. In his mind, however, he did not belong at all to mediation theology. For Baur, mediation theology tried to mediate between orthodox Christian doctrines and the new science, and it produced bad history as well as bad theology. But he mediated Christianity and Hegelian philosophy, and in this sense he was a mediation theologian.[73] With the help of his Tübingen School of students and coworkers he was the most important critical historian-theologian of the nineteenth century.[74] He called his method "historical critical" or "purely historical"; his intent was to investigate and relate history objectively "as it had been." New Testament interpretation must be based on clear objective knowledge; otherwise interpretation will be expected to demonstrate what faith believes.[75] Even though his conclusions were often wrong, more than any other historian of the century he laid the tracks, so to speak, for all future historical-critical work on the New Testament. He argued that certain supposed letters of Paul were not by Paul (he thought only Galatians, Romans, and the two Corinthian letters were authentic), that the Acts of the Apostles represented a compromise between Judaistic and Hellenistic Christians, and that the Synoptic Gospels were composed not primarily as myth, as Strauss had argued, but according to each author's particular interests and point of view. The effect of this

72. *Die Tübinger Schule. Ein Sendschreiben an Herrn Dr. F. C. Baur* (Leipzig: Breitkopf und Härtel, 1855), 94. On historical figures, see esp. Hase, *Neue Propheten*, 2nd ed. (Leipzig: Breitkopf und Härtel, 1861): Joan of Arc, Savonarola, Anabaptism.

73. Baur's successor at Tübingen, Carl Weizsäcker, called Baur a mediation theologian because Baur located the essence of Christianity in the (Hegelian) universal: *Jahrbücher für deutsche Theologie* 7 (1862): 811f. On Baur, see Peter Hodgson, *The Formation of Historical Theology: A Study of F. C. Baur* (New York: Harper, 1966); Peter Hodgson, ed. and trans., *Ferdinand Christian Baur on the Writing of Church History* (New York: Oxford University Press, 1968); F. C. Baur, *The Church History of the First Three Centuries*, trans. Allan Menzies, 2 vols. (London: Williams & Norgate, 1878–79). See also R. W. Mackay, *The Tübingen School and Its Antecedents* (London: Williams & Norgate, 1863); Horton Harris, *The Tübingen School* (Oxford: Clarendon, 1975); Christoph Senft, *Wahrhaftigkeit und Wahrheit; die Theologie des 19. Jahrhunderts zwischen Orthodoxie und Aufklärung* (Tübingen: Mohr Siebeck, 1956), 47–86.

74. The most significant members of the Tübingen School were Edward Zeller (1824–1909) and Albert Schwegler (1819–57). Zeller was the editor of the school's journal, *Theologische Jahrbücher*. D. F. Strauss was associated with the school but remained independent of his one-time teacher, Baur. A Hegelian systematic theologian related to the school was the Zurich theologian Aloys E. Biedermann (1819–85); on him, see Claude Welch, *Protestant Thought in the Nineteenth Century*, 1:160–67.

75. Baur, *Vorlesungen über neutestamentliche Theologie*, ed. F. F. Baur, reprint of 1st ed. 1864 (Darmstadt: Wissenschaftliche Buchgesellschaft, 1973), 33ff.

work—together with Strauss's *Life of Jesus*—forced theology in the last half of the century to spend a great deal of time exploring and confirming or refuting its claims and trying to comprehend its consequences.

Baur was thoroughly Hegelian in his theology, so much so that he is often accused of having imposed the Hegelian dialectic of thesis-antithesis-synthesis on his histories. Certainly Hegel's dialectic opened his eyes to "antithetical" historical conflicts, especially in early Christianity, conflicts that had typically been smoothed over in previous theology. He also found moments in the historical church that brought the antitheses into new unity. His church history is largely a dialectic of movement forward from conflicts to ever-new resolutions. One important result was his view that historical development in the post–New Testament period raised Christianity to a higher level than its origin: Christianity became a way to explain the world instead of only a way of salvation. Another result was the reduction of the significance of the New Testament canon, insofar as the history of dogma progressed in ever-higher understanding of Christian truth. Baur also said the canon contained the writings that over time have been and will continue to be recognized by the church to be the "most original and generally valid expressions of the Christian mind."[76] But this too conforms to Hegel's regard, especially in the *Philosophy of Religion,* for the "immediacy" of Christian revelation [chap. 2.3].

In the concluding part of *Die christliche Lehre von der Dreieinigkeit und der Menschwerdung Gottes* (The Christian Doctrine of the Trinity and the Incarnation of God), published in 1843, Baur affirms with Hegel that God comes to consciousness of God in human self-consciousness. God is Spirit, and Spirit as process does not return to the absolutely "unconditioned" [*Unbestimmte*] but gives itself finite forms and therefore also consciousness. "The process consists essentially of God 'determining' or 'conditioning' God's self into finite Spirit."[77] It is only the determinations or conditions of finitude that make personhood or self-consciousness possible, and so it is also with God, who comes to consciousness and personhood in human consciousness. All concepts of God must be developed in human consciousness, and so it is also with God's self-knowledge. The difference between the consciousness or personhood of God and that of human being is that God's personhood is the self-consciousness of the absolute unity of the process, "absolute rest in its [the process's] motion."[78]

Baur agrees with Strauss that the Hegelian Spirit cannot possibly be contained or incarnated in a single individual, the person of Christ, but can only involve all humanity and all of history. "The whole process of world history would have to disappear immediately if God or the Absolute could finalize itself in absolute

---

76. Baur, *Lehrbuch der christlichen Dogmengeschichte,* reprint of the 3rd edition of 1867 (Darmstadt: Wissenschaftliche Buchgesellschaft, 1968), 365. Cf. Christoph Senft, 72–86.

77. F. C. Baur, *Die christliche Lehre von der Dreieinigkeit und der Menschwerdung Gottes in ihrer geschichtlichen Entwicklung. Dritter Teil: Die neuere Geschichte des Dogma, von der Reformation bis in die neueste Zeit* (Tübingen: C. F. Osiander, 1843), 907.

78. Ibid., 930f.

unity in a single individual as in a particular moment. Therefore it is utterly impossible that the Idea in the infinity of its totality is identical with a single individual."[79] What is most important in Christian history is not the individual person of Christ but faith in Christ, that is, the "representation" [*Vorstellung*] of the risen Christ that is the concept in historical form.[80] Therefore, Baur says that, according to Hegel's *Phenomenology*, "what lies behind this faith objectively may rest in itself, namely the 'in itself' of the [historical] person of Christ." According to Baur, the difference between this historical person and faith is like the difference in Kant's philosophy between the unknown "thing in itself" and what actually appears for perception.[81] Regarding the resurrection of Christ, he says, "What the resurrection is in itself lies outside the realm of historical investigation," whether one regards it as a psychological event in the minds of the disciples or as an objective miracle. Historical investigation rather has to do with the faith of the believing disciples, which can be investigated in the texts of the New Testament.[82] In another place he writes, "What lies behind this faith remains veiled in mystery."[83]

In Jesus the "concept" of God and the "knowledge" of the concept unite, but "the concept is the absolutely determining [*das absolut Bestimmende*] and the reality [of the person of Christ] is reduced to mere appearance." "No matter how high one places this individual [Christ], because of the concept of the unity [of all things in God] that comes to consciousness in him, this individual must stand in a subordinate relationship to the concept, and a God-human in the sense intended by the church's doctrine contains an insoluble contradiction."[84] But the contradiction becomes insignificant in the higher development of Christian thought, in the connection of faith and reason or theology and philosophy. God has bound these together in such a way that they go "deep into one another," and they have lived through the historical process of the development of Christianity together. Today their connection is of greatest importance, an importance threatened by conservative trends in the contemporary church and theology, trends that reverse this progress. "To tear them apart [sc. faith and reason, theol-

79. Ibid., 963. [Cf. chap. 2.3 and 2.5.]

80. [Cf. *Vorstellung* and "Idea" in Hegel, chap. 2.3.] Cf. Baur, *Lehrbuch der Dogmengeschichte*, 18: "Christianity entered the world . . . in the form of religion, of revelation, the immediately self-positing absolute God-concept. Because of its utter givenness the subjective consciousness could only relate to it in faith. Therefore Christian dogma has its point of departure in faith. It is faith in the manner of representation [*Vorstellung*], and all thought that relates to dogma . . . has its final determining principle only in faith."

81. Ibid., 971. Cf. Baur's *Kirchengeschichte des Neunzehnten Jahrhunderts* (Church History of the Nineteenth Century), ed. Eduard Zeller, 2nd ed. (Leipzig: Fues, 1877), 398: "Concept and appearance are immediately one only in representation [*Vorstellung*]." See, e.g., further Baur, *Lehrbuch der Dogmengeschichte*, 18.

82. Baur, *Kirchengeschichte der drei ersten Jahrhunderte*, 3rd ed (Tübingen: L. F. Fues, 1863), 39f. This section of the text is translated in Hodgson, *The Formation of Historical Theology*, 235.

83. Baur, *Die christliche Gnosis* (Tübingen: C. F. Osiander, 1835), 712. [Cf. Strauss, chap. 2.5.1.]

84. Baur, *Die christliche Lehre von der Dreieinigkeit*, 992f., 995, 998.

ogy and philosophy]," to conclude that historical development "has had no result at all," would be to leave them in the contradiction in which they now stand in the "consciousness of the time," namely, the contradiction of church on the one hand and science or reason on the other.[85] With this Baur ends *The Christian Doctrine of the Trinity and the Incarnation of God.*

In his later *Vorlesungen über neutestamentiche Theologie* (Lectures on New Testament Theology) Baur developed a more "positive" view of Jesus than he had before, although he denied there was any significant difference. He does not try to give a life of Jesus but a presentation of his "teaching" or, as he also says, the "religion" of Jesus. He bases his presentation on Matthew's Gospel, which according to Baur contains, in spite of later additions, the oldest and most authentic teaching of Jesus. All subsequent development of Christian dogma or theology depends on Jesus' teaching as its "basis and presupposition."[86] Now Jesus' teaching or his religion is at least as important for Christianity as the post-Easter faith of the apostles. Its essence is contained in the relationship of Jesus to the "Father." This relationship has nothing to do with reflection or speculation but is an "immediate consciousness" of God. But the key element is the concept, which is meant by the word "idea" [*Idee*] in the following quotations.[87]

"In the idea of the Father lies . . . the ethical obligation . . . to become similar to God in all moral perfections." "The absolute idea of God is brought to its definite concept and its adequate expression in the idea of the ethical." "If the Father is the ethical idea in itself [*an sich*] . . . , the Son can only be comprehended as the idea that realizes itself [i.e., makes itself real in the concrete], and the more perfectly the idea is realized, all the more perfectly is the unity of the Son with the Father given."[88] This is, Baur writes, "the substantial core of Christianity, to which all else, however great its significance, stands in a more or less secondary relationship, . . . [and it] is in itself already the whole of Christianity." It makes itself known "in the simple sentences of the Sermon on the Mount as the purest content of the teaching of Jesus." It has the "form of religion" in the "righteousness" in the sermon, for righteousness stands in the "most immediate relationship" to the kingdom of God and has therefore to do not only with the relationship of human beings to each other but also with their relationship to God. The human will is submitted to God in complete reconciliation with God.[89] "Father" and "Son" relate to each other, as in Hegel, as concept and concrete appearance, and Baur's discussion of Jesus' ethics has its parallel in what Hegel says about the Sermon on the Mount and the kingdom of God in the *Philosophy of Religion* [chap. 2.3]. In

85. Ibid., 998f.

86. *Vorlesungen über neutestamentiche Theologie,* 45. These lectures were begun in the early 1850s and published posthumously in their final form at Baur's death.

87. In the following quotations "idea" is the translation of Baur's word *Idee,* which means "concept." [See Chap. 2.3, note 80, on the difference between "Idea" and "Idee."]

88. *Vorlesungen,* 116f.

89. Ibid., 64–70.

the *Phenomenology* Hegel characterized the attitude and behavior of Christ and the early Christians in terms of complete unity with God. Evil has no place here.[90]

In a work written close to the end of his life, *Kirchengeschichte des 19. Jahrhunderts* (Church History of the Nineteenth Century), Baur gives a pessimistic assessment of theology and church, and in doing so he gives an evaluation of the significance of new developments, especially the work of the Young Hegelians, Feuerbach and Strauss. Summing up the influence especially of Feuerbach, he writes that "the principle of our time is human self-consciousness as the absolute power over everything, as the most immediate thing humanity has to hold to; but if one does not set the truth of self-consciousness in the general or universal [*das Allgemeine*]—which is the chief matter in Hegel and which is the presupposition of all thinking and willing—then everything that gives life unity and connection is dissolved into the raw dominance of egotism."[91] For Baur, Strauss is too negative in what he states as the results of his historical work.[92] For the present there remains the dilemma of the "irreconcilable" difference between "the old faith and modern science." "Therefore," Baur writes in dry resignation, "it can only be left to each person to find a way beyond this and hence subjectively [in his or her own mind] to resolve the bifurcation that has come into the general consciousness of our time" [cf. Strauss, chap. 2.5.1]. Never before has this division caused a complete break between science and church as now seems to be the case. Baur laments the current situation as one in which, instead of conducting the conflict about what is "positive" in Christianity with scientific means, the traditional church itself has become the "positive fact."[93] The remainder of the book is a rather harsh critique of the contemporary churches and of both confessional and mediation theology. Neither meets the contemporary need for free, unbiased science, which is the only means of truly moving forward. The mediation theologians, who claim value-free science, "no longer have the right mind for the old [orthodox] system but also do not have the energy and courage to raise themselves to a new one; they know that they are not one with the church, and yet they do not risk breaking with it."[94] And neither does Baur.

---

90. *Phenomenology of Spirit*, 469f., 471f.
91. *Kirchengeschichte des 19. Jahrhunderts*, 416; cf. 373, where Baur says that for Hegel the ego sacrifices itself because its true self is the general or universal [*das Allgemeine*]. "The I knows itself as 'Allgemeines,' and this 'Allgemeine' is God as the absolute Spirit that gives itself the determination of being subjective Spirit [the ego]." [Cf. Hegel, chap. 2.3.]
92. Ibid., 416ff.
93. Ibid., 426f.
94. Ibid., 427–34.

Chapter 4

Ritschlianism and Liberal Theology

4.1 NEO-KANTIANISM: F. A. LANGE AND HERMANN LOTZE

The era of Bismarck saw a significant leap forward not only in the expansion of industrialization but also in empirical science, especially after Darwin's work was introduced in the early 1860s. Now a "realist" philosophy, Neo-Kantianism, emerged as dominant. One of its characteristics was a growing division between the understanding of human spirit [*Geist*] and nature, which was increasingly seen as the object of technical science. Neo-Kantianism can be more narrowly or more broadly defined, insofar as it names both a specific school and a broad trend of philosophical thought. Like Kant it separated moral reason and religion from what Kant had called "pure reason," the scientific understanding of phenomena. Kant's "thing in itself" was maintained as a term referring to the force or forces that underlie phenomena. With his 1866 publication *Geschichte des Materialismus* (History of Materialism), Friedrich Albert Lange (1828–75), the initiator of the Marburg School of Neo-Kantianism, is credited more than any other with giving the new philosophical movement definition. Lange argued that both the phenomenal world of nature and the capacity with which we perceive it are "products of our organization" (our minds), but all such products are "mere pictures of what is truly present," that is, of the "vibrations and motions of every kind with which we must think the surrounding media are filled."[1] Science is limited to the investigation of empirical phenomena and as a consequence has to do with partial aspects of the whole in which humanity lives. Only metaphysics, religion, and the practical philosophy of the motivations and goal of human actions have ideas of the whole. But none of these can claim scientific truth for their ideas of the whole.[2] They do, however, have a kind of truth: "poetic" truth, validated first by their "ethical value" (in parallel to the "good" of Kant's moral will) and by the need of humanity for such ideas and ideals of the whole. This is a kind of pragmatism, which is common in Neo-Kantian religious thought [cf. Feuerbach, chap. 2.5.2]. Lange speaks of religious visionaries and prophets, mystery and holy awe, and the ideas that produced the great domes of the Middle Ages. "Poetic truth" is exclusively a product of the creative imagination, and it changes over time. Religion changes its forms in response to the progressive development of the scientific view of the world [cf. Fries, chap. 2.8]. One knows today, Lange says, that traditional dogmas cannot be scientifically true, although they may retain poetic validity.[3] Even though the present is a time when old religious forms are losing their appeal, a "time of harvest" will come when a "lightning flash of genius" will again "create out of the atoms a whole."[4]

Theology was most influenced by variations in Neo-Kantianism that offered more positive ways to understand religion, especially by the work of Rudolf Hermann Lotze (1817–81), who was Albrecht Ritschl's colleague at Göttingen. A sign of the new empiricism is his acceptance of Darwinian human evolution from ape-like primates.[5] Lotze is especially known for his theory of values or the good. According to Lotze the mistake of traditional metaphysics, including Idealism, lies in its belief that abstract ideas are realities [cf. Schelling, chap. 2.4.2], when in fact they are no more than subjective deductions derived from the experience of a world in constant change.[6] According to Lotze, what is real is what is given in experience or the phenomena we perceive; yet what is given is also more than the phenomena. This "more" must be assumed in order to account for the vitality of life that we experience in phenomena. There must be a multitude of living forces underlying phenomena, which, because of their interactive relation to each

1. F. A. Lange, *Geschichte des Materialismus*, 1st ed. (Iserlohn: J. Baedeker, 1866), 497, 491. A later correction was that "our organization" is itself a product of what makes the phenomenal world, which reduces the implication of subjective idealism, i.e., that the world is the product of the ego [Fichte, chap. 2.2.2].

2. Ibid., 272, 538.

3. Ibid., 538–57. See the translation of the expanded and revised 2nd ed. of 1873: *History of Materialism*, trans. E. C. Thomas, 3 vols. (London: Trübner & Ludgate Hill, 1879–81), 3: 280–91, 335–62.

4. *Geschichte des Materialismus*, 552.

5. On Darwin, see Lotze, *Metaphysic*, trans. Bernard Bosanquet, 2nd ed., 2 vols. (Oxford: Clarendon, 1887), 2:158f.; *Microcosmus*, trans. Elizabeth Hamilton and E. E. Constance Jones, 2nd ed. (New York: Scribner & Welford, 1887), 1:526f. See also Lange on Darwin, *Geschichte*, 397–403.

6. Lotze, *Metaphysic*, 1:192–230; *Microcosmus*, 2:318–60; *Outlines of Logic and the Encyclopaedia of Philosophy*, trans. George Ladd (Boston: Ginn, 1887), 164–69.

other, are parts of one great living spiritual reality, God, who unites them in a purposeful whole. God is the "one infinite being" and omniscient and omnipotent person. God must be person, insofar as God, like human beings, is a spiritual reality that maintains identity in change.[7] The phenomena we perceive as the world of nature, including human bodily life, form a mechanism of causes and effects. But human life is both natural and spiritual. Experience teaches us the higher value of spiritual over bodily reality, especially the value of morality.[8] Religiousness or faith, which is a natural human need, directs us to attempt to comprehend the whole in which we live and our purpose in it.[9] Humanity learns to avoid natural egotism (sin) and to be guided by the idea of value and the highest good, God, whose ethical qualities are summarized in eternal "living love" and in whom the purpose of life and happiness are found.[10]

In Lotze's judgment the Platonic ideas represent the classical mistake of all metaphysics. Like Plato, all subsequent metaphysics finds reality in ideas that are "behind" the real, phenomenal world. For Lotze, God is not above and behind the world, but present in it as its life source. The living "one infinite being" is "unconditioned," insofar as it is not dependent on anything else. What Lotze intends is the vitality of the whole, the living God in all reality as the conscious and personal unity that directs it toward the highest good.[11] He interprets Christianity accordingly. Since God is "the supreme principle of good," Christian dogmas should be reformulated to conform with this principle, as our "feeling" confirms. They should not conflict with modern science, for otherwise they are alienated from the reality of the modern world.[12] In his lectures on philosophy of religion Lotze limits the content of religious truth to three points: "We name (1) the moral laws the will of God; (2) the individual finite spirits [human beings] not products of nature but children of God; (3) reality not simply the course of the world but a Kingdom of God." These three points are the basic content of Christian revelation. He accepts the uniqueness of Christ's relationship to God, while he finds the doctrine of the substitutionary atonement by the sacrifice of Christ incompatible with modern thought. Christian faith, he says, delivers us from fear and hopelessness by teaching that the evil we experience is a divine discipline and a preparation for life after death.[13]

---

7. Lotze, *Microcosmus*, 2:600f., 672–87. The perception of space is for Lotze subjective (as for Kant), but temporal sequence is only partly subjective: ibid., 603f., 708ff. For his view of the "One Infinite Being" Lotze recognizes partial antecedents in Spinoza and the early Schelling, but they err in describing the relationship between the Absolute and concrete life as a "dualism" instead of a unity: *Metaphysic*, 2:4ff.; *Grundzüge der Religionsphilosophie*, 2nd ed. (Leipzig: Hirzel, 1884), 27.

8. *Microcosmus*, 1:682–714. Natural reality is "organized by relations of reciprocal conditioning." Ibid., 710.

9. Ibid., 2:115f., 475–94 (Christianity), esp. 486f.; cf. 305–60 ("Truth and Science").

10. Ibid., 671ff., 699, esp. 721ff.

11. Ibid., 663–69, 677, 699, 728; cf. 480: "the spiritual world which though unseen is everywhere." Cf. *Metaphysic*, 1:165: "the unconditioned Being which must lie at the foundation of this process of the conditioned." Cf. further Lotze, *Grundzüge der Religionsphilosophie*, 12f.

12. *Microcosmus*, 481–88.

13. *Grundzüge der Religionsphilosophie*, 86–95.

4.2 ALBRECHT RITSCHL

Early in his academic career Albrecht Ritschl (1822–89), professor of theology at Göttingen, studied under several mediation theologians of the previous generation, among them Richard Rothe, but he soon became a student of F. C. Baur and Baur's Tübingen School.[14] His first major work was in New Testament criticism. He was inclined to a more traditional interpretation of the authenticity of the New Testament authorship and history than was Baur, which eventually led to a break.[15] The biography by his son notes that in 1864 he read Lotze's *Microcosmus* "with great enjoyment." Not until later, however, did he associate himself with Lotze in his publications, namely, in the 1881 publication *Theology and Metaphysics,* and in the third volume of the second edition (1883) of his major work, *The Christian Doctrine of Justification and Reconciliation.*[16] Particularly in its relationship to Lotze, Ritschl's theology appears as a new form of mediation theology. The first volume of *Justification and Reconciliation* is a critical history of these doctrines since the Middle Ages; the second treats the doctrines in the New Testament. In the third volume Ritschl gives his own theological interpretation. It was especially the popularity of this third volume, first published in 1874, that brought about the formation of the Ritschlian School of theologians. The English translation of the third edition of this volume is the work discussed here.[17]

In the introduction Ritschl addresses the "scientific" nature of theology. "Revelation must be given" in order that theology can interpret it scientifically.[18] "The formally correct expression of theological propositions depends on the method we follow in defining the objects of cognition, that is, on the theory of knowl-

14. Recent works on Ritschl: Philip Hefner, *Faith and the Vitalities of History* (New York: Harper & Row, 1966); David Mueller, *An Introduction to the Theology of Albrecht Ritschl* (Philadelphia: Westminster, 1969); James Richmond, *Ritschl: A Reappraisal; A Study in Systematic Theology* (Glasgow: Collins, 1978); Rolf Schäfer, *Ritschl* (Tübingen: Mohr Siebeck, 1968); see also Claude Welch's chapter on Ritschl in *Protestant Thought in the Nineteenth Century,* 2:1–30.

15. The break with Baur came with the 2nd edition of Ritschl's *Die Entstehung der altkatholischen Kirche* (Bonn: Adolph Marcus, 1857), in which Ritschl directly attacks several of Baur's key theses and conclusions, e.g., the inauthenticity of Acts: see 104, 123, 128, 138, 149. The definitive biographical work on Ritschl is by his son, Otto Ritschl, *Albrecht Ritschls Leben,* 2 vols. (Freiburg: Mohr Siebeck, 1892, 1896); on Ritschl and Baur, see vol. 1, chaps. 5–8. See also Horton Harris, *The Tübingen School* (Oxford: Clarendon, 1975), 101–12. Martin Kähler calls the early Ritschl "a complete Hegelian": *Geschichte der protestantischen Dogmatik,* 209.

16. *Ritschls Leben,* 2:20. We use the English translation of the short work, *Theology and Metaphysics,* by Philip Hefner in Ritschl, *Three Essays* (Philadelphia: Fortress, 1972), 151–217. The other two essays are *Instruction in the Christian Faith* (originally conceived as a catechism) and the Prolegomena to the *History of Pietism.* Lotze's infuence is probable in Ritschl's discussion of the misuse of metaphysics in theology in an article from the year 1865: A. Ritschl, *Gesammelte Aufsätze,* ed. Otto Ritschl, 2 vols. (Freiburg and Leipzig: Mohr Siebeck, 1893, 1896), 2:27–30; cf. an article from the year 1871: 1:149f.

17. Ritschl, *The Christian Doctrine of Justification and Reconciliation,* trans. H. R. Mackintosh and A. B. Macaulay, 3 vols. (Edinburgh: T. & T. Clark, 1902). The original publication is *Die christliche Lehre von der Rechtfertigung und der Versöhnung,* 3 vols. (Bonn: Marcus, 1870–74). Ritschl himself prepared the 2nd and 3rd editions, each with additions.

18. *Justification and Reconciliation,* 3:24.

edge." He expressly identifies his own theory of knowledge or perception with Lotze's. Human life, he says, is guided by good or value, and the highest good is God. He rejects the method of metaphysics that reasons abstractly about God and ideas "behind" reality.[19] The key to comprehending God and the purpose of human life lies in human being's discernment in making value judgments. Science and religion are "different functions of spirit." While "religious knowledge" consists in value judgments, "scientific knowledge seeks to discover the laws of nature and spirit through observation." Natural science has to do with the "mechanical regularity of sensible things" interpreted by the law of causality. This is its limitation. The more important task, comprehending the unity of the world, is motivated by religion.[20] "Religious knowledge of God can be demonstrated as religious knowledge only when God is conceived as securing the believer such a position in the world as more than counterbalances its restrictions. Apart from this value judgment, there exists no knowledge of God worthy of this content."[21]

Kant is correct in saying, in the *Critique of Judgment,* that human moral freedom and the hope of happiness require the existence of the moral creator and "supreme good," God, who "sets the final end before us." However, Kant is mistaken in thinking that "practical" reason is separate from theoretical or scientific reason and that its perceptions are not scientifically valid. The moral will is a reality within the field of scientific perception; knowledge of it is knowledge of the "laws of spiritual life." All higher human life demonstrates that "spiritual life is the end, while nature is the means." Ritschl concludes: "Now we must either resign the attempt to comprehend the ground and law of the coexistence of nature and spiritual life, or we must . . . acknowledge the Christian conception of God as the truth by which our knowledge of the universe is consummated." And "by following this path we find that science is bound to accept the Christian idea of God."[22]

Ritschl was above all a historian, and the bulk of his work is in history. Although his work spread over the whole of church history, he had special appreciation for Luther and the Reformation. He was, however, selective in what he appreciated; he excluded both Luther's allegiance to the pre-Reformation confessions of the church and his eschatology.[23] The pre-Reformation confessions, which were part of the orthodox Lutheran tradition, were in Ritschl's view formulated in terms of antique metaphysics. Theology should have to do only with

19. Ibid., 14–25. In *Theology and Metaphysics* Ritschl discusses the same points with reference to Lotze and with emphasis on the theory of perception and the rejection of metaphysics. Ritschl calls the God of metaphysics the "shadow of the world" (180) and metaphysics itself, as implicitly a devaluation of this world because the truth is beyond it, "Buddhist" (161).

20. Ibid., 194, 207–9.

21. Ibid., 212f.

22. Ibid., 219–24. Ritschl's theory of faith as value judgment later earned him the criticism that his system is an "inversion of faith" that puts human being in the center and makes God "an instrument, not an end" (H. Richard Niebuhr, *The Meaning of Revelation* [New York: Macmillan, 1962], 31).

23. On Ritschl's interpretation of Luther, see esp. David W. Lotz, *Ritschl and Luther* (Nashville and New York: Abingdon, 1974).

the presentation of God and Christ as given in Scripture and mediated by the church, not with supposed metaphysical realities "behind" them. Such notions, he said, have corrupted theological thinking since the postapostolic age of the church.[24] Ritschl saw two conflicting confessional directions in Luther's Christology. One affirmed the divine person of Christ, as expressed in the pre-Reformation confessions. The other, the one more important for Luther, is the doctrine of Christ the redeemer who awakens trust in himself and in God. This confession of personal trust, which is experiential, is something other than the traditional confessional metaphysical statements about, for example, the preexistence of Christ "eternally begotten of the Father" in the Nicene Creed. Luther left the conflict between the two confessional directions unresolved. His close associate Philip Melanchthon, however, taught that the doctrine of the work of Christ the redeemer was primary.[25] Ritschl finds that the New Testament agrees with this primary direction of Christology in Luther and in Melanchthon: Christ the redeemer is central, and all attributes of his divinity are directly related to this. The apostles' witness to the resurrection of Christ confirms what the believer today knows through the trust-awakening experience of faith, namely, that Christ mediates justification and reconciliation, which result in the believer's spiritual freedom and dominion over the world.[26] And Christian freedom is never that of the isolated individual, but life in the community that Jesus founded, as Schleiermacher taught.[27]

With reference especially to the early Luther (e.g., *The Freedom of a Christian*, 1520), Ritschl teaches that Christian freedom is essentially freedom for life in the world, that is, for vocation. Vocation is the service of the moral kingdom of God in one's own concrete life and circumstances: in the family, at work, in the community, in the state. Each person, in fulfilling her or his vocation, serves the progressive development of the kingdom of God, which is God's purpose for the world. (Religion generally is "an interpretation of man's relation to God and the world, guided by the thought of the sublime power of God to realize the end of [the] blessedness of man.")[28] Christian vocation includes the love and trust of God and the love of neigh-

---

24. *Justification and Reconciliation*, 3:6f., 211–13, 226.

25. Ibid., 396, where Ritschl quotes from Melanchthon's *Loci communes*, "to know Christ is to know his benefits." Cf. ibid., 394ff. In the *Loci* of 1521, Melanchthon writes against Catholic dogmas: "This is to know Christ, to wit, to know his benefits and not as they teach, to perceive his natures and the mode of his incarnation" (*The Loci Communes of Philip Melanchthon*, trans. Charles Leander Hill [Boston: Meador Publishing Co., 1944], 68).

26. Ibid., 391–406; *Three Essays: Instruction in the Christian Religion*, §§20–24. Ritschl rejects the possiblity of a depiction of the "religion of Jesus" for the purpose of the imitation of his religion, for only he is the author of forgiveness: *Justification and Reconciliation*, 3:2. Jesus is "for himself" with his "own personal self-end" in relationship to God (ibid., 442ff.). Ritschl's main biblical text for "spiritual dominion" is Mark 8:36f.: ibid., 223. See also Ritschl's summaries on justification and reconciliation: ibid., 78f., 85, 139.

27. In *Die Lehre von der Rechtfertigung und der Versöhnung*, 3rd ed. (Bonn: Adolf Markus, 1889), 1:555, Ritschl remarks that Schleiermacher's "epoch making significance lies in his idea that all individual spiritual life can only be rightly understood in the relation . . . to the community." Cf. ibid., 496.

28. *Justification and Reconciliation*, 3:194f. [Cf. mediation theology in chap. 3.]

bor that bonds the community into one purpose.[29] Traditional theology has laid far more weight on personal justification and redemption than on the "ethical interpretation of Christianity through the idea of the Kingdom of God." For Ritschl both are necessary: they are the "two principal characteristics of Christianity," so that Christianity is to be understood as "an ellipse which is determined by two foci."[30]

The development of the moral kingdom among Christian nations is also a purpose of the kingdom of God. It was prepared in history by the development of "the moral fellowship of the family, national fellowship in the state, and, lastly, the combination of several nations in the World-empire." "The Christian concept of the Kingdom of God stands in closest analogy with all these graduated forms, and is in part genetically derived from them." Ritschl refers especially to the preparatory developments in the Roman Empire, both its government and its law, including the "legal recognition of the individual."[31] The "justitia civilis," the state, is a "necessary and integral part of God's moral order."[32]

Ritschl was, like Hegel, highly critical of pietism because of its otherworldly character. Like both the monasticism and the ascetic Anabaptism of the Reformation period, pietism has the very opposite view from Ritschl of vocation in the world. None of the three frees the Christian for life in the real world. Like metaphysics they occupy themselves with what is "behind" or beyond it.[33] The criticism of pietism is closely related to Ritschl's criticism of eschatology. As a New Testament theologian, and like his former teacher, F. C. Baur, Ritschl thought early Christian eschatology, as a negation of the world, was a distortion of Jesus' ethical teaching of the kingdom of God. Jesus, he said, meant the kingdom as a reality in this world.[34] For Ritschl, however, progress toward the kingdom was not destined to bring complete reconciliation and happiness on earth. These were to be found after death in heaven, one's final spiritual destination.[35] Ritschl's understanding of

29. Ibid., 8–14, 661–70 (and throughout). The kingdom, the "highest good," unites the redeemed in the moral community. In the community of love, the purpose of each person belongs to the purpose of all the others. Ibid., 320, 511–14, 520f., 548–50. Trust in God and God's providence: 321, 326.

30. Ibid., 10f.

31. Ritschl adds that the benefits of Rome's legacy were "lamentably counterbalanced by the prevalence of slavery, that fountain of every kind of immorality" (Ibid., 311).

32. *Justification and Reconciliation,* 3:309, 312f., 316. On civil justice: *Three Essays: Instruction,* §60ff.; *Justification and Reconciliation,* 3:315f.

33. Ritschl, *Three Essays,* 53–139 (from the Prolegomena to Ritschl's *History of Pietism*), 157f., 183 (from *Theology and Metaphysics*). See also *Justification and Reconciliation,* 3:18f., 112–14, 155ff. Other than the "Prolegomena" Ritschl's history of pietism is not translated: *Geschichte des Pietismus,* 3 vols. (Bonn: Adolf Markus, 1880–86); on pietism, see *Justification and Reconciliation,* 1: chap. 10.

34. *Three Essays: Instruction,* §§1ff., 76f. See also *Justification and Reconciliation,* 30ff.; against end-time eschatology: 613. Cf. the similar views of F. C. Baur, *Vorlesungen über neutestamentliche Theologie:* on Jesus and end-time eschatology: 105–12; on Jesus' ethics of the kingdom of God: 51, 62–75; on his messianic self-consciousness: 75–105. For Baur (ibid., 129ff.; cf. 67), the significance of Christ's death as a sacrifice of forgiveness and reconciliation first arises in post-Easter doctrine; for Ritschl, forgiveness and reconciliation are proclaimed by Jesus himself: *Justification and Reconciliation,* 2: §7; 3: §55f. See also Gerald W. McCulloh, *Christ's Person and Life-Work in the Theology of Albrecht Ritschl* (New York: University Press of America, 1990).

35. *Three Essays: Instruction,* §§17, 76; *Justification and Reconciliation,* 3:§52.

the life of the spirit and of spiritual dominion over nature is reflected in his interpretation of the New Testament miracles, which is similar to Schleiermacher's: they are "not contrary to nature," but they should also not be explained by science, for they are expressions of spiritual value. To explain them scientifically is to prejudge what may only be encountered in spiritual reality, not in nature.[36]

Theology must present the truth and rule of God as eternal, not as we perceive it "under the form of time."[37] The "Christian world-view" is a "unified world-view" and must be presented as a whole, rather like Lotze's purposeful whole of God and world. Ritschl expresses this whole as a "completed" or "closed world-view" [eine geschlossene Weltanschauung], and as a "completed" or "closed whole" [ein geschlossenes Ganze].[38] As in Hegel's rational knowledge of the Absolute, there are no gaps and no mysteries; each piece fits logically and even with simplicity within the whole. Instruction for the Christian laity is also relatively simple and straightforward: believe in God's love (justification and reconciliation) and the moral law, do your duty in the "natural orders" of world-life (family, vocation, state, etc.), and realize personal spiritual dominion in the certainty of the future completion of this dominion in heaven.[39]

The "natural orders" of life in the world have the value of being good, much as for Hegel the given world was reasonable. One example of good order for Ritschl is that the rule of princes over the church is a right arrangement, insofar as it keeps the church from being "a state within the state" and, in freeing the pastors from politics, protects their moral authority.[40] There is for Ritschl no serious contrast between church and world. If one makes sound, reasonable value judgments, one must be Christian; and a reasonable world must be a Christian world. Ritschl's requirement of a moral Christian order for the state suggests a social consciousness and social reform. He made no proposals for such reform, but he directed all responsible parties to do their duty for the kingdom of God.

Ritschl attracted talented theologians to his theology, above all, Wilhelm Herrmann and Adolf Harnack. Ritschlianism rapidly gained popularity, and soon almost an entire generation of German and Swiss pastors identified themselves with it. In relatively close connection with the Ritschlians, the history of religions school of critical historical research developed. Often called New Protestantism,

---

36. *Three Essays: Instruction*, §25; *Theology and Metaphysics*, 193f., 203–6.

37. *Justification and Reconciliation*, 3:322–25.

38. Ritschl, *Die christliche Lehre von der Rechtfertigung und Versöhnung*, reprint of the 2nd ed. of 1888 (Hildesheim: George Olms, 1978), 3:187, 189. The English translation gives for both expressions: "completely rounded view of the world": *Justification and Reconciliation*, 3:200, 203; cf. 617.

39. Such instruction is actually typical of Protestant lay instruction in the nineteenth century. It parallels the tradition of common-sense evangelicalism in the United States. See, e.g., the "simple" gospel of Christianity and moral cultural values in the representative figure of Robert Baird (1798–1863) in Mark Noll, *America's God* (Oxford: Oxford University Press, 2002), 441–43; cf. 233–38.

40. *Three Essays: Instruction*, §88. In an interesting parallel, one historian says that Bismarck sensed in both the Catholic and Protestant churches "the desire for power" of a *Nebenregierung*, i.e., a government alongside that of the state or, as one can also say, a state within the state (Heinrich Hermelink, *Das Christentum in der Menschheitsgeschichte*, 2:602). On natural orders, cf. *Justification and Reconciliation*, 3:516.

together they dominated German theology from the end of the nineteenth century until the end of World War I, and their influence extends into the present.

4.3 WILHELM HERRMANN

Wilhelm Herrmann (1846–1922) studied in Halle with August Tholuck and was for most of his life professor of theology in Marburg, where he counted Karl Barth and Rudolf Bultmann among his students. During his academic career his appreciation grew for Schleiermacher's theology, namely, as theological thought grounded in the personal experience of the reality of Christ. He was well known for the spiritual edification of the reflection periods following his lectures, something that is attributed to the influence of Tholuck and the Awakening. He had considerable impact on the spiritual and academic formation of a generation of pastors. His most popular work, *The Communion of the Christian with God*, received attention in England and America.[41] He was one of the first theologians to be drawn to Ritschl.[42] Like Ritschl he agreed in the main with the Neo-Kantian critique of metaphysics, finding in it support for Luther's separation of reason and faith. Luther's distinction between the gospel on the one hand and human reason and the law on the other is a dominant theme in all of Herrmann's works.[43]

At Marburg, Herrmann was in conversation with the two most important Neo-Kantian philosophers of the time, Hermann Cohen (1842–1918), who was F. A. Lange's successor, and Paul Natorp (1854–1924). The Marburg School of Neo-Kantianism abandoned Kant's concept of the "thing in itself" as a remnant

41. *The Communion of the Christian with God*, ed. Robert Voelkel, reprint of the 2nd English edition of 1906 (Philadelphia: Fortress Press, 1971). Other translated works are *Faith and Morals*, trans. Donald Matheson and Robert W. Stewart, 2 vols. (New York: G. P. Putnam's Sons, 1904); *Systematic Theology*, trans. Nathaniel Micklem and Kenneth Saunders (London: George Allen & Unwin, 1927) (The German edition of this work, *Dogmatik*, was posthumously published from lecture notes in 1925); and with Adolf Harnack, *Essays on the Social Gospel*, trans. G. M. Craik (New York: G. P. Putnam's Sons, 1907). On Herrmann, see Robert Voelkel, *The Shape of the Theological Task* (Philadelphia: Westminster, 1968); Helmut Thielicke, *Modern Faith and Thought*, 344–61; Bruce L. McCormack, *Karl Barth's Critically Realistic Dialectical Theology*, 49–68; Simon Fisher, *Revelatory Positivism?* 123–69 [see McCormack and Fisher in the section on K. Barth in chap. 6.1 note 3]; Peter Fischer-Appelt, *Metaphysik im Horizont der Theologie Wilhelm Herrmanns* (Munich: Christian Kaiser, 1965).

42. See the references to Herrmann in Otto Ritschl's biography, *Ritschls Leben*. Herrmann can affirm with Ritschl that "value judgment" is the basis of the religious view of the world (Herrmann, *Die Religion im Verhältnis zum Welterkennen und zur Sittlichkeit* [Halle: Max Niemeyer, 1879], 84–91). For Herrmann as for Ritschl, one finds in Jesus "the power to triumph inwardly over the circumstances upon which we remain outwardly dependent"; it liberates us "from all fear of man." And for Herrmann an important task of the church was "to permeate culture with the power of true religion" (*Systematic Theology*, 15, 52f.).

43. Law and reason define the reality of the "natural" world. Like Schleiermacher, Herrmann divides his work on ethics into two parts, "natural" or "philosophical" and "Christian." As most Lutheranism in this period, he sees the state as a natural institution based on a *Volk* and its culture. It has the task of maintaining *Volk* and culture among the nations. Self-assertion, including if necessary war, is the state's character—not love. It should be neither a democracy nor rule by a single person (Herrmann, *Ethik*, 4th ed. [Tübingen: Mohr Siebeck, 1909], §28, 204–14).

of prescientific myth. What they understood as the "limitation" of science had to do only with the unending series of problems science faces. Cohen found the significance of religion in moral value.[44] For Natorp, religion is a "feeling" of unity, but this feeling has no relationship to a transcendent reality. It is universally human and has its own province of mental life (as in Schleiermacher's *Speeches*). Religion errs when it develops from feeling what it thinks is a knowledge of God. Science corrects the error.[45] For Herrmann, Cohen's and Natorp's perception of both science and religion was deficient. In his work of 1879, *Die Religion im Verhältnis zum Welterkennen und zur Sittlichkeit* (Religion in Relationship to World-Perception and to Morality), Herrmann revives Kant's argument that in the natural sciences there is an unending regression of causes and effects in which everything is conditioned by something else. In "feeling," however, we have a sense of the "unconditioned" as the negative boundary of conditioned things and a sense of the human soul as beyond or not subject to causal explanation. Moreover, the sciences work on the assumption of purpose and meaning in nature. Such presuppositions are not given in science itself but "arise in the feeling and willing human spirit." The life of the spirit or soul is in truth therefore the presupposition of the sciences. An important aspect of the life of the soul is the search in moral earnestness for the meaning of life.[46]

In his later lectures on *Systematic Theology* Herrmann says that prior to faith persons are led by their inner lives, their moral seriousness, to search for the final purpose of their being and actions. There is "craving for religion" and "despair" in not finding the needed answer. This is also necessary, for "religion can only arise with the will to truth."[47] It is a preparatory step toward the acceptance of revelation. *The Communion of the Christian with God* closes with a section on science and faith that affirms—with Schleiermacher—that "science has no part" in the "thoughts of faith," and no "bridge" exists between faith and "all that science can acknowledge to be real." Faith, Herrmann says, is based on a particular personal experience of God that is God's gift to the Christian within the given world. "Where we are, there is the world." Hence it is illusion to think one can find God beyond the world; instead one has found only "a part of the world" or an abstraction of it.[48]

According to Herrmann, Christian faith is given through personal encounter with Jesus, the "ground" of faith. This encounter is defined more specifically as

<hr/>

44. Simon Fisher, *Revelatory Positivism?* 19–122, esp. 33f., 22–26, 38f.; cf. 265. See also Andrea Poma, *The Critical Philosophy of Hermann Cohen*, trans. John Denton (Albany: State University of New York, 1997), on Herrmann: 118, 162, 201, 215.
45. Paul Natorp, *Religion innerhalb der Grenzen der Humanität* (Tübingen: Mohr Siebeck, 1908), 38–61, 99–102.
46. *Die Religion im Verhältnis zum Welterkennen und zur Sittlichkeit*, 15–67, esp. 50–53; 356–59. See also Herrmann's essay on Cohen and Natorp in Herrmann, *Gesammelte Aufsätze*, ed. F. W. Schmidt (Tübingen: Mohr Siebeck, 1923), 377–405.
47. *Systematic Theology*, 19, 37f. In faith one is freed "from care and despondency." Ibid., 52.
48. Herrmann, *Schriften zur Grundlegung der Theologie*, ed. Peter Fischer-Appelt, 2 vols. (Munich: Christian Kaiser, 1967), 1:187. Cf. *Systematic Theology*, 31f.

the encounter with Jesus' "inner life," his constant communion with God, which is expressed in the Gospels' "picture" of Jesus' life and teaching [cf. Rothe, chap. 3.2].[49] The encounter occurs not only by means of this picture of Jesus but also through the proclamation of the church and the personal lives of Christians. Being drawn into this reality, into communion with God, persons of faith know the kingdom of God, which in Jesus' teaching is "above all the rule of God in one's own heart." They enter into a life of prayer and of works of obedience to a power that they know is superior to any other in the world and that rules over them all. The encounter with Jesus' inner life is something other than belief in the miracles and doctrines of the New Testament or the dogmas of the church. Belief in these is not a requirement for salvation. Salvation is received with the forgiveness of sins in the encounter with Jesus, as Jesus forgave sins during his lifetime on faith in him alone. To require faith in miracles and dogmas where the modern moral conscience finds them incredible would be to require a legalistic work and a sacrifice of moral honesty. The miracles are rather to be understood as symbols of the miracle of faith in which God opens a new and wonderful dimension of reality above the natural.[50] We cannot believe as Jesus did in the near end of the world, but we can well understand the relationship of this belief to his ethics of inner freedom from the world.[51] In contrast to problematic miracles and doctrines, Jesus' communion with God is "marvelously simple" in calling forth faith, which is trust in Jesus and through him in God. This trust means personal new birth. Trust is an act of our free will, yet it coincides with the gift of revelation in which we know ourselves "in the grip of a spiritual power" on which we are "utterly dependent."[52] It "sets us in a new existence."[53] The modern scientific world requires validation of what is believed. Faith is validated by the encounter with Jesus.[54]

Herrmann's statement of the "evangelical principle of the authority of Scripture" follows from what is said above: "What we should apprehend in the Scriptures as the indispensable means of salvation is what God is seeking to say to us through the personal life revealing itself there." What cannot be connected with this is not Word of God.[55] "We can only speak of God by speaking of what God

49. The primary source for the following paragraph is *Communion of the Christian*, 40–63, 72f., 76–84, 100–108, 120, 230, 243–52, 328–49.

50. *Schriften zur Grundlegung der Theologie*, 2:170–205, esp. 202–5, 175–83.

51. Ibid., 1:217–37. In *Faith and Understanding*, 265–69, Rudolf Bultmann gives a summary of Johannes Weiss's rather identical understanding of the relationship of Jesus' expectation of the end of the world to his ethics. Weiss was Herrmann's colleague in New Testament at Marburg. [See Bultmann, chap. 6.3.]

52. *Systematic Theology*, 35f. God's love characterizes God's "power over the world" (Herrmann, *Gesammelte Aufsätze*, 487).

53. *Schriften zur Grundlegung der Theologie*, 2:314, 164.

54. See the discussion in *Communion of the Christian*, 66–115.

55. *Systematic Theology*, 59; cf. 58–65. For Herrmann the christological doctrines of Paul and John interpret Jesus' divinity in light of his person and work, as does the Nicene Creed. The Chalcedonian formula of the two natures of Christ is, however, metaphysical. Herrmann does not accept it. Ibid., 139–45.

does to us." At the same time, sound historical criticism is "a requirement of truthfulness."[56] The "factual" Jesus of history is indispensable for faith, for in him the truth of God comes into concrete history.[57] But our encounter with or personal experience of Jesus is not about objective historical facts; it is rather about a different, personal dimension of history: "Nothing in history can belong to us but what we ourselves experience."[58] The picture of Jesus that faith carries in its inner life, its heart and conscience, is "absolute truth" compared to the "relative truth" of the constantly changing results of historical research. As modern science frees us from seeking God in nature, so also it frees us from seeking support for faith in objective history.[59]

Personal encounter with the Jesus of the Gospels is not the encounter with the resurrected Christ, who is hidden from us. Truthfulness requires, Herrmann says, that we be clear on this point. In faith there is indeed hope for heaven, as the spirit "struggles to rise above the earth," but we cannot know what really happened in the contradictory and obscure reports of the resurrection appearances in the New Testament. In any case they show how the power of the person of Jesus impressed itself on the minds of the disciples after his death. But faith does not need to believe these appearances as historical fact, because its own personal experience witnesses to Jesus' undying, immortal life. In this sense, says Herrmann, faith today can joyfully accept the reports of the resurrection appearances.[60] While faith has its own special history in each individual person, it bonds Christians together in Christian community, the church.[61]

4.4 ADOLF HARNACK

Adolf Harnack (1851–1930) was, after prior positions at other universities, professor of church history at the university in Berlin.[62] In both the extent and the importance of the works he published or edited, he was the most significant church historian of his age. Twice he refused a call to Harvard. A member of the

---

56. *Schriften zur Grundlegung der Theologie*, 2:163. According to Herrmann's *Ethik*, §30, 220f., truthfulness is the moral consciousness of religion or faith and the reverent respect for reality that we have when we experience ourselves placed before God and love God. It is the inner clarity from which all moral striving proceeds and is therefore the root of all virtue.

57. *Communion of the Christian*, 102–5; cf. 16–18; 288–96. Cf. *Gesammelte Aufsätze*, 290f.; *Systematic Theology*, 65.

58. Herrmann, *Die mit der Theologie verknüpfte Not der evangelischen Kirche und ihre Überwindung* (Tübingen: Mohr Siebeck, 1913), 24, as quoted by Rudolf Bultmann in *Faith and Understanding*, 134 [chap. 6.3].

59. *Systematic Theology*, 76f.; cf. 16–18. [Cf. *fides divina* and *fides humana* in Rothe, chap. 3.2]. Martin Kähler [chap. 5.1] and George Wobbermin [chap. 4.6 note 81] developed similar theories of two kinds of history, scientific and existential or faith history.

60. *Communion of the Christian*, 293f.; *Systematic Theology*, 125–29.

61. *Systematic Theology*, 32, 148–51.

62. The authoritative biography is Agnes von Zahn-Harnack, *Adolf von Harnack*, 2nd ed. (Berlin: Walter de Gruyter, 1951). In English, see Wayne Glick, *The Reality of Christianity. A Study of Adolf von Harnack as Historian and Theologian* (New York: Harper & Row, 1967).

Prussian Academy of Science and the founding president of the Kaiser Wilhelm Society for the Promotion of the Sciences, he was thoroughly at home in the university culture of Berlin. He was recognized as one of its most prestigious members. For years he was counselor to ministries of the court and to the kaiser himself. He helped write the kaiser's address to the German people calling them to the First World War. He was ennobled "von Harnack" in 1914. He was also aware of the severe social problems in industrial Germany. From 1902 until 1911 he was chairperson of the Evangelical-Social Congress, in which he steered a moderate liberal course away from its earlier socialist direction. He emphasized the need for expert information in dealing with social problems, a characteristic of the German tradition of government by highly educated ministries.[63] For the church in Berlin he was too liberal on church issues to be taken into its leadership. He suggested updating the church's Greek and Roman creeds because they made concepts from Greek metaphysics and the doubtful assertion of the virgin birth the test of faith. In his late work (published 1920) on the second-century heretic Marcion, he went so far as to say only the New Testament should be considered canonical.[64]

One has the advantage with Harnack of having a single book in which he states his theological position, *What Is Christianity?* The original title of the book is *Das Wesen des Christentums,* which is literally translated "The Essence of Christianity."[65] It is based on lectures given in 1899–1900, published in 1900 and immediately translated into English. Easily accessible for Christian laity, it is one of the most popular theological works ever written. It has appeared in many different languages and been reprinted numerous times. Unlike Ritschl and Herrmann, Harnack did not write about contemporary philosophy, but he shares their Neo Kantian orientation. Metaphysics, he says, was introduced into theology when Christianity changed clothes, so to speak, as it moved from Jewish culture to Greek-Hellenistic culture and the gospel was accommodated to this new culture. Christianity outgrew this accommodation when it spread later to other cultures and finally to modern culture (200ff.).[66]

In other ways Harnack demonstrates his Ritschlian orientation. The real content of the gospel is free of all science; its realm is that of the human spirit, and

---

63. See Harnack and Wilhelm Herrmann, *Essays on the Social Gospel.* Most of this work is Harnack's.

64. On the Old Testament, see A. Harnack, *Marcion: The Gospel of the Alien God,* trans. John E. Steely and Lyle D. Bierma (Durham: Labyrinth Press, 1990), 137f.; on Harnack's critique of the Apostles' Creed, see Martin Rumscheidt, ed., *Adolf von Harnack. Liberal Theology at Its Height* (London: Collins, 1989), 200–303; Wayne Glick, *The Reality of Christianity,* 56f.

65. A. von Harnack, *What Is Christianity?* trans. Thomas Bailey Saunders, 1st English ed. 1901 (Philadelphia: Fortress, 1986). The page numbers in the following text refer to this edition. "The Essence of Christianity" was the title of Feuerbach's notorious work, as Harnack well knew. Major historical works by Harnack are in translation: *History of Dogma,* trans. of 3rd German ed. 1900 by Neil Buchanan, 7 vols. in 4 (New York: Dover, 1961); *Outlines of the History of Dogma,* 1st English ed. 1893, trans. Edwin Knox Mitchell (Boston: Beacon Hill, 1959); *The Expansion of Christianity in the First Three Centuries,* trans. James Moffatt, 2 vols. (London: Williams & Norgate; New York: G. P. Putnam's Sons, 1904).

66. Cf. Harnack, *History of Dogma,* 1: chap. 4.

it is experiential: one can confess only the religion that one has experienced (147f.). Faith recognizes that it is not "yoked to blind necessity" or the natural world of cause and effect (30). In whatever situation of worldly life Christians find themselves, they may know that the gospel has all worldly oppositions ultimately "beneath it," such as wealth and poverty, so that like Paul they may "dominate all earthly things and circumstances" (17). Jesus lived in the calm of absolute certainty "above the earth and its concerns" (35f.). The Gospels give a picture of Jesus that shows us not his life story but his teaching, "how his life issued into the service of his vocation," and the impression he made on his disciples (31). New Testament eschatology essentially belongs to the Jewish environment of Christianity, not its essence (52ff.). The aim of the gospel, the conversion of everyone in the world, is "progressively realized through the centuries" (191). It is the "great far-off event, the realized dominion of the Good" (151). Like Ritschl he affirms Luther's doctrine of the Christian freedom of a life of worldly vocation in the "earthly ordinances" in opposition to all forms of asceticism, including pietism. He agrees with Ritschl that Luther did not draw the consequences of his theology, and his thought therefore remains in medieval conceptuality (280).[67] The resurrection of Christ is not scientifically verifiable; instead the certainty of it is gained through faith in communion with the Spirit of Christ (160–63).[68]

In his attention to social righteousness, especially to the relief of the hard lot of the poor (cf. 91–123), Harnack expands thought on moral duty to the kingdom of God. Although the gospel raises each person to spiritual dominion over the world, it "aims at founding a community . . . as wide as human life and as deep as human need. . . . Its object is to transform the socialism which rests on the basis of conflicting interests into the socialism which rests on the consciousness of spiritual unity. In this sense its social message can never be outbid." This belongs to Jesus' proclamation of the kingdom of God and the infinite value of every human soul, with the consequence that "the Gospel is a social message, solemn and overpowering in its force; it is the proclamation of solidarity and brotherliness in favor of the poor" (100f.). "Jesus regarded the possession of worldly goods as a grave danger to the soul, as hardening the heart, entangling us in earthly cares. . . . 'A rich man shall hardly enter the kingdom of heaven'" (93f.).

The unique contribution of Harnack's theology is his understanding of the relationship of human nature, the gospel, and history. With the Augustinian tradition he says, "The heart is restless until it finds rest in God" (8f.). The essential nature of human being remains constant throughout time, while culture changes. The essential and eternal message of the gospel of Jesus is directed to this essential human nature. But the essential gospel is always also enveloped in the form of a specific historical culture. For example, in the Hellenistic world Christianity gave itself a new form by thinking in terms of Greek metaphysics. The task of the historian of Christianity is to recognize what is essential in Christianity and to

67. Cf. ibid., 7:169ff.
68. Cf. ibid., 1:85ff.

show how this essence took form or shape in the history of specific Christian cultures. Therefore Harnack distinguishes between the "husk" (historical culture) and the "kernel" (essential gospel) of Christianity (12ff., 55).[69] His famous definition of the gospel's essence, derived from Jesus' teaching, is composed of three points, each of which is implicit in the other two: "firstly, the kingdom of God and its coming; secondly, God the Father and the infinite value of the human soul; thirdly, the higher righteousness and the commandment to love" (51). The "coming" of the kingdom has nothing to do with apocalyptic eschatology; it rather means that with the message of Jesus God comes into and grasps the soul of the individual person (56). This inner coming of the kingdom is God's gift, not a product of culture; "it is the most important experience" a person can have. It is "the inner link with the living God" and it transforms the person for commitment to the work of Christian love in the world. "It permeates and dominates [a person's] whole existence, because sin is forgiven and misery banished" (62). Harnack often makes the point that this experience is "simple." Repeatedly he says it is "inner," in the "heart" of the Christian person. It gives the person dominion over the world and hence inner peace in all circumstances. It is "eternal life in the midst of time" (8).

There is a certain similarity between Harnack's "essence of Christianity" and Marcion's theology, the subject of his last major work, in which Harnack is also responding to the devastation of World War I and the collapse of the order in which he had played such an important role. The savior Christ of Marcion's theology was wholly other than the creator, who had made a miserable world and ruled it with the legalism of law. Harnack sympathizes with Marcion, but he does not endorse a "modern Marcionism" that would set grace and freedom over against the sinful created world; he will not abandon the hope of the transformation of the world by Christianity.[70]

4.5 WALTER RAUSCHENBUSCH

The most enduring of the American Ritschlians has been Walter Rauschenbusch (1861–1918), Baptist minister and professor of theology at Rochester Theological Seminary. He was the son of a German Baptist minister; at the age of seventeen he entered a Gymnasium in Germany in order to receive the traditional German preparation for ministry. After seminary in Rochester he was for thirteen

69. Cf. Kant's concept of the "shell" of religion in chap. 2.1.3. Hegel speaks of the "husk" of forms that have lost their meaning (*Encyclopedia*, 4). Cf. Ritschl, *Justification and Reconciliation*, 3:613: "We have been accustomed to regard the early Christian expectation of the nearness of the world's end as belonging to the shell and not to the kernel. And there the matter will rest, for that anticipation has not acted prejudicially on any of the positive social duties which follow from Christianity."

70. Harnack, *Marcion*, esp. 142–45. Harnack identifies the Russian mystic Leo Tolstoy (1828–1910) with "modern Marcionism." See *The Religious Writings of Leo Tolstoy* (New York: Julian Press, 1960). In her biography, 398–400, Agnes von Zahn-Harnack discusses the spiritual kinship Harnack felt with Marcion.

years pastor of a church in the rough and destitute Hell's Kitchen area of New York City, where his social conscience was formed.[71] He was well versed in German theology. Ritschlianism became influential in American theology in the 1890s and for some even before; Ritschlian influence on Rauschenbusch was American as well as German.[72] Of particular importance was the publication of Adolf Harnack's *What Is Christianity?* published in English in 1901, one year after its first publication in Germany. Historical works by Harnack had appeared earlier.

Rauschenbusch's theological orientation in his first and most famous work, *Christianity and the Social Crisis,* first published in 1907, is clearly Ritschlian.[73] His main theological source is Harnack. "The Kingdom of God is the true human society; the ethics of Jesus taught the true social conduct which would create the true society" (71). But "Jesus was not a social reformer. Religion was the heart of his life, and all that he said on social relations was said from the religious point of view. He was . . . the inaugurator of a new humanity. But as such he bore within him the germs of a new social and political order" (91). "Jesus had realized the life of God in the soul of man and the life of man in the love of God. . . . He had to teach men to live as children in the presence of their Father . . . [and] that they must enter a new world of love and solidarity and inward contentment" (48). The pursuit of wealth is for Jesus a "profound danger to the better self" (74), and his "fundamental sympathies are with the poor and oppressed" (82).

Jesus' "scientific insight" is his recognition of the "law of organic development," the progressive, gradual growth of the kingdom of God (59f.). Christian history is this progressive development. Rauschenbusch rejects early Christian apocalyptic eschatology as an influence of Jesus' religious environment (59, 112, 115), but not the millennial hope in the return of Christ expressed within it, for the gospel is a message of hope for the social world (103–11). As the church made the transition to acceptance in the Greco-Roman world, it became, through the interest of this culture in immortality, otherworldly and ascetic. Gradually the priority of the kingdom of God was replaced by agreement with church dogma and then by the church itself. With time the church joined with the state in preserving the existing social order (160–94). Luther, in his early work an advocate of reform, later turned to dogmatism and disavowed the cause of the lower classes

71. Christopher H. Evans, *The Kingdom Is Always Coming: A Life of Walter Rauschenbusch* (Grand Rapids: Eerdmans, 2004); Paul M. Minus, *Walter Rauschenbusch: American Reformer* (New York: Macmillan, 1988).

72. See, e.g., Shailer Mathews, *The Social Teachings of Jesus* (New York: Macmillan, 1897). On Mathews: William D. Lindsey, *Shailer Mathews' Lives of Jesus* (Albany: State University of New York Press, 1997). See also William Adams Brown, *The Essence of Christianity* (New York: Charles Scribner's Sons, 1902).

73. *Christianity and the Social Crisis* (New York: Macmillan, 1907). Page references in the following text are to this work unless otherwise noted. It is only in his last work, *A Theology for the Social Gospel* (New York: Macmillan, 1917), that Rauschenbusch openly speaks of Ritschlian influences: 92–94, 124f., 138f.; cf. 265. The social gospel movement had begun much earlier in America, as soon as an industrial poor became an evident problem, and this tradition was also formative for Rauschenbusch's ethics. See, e.g., Donovan E. Schmucker, *The Origins of Walter Rauschenbusch's Social Ethics* (Montreal and Kingston: McGill-Queen's University Press, 1994).

(334).[74] Key areas of progress in the modern world are democracy and the sciences, and the turn toward the world itself that they represent (194–210). In the modern period "Protestantism has lost its ecclesiastical character and authority. But at the same time Protestant Christianity has gained amazingly in its spiritual effectiveness on society" (207)[cf. Ritschlianism, chap. 1.3].[75]

Rauschenbusch's realistic analysis of the social situation and his call to Christian action exceeds anything comparable in German theology from this period until after World War II. He portrays the inhumanity of American business and industry and the severe oppression of the industrial poor, the racism of the society, and the consequences that must be avoided. "If the church cannot Christianize commerce, commerce will commercialize the church" (314). "The church in the past has been able to appeal to a good and just God. . . . If that unconscious religion of the average man [inherited from tradition] once gives way to a sullen materialism, there will be a permanent eclipse of the light of life among us. This is the stake of the church in the social crisis" (316). "If the church tries to confine itself to theology and the Bible, and refuses its larger mission to humanity, its theology will gradually become mythology and its Bible a closed book." "Individualist Christianity has lost sight of the great idea of the kingdom of God" (339f.).

Rauschenbusch's hope for real change rests in his belief in the work of God in Christian persons. "Christianity bases all human relations on human love, which is the equalizing and society-making impulse." In contrast, "competitive industry and commerce are based on selfishness" (309f.). He appeals to love practiced in "communistic" efforts, a term that for Rauschenbusch means cooperative work in society in opposition to selfishness (390–98, 407, 413f.). Rauschenbusch is, with considerable reserve, optimistic about such a possibility, not in the sense that he sees convincing proof of progress in the right direction, but in the sense of his belief in the effect of Jesus in a Christian society (e.g., 348). He is well aware that the effort may not be sufficient and that "the new era may die before it comes to birth" (xii). But "sometimes the hot hope surges that perhaps the long and slow climb might be ending" (421). It requires commitment and work. Christian preachers should have "the prophetic insight which discerns and champions the right before others see it" (363). His famous concluding paragraph to *Christianity and the Social Crisis* begins with the words, "Last May a miracle happened." Spring blossomed, having long been prepared by nature's processes—a parable of

74. Although his emphasis on social reality is greater than Harnack's, Rauschenbusch's history of the church is based on Harnack, to whose work he refers, esp. p. 112: *The Expansion of Christianity in the First Three Centuries*. For the history after these centuries, the main sources are very probably Harnack's *Outlines of the History of Dogma* and the last half of *What Is Christianity?*

75. Like Ritschl and Harnack [chap. 1.3], Rauschenbusch advocated the strong national state, which should pursue wealth and power, as seen for example in his support of the Spanish-American War and the resulting acquisition of Spanish colonies. *Christianity and the Social Crisis*, 281; see Evans, *The Kingdom Is Always but Coming*, 139. Rauschenbusch makes a remarkable Darwinian comment in *Christianity and the Social Crisis*, 274f.: "The intellectual standard of humanity can be raised only by the propagation of the capable. Our social system causes an unnatural selection of the weak for breeding, and the result is the survival of the unfittest." Cf. *Christianity and the Social Crisis*, 174.

the growth of the kingdom of God. "Perhaps" the time has come for "that great day of the Lord for which the ages waited" (422).

In his last book, *A Theology for the Social Gospel*,[76] Rauschenbusch elaborates on themes in his earlier work, often anticipating developments in later Christian ethics, especially the work of Reinhold Niebuhr [chap. 7.2]. He writes, for example: "Theology has not given adequate attention to the social idealizations of evil, which falsify the ethical standards for the individual by the authority of his group or community, deaden the voice of the Holy Spirit to the conscience of individuals and communities, and perpetuate antiquated wrongs in society. The social idealizations are the real heretical doctrines from the point of view of the kingdom of God" (78). He reflects on the false optimism of the eighteenth century's "age of reason," an optimism that was profoundly shaken by the mass disaster of the Lisbon earthquake of 1755 that killed 30,000 people. He sees a similar disaster in World War I, in the midst of which he wrote this book. He evokes the image of millions sitting like Job in ashes, "challenging the injustice of the God who has afflicted them by fathering the present social system" (181). Rauschenbusch still believes in and hopes for reform, although one misses that surge of "hot hope" in *Christianity and the Social Crisis*. Now the emphasis is rather on the prophetic task of the gospel in a darkening world.

4.6 ERNST TROELTSCH

The history of religions school pursued the question of how the Old and New Testaments are related to the religions of surrounding cultures, a question first opened by investigations of the relationship of pre-Christian mythologies to Christianity in the previous century. The school has its roots in Ritschlianism and in the emergence of comparative religion studies, especially at the University of Göttingen. One of its main sources of inspiration was Paul de Lagarde (1827–91), professor of Hebrew and Near Eastern languages, who counted Ernst Troeltsch and others associated with the history of religions school among his students. Reminiscent of Kant and Fries [chap. 2.8], Lagarde says that all true religion is a matter of timeless elements, "eternal laws," and is essentially "gospel" and "life." It includes relationship to the eternally present God, the awareness of sin, of repentance and forgiveness, of love and duty, and of the "kingdom of God" as the sum of goodness. For Lagarde neither Catholicism nor Protestantism is still viable, because they are too much tied to the thought of the past. While Jesus demonstrates gospel, he was made into the Christ of historical Christianity by the mixing in of Jewish, Greek, and Roman ideas. The religious task in modernity is to reformulate gospel in living ideas of German culture, something that is

76. Page numbers in the following text refer to this work (see bibliographic information in note 73).

to be accomplished by a future genius.[77] Lagarde's thinking about the elements of religion is not unusual among the members of the history of religions school. One sees its traces also in Troeltsch.

Another important source for the history of religions school was Wilhelm Dilthey (1833–1911), professor of philosophy in Berlin. Dilthey demonstrated that the richness of "life experience," of both individuals and cultures, could not be sufficiently grasped by the universal methods of natural science. It must rather be understood in its historical particularity, each instance for itself. Accordingly he raised the question of how or by what means we understand one another, other cultures, and other periods of history. His answer was that understanding is made possible because all humanity has essentially the same structure of being, although even the way we define this structure depends on our particular life experience. Metaphysics is an expression of life experience and changes with fluctuations of human history. In exploring the way historical understanding happens, Dilthey revived interest in Schleiermacher's hermeneutics as a theory of understanding. Most importantly he brought the problem of historical relativism to prominence.[78]

Ernst Troeltsch (1865–1923) had been Ritschl's student at Göttingen and was significantly influenced by Lotze and especially by Dilthey. For several years he was professor of theology at Heidelberg; in 1915 he accepted a position as professor of philosophy in Berlin. After World War I he served three years as an undersecretary in the ministry for education; his politics are described as national liberal.[79] He was an important contributor to the development of comparative religious studies, although his main interest was the history of European religion.

77. Lagarde, *Über das Verhältnis des deutschen Staats zu Theologie, Kirche und Religion* (Göttingen: Dieterich, 1872), 16ff., 28ff., 36–39, 60–62; reprinted in Lagarde, *Deutsche Schriften,* 5th ed. (Göttingen: Dieterich, 1920). [Cf. Strauss's *Old Faith and the New,* chap. 2.5.1.] One of his appreciative students was the New Testament historian Wilhelm Bousset (1865–1920), professor of New Testament at Marburg and Giessen. Other major figures of the school were the Old Testament scholar Hermann Gunkel (1862–1932) and, in New Testament, William Wrede (1859–1906). The importance of these figures for the development of biblical studies can hardly be overestimated. As theologians they were typical of their time. A Bousset scholar writes: "Bousset was a 'modern' Protestant, that is, he did not find his faith in the doctrines of the church. The idea of salvation as proclaimed by Paul and Luther, humanity's total depravity, the divinity of Christ, the belief in miracles, the sacrificial death of Christ—these are all statements that a modern Protestant living in the world of modern culture cannot agree with. But they also do not belong to the simple gospel of Jesus." Anthonie F. Verheule, *Wilhelm Bousset, Leben und Werk* (Amsterdam: Uitgeverij Ton Bolland, 1973), 375.

78. An introduction is Dilthey's own work, *Pattern and Meaning in History,* edited and introduced by H. P. Rickman (New York: Harper & Row, 1962). See also Wilhelm Dilthey, *Introduction to the Human Sciences,* ed. Rudolf Makkreel and Frithjof Rodi (Princeton, NJ: Princeton University Press, 1989).

79. Recent works on Troeltsch: Hans-Georg Drescher, *Ernst Troeltsch: His Life and Thought,* trans. John Bowden (Minneapolis: Fortress, 1993); Robert J. Rubanowice, *Crisis in Consciousness* (Tallahassee: University Presses of Florida, 1982); Wilhelm Pauck, *Harnack and Troeltsch* (New York: Oxford University Press, 1968); John Powell Clayton, ed., *Ernst Troeltsch and the Future of Theology* (Cambridge: Cambridge University Press, 1976); Benjamin A. Reist, *Toward a Theology of Involvement: The Thought of Ernst Troeltsch* (Philadelphia: Westminster, 1966); Thomas Ogletree, *Christian Faith and History: A Critical Comparison of Ernst Troeltsch and Karl Barth* (Nashville: Abingdon,

In his philosophical theology Troeltsch was an Idealist for whom the Absolute—itself a culturally relative concept, yet a relatively correct one—stands above the relativities of history as their origin and goal, but a goal that transcends the finitude of historical life. According to Troeltsch's lectures on *The Christian Faith,* the Absolute is the original unity of humanity and God, "the divine life" (or "absolute life"), and all religion is related to it. In concrete history, original unity divides into a "spiritual world" and a "natural world." Human being, a mixture of nature and spirit, struggles to rise from being dominated by natural forces to higher spiritual and ethical life. But there is great suffering and misery in natural life, and Troeltsch questions whether hope is real for the multitudes in his time that live in terrible circumstances. In the wandering of "Spirit" through an indefinitely long process of "growth," which for Troeltsch also encompasses the suffering of the many, the divine essence overcomes the division of natural and spiritual. Gradually in and with human being what is divided, nature and spirit, is elevated to "divine communion." Spirit "returns" to God (original unity), which is "God's own self-redemption." "God fully becomes God . . . through being believed and loved by finite spirits."[80] The key concepts are evidently from Hegel [chap. 2.3] and Neo-Kantianism (the division of nature and spirit [chap. 4.1]).

Troeltsch perceived a problem of unrecognized historical relativity in the Ritschlian modernization of some but not all traditional dogmas. The theology of Ritschl and Herrmann, he said, is at bottom a "biblicist-authoritarian dogmatics with a modern historical theology and philosophy of religion."[81] It does not rightly understand itself as a phenomenon of the modern world. According to Troeltsch the whole history of dogma, theology, and the church—not just this or that aspect of them (as in Ritschl and Herrmann)—should be understood as a development or an evolution, so that everything in this history is seen as relative to its stage in the historical process. As such it can and should be investigated purely historically. All ages have, in their own way, modernized or, as he says, "simplified" according to their point of view.

1965); Karl Barth, *Church Dogmatics* IV/1:383–87; Brian Gerrish, "Protestantism and Progress," in H. Renz and F. W. Graf, eds., *Troeltsch-Studien,* vol. 3 (Gütersloh: Gerd Mohn, 1984), 35–53.

80. *The Christian Faith, Based on Lectures Delivered at the University of Heidelberg in 1912 and 1913,* trans. Garret E. Paul (Minneapolis: Fortress, 1991), 177–94, esp. 178, 193; cf. 59f., 123, 152ff. God's "world-goal" is "the development of the God-filled personality; and all who acknowledge this should set their lives on this goal" (Ibid., 304, cf. 206). Cf. Troeltsch, *Religion in History,* trans. James Luther Adams and Walter F. Bense (Minneapolis: Fortress Press, 1991), on Hegel, 92, 260; on the Absolute, 60, 67, 105, 148ff.

81. Troeltsch, *The Christian Faith,* 16. Cf. Troeltsch, *The Absoluteness of Christianity and the History of Religions,* trans. David Reid (Richmond: John Knox, 1971), 82; *Religion in History,* 42. Troeltsch especially challenged Herrmann's claim to establish the validity of Christianity through the encounter with Christ ("faith cannot establish historical facts"), as, e.g., in *The Christian Faith,* 92f., where Troeltsch also rejects a new and influential theory of history put forward by George Wobbermin (1869–1943), in *Geschichte und Historie in der Religionswissenschaft* (Tübingen: Mohr, 1911), 5–15, namely, that there are two kinds of history, *Historie,* the subject of scholarly investigation, and *Geschichte,* experienced history [cf. Herrmann, chap. 4.3, and M. Kähler, chap. 5.1]. See Brent W. Sockness, *Against False Apologetics: Wilhelm Herrmann and Ernst Troeltsch in Conflict* (Tübingen: Mohr Siebeck, 1998).

Troeltsch illustrates what he means in the following, in which he partly agrees with Ritschl: "We concur with Luther's emphasis on solace in the midst of sin while we relegate everything medieval and scholastic to the margins of our consciousness, despite the fact that things medieval and scholastic were quite important to him. . . . There is clearly something at work [in our religion] besides the Bible and the tradition: the modern world's own thought and spiritual insight. This is also true of Harnack's beautiful, but quite unhistorical, formulation of the essence of Christianity."[82] In fact Harnack's "essence" is for Troeltsch apparently the best modern formulation of the meaning of Christ, insofar as he himself formulates this meaning in an almost identical way.[83] The difference is that for Harnack the "essence" is the historical core of the message of Jesus, while for Troeltsch it is a modern interpretation of that message.

How does one understand the "absoluteness" of Christianity in the situation of such historical relativity? Historical meaning is constantly subject to reinterpretation, to the modernizing of each age. According to Troeltsch, "absolute, unchanging value, conditioned by nothing temporal, exists not within but beyond history and can be perceived only in presentiment [*Ahnung*] and faith."[84] Presentiment and faith are phenomena of a "religious apriori," a term that Troeltsch coined [cf. "a priori" in Kant, chap. 2.1]. The "religious apriori" is a natural religious relationship to the Absolute in every human being, in a "a rational core that lies behind the working of the soul." The relationship of this "rational core" or of the "religious apriori" to the Absolute makes possible a "metaphysic of the noumenal character" of human being.[85] Through scientific analysis of this character—which is possible because the "core" is rational—Troeltsch could answer the problem of relativism. The "religious apriori" has to do only with practical personal life, not theoretical reason or science. "The danger of relativism" is avoided by the recognition of a "non-theoretical validity." This awareness "enters the awakened consciousness in the form of a specifically religious assurance and decision. This is not relativism but subjectivism. It is the renunciation of decisions based on theoretically constructed criteria, and the affirmation of decisions based exclusively on the personal sense of truth." It is, however, not only subjectively personal, insofar as it binds "everyone capable of perceiving it and actualizing it in a personal fashion." "It is set in a metaphysical background that cannot be constructed

---

82. *The Christian Faith*, 32.

83. Jesus' "profoundest impact" is "his religious and ethical proclamation of the value of the soul and the Kingdom of God in brother-love, as well as his extraordinary consciousness of mission and his struggle for a divinely induced world-renewal—all these are clearly historical" (Ibid., 88). "[Jesus] expected a miraculous transformation of the world, but this . . . was no more than a true, genuine and free surrender to the will of God and the God-pleasing brotherly love that results" (Ibid., 121). Redemption in Christ occurs through our connection with his person as mediated by the community; hence, Troeltsch says, "it is always contemporary" (Ibid., 275).

84. *The Absoluteness of Christianity*, 90. Elsewhere Troeltsch defines historical criticism in terms of its presupposition in our experience, especially our understanding of what is possible and probable; that is, it is based on analogy to our experience. See Troeltsch, "Historical and Dogmatic Method in Theology," in *Religion in History*, 11–32, esp. 13f.

85. *Religion in History*, 36.

by means of a theoretically compelling logic but must be grasped, just as it is solely revealed, in personal commitments. This background consists in a vigorous movement of reason as such, which bursts forth in ever-new creations and into whose creative teleology the soul can intuitively enter."[86] In this discussion the key concepts are rather clearly from Fries [chap. 2.8].

Religious-metaphysical statements about God are not scientific (theoretical) but "mythological, poetic and symbolic" [cf. Fries and Lange, chap. 4.1]. Theology has the task of assuring "a place for the practical-symbolic mode of knowledge, which is directed toward ultimate religious truth, beside the empirical mode of knowledge of the exact sciences." "Faith will continue to adopt its myths to the scientific view of the world, eliminating or re-interpreting whatever is essentially inconsistent with this view." One must concede, he says, that this involves the possibility that Christianity could dissolve along with its myths. "Analysis of these things is the most pressing task of theology today."[87]

In the foreword to *The Absoluteness of Christianity,* Troeltsch had briefly addressed the problem of how "a theology grounded in the history of religion," that is, in historical development and relativity, can be taught to theological seminarians "who desire to serve a church for which there is a definite historical authority"—in Protestantism, the Bible. His answer is that in such a case theology must practice "a cautious, careful, and sensitively reforming accommodation."[88] One is reminded of D. F. Strauss's advice to the enlightened clergy on the education of their congregations in the conclusion of his *Life of Jesus* [chap. 2.5.1]. In any case, for Troeltsch faith and science cohere ultimately in the unity of truth in the Absolute, and scientific investigation is not antithetical to the interests or reality of religion.[89] Religion or faith has no need to fear the use of science in religious matters, rather the opposite. In a later essay Troeltsch writes: "With the central place it gives to the personality of Jesus Christ Christianity does not have something special which distinguishes it from all other religions and makes redemption possible here alone. Rather, in this it only fulfills . . . a general law of man's spiritual life." Traditional dogma has collapsed in the modern period, but the church needs "Jesus' person and teaching," which historical science must secure, "otherwise Christianity will not go on."[90]

---

86. Ibid., 67f.

87. From the essay "Faith," in *Religion and History,* 128–30. Cf. *The Christian Faith,* 11: Theology "must seek an inner transformation of the religious life analogous to the transformation of the scientific world-picture."

88. *The Absoluteness of Christianity,* 29.

89. "There are only universally scientific, rather than specifically theological modes of understanding. The uniqueness of Christian theology lies, then, in the nature of its subject matter, not in special methods of research and validation" (*Religion in History,* 43). In the same essay, "On the Question of the Religious Apriori," he says that the main points of the plan of his work "have already been sketched by our idealistic philosophy. I continue the approach that prevailed before Hengstenberg and the Restoration" (Ibid., 44) [see chap. 1.2].

90. "The Significance of the Historical Jesus for Faith," *Ernst Troeltsch, Writings on Theology and Religion,* trans. Robert Morgan and Michael Pye (London: Duckworth, 1977), 201f.; see Troeltsch's comments on Strauss, 183, 186, 192. On general laws of spiritual life, cf. Paul de Lagarde earlier in chap. 4.6.

Troeltsch is especially known for his *Social Teachings of the Christian Churches*, in which he adopts the sociology of his friend Max Weber in investigating the relationship between the social-economic-political world and the behavior of the church within and toward this complex world.[91] In the "Results" of *Social Teachings*, Troeltsch summarizes his findings, abstracting from church history three social types of the church: "sect," characterized by withdrawal from the world for the sake of the ideal kingdom of God and the sect's own holiness; "church," characterized by the church's penetration of culture and hence also fusion with culture, and the institutional form of this fusion; and "mystic" or inward spirituality, with which Troeltsch also identifies modern religious individualism (and himself).[92] He sees all three types flowing together in contemporary Protestantism. However, they have not produced a new Protestant social ethic, the problem with which the work ends. The churches are not providing ethical guidance in meeting the social problems of the modern industrial world. In earlier epochs they had provided guidance, in the synthesis of reason and faith in medieval Catholicism and in the work ethic of post-Reformation Calvinism. What is always needed in political and economic life is a creative interaction between the ethically indispensable ideals of religion, as in the concept of the kingdom of God (or however "the Absolute" is expressed), and the often-brutal facts of concrete natural life. "Nowhere does there exist an absolute Christian ethic . . . ; all that we can do is to learn to control the world-situation in its successive phases just as the earlier Christian ethic did in its own way."[93] Troeltsch recognizes Richard Rothe's attention to the relationship of Christianity to secular ethics as an important precedent [chap. 3.2].[94]

Among Troeltsch's final works is a series of lectures given at universities in England in 1922, a year before his death. In his first speech he speaks of the individuality of the religions in specific times and places. The great world religions, each with its own historical formation, continue to develop their uniquely individual potentialities, and Christian missions must respect these historical boundaries.[95] In the second speech he addresses the increasingly difficult problem of the ethical formation of economic-social-political life in the modern world.[96] Here

91. Ernst Troeltsch, *The Social Teachings of the Christian Churches*, trans. Olive Wyon, 2 vols. (New York: Harper & Brothers, 1960); cf. Drescher, 222ff.; see also Troeltsch, *Protestantism and Progress*, trans. W. Montgomery, 1st ed. 1912 (Boston: Beacon Hill, n.d.). Troeltsch employs sociological methods of Max Weber. See Wolfgang J. Mommsen and Jürgen Osterhammel, eds., *Max Weber and His Contemporaries* (London: Unwin Hyman, 1987), 209–13, 215–33.

92. Cf. *Religion in History*, 51: "Alongside the church there exists a purely intellectual and literary Protestantism that indistinguishably blends into religious movements outside the church. . . . While it is difficult to define . . . , it . . . apparently comprises the progressive and vital religious forces, at least in Germany and the Anglo-Saxon countries. . . . Despite its essentially academic and literary nature, it remains in touch with popular religion, which is organized on cultic and social lines." Cf. Rothe's "Christianity outside the Church" [chap. 3.2].

93. *Social Teachings*, 2:993–1013; quotation 1013.

94. Troeltsch, *Zur religiösen Lage, Religionsphilosophie und Ethik* (Tübingen: Mohr Siebeck, 1913), 569f.

95. *Christian Thought: Its History and Application*, trans. Baron F. von Hügel, 1st German ed. 1923 (New York: Meridian, 1957), 53ff., 61–63; on mission: 58; cf. *The Christian Faith*, 298f.

96. *Christian Thought*, 70–93. Cf. *Religion in History*, 173–236, 260–63.

"spirit" attempts—without success—to dominate "nature," understood as raw
and egotistic materialism. In the third speech his focus is the sphere of values, of
goods and purposes in Christian culture broadly understood. He especially mentions the "idea of personality," which is a "western belief" and "the truth for us,"
but not for Eastern religions.[97] In the fourth speech he observes that the churches
no longer provide cultural adhesion and ethical guidance for the contemporary
world. Only individual conviction determines the course of values and ethics.
But Troeltsch nevertheless looks forward to a new ethical "synthesis" molded by
leading personalities who will "establish its final religious and metaphysical convictions." It will be a historically relative, pragmatic compromise between the
absolute values of the kingdom of God and the forces of the social-economic-
political world, a compromise that intends to effect what is realistically possible
and is validated by the ability to give these forces ethical direction.[98]

4.7 RUDOLF OTTO

Rudolf Otto (1869–1937) was, like Troelsch, educated at Göttingen under
Ritschlian influences and soon became associated with the history of religions
school. He was professor of theology in Breslau and then in Marburg as the successor of Wilhelm Herrmann. During the war years he served as a member of
the Democratic Party in the Prussian parliament. In 1922 he founded the Inter-
Religious League (*Religiöser Menschheitsbund*) as an organization for cooperation
among the world religions for common ethical commitment; it failed for lack of
support. In the 1930s he initially supported the German Christian movement
[chap. 1.4] but apparently regretted it later, spending his last years in depression.[99] Otto is widely regarded as a founder of modern comparative religions
studies. As a young theologian he concentrated on the historical criticism of the
Bible but was soon led to Romanticism and Idealism. He became an advocate of
the philosopher J. F. Fries and his theological follower W. M. L. de Wette [chap.
2.8]. He valued, not without criticism, the first edition of Schleiermacher's
Speeches on Religion, which he republished in 1906.[100] His most important work
was *The Idea of the Holy*, which quickly went though many editions and whose
translations soon made his name known throughout the world.

97. *Christian Thought*, 119–21. In this speech, 102, Troeltsch states that the origin of moral conscience is "outside time," a Kantian concept that appears both in Schelling and in the theologian
Julius Müller [chaps. 2.1, 2.4.1, 3.1]. According to *The Absoluteness of Christianity*, 89, 112ff., a comparison of the world religions shows the relatively superior value of Christianity, especially in its concept of personal being or personhood.

98. *Christian Thought*, 138ff., 142; cf. 90, 177. Cf. Troeltsch's assessment of Christianity's inability positively to inform or influence current society as it had in the past, in his essay from the year
1922, "The Social Philosophy of Christianity," in *Religion in History*, esp. 229–34.

99. Melissa Raphael, *Rudolf Otto and the Concept of Holiness* (Oxford: Clarendon, 1997), 20,
76–79. As Raphael suggests, Otto's concept of the nonrational was probably a stimulus for Nazi religious thought.

100. His work on Fries and de Wette is cited in chap. 2.8, note 244.

In *The Idea of the Holy*[101] Otto faults Schleiermacher for the shortsightedness of his expression "feeling of dependence." Since dependence indicates condition, it is a "feeling of being conditioned" and hence of being effected by a cause. This, says Otto, is a secondary rational thought that can only follow a prior nonrational religious experience or feeling, namely, the "immediate experience of the noumenous" or of the transcendent God, "the Holy."[102] Such immediate experience of noumenal reality is primary in religion. Otto identifies and gives Latin names to three characteristics of immediate religious experience: (1) the feeling of the "wholly other" as the mystery of the "noumen" that has no place in our scheme of reality: the *mysterium*; (2) the "trembling of the soul" before the awesome, terrible, and consuming power of this noumen: the *tremendum*; (3) and the fascinating and intoxicating attraction of the noumen: the *fascinans*. These Otto finds in all religions in progressive degrees, beginning with religious feelings such as the fear of ghosts, and progressing finally, in the case of the *mysterium*, to the idea of God as above the world; in the case of the *tremendum*, to the idea of the dreadful power of God before which nothing can stand; and in the case of the *fascinans*, to the idea of God's love and hence of comfort, of bliss and beatitude.[103] Among other failures, recent theology—Otto mentions Schleiermacher and Ritschl—has failed to recognize the power of the *tremendum* and its biblical tradition of the "wrath of God." Earlier theologians, such as Luther, did recognize it.[104]

Like Fries and de Wette, Otto names noumenal consciousness *Ahnung*. He also calls it "creature consciousness." It is given a priori in the mind as the depth-dimension of the human soul. Noumenal reality in itself is nonrational and in its most powerful effects irrational. With reference to Fries, Otto makes use of Kant's concept of "schematization." For Kant, through the "schemata" the mind applies the categories of understanding to the "thing in itself" in order to produce the phenomena we perceive [chap. 2.1.1]. According to Otto, the religious mind "schematizes" the noumena in the act of producing the ideas or concepts that give the noumena intelligible expression, such as "the wrath of God" or the concept

101. *The Idea of the Holy*, trans. John W. Harvey, 1st ed. 1923 (London: Oxford University Press, 1950). The original German, *Das Heilige*, was first published in 1917. See also Otto, *Religious Essays, A Supplement to the 'Idea of the Holy,'* trans. Brian Lunn (London: Oxford University, 1931); *India's Religion of Grace and Christianity Compared and Contrasted*, trans. Frank Hugh Foster (New York: Macmillan, 1930). English interpretations are Robert F. Davidson, *Rudolf Otto's Interpretation of Religion* (Princeton, NJ: Princeton University Press, 1947); Todd A. Gooch, *The Numinous and Modernity* (Berlin: Walter de Gruyter, 2000); Steven Ballard, *Rudolf Otto and the Synthesis of the Rational and the Non-Rational in the Idea of the Holy* (Frankfurt: Peter Lang, 2000); Adina Davidovich, *Religion as a Province of Meaning* (Minneapolis: Fortress, 1993), 149–220. See also Hans-Walter Schütte, *Religion und Christentum in der Theologie Rudolf Ottos* (Berlin: Walter de Gruyter, 1969).

102. *Idea of the Holy*, 20, cf. 146–50, 155f. The meaning of the word "noumenous" (noumen, noumenal, noumenon, noumena) is explained in the chapter on Kant earlier in this book [2.1.1].

103. Ibid., 12–35.

104. Ibid., 18, 95–108; cf. 83: without the true holiness of God, the Gospel of Jesus is turned "into a mere idyll," which is meant as a criticism of theologians who only talk of the love of God. In Otto's three basic elements of the Holy, concepts in Romanticism and early Idealism are recognizable, e.g., the beautiful and the sublime, the wonderful and the terrible.

of the noumenous itself.[105] Schematization evolves over time as the religions develop historically. The different religions are characterized by the language for noumenal reality that they produce. Theoretically all human beings have this productive capacity, but in reality it is the person especially gifted for noumenal "cognition"—first the artist and then the prophet—who produces expressions of the Holy for the many. At the highest stage, exceeding the prophet, is the "Son."[106]

Christ and Christianity are the highest religious expressions of noumenal reality. In Christianity—and to a lesser degree in the other world religions—two lines of evolutionary development converge: the cognition of the noumenal, expressed in concepts such as the wrath and love of God, and the ethics of "the good" that are derived from humanity's a priori moral sense. As these lines converge, first in Old Testament prophecy and then in Christianity, the ideals of obligation, justice, and goodness "become the 'will' of the noumen, and the noumen their guardian, ordainer and author." The Holy becomes good, and the good becomes sacred. The result is "civilized religion," a "healthy harmony" of the rational and irrational.[107]

According to a later book, The Kingdom of God and the Son of Man, first published in 1934, Jesus' proclamation of the kingdom of God is not in the first place the proclamation of a moral kingdom but of the noumenal power of God as the reality of the Holy. This "charismatic" power swept the first Christians into a new reality, the miraculously experienced new birth that permeates and is the Holy Spirit of the New Testament. "The Kingdom of God, as already at hand, is . . . the in-breaking miraculous power of the transcendent." The charismatic gifts that appear in Paul's letters are signs of this power, not however as absolutely miraculous, but as "the mysterious heightenings of talents and capacities, which have at least their analogues in the general life of the soul." The most charismatic person of all is Christ. Otto interprets the miracle of the walking on the sea as an apparition "connected on the side of the charismatic with an act . . . of charismatic second sight, of [Jesus] recognizing the need in which the disciples find themselves."[108] Christianity lives today because of the gift of "divination" by which the "Spirit recognizes the Spirit," that is, Spirit in the contemporary Christian recognizes the Holy in the New Testament.[109]

4.8 WILLIAM JAMES

William James (1842–1910), professor of philosophy at Harvard, was also important for the development of the discipline of comparative religions. He had

---

105. *Idea of the Holy,* 45, 140; cf. 31; see also Otto, *The Philosophy of Religion,* 93 [chap. 2.8].
106. Ibid., 177f.
107. Ibid., 109f., 141f.; cf. 56.
108. *The Kingdom of God and the Son of Man,* trans. Floyd V. Filson and Bertram Lee Woolf (Grand Rapids: Zondervan, n.d.), 334, 340, 370f. Cf. the quasi-scientific explanation of the miracles in Schleiermacher.
109. *Idea of the Holy,* 143–74.

studied in Europe, knew German philosophy well, and could read several languages. He is known for applying empirical and pragmatic methods of research to religious studies. Empiricism had long been a characteristic of English-speaking philosophy, but pragmatism accentuated its "inner worldly" aspect. It defines truth in terms of both empirical demonstration and pragmatic process: truth is instrumental for the benefit of human life, and it is a value in and for human life that evolves or is developed as human life evolves.[110] Charles Peirce (1839–1914), the founder of American pragmatic philosophy and the major source for James's pragmatism, was also well versed in German philosophy. He regarded Schelling's philosophy of nature, especially in the original unity of subject (thought) and object (world), as of key importance for his own philosophy, and he influenced James's thought about an original unity.[111] What James thinks of this unity is expressed, rather as in Lotze [chap. 4.1], as an utterly unconditional noumenal presence underlying and producing the world of experience. There is a communication from this presence to "feeling" in human experience, but it is not clear conceptual communication, so that what one knows of this noumenal presence can be expressed only in metaphor.

In the "results" of his famous and influential work *The Varieties of Religious Experience* (first edition 1902),[112] James draws the conclusion that religion has nothing to do with science or with the understanding. It is rather "feeling" and has a multitude of forms, in accord with differences among persons. "Individuality is founded in feeling." However, the primary expression of the forms is given through the great religious figures of history. Unlike Schleiermacher, who ranked the other religions below Christianity, James thinks the feelings and conduct of Stoic, Christian, and Buddhist saints "are almost always the same" and their lives are "practically indistinguishable."[113] He lists effects that religious feelings among different persons have in common: "an assurance of safety, a temper of peace, and, in relation to others, a preponderance of loving affections." In another place he lists the effects as goodness, beauty, justice, and moral law.[114] The more morality is religious in nature, the greater the moral progress in human society. In religion there seem to be no evil effects, which James defines as the experience of meaninglessness.[115] His view of the effects and values of religion is evidently drawn not

---

110. See James, *Pragmatism,* 1st ed. 1907 (Cambridge: Harvard University Press, 1975), 28–334; on religion: *The Will to Believe,* 1st ed. 1897 (Cambridge: Harvard University Press, 1979).

111. Bruce Wilshire, "The Breathtaking Intimacy of the Material World," in Ruth Anna Putnam, ed., *The Cambridge Companion to William James* (Cambridge: Cambridge University Press, 1997), 104–7. On James, see also Ellen Kappy Suckiel, *Heaven's Companion: William James' Philosophy of Religion* (Notre Dame, IN: Notre Dame University Press, 1996); Richard M. Gale, *The Divided Self of William James* (Cambridge: Cambridge University Press, 1999); Stanley Hauerwas, *With the Grain of the Universe: The Church's Witness and Natural Theology* (Grand Rapids: Brazos, 2001), 43–86.

112. William James, *The Varieties of Religious Experience* (Cambridge: Harvard University Press, 1985), 302–408.

113. Ibid., 395–97.

114. Ibid., 53ff., 382f., 384, 399ff.

115. Ibid., 109–38 ("The Sick Soul"); 41ff. See esp. Suckiel, 97–112; *Cambridge Companion to William James,* 260–65, 273–81. James experienced periods of severe depression.

only from his broad reading in philosophy of religion, but also from what he knew of religion in his own experience and in Protestant New England culture. His individualist definition of religion seems rather Puritan: "the feelings, acts, and experiences of individual men in their solitude, so far as they apprehend themselves to stand in relation to whatever they may consider the divine."[116]

However, "whatever they may consider the divine" is not what is truly religious. It is rather only the conceptual interpretation of what is truly religious or, as he says elsewhere, it is what is true "for you."[117] Higher reality, or what James once calls the "higher part of the universe," is conceptually interpreted only in metaphors of personal meaning. With whatever conceptual metaphors higher reality is interpreted, insofar as they are true "for you," they are what James calls "over-beliefs." Over-beliefs are comprised of not only the belief systems of the various religions but also all philosophical ideas about the origin of religion. The idea of God is an over-belief.

All religion has to do with the human "need" for an answer to what is wrong in human life [cf. Feuerbach, chap. 2.5.2]. Employing a new concept in psychology, the "subconscious," James says empirical research indicates that there is in the subconscious of religious people a "higher" self that has an instinctive sense of what salvation from wrong is or means. This higher self opens into what James calls a "more" than the self that actually works the salvation that instinct anticipates. It must be real, he reasons, because it produces those real effects that give meaning to life, for example, morality. "God" is in the first place a beneficial idea that helps people answer the problems of life. Secondly, "God" is James's philosophical term for this mysterious "more." Because we know of it only in experience, and because all experience is in space and time, he concludes that God must be in space and time and therefore an aspect of finite reality.[118] Again: the "effects" (security, love, morality, etc.) of religion are real, while the "more" is James's interpretation of their origin. This is recognizably related to Fries's concept of *Ahndung* and the metaphorical expression of noumenal reality [chap. 2.8] and their parallels in Rudolf Otto, although for James the only truth that can be validated are the effects of the "more."

While concepts of divine reality vary among the religions, for James they all refer to the mystery that is God. A natural comparison is with Ernst Troeltsch, who was impressed by James's empirical analysis of religion and largely agreed with it. He even identified himself with James as a philosopher of religion who respected the existing dominant religion while being himself a spiritual individ-

116. *Varieties of Religious Experience,* 34.

117. James, *A Pluralistic Universe,* 1st ed. 1909 (Cambridge: Harvard University Press, 1977), 148.

118. *Varieties of Religious Experience,* 397–408. On James's concept of God as finite and on his understanding of religious experience as a dynamic spiritual-material unity see esp. the essays by Richard Rorty and Bruce Wilshire in *The Cambridge Companion to William James,* 83–124. We have already commented on the appropriation through Peirce of Schelling's subject-object unity. It is also related to Romanticism's sense of divine presence [chap. 2.2]. James valued Emerson's language about the immanence of the "over-soul" in the beauty of nature, although Emerson's "over-soul" is for James just another variety of over-belief. Ibid., 34f., 53, 392f. [chap. 2.9].

ualist. He agreed with James that the scientific analysis of religion is beneficial for both religion and science, and that one should regard personal experience as primary in religion. But Troeltsch criticized James's method for being so limited to the empirical that it could not claim validity for concepts of higher reality. When James spoke of "God" as the mystery of reality, his definitions required that "God" be classified as only an "over-belief," not a valid concept of the mystery. For Troeltsch, higher concepts—whatever their relativity as cultural-religious phenomena—are necessary for religion and owe their origin ultimately to the reality of "the Absolute." Indeed Troeltsch concluded that the consequence of James's empiricism had to be agnosticism and the destruction of religion.[119]

James had significant influence on American liberal theology in the early twentieth century, especially at the University of Chicago, although here too "over-belief" was a problematic concept.[120] With time he was also appreciated as being something of a religious-cultural prophet. In the 1950s the American historian Daniel Boorstin could characterize religion in the United States just as James had defined it, as "intensely personal" and "instrumental," based on its beneficial effects. Each sect "serves the personal need of its member and helps him quiet his personal uneasiness." And "we assume that the greater the person and the stronger the personality, the more he would need a religion tailor-made to his personality."[121]

4.9 ALBERT SCHWEITZER

"O this genteel, refined culture that speaks so edifyingly of human dignity and human rights and disregards and tramples these human rights and dignity among millions and millions. . . . Our Christianity will become a lie and a disgrace, if not all that has been done out there [in the colonies of the colonial powers] is not atoned for, if not for every person who has acted brutally in the name of Jesus Christ, a helper in the name of Jesus Christ comes, for every person who has stolen, one who contributes, for every person who has cursed, one who blesses."[122] The words are from a speech Albert Schweitzer (1875–1965) gave in January 1906, the year he decided to become a medical doctor in Africa. Through

119. Troeltsch, *Zur religiösen Lage, Religionsphilosophie und Ethik*, 364–85. The essay on James cited here was published in English in the *Harvard Theological Review* 5, no. 4 (October 1912): 401–22. Cf. James on the Absolute as an over-belief, in *Pragmatism*, 41.

120. On theologians influenced by James, see Gary Dorrien's chapter, "In the Spirit of William James," in *The Making of American Liberal Theology*, 2:216–85.

121. Boorstin, *The Genius of American Politics* (Chicago: University of Chicago Press, 1958), 140ff.

122. H. Steffahn, *Albert Schweitzer in Selbstzeugnissen und Bilddokumenten* (Reinbek, 1979), 72f., as quoted by Günter Altner, "Albert Schweitzer" in Martin Greschat, ed., *Gestalten der Kirchengeschichte*, vol. 10/1:278f. On Schweitzer, see Werner Picht, *The Life and Thought of Albert Schweitzer*, trans. Edward Fitzgerald (New York: Harper & Row, 1964); George Seaver, *Albert Schweitzer: The Man and His Mind* (New York: Harper & Brothers, 1947); Erich Grässer, *Albert Schweitzer als Theologe* (Tübingen: Mohr Siebeck, 1979).

firsthand experiences he became a major critic of the economic and political policies of the European colonial powers in Africa. His work for world peace, especially for the abolition of atomic weapons, brought him the Nobel Peace Prize in 1952. He was also known as an important interpreter of the organ works of Johann Sebastian Bach. His first profession was theology, and he served for a short while as pastor in his native Alsace, then a province of Germany. He became a lecturer at the University of Strassburg, where he wrote his most famous theological work, *The Quest of the Historical Jesus,* also published in 1906. He completed his medical degree and left for Africa in 1913, in the service of a French missionary society. He spent the rest of his life at the Lambaréné mission, although he traveled several times for extended stays in Europe.

The *Quest* is first of all a history of works on the life of Jesus from the time interest in the subject arose in the eighteenth century to Schweitzer's own time. He gives his interpretation in its closing chapters. According to Schweitzer, Jesus proclaimed the near end of the world in the coming kingdom of God, for which humanity had to prepare by practicing the higher righteousness of the love commandment and the Sermon on the Mount. With time Jesus became convinced that his death would accelerate the coming of the kingdom. "[Jesus] lays hold of the wheel of the world to set it moving on that last revolution which is to bring all ordinary history to a close. It refuses to turn, and he throws himself upon it. Then it does turn; and crushes him. . . . The wheel rolls onward, and the mangled body of the one immeasurably great man, who was strong enough to think of himself as the spiritual ruler of mankind and to bend history to his purpose, is hanging upon it still. That is his victory and his reign." For Schweitzer, Jesus is essentially a tragic hero, for like the heroes of Greek tragedy he is crushed by the hard reality of this world—the ancient and powerful god—he could not overcome.[123] Jesus' mind and teaching were completely dominated by his eschatological expectation of the supernatural coming of the kingdom of God, and after his death this expectation is carried over into the disciples' subjective visions of his resurrection.[124]

For Schweitzer, in opposition to the Ritschlian interpretation, the ethical teaching of Jesus and the New Testament church cannot be separated from their eschatological belief in the near end of the world. But this is only a partial dis-

---

123. Albert Schweitzer, *The Quest of the Historical Jesus,* trans. W. Montgomery, 1st English ed. 1910 (New York: Macmillan, 1968), 371. There are other indications in *The Quest* that Schweitzer saw Jesus as a tragic hero (see, e.g., 255), and one encounters tragic situations fairly often in his works. Tragedy is a major subject in Nietzsche (esp. *Birth of Tragedy*), who was a formative influence on Schweitzer in his student period. The image of the "wheel" that "crushes" is perhaps drawn from the end of D. F. Strauss's *Der alte und der neue Glaube,* 4th ed. (Bonn: Emil Strauss, 1873), where Strauss says the universe is a "machine with iron-toothed wheels" ready to crush the incautious person. Friedrich Nietzsche, in *Thoughts out of Season,* trans. Anthony Ludovici (New York: Russell & Russell, 1964), 56, turns the image back on Strauss as one caught in the wheels of his own machinelike universe. Albrecht Ritschl uses the image in a similar way in his criticism of Strauss's book, in *Justification and Reconciliation,* 3:619.

124. Schweitzer, *The Kingdom of God and Primitive Christianity,* trans. L. A. Garrard (New York: Seabury, 1968), 131ff.

agreement with the Ritschlians, insofar as for Schweitzer the separation is nevertheless necessary for the understanding of Jesus' significance in the modern world, for which New Testament eschatology is incredible. The initial movement toward separation is, however, visible for Schweitzer in Paul's preaching that the end time of the kingdom has already begun with Christ's death and resurrection. This interpretation opens the possibility, taken up by the later church, of extending the culmination or final act of the end time into the indefinite future.

The Holy Spirit is the bridge, so to speak, over which the gospel crosses into the modern period. It transcends temporal conditions and enters creatively into what Schweitzer calls the "mysticism" of the individual believer. Through this personal mysticism the essence of Christ, his ethical person, comes into the life of the modern Christian. Jesus' expectation of the kingdom now becomes meaningful as a symbol of the transcendent nearness of the Christian God. Paul knew union with Christ by the power of the Spirit; from it still follows, as Paul taught, the active life of love. This mystical union with Christ and the active ethics of love are the core of Schweitzer's faith.[125] Ethics is by no means secondary. Christianity "must insist on the fact that the ethical is the highest type of spirituality."[126] The Sermon on the Mount is "the incontestable charter of liberal Christianity."[127]

Christianity's personal God, defined as "ethical will," is opposed by a great force, the natural world and human history (the "wheel" that tragically crushed Jesus).[128] There is a dualism in Schweitzer's thought that has faith, hope, and optimism on one side and deep pessimism on the other, a dualism that suggests the Marcion of Harnack's late work [chap. 4.4]. Philosophy and theology must acknowledge, Schweitzer says, that we do not and cannot know the "meaning of the world," and for this reason it is no longer possible to explain human existence from ideas about its meaning. No purpose is to be found in the course of nature, which we face "absolutely perplexed." In the last part of the nineteenth century, Schweitzer writes, philosophy tried to meet this problem by speaking of a "twofold truth," one of natural science, which is limited in what it can know, and one of value. Ritschl's theory of value judgments was placed alongside "the scientific conception of life." Such twofold truth cannot be considered valid. Humanity must rather accept the limitations of the scientific knowledge of the world without speaking of a completely different access to truth in value judgments or

125. Schweitzer, *The Mysticism of Paul the Apostle*, trans. William Montgomery (New York: Henry Holt, 1931), 377–80, 384–86. On Harnack, see esp. Schweitzer, *Out of My Life and Thought*, trans. C. T. Campion, 2nd ed. (New York: Henry Holt, 1933), 33. Schweitzer was critical of Harnack's work on the New Testament but accepted his kernel-and-husk view of church history: *Mysticism of Paul*, 369, 371; Schweitzer, *Paul and His Interpreters*, 1st English ed. 1912, trans. W. Montgomery (New York: Schocken, 1964), vi, 81 (and elsewhere). See also Picht, *Life and Thought of Albert Schweitzer*, 222f.

126. Schweitzer, *Christianity and the Religions of the World*, trans. Johanna Powers (New York: George H. Doran, 1923), 91.

127. *Out of My Life and Thought*, 73f.

128. *Christianity and the Religions*, 83.

in some other way. Traditional metaphysics and theology are, he says, like the eschatological end time expectation of Jesus: they attempt to solve a riddle—the meaning of the world and of human history—that cannot be solved. Yet within us, says Schweitzer, is the "will to live." If we follow where the thought of this "will" leads in all consequence and in depth, we see that all of life is "will to live," and we come to affirm life as it is, whether the course it takes is horrible or beautiful.[129] This affirmation is "reverence for life."

With this thought Schweitzer turns, in spite of what he had said elsewhere, to metaphysics. "In my deepened world- and life-affirmation, I manifest reverence for life. With consciousness and with volition I devote myself to Being. I become of service to ideas which it thinks out in me. . . . Reverence for life means to be in the grasp of the infinite, inexplicable, forward-urging will in which all being is grounded."[130] The language and conceptuality are those of early Idealism.[131] But Schweitzer rejects concepts of the "Absolute" and the "totality of Being" as abstractions to which one can have no real personal relation and as such are ethically unproductive [cf. Lotze, chap. 4.1]. "There is no Essence of Being, but only infinite Being in infinite manifestations. It is only through the manifestations of Being . . . that my being has any intercourse with infinite Being." By devoting myself to those beings on whom I can have influence and who need my help, "I make spiritual inward devotion to infinite being a reality and thereby give my own poor existence meaning and richness. The river has found its sea."[132] "Whenever my life devotes itself in any way to life, my finite will to live experiences union with the infinite will in which all life is one." In reverence for life my will to live is "obedient to this higher revelation" and is "religiousness," "a living and never-ceasing divine service."[133]

This is for Schweitzer the connection with Jesus, for reverence for life is "will to love." "The essential element in Christianity as it was preached by Jesus and as it is comprehended by thought, is this, that it is only through love that we can attain to communion with God. All living knowledge of God rests on this foun-

---

129. Schweitzer, *Civilization and Ethics*, trans. C. T. Campion and Charles B. Russell, 3rd ed. (London: Adam & Charles Black, 1946), 203–13. On metaphysics, see Schweitzer, *Decay and Restoration of Civilization*, trans. C. T. Campion, 1st English ed. 1923 (London: A. & C. Black, 1947), 6. See also George Seaver, *Albert Schweitzer, Christian Revolutionary* (New York: Harper, 1944), which has chapters on Schweitzer's critique of philosophy.

130. *Civilization and Ethics*, 214. On p. 243 one finds Schweitzer's famous description of his reverence for the life of plants and insects. "He tears no leaf from a tree, plucks no flower, and takes care to crush no insect. . . . If he walks on the road after a shower and sees an earthworm which has strayed onto it, he bethinks himself that it must get dried up in the sun, . . . so he lifts it from the deadly stone surface, and puts it on the grass. If he comes across an insect which has fallen into a puddle, he stops . . . in order to hold out a leaf or a stalk on which it can save itself."

131. Cf. the early Schelling, *Werke*, 6:140: "The [infinite] All is the knower in me." The modern German concept of the will, which originates in Fichte [chap. 2.2.2], is for Schweitzer taken from Nietzsche and Schopenhauer. [Cf. also D. F. Strauss's view of the universe, chap. 2.5.1.]

132. *Civilization and Ethics*, 237f.

133. Ibid., 246; cf. 277.

dation: that we experience him in our lives as will to love."[134] But there is no resolution of the ambivalence or rather opposition in the relationship of spiritual
and natural. In the natural world "Christianity finds a will which does not answer
to the will of the ethical God and which, therefore, is evil."[135]

"The spirit of Jesus in us has entered the world as creating spirit, and so the
truth has again proven that it is, finally, the highest good and can bring humanity progress."[136] But progress cannot take place without the recognition of the
gap between the good and passionate intentions of personal ethics and society's
impersonal and increasingly unethical direction. This problem and the way to
overcome it must be addressed.[137] Conscientious secular reason and religious
faith must converge in reverence for life and in ethics. In reverence for life profound secular thought becomes religious and the "religious world-view" becomes
philosophical. The result of both is "true humanism."[138] Whether reverence for
life is identified with Christianity and its "ethical God" or not, it is the highest
good for the world. Whether or not it will prevail against the forces of destruction or suffer Jesus' tragic fate is an open question.[139]

4.10 FRITZ BURI

Fritz Buri (1907–95), a Swiss, was appointed professor of theology at the University of Basel in 1951 as a liberal balance to Karl Barth. Together with his teacher,
Martin Werner (1887–1964), professor of theology at Bern, he was an advocate
of the theology of Albert Schweitzer, although he did not share Schweitzer's pessimism. It was not a departure from his agreement with Schweitzer—in biblical
criticism, ethics, and cultural criticism, and in the symbolic interpretation of
Christ's proclamation of the imminent coming of the kingdom of God—
when Buri later became a student of the influential philosopher and psychologist
Karl Jaspers (1883–1969), who joined the philosophical faculty at Basel after
World War II. In fact Jaspers's philosophy of religion is very close to Schweitzer's
thought.

---

134. *Out of My Life and Thought*, 274–77.
135. *Christianity and the Religions of the World*, 82; cf. 86.
136. From Schweitzer's 1905 lecture on the "History of the Life of Jesus Research from Reimarus
to the Present," quoted from the unpublished archives by Grässer, *Albert Schweitzer*, 263. A recent
publication from the archives is *Albert Schweitzer: Leben, Werk und Denken, 1905–1965, Mitgeteilt
in seinen Briefen* (Heidelberg: Lambert Schneider, 1987); see also Schweitzer, *A Place for Revelation:
Sermons on Reverence for Life*, trans. David L. Holland (New York: Macmillan, 1988).
137. *Civilization and Ethics*, 223–27.
138. Ibid., 30, 277; *The Decay and the Restoration of Civilization*, 105; cf. *Out of My Life and
Thought*, 273f.
139. See Schweitzer's 1934 article "Religion in Modern Civilization," in George Seaver, *Albert
Schweitzer*, 335–42, esp. 335f.; cf. Schweitzer, *On Nuclear War and Peace*, ed. Homer A. Jacobs (Elgin,
IL.: Brethren, 1988).

Buri's "theology of responsibility" is accessible in a short work to which he adds an introduction for the American theological public: *Thinking Faith: Steps on the Way to a Philosophical Theology.*[140] "Thinking faith" is not the objective thinking of science. "There is no thinking without objects but there are objects of thought which are not merely objects, for they point to what is not objectifiable." Human thought encounters a "boundary" that cannot be crossed in three all-important interrelated aspects or dimensions of human existence: (1) Being-in-Totality, which exceeds any attempt to conceive it objectively; (2) the human soul or personal self; and (3) Transcendence, which like Being-in-Totality is "unconditioned" and with which the soul exists in a nonobjectifiable relationship.[141] Transcendence communicates meaning indirectly in the "symbols" of the world religions, in their historical myths and liturgical forms. Christianity's historical myths of creation, the resurrected Christ, and the near kingdom of God are not factually true but symbols through which comes the "summons" of Transcendence to faith and responsible being in ethical community (58ff., 93ff.).[142] Grace is the event of truly hearing and therefore following the summons (56). In the church laypersons may understand themselves and their faith simply through the church's symbols, but "thinking faith" recognizes the symbols as symbols in their relationship to Transcendence. In either case it is by the grace of hearing the "voice" spoken in the symbols that one understands one's life as existence in faith. Prayer is "the true form of existence" as unceasing personal relationship to God.[143] To the voice of the summons one owes the recognition that the "Thou" of the other person belongs to one's own personhood, and that one's own personal decision in assuming responsible personhood in community, in both church and world, is free and unconditional.[144]

Christian dogmatics and ethics have among their tasks that of preventing the mistakes of orthodoxy and nihilism, both of which take away the freedom of human responsibility: orthodoxy, by having belief and behavior already decided; nihilism, by saying nothing is true (69f.). Christian responsibility requires engagement with modern philosophy and the criticism of traditions, and it requires openness to the global community.[145] Buri pursued dialogue with other religions,

140. Trans. Harold H. Oliver (Philadelphia: Fortress, 1968). Page references in the following text are to this work. See also Buri, *Theology of Existence*, trans. Harold H. Oliver and Gerhard Onder (Greenwood, SC: Attic Press, 1965); *How Can We Still Speak Responsibly of God?* (Philadelphia: Fortress, 1968); *Christian Faith in Our Time*, trans. Edward Allen Kent (New York: Macmillan, 1966). Buri's chief work is his three-volume *Dogmatik als Selbstverständnis des christlichen Glaubens* (Bern: Paul Haupt, 1956, 1962, 1978). A monograph on Buri is Charley D. Hardwick's *Faith and Objectivity* (The Hague: Martinus Nijhoff, 1972).

141. Cf. Schleiermacher's dialectic, chap. 2.7.1 above.

142. Buri, *Der Pantocrator: Ontologie und Eschatologie als Grundlage der Lehre von Gott* (Hamburg-Bergstedt: Herbert Rich Evangelischer Verlag, 1969), 15.

143. Ibid., 155–57.

144. Cf. *How Can We Still Speak Responsibly of God?* 53ff.

145. In his perceptive untranslated work *Gott in Amerika*, 2 vols. (Bern: Paul Haupt, 1969, 1972), Buri discusses theology in the United States in the 1960s, including the "death of God" theology and the social criticism of the civil rights movement.

which perceive the summons of Transcendence and its grace through their own religious symbols (91). One of his most important works is his book on the Christian-Buddhist dialogue in Japan: *The Buddha-Christ as the Lord of the True Self: The Religious Philosophy of the Kyoto School and Christianity*.[146] In an earlier work he had called for the openness of Christianity to new forms of faith that may develop from these dialogues, which he expresses as the demonstration of the ability of "the Pantocrator," Christ as the ruler of the world, to be the Pantocrator "in science, philosophy and the religions of the world."[147]

The key concepts in the definition of the three boundary areas of human existence correspond to concepts in Karl Jaspers's philosophy and in Jaspers's interpretation of Kant.[148] They are related to Fichte's moral Idealism, Schleiermacher and, in the concept of the communication of Transcendence, to Fries's and Rudolf Otto's philosophies of religion. But in contrast to the Romantic spirit of the early Schleiermacher, Fries, and Otto, like Jaspers Buri emphasizes the relationship of theology to reason and the sciences. His closest theological contemporary was Paul Tillich.

4.11 ALFRED NORTH WHITEHEAD

Alfred North Whitehead (1861–1947) was at first a mathematical theoretician who worked with the mathematician and philosopher Bertrand Russell (1872–1970). He taught first at Cambridge and then at the University of London, and in 1924 followed a call to Harvard.[149] His three major works on metaphysics and religion, which mediate modern science and religion, were written and published in a relatively short time between 1925 and 1929. Whitehead was not actually a student of German Idealism, so the similarities are more likely due to the Platonic tradition in British philosophy. In his first book on metaphysics, *Science and the Modern World*, he defines God with reference to Spinoza's doctrine of one substance. Similar to Plato and the early Schelling [chap. 2.2.2], he interprets this one substance as irrational activity and eternal possibility limited

146. Trans. Harold H. Oliver (Macon, GA: Mercer University Press, 1997).

147. *Der Pantocrator*, 14.

148. See esp. Jaspers, *Philosophical Faith and Revelation*, trans. E. B. Ashton (London: Collins, 1967); *The Perennial Scope of Philosophy* (New York: Philosophical Library, 1949); on Jesus: *The Great Philosophers*, trans. Ralph Mannheim (New York: Harcourt, Brace & World, 1962), 74–97. See also Kurt Hoffmann, "The Basic Concepts of Jaspers' Philosophy," in Paul Arthur Schilpp, ed., *The Philosophy of Karl Jaspers* (New York: Tudor, 1957), 95–113. Jaspers had been a devoted student of Max Weber.

149. A brief autobiography is included in Paul Arthur Sharp, ed., *The Philosophy of Alfred North Whitehead* (New York: Tudor, 1951), 3–14. Whitehead's student Charles Hartshorne and Hartshorne's student John B. Cobb Jr. are two prominent theologians in America who have, in a new form of mediation, developed Whitehead's thought theologically: Charles Hartshorne, *Man's Vision of God* (Chicago: Willet, Clark & Co, 1941); *The Divine Relativity* (New Haven, CT: Yale University Press, 1948); John B. Cobb Jr., *A Christian Natural Theology* (Philadelphia: Westminster, 1965). Cf. Wolfhart Pannenberg's critique of Whiteheadian theology, *Metaphysics and the Idea of God*, trans. Philip Clayton (Grand Rapids: Eerdmans, 1990), chap. 6.

by a power or principle of limitation. Through this principle, substance "determines" or conditions itself into particular finite existence. It introduces "contraries, grades and oppositions" into the open possibilities of substance. It aims, with its ordering of the possibilities, at producing an existing world, including the division of good and evil in human history. "What further can be known about God must be sought in the region of particular experiences." The various world religions and philosophies name God according to their experiences.[150]

In interaction with science, religious expression discards (or should discard) outdated mythical and dogmatic explanations of God. Religion also learns (or should learn) that it does not primarily have to do with ethical conduct. "Religion is the vision of something which stands beyond, behind, and within, the passing flux of immediate things; something which is real, yet waiting to be realized; something which is a remote possibility, and yet the greatest of present facts; something that gives meaning to all that passes, and yet eludes apprehension; something whose possession is the final good, and yet is beyond all reach; something which is the ultimate ideal, and the hopeless quest. The immediate reaction of human nature to the religious vision is worship."[151] In this statement the meaning of religion seems to lie in the infinite nature of God, beyond human finitude but with which human finitude is ontologically connected and toward which it reaches [cf., e.g., James, chap. 4.8].

In Whitehead's next book, *Religion in the Making*, he further defines the concept of God, and in such a way that one hears echoes of Hegel [chap. 2.3]. God is "the completed ideal harmony" of the creativity and possibilities of the actual universe.[152] God is an "actual" or "definite entity" or, in traditional metaphysical language, a real being. If God were not his actual entity, there would be no real creativity and nothing to control infinite possibility (152). God includes all possible concepts and, because of this, is omniscience. In the valuation of possibilities God has always already decided for good against evil, and God's aim in creation is the "transmutation of evil into good." God transcends the temporal world, and "the consciousness which is temporal in us, is universal in him." Religious feelings, which can be quite strong, are unreliable in the interpretation of religion (144–60).

In a third work, *Process and Reality*, Whitehead says that God is affected by events in the world. Applied to human life, the argument can be summarized as follows. While God interacts with the world as its principle of limitation—that is, of possibility, value, and direction toward what is good—human being makes free choices that take the events in one direction instead of another. There must therefore be a corresponding adjustment in God's action that accommodates the new situation and gives new creative possibilities for development toward what

---

150. *Science the Modern World*, 1st ed. 1925 (New York: Free Press, 1967), 177–79.
151. Ibid., 189–92.
152. *Religion in the Making* (New York: Macmillan, 1926), 119f.; cf. 156f. Page references to the end of the paragraph are to this work.

is good.[153] For ethics this opens a dimension of dealing with situations that envisions and tries to actualize creative solutions rather than, for example, relying on methods from the past. The argument has a parallel in Hegel, for whom the dialectic of "Spirit" is inherently directed toward new syntheses as forms of reconciliation, and for whom Spirit includes all possibilities of actual being.[154]

153. *Process and Reality* (New York: Macmillan, 1929), 524ff. Cf. Cobb, *Christian Natural Theology*, 251: God "constantly readjusts his aim to the partial successes and partial failures of the past so that some new possibility of achievement always lies ahead."
154. On Hegel and Whitehead, see George R. Lucas Jr., *Two Views of Freedom in Process Thought: A Study of Hegel and Whitehead* (Missoula, MT: Scholars Press, 1979), esp. 123ff., and George R. Lucas Jr., ed., *Hegel and Whitehead* (Albany: State University of New York, 1986).

Chapter 5

Antecedents of Dialectic Theology

5.1 MARTIN KÄHLER

In his student days Martin Kähler (1835–1912), professor of systematic theology and New Testament at Halle, studied under Richard Rothe, August Tholuck, and Julius Müller [chap. 3]. Like them he was a product of the Awakening; like the Ritschlians he became critical of the kind of mediation theology these teachers represented. He was also influenced by the biblical theology of Johann Tobias Beck [chap. 1.2]. The work for which Kähler is famous is *The So-Called Historical Jesus and the Historic Biblical Christ,* first published in German in 1892.[1] In the original title, *Der sogenannte historische Jesus und der geschichtliche, biblische Christus,* a distinction is made between *historisch* and *geschichtlich.*[2] Both words mean "historical." *Geschichtlich* is a Germanic word

---

1. Trans. Carl E. Braaten (Philadelphia: Fortress, 1964). Page numbers in the following text refer to this work unless otherwise noted. Significant works on Kähler's theology are in German, esp. Hans-Georg Link, *Geschichte Jesu und Bild Christi* (Neukirchen: Neukirchener Verlag, 1975); see also Johannes H. Schmid, *Erkenntnis des geschichtlichen Christus bei Martin Kähler und bei Adolf Schlatter* (Basel: F. Reinhardt, 1978).

2. Cf. Wilhelm Herrmann [chap 4.3] and George Wobbermin [chap. 4.6 note 81].

with a nuance of "story," while *historisch,* like its English equivalent, comes from Latin. Kähler uses the terms to distinguish between the life of Jesus as produced by critical-historical research (*historisch*), which in his view falsifies the biblical view of Jesus, and the true historical (*geschichtliche*) "picture" of Jesus, the Christ of faith in the New Testament [cf. "photograph" in Rothe, chap. 3.2]. For Kähler the falsification resulted from psychological and biographical interpretations of Jesus for which no actual historical data in the Bible existed (a complaint made against earlier lives of Jesus by D. F. Strauss). Controversy swirled around Kähler's claim that "the entire life of Jesus movement" is "a blind alley" (46). Historical-critical work on the life of Jesus produces nothing but changing results, both from critic to critic and from generation to generation. And Christian faith has never and does not now rest on the results of historical criticism [cf. Herrmann, chap. 4.2]. For Kähler (in distinction from Herrmann) the true historical Jesus of the Bible is "the crucified, risen and living Lord." He is "the Christ of the apostolic preaching, of the whole New Testament" (64f.). The attempt to go behind the New Testament witness to a supposedly more human Jesus, as had occurred in the lives of Jesus of the time, is based on the assumption that Jesus is "like us," and not, as the Bible presents him, "unlike us" in his sinlessness and his being savior, that is, his supernatural quality (52ff.). The New Testament and the history of the church show clearly that he evoked "childlike" faith, a trust that depended only on the New Testament "picture" Christ (66ff., 79). According to Kähler one cannot, as in Herrmann, isolate an "inner life" of Jesus that is "behind" the New Testament's presentation or picture of Christ as the risen Lord (77).

Kähler's critique of problematic historical criticism was also directed at the earlier mediation theology's attempts at reconciliation with historical criticism. He relates that Tholuck once told a student that if John the disciple could be proven not to have written the Gospel, it would be "an almost insuperable blow to Christianity." This, says Kähler, is indicative of this theology's "wait and see attitude" toward criticism and, more subtly but definitely, of its fear and restriction of criticism (107). According to Kähler there must be another "foundation" for the confidence in the New Testament sources. "There must be for everyone a reliable means of access to the Christ of the whole Bible" (121f., 63f.). This access is apostolic preaching of the living Lord (71).[3] But Kähler was not an opponent of historical criticism. He considered its development "a divine dispensation for the church," a judgment he bases on "trust in God's educative rule over the church" (148). The historical critical discovery of oral traditions, for example, has shown they are an undeniable component of the New Testament; they are "trustworthy" in what they communicate (142). Criticism also supports the apostolic proclamation. The doctrine of biblical inerrancy, for example, begins

---

3. Kähler's systematic work, *Die Wissenschaft der christlichen Lehre* [see later in this chapter], §§49–52, affirms the doctrine of the internal witness to Scripture by Holy Spirit, *fides divina* (cf. p. 703).

by declaring the Bible revelation, only after which follows a corresponding appropriation of its content. This is essentially the same procedure as beginning with doctrinal propositions that must be accepted. In both cases a "law" is imposed on faith. Rightly one begins with the Christ whose death and resurrection mean the justification of the sinner (134ff., 95).

Kähler's large systematic work, *Die Wissenschaft der christlichen Lehre* (The Science of Christian Doctrine),[4] is a comprehensive treatment of the presuppositions and content of Christian doctrine and ethics. He explains that theology, the "science" of Christian doctrine, must be given its content, the revelation, through faith, and it has the task of relating this content to the rest of science (§§1ff., 18, 36). In the section entitled "Apologetic" or "Presuppositions of Faith in Justification," Kähler follows a familiar path in nineteenth-century theology; he develops a "theological anthropology": a doctrine of religion and the God-consciousness prior to faith (§114ff.). He does this only after he defines Christianity as the objectively true religion and justification as God's objective act in the death and resurrection of Christ, so that theological anthropology is developed in the light of this truth (§§99–113). God-consciousness and religion are essentially receptive; they are the "structures" for receiving Christian revelation (§§117–127).

Kähler notes that the term "unconditioned" only makes a negative statement about God. If the theologian uses it to define God as a divine being that "conditions" human or finite life, then it is comparable to the concept of the *Allgemeine,* an abstract general concept of God [cf. chap. 2.3]. But God is not defined by such conceptions. If God were, God "would belong to our world," because God would be defined by a human concept [cf. Herrmann]. However if one says that God grounds and conditions God, so that all definition in God is God's own [cf. Dorner, chap. 3.3], then one may say that God is the unconditioned. For now there is no thought of God being conditioned by finitude. And one may also say that God conditions or determines human life (§§187–90). Kähler emphasizes that God is personal and living (§189ff.), the God of Christ's resurrection (§382) and his second coming (§522ff.). The miracles of Jesus have to do with the purpose of God in revelation. There are problematic aspects of the miracles, which "are reserved to more comprehensive and deeper-going insight" (§219).

Throughout the *Wissenschaft der christlichen Lehre* the dominant theme is the sovereign purpose of God in the history of salvation and the world. Kähler lifts up the church's task of mission to the world (§§99ff., 213, 492f.).[5] Christian fellowship is "higher than the membership of a folk" (§753). "The requirements of the moral consciousness find their all-encompassing satisfaction only in the conviction that our world is a purposefully determined whole and that each personal individual life is in a relationship of interaction with it." This and other

---

4. 3rd ed. (Leipzig: Deichert, 1905). References to sections (§) in the following text are to this work.
5. *Schriften zu Christologie und Mission,* ed. Heinzgünter Frohnes (Munich: Christian Kaiser, 1971), is an extensive collection of Kähler's writings on missions.

similarities to Ritschl's theology have caused comparison of the two since Kähler's time.[6] Kähler is, however, different from Ritschl, not only in his concentration on mission and conversion, but also in his pessimism in regard to the situation of the established churches and the state of Christianity in Germany. In his view Germany was in sore need of missions.[7]

5.2 FRANZ OVERBECK

Franz Overbeck (1837–1905), professor of church history and New Testament at Basel, is known for his friendship with the controversial philosopher Friedrich Nietzsche (1844–1900) and for his attack on the theology of his time, particularly that of the Ritschlians, as symptomatic of the "end of Christianity." Prior to teaching at Basel he had been a lecturer in early church history at Jena, where his academic patron was Karl Hase [chap. 3.4]. He valued the criticism of F. C. Baur and his Tübingen School, but he was not a Hegelian. In fact the influence neither of Hase nor of Baur provides sufficient ground for understanding his basic conception of theology and church history.[8]

At the beginning of his academic career Overbeck was interested especially in early monasticism, which tried, "by the sweat of its brow" but without success, to continue the "denial" of the world it inherited from New Testament eschatology. A constant theme of Overbeck's work is that early Christianity's vision of the resurrected Christ, which had the meaning of a new world, is in complete contradiction with a continuation of the old world or eon and its culture, which is the product of human sinfulness. In an important example, Overbeck says that Christianity's original vision of a new world meant real hope for the slaves of the Roman Empire.[9] Overbeck concentrated his work on two related subjects: the history of the transition from the eschatological vision of early Christianity to the church "of this world," and the criticism of theology as being "of this world."

---

6. *Wissenschaft der christlichen Lehre*, §262. Kähler also speaks of judgments of faith as "value" judgments (§610). See Link, 333–44. See also Kähler's discussion of Ritschl, *Geschichte der protestantischen Theologie im 19. Jahrhundert*, 240–63, cf. 263–76.

7. See, e.g., *Schriften zu Christologie und Mission*, 351–68.

8. On the following, see the introduction to Franz Overbeck, *On the Christianity of Theology*, trans. John E. Wilson (San Jose: Pickwick Publications, 2002), and the work itself, esp. chap. 1. It is a translation of the 2nd ed. of *Über die Christlichkeit unserer heutigen Theologie*, 1st ed. 1873 (Leipzig: C. G. Naumann, 1903; reprint Darmstadt: Wissenschaftliche Buchgesellschaft, 1963). The other work for which Overbeck is most known is *Christentum und Kultur*, a selection of Overbeck's notes strongly edited by C. A. Bernoulli (Basel: Benno Schwabe, 1919; reprint Darmstadt: Wissenschaftliche Buchgesellschaft, 1963). A new edition of Overbeck's works, *Franz Overbeck Werke und Nachlass* (Stuttgart: Verlag J. B. Metzler, 1994ff.) has been published by the Franz Overbeck Commission in Basel. On Overbeck, see also Martin Henry, *Franz Overbeck, Theologian?* (Frankfurt: Peter Lang, 1995); Niklaus Peter, *Im Schatten der Modernität, Franz Overbecks Weg zur Christlichkeit der heutigen Theologie* (Stuttgart: J. B. Metzler, 1992).

9. Overbeck, *Studien zur Geschichte der alten Kirche*, 1st ed. 1875 (Darmstadt: Wissenschaftliche Buchgesellschaft, 1965), 225. Cf. *Christianity of Theology*, 26, 97f.

He was aware of a kinship with D. F. Strauss's criticism of Schleiermacher and mediation theology as being "half faith, half science." For if faith is originally determined by the belief in the resurrected Christ and the end of this world, then all "science" [*Wissenschaft*],[10] which has to do with the development of thought in this world, must be foreign to faith. Therefore, he said, theology contains in its science an element that is actually hostile to faith, insofar as science inherently affirms the existing world. And with its science theology makes life possible for Christianity in a world that Christianity in truth denies.[11]

Overbeck scores the fact that contemporary theology, while it lives within current "this-worldly" culture, is interested in the "religion of Jesus" that one might in some way adopt as one's own. For example, Harnack's understanding of the religion of Jesus is fully accommodated to life in present-day culture [as Harnack also intended]. Historically the belief of Christianity in Christ, beginning with the New Testament, was only interested in his significance as the savior, something no one could imitate.[12] Moreover, theology in the modern period is a matter of many different individual theologies that are in constant conflict with one another. All of this is evidence that the "old world," the only world theology knows, continues to exist. Theology should recognize the contradiction between itself and Christianity's original proclamation, but instead it "draws Christianity down" into this world; that is, it forces Christianity to live as a member of it. For Overbeck, no theologian exemplified this more or better than Harnack.[13] It is for this reason that Overbeck speaks of the "end of Christianity": it is being dissolved into the cultural ideas and values of the modern world.[14] No different is his understanding of the life of the church, where there are a "thousandfold practical compromises" lying "before us in daily life." He nevertheless suggests that "wise pastors" will "heed their practical vocation" and keep their distance from the conflicts of theology.[15]

Not all theology suffers in Overbeck's view from such "worldliness," although he does not say much about this. In his earlier thought he spoke of Luther's 1532 commentary on Galatians as a powerful work of Christian "poetry," not history and hence not science or *Wissenschaft*.[16] So in this regard the Galatians commentary

10. *Wissenschaft* is meant in the broad sense of the humanities (philosophy, history) as well as the natural sciences.

11. *Christianity of Theology*, 70. For Overbeck Christianity did however "de-divinize" or secularize the world, insofar as its effect on the world resulted in the destruction of belief in the gods (Ibid., 97). (Cf. Schelling, *Werke*, 14:175, 239.)

12. *Christianity of Theology*, 90. Ritschl's *Justification and Reconciliation*, published after this work by Overbeck, also expresses this [chap. 4.2].

13. *Christianity of Theology*, 107, 148–52; *Christentum und Kultur*, 198–240, cf. similar comments on Ritschl, 165–68, 172, 176f.

14. *Christentum und Kultur*, 289, cf. *Christianity of Theology*, 134, cf. Kierkegaard, *Sickness unto Death*, 91f.

15. *Christianity of Theology*, 56.

16. Cf. poetic form in the early Schelling [chap. 2.2.5] and Richard Rothe [chap. 3.2]. This is not an uncommon term for religious language in the nineteenth century. It meant what was not *Wissenschaft*.

is not theology as Overbeck defines it. In the same essay he writes, "The Socinians and Arminians openly said that they wanted to found the religious value (fides divina) of the biblical books on their historical credibility (fides humana). Precisely this the orthodox theologians did not want to do, and entirely correctly."[17]

Overbeck's most important historical publication is Über die Anfänge der patristischen Literatur (On the Beginnings of Patristic Literature).[18] It has to do with the period of transition in the life of the church from an existence that, especially in the New Testament period, had little or nothing to do with the world of culture and was not recognized by it, into an existence that took Greco-Roman culture into itself and came to be recognized as a factor in this culture. The canon of the New Testament is an Urliteratur (original literature) "that Christianity created so to speak by its own means [not those of the culture], insofar as this literature grew exclusively on the basis of and within the particular interests of the Christian community prior to its mixture with the surrounding world" (36). In another place he attributes authorship in the New Testament to the inspiration of the Holy Spirit.[19]

The beginning canonization of New Testament writings is a symptom of the transition, as is the work of the first Christian apologists, which addresses non-Christians. "Patristic literature" comes into being when a canon is presupposed, and when Christian writers adopt given cultural ("profane") forms of literature to communicate not with non-Christians, but with new Christians (47ff.). Forms of secular history and philosophical literature, found previously in apologetic theology, are now used to teach new converts. Overbeck's example is Clement of Alexandria (deceased before the year 216), who teaches the Christian faith to an increasingly large "heathen" public within the church. This public is made up of a mass of educated new Christians—educated in Greek culture—who have not had the same Christian experience as the early Christians of the New Testament and the immediately following postapostolic period. They are not only relatively ignorant of what the New Testament is about, but they also have a specific frame of reference for understanding it in their own culture and its Wissenschaft.

17. Introduction to the Christianity of Theology, 19f., which gives a summary of Overbeck's introductory address at the University of Basel in 1870: Entstehung und Recht einer rein historischen Betrachtung der neutestamentlichen Schriften, now published in Franz Overbeck Werke und Nachlass, vol. 1, Schriften bis 1873, ed. Ekkehard Stegemann und Niklaus Peter (Stuttgart: J. B. Metzler, 1994), 75–106. The exposition of the doctrine of justification by faith in the Galatians Commentary is for Luther an "inexhaustible and deep content that extends into the immeasurable [das Ungemessene]" (93). On fides divina and fides humana, see Rothe, Dorner, and Hase in chap. 3.

18. (Darmstadt: Wissenschaftliche Buchgesellschaft, 1966), 36. The work originally appeared in the Historische Zeitschrift 48 (1882):417–71. References in the following are to the Darmstadt edition. Prior to coming to Basel, Overbeck translated into German Clement of Alexandria's main work, which was posthumously edited and published: Titus Flavius Klemens von Alexandria, Die Teppiche (Stromateis), ed. C. A. Bernoulli und Ludwig Früchtel (Basel: Benno Schwabe, 1936).

19. See translator's introduction to Christianity of Theology, 25, where Overbeck's 1879 lecture, Geschichte der christlichen Literatur bis Eusebius, is quoted.

Clement wrestles with the problem of the inadequacy of the forms of his teaching, especially of his theology of the universal Logos, which is derived mainly from Greek philosophy. He is aware of the hermeneutical problem of discussing the Christian faith in forms derived from Greek culture (66). The canonical expression of Christianity is the New Testament, which contains highest truth, yet this truth lies beyond the initial understanding of Clement's new Christians. His effort is to develop a method by which the educated heathen may be led to discover the truth of the New Testament, which in the context of Greco-Roman literature or philosophy can only be paradoxical.

For Overbeck, patristic literature marks the transition to all postcanonical Christian literature and to theology in the proper sense of the word. (Paul is not a theologian but an apostle.) In this context, especially in Overbeck's understanding of Clement's relationship to the canon of the New Testament, it is noteworthy that Overbeck saw "no value" in "purely abstract definitions of religion."[20] Original Christianity is a particular and specific phenomenon; abstract concepts of religion are products of philosophy as *Wissenschaft*.[21]

In the centuries following Clement and in the Middle Ages, the sciences stood in the service of a church powerful enough to order the sciences under the rule of faith, even as the church accommodated itself to these sciences. In the modern period, the sciences are emancipated from the church, so that the church once again finds itself in a situation that is to a certain degree similar to Clement's.[22] Perhaps it is an indication of Clement's dilemma in Overbeck's own time when Overbeck uses the paradoxical image of "placing oneself in the air" (*sich in die Luft stellen*) to express what does not stand on the ground of *Wissenschaft* or of cultural values and norms.[23] In any case Overbeck's work on Clement understands theology as something that develops not in the New Testament but in the patristic period, and in his view it has always been "modern" or "timely,"

20. From a letter to A. E. Biedermann, in Paul Burkhardt, "Aus der Korrespondenz von A. E. Biedermann (1819–1885)," *Aus fünf Jahrhunderten schweizerischer Kirchengeschichte. Zum 60. Geburtstag von Paul Wernle* (Basel: Beno Schwabe, 1932), 346. See the discussion of this letter in the translator's introduction to *Christianity of Theology*, 1f. Cf. the later Schelling's critique of Hegel [chap. 2.4.2]; cf. Kierkegaard [chap. 2.6].

21. As the New Testament is *Urliteratur*, so its history is *Urgeschichte*, an original Christian history which, in comparison with all following Christian history, is not only unique but also, as Overbeck enigmatically said, "more than history." *Christentum und Kultur*, 20–28. A characteristic of Christian *Urgeschichte* is that so little historical knowledge or data exists about it, other than what is in the New Testament writings themselves. A "historical literature" like that in the Greco-Roman world of the time is missing. Overbeck's thesis is "a literature has its history in its forms, therefore every real history of literature will be a history of forms [*Formengeschichte*]" (*Über die Anfänge der patristischen Literatur*, 12).

22. *Christianity of Theology*, 74: "Broadly conceiving the human significance of the matter, support for Christianity is either a matter for all the sciences, as was earlier the case, or for none at all, as is presently the case. For theology today not even the appearance of support can exist."

23. *Christentum und Kultur*, 77. Overbeck may have taken the expression "in the air" from D. F. Strauss, who says that Schleiermacher, in eliminating the orthodox-supernatural explanation of Jesus' sinless perfection, has no real basis for asserting it, hence the assertion "stands in the air" (*Der Christus des Glaubens und der Jesus der Geschichte*, 33).

culturally and scientifically up to date.[24] One could also say it has always been apologetic theology and hence mediation theology.

Late in life, after he retired from his professorship at Basel, Overbeck, in manuscripts that were published long after his death, made a point of denying faith— or at least seeming to deny it, for his denials are ambiguous. He writes for example, "I was professor of theology, but as such [*dabei*] neither a theologian nor a Christian."[25] The words can be taken in two ways: simply that he was neither a theologian nor a Christian, or that as a theologian he professed neither theology (which he opposed) nor Christianity (which according to Overbeck no theologian as such professes). Was he intentionally leaving theological posterity a riddle?[26] According to Karl Barth, who did not discuss this question, Overbeck did address "unanswered" or "insufficiently answered" questions to theology.[27]

The ambiguities in his late writings may in some way reflect ambiguities in the late works of his friend Nietzsche, whose sharp critique of Christianity is related to Overbeck's criticism of modern theological Christianity. In spite of more than a century of scholarship, Nietzsche's late works are still enigmatic. His famous statement of the "death of God" depicts God as subject to the changes of time and to changing ideas.[28] In *The Birth of Tragedy* Nietzsche wrote: "For it is the fate of every myth to insinuate itself into the narrow limits of some alleged historical reality, and to be treated by some later generation as a solitary fact with historical claims. . . . For this is the manner in which religions are wont to die out: when . . . under the stern, intelligent eyes of an orthodox dogmatism, the mythical presuppositions of a religion are systematized as completed sum of historical events, and when one begins apprehensively to defend the credibility of

24. *Christentum und Kultur,* 292. Insofar as Overbeck's view of the transition to theology in church history is in effect a kind of "fall" from New Testament Christianity, it bears some resemblance to the *Magdeburger Centurien* of the Lutheran church historian Matthias Flacius (1520–75), whose history represents Roman Catholicism as a fall from the pure teaching of the early church. It also resembles histories in Pentecostalism that see a loss of the Holy Spirit in the church after the New Testament period (to be given again in the end times). And one is reminded of Karl Hase's saying that all great histories end tragically.

25. Quoted from Overbeck's unpublished manuscripts in the introduction to *Christianity of Theology,* 27f.

26. Among the pieces of the puzzle is Overbeck's handwritten copy of John Henry Newman's hymn "Lead and Guide Me," left among other quotations from various sources for his posthumous editor to read, now located in the unpublished archives: Franz-Overbeck-Nachlass, A 271, Handschriften-Abteilung der Universitätsbibliothek Basel.

27. Karl Barth's essay title, "Unerledigte Anfragen an die Theologie," stems from his debate with Eberhad Vischer about Overbeck in *Die christliche Welt,* 1922 (see the introduction to *Christianity of Theology*). Vischer later published an autobiographical essay by the late Overbeck. Vischer gave it the title, *Selbstbekenntnisse* (Basel: Benno Schwabe, 1941). Visher's introduction includes the information that toward the end of his life Overbeck was awarded and accepted a Doctor of Divinity degree from the University of St. Andrews in Scotland. This award (like the oath of office Overbeck took on becoming a member of the Basel theological faculty) included a confessional affirmation of Christianity.

28. E.g., in the section "The Madman," in *The Joyful Wisdom (La Gaya Scienza),* trans. Thomas Common (New York: Russell & Russell, 1964), §125, pp. 167f.

the myth, while at the same time opposing all continuation of their natural vitality and luxuriance; when accordingly, the feeling for myth dies out, and its place is taken by the claim of religion to historical foundations."[29] Here Nietzsche reflects, from a rather different perspective, one aspect of Overbeck's view of the history of theology.

29. *Birth of Tragedy*, trans. Wm. A. Hausmann (New York: Russell & Russell, 1964), §10, p. 84. Nietzsche's late works are anti-Christian but have a certain prophetic quality. His concepts and images are mythological and consistently reflect aspects of the philosophy of nature. Interpretations of mythology in the nineteenth century, especially in early Romanticism and Idealism, must be taken into account in the attempt to understand him. See, e.g., J. E. Wilson, *Schelling und Nietzsche* (Berlin: Walter de Gruyter, 1996).

Chapter 6

Dialectic Theology

"Dialectic theology" emerged among a group of young theologians in the years after World War I; most of its advocates were to experience the far greater catastrophes of the next war. They agreed with their Neo-Kantian and Ritschlian teachers on the impossibility of a scientifically valid philosophical metaphysics, but in almost all other areas they were quite critical of them. One characteristic mark of dialectic theology is an interest in Kierkegaard that far exceeded the attention given him in previous decades. It has often been noted that this interest fell together with a broad postwar cultural pessimism and, especially among the dialectic theologians, skepticism about the Christian character of Western culture. Franz Overbeck is another theologian given attention he did not have before. The critical philosophy of Nietzsche was read with renewed interest, and the novels of the nineteenth-century Russian Fyodor Dostoyevsky (1821–81) were discovered as it were for the first time. Kierkegaard was also an important source for the postwar development of philosophical existentialism [Martin Heidegger, see chap. 6.3]. Kierkegaard's contrast of authentic existence or faith with Hegel's absolute reason has a parallel in the existentialists' reaction against the total comprehension of existence in scientific thought. In connection with existentialism there emerged new reflection on how one's relationship to things, persons, or God determines

171

the way one perceives and behaves toward them, as expressed for example in the alternatives "I-It" and "I-Thou."[1] In the wake of Neo-Kantianism, philosophy in support of scientific modernity and its rapid technical progress continued with new developments in empirical analysis.

6.1 KARL BARTH

Karl Barth (1886–1968) was born into a Swiss Reformed pastor's family; his father later became a professor of theology in Bern.[2] His university education was in Germany and mainly in Marburg, the most liberal and progressive theological faculty of the time. Here he studied under Wilhelm Herrmann, the Neo-Kantian philosophers Hermann Cohen and Paul Natorp, and some of the period's most important biblical scholars. He also studied under Harnack in Berlin, and he served on the staff of the Ritschlian newspaper/journal, *Die christliche Welt*. As a young pastor in Switzerland he became a religious socialist and an active member of the Social-Democratic Party. Work for the kingdom of God meant commitment to work on behalf of the poor for social justice. Later, around the time of the Russian Revolution in 1917, he moved away from "religious-socialist" theology ("hyphenated theology" as he was to call it). He began stressing the independence of the gospel from political programs, but he still insisted on the gospel's revolutionary nature. His first work of major importance was the second edition of his commentary on Paul's letter to the Romans, published in 1922.[3] Through this work he became the leader of the new dialec-

1. This is commonly associated with the 1924 work of the Jewish philosopher-theologian Martin Buber, *I and Thou*, trans. Ronald Gregor Smith (New York: Collier-Macmillan, 1958). The analysis of "I-It" was particularly important for the critique of the inhumanity of modern technical society generally.

2. The standard biography is by Eberhard Busch, *Karl Barth*, trans. John Bowden (Philadelphia: Fortress, 1975). Recent introductions to Barth are given in George Hunsinger, *How to Read Karl Barth* (New York: Oxford, 1991); Eberhard Busch, *The Great Passion: An Introduction to Karl Barth's Theology*, trans. Geoffrey W. Bromiley (Grand Rapids: Eerdmans, 2004); Eberhard Jüngel, *Karl Barth, A Theological Legacy*, trans. Garrett E. Paul (Philadelphia: Westminster, 1986); Geoffrey W. Bromiley, *Introduction to the Theology of Karl Barth* (Grand Rapids: Eerdmans, 1979); see also the works mentioned in the following footnote. Recent interpretations of Barth's theology are George Hunsinger, *Disruptive Grace: Studies in the Theology of Karl Barth* (Grand Rapids: Eerdmans, 2000); Eberhard Jüngel, *God's Being Is in Becoming*, trans. John Webster (Grand Rapids: Eerdmans, 2001); Gary Dorrien, *The Barthian Revolt in Modern Theology: Theology without Weapons* (Louisville, KY: Westminster John Knox, 2000); John Webster, ed., *The Cambridge Companion to Karl Barth* (Cambridge: Cambridge University Press, 2000).

3. *Der Römerbrief*, 2nd ed. (Munich: Christian Kaiser, 1922); ET: *The Epistle to the Romans*, trans. Edwyn C. Hoskyns from the 6th German edition (Oxford: Oxford University Press, 1933). The first German edition (Bern: G.A. Bäschlin, 1919) has been reprinted (Zurich: EVZ-Verlag, 1963). Some recent works on Barth's development as theologian are: Simon Fisher, *Revelatory Positivism? Barth's Earliest Theology and the Marburg School* (Oxford: Oxford University Press, 1988); Bruce McCormack, *Karl Barth's Critically Realistic Dialectical Theology: Its Genesis and Development 1909–1936* (Oxford: Clarendon, 1995); T. F. Torrance, *Karl Barth, an Introduction to His Early Theology,*

tic theology.[4] Following its publication he was called to a series of university positions in Germany: first to a position for Reformed theology in the Lutheran faculty at Göttingen, then to the predominantly Catholic theological faculty at Münster, then to Bonn in the United Church. Because of his opposition to the Nazi government he was officially "retired" in 1936, and his writings were banned. In this same year he moved to the Reformed theological faculty at the University of Basel in Switzerland. In 1931 Barth had begun his major work, the *Church Dogmatics*, which was unfinished at his death.[5]

6.1.1 The Second Edition of *Romans*

A remarkable coincidence of influences led Barth to write the heavily revised second edition of *Romans*: Kierkegaard, Overbeck, and the Awakening pastor Johann Christoph Blumhardt (1805–80) and his son Christoph Blumhardt (1842–1919). Barth's theologian-friend Edward Thurneysen (1888–1974) had earlier introduced him to the religious-socialist and pastor-theologian in Zurich, Hermann Kutter (1863–1931), who was also a bridge to the Blumhardts, especially to Christoph Blumhardt, Kutter's "spiritual father."[6] Probably through Blumhardt, Kutter came to value the biblical realism of Johann Tobias Beck [chap. 1.2], in particular Beck's depiction of the contrast between Christ's teaching of the kingdom of God and Christianity as it ordinarily exists. This was also a theme of the Blumhardts' preaching, and it was related to Overbeck's critical theology. Especially the elder Blumhardt proclaimed the imminent coming of the kingdom of God and the spiritual gifts of the end time, while his son applied his father's message concretely to political action for social justice.[7] Kutter contrasted

---

1910–1931 (London: SCM, 1962); Ingrid Spieckermann, *Gotteserkenntnis: Ein Beitrag zur Grundfrage der neuen Theologie Karl Barths* (Munich: Christian Kaiser, 1985). W. R. Ward's *Theology, Sociology and Politics: The German Protestant Social Conscience 1890–1933* [cf. chap. 1.4] shows the position of Barth's socialist theology within the context of the political and social thought of the period. Much contested is Friedrich-Wilhelm Marquardt's work on Barth and socialism: *Theologie und Socialismus: Das Beispiel Karl Barths* (Munich: Kaiser-Grünewald, 1972). (In the 1st ed. of *Römerbrief,* p. 332, Barth predicts a new birth of "Marxist dogma as world-truth, when the socialist church will be resurrected in a socialist world.") Marquardt is discussed in *Karl Barth and Radical Politics,* trans. George Hunsinger (Philadelphia: Westminster, 1976), and Jüngel, *Karl Barth,* 82–104.

4. James M. Robinson, ed., *The Beginnings of Dialectic Theology.* A new journal, *Zwischen den Zeiten* (Between the Times), was established for dialectic theology by Barth, Edward Thurneysen, and Friedrich Gogarten, published 1923–33.

5. Karl Barth, *Church Dogmatics,* trans. G. W. Bromiley et al., 4 vols. in 13 and Index (London: T. & T. Clark, 2004). (References to this work in our text are to the volume and page or section number.) Barth's German works, other than the *Church Dogmatics,* are being published in the *Karl Barth Gesamtausgabe,* currently 41 vols. (Zurich: Theologischer Verlag, 1971ff.).

6. Andreas Lindt, "Hermann Kutter," in Martin Greschat, ed., *Gestalten der Kirchengeschichte,* 10/1, 128.

7. See Barth's essay on the elder Blumhardt in *Protestant Theology in the Nineteenth Century.* On the younger Blumhardt, see Robinson, ed., *Beginnings of Dialectic Theology,* 40–45, and R. Lejeune, *Christoph Blumhardt and His Message* (Woodcrest: Plough Publishing, 1963). See also Busch, *Karl Barth,* 83–87.

Jesus' preaching of the kingdom with "religion," which he condemned as a symptom of the alienation of humanity from true life.[8]

In the second edition of his commentary on *Romans*,[9] Barth rejects the identification of the Christian gospel with socialist revolution (476ff.), because the socialist revolution remains in and of this world, while the gospel is truly revolutionary (530). But there is a far greater rejection involved in the work, namely, a radical break with the whole of the "mediation" tradition in nineteenth-century theology, the tradition that mediated traditional Christianity with philosophy. It had begun in Idealism and had been continued into the twentieth century by the Ritschlians and the theologians of the history of religions school. For Barth, the contrast could not be greater between God, Christ, and the gospel on the one hand and all human philosophical and religious endeavor on the other. (The contrast is what defines "dialectic.") Kierkegaard was particularly significant for Barth's understanding of this distinction. He takes from Kierkegaard the understanding of the "infinite qualitative difference" between this world's reasoning and faith as "paradox" and "encounter" with God in Christ, and the concept of revelation as the "moment" that is not explained within historical time. Only God's act can lay the foundation of faith in Christ.[10] He also takes from Kierkegaard the equally infinite difference between the so-called gods of this world and the holy and "wholly other" God of the Bible who "dwells in unapproachable light" (1 Tim. 6:16) (e.g.,109–12). In Reformed orthodoxy a similar thought had been formulated in the expression, "the finite cannot contain the infinite."[11]

Although Overbeck had denied that theology could be a "true" theology—for Barth theology is, as he finds it in Paul, the Word of God (422)—Barth takes from Overbeck his conviction that theology and church must avoid "compromises" (36f.) with culture and its sciences, for this would mean finding some

8. Kutter, *Das Unmittelbare* (The Immediate) 1st ed. 1902 (Basel: Kober, 1921), the last part of which (276–347) has to do with the difference between "religion" and Christianity. The book is based on the Marxist thesis (esp. chap. 2) that humankind lived originally in harmony with itself and nature in the "immediacy" of natural life. With the development of capitalism, it experienced increasing alienation from and fragmentation of "the immediate." But progress in philosophy, theology, and society has led in the present to the dawning realization that the real meaning of life, the "immediate," can be won through the rebirth of original faith that God is in Christ and believers are in Christ (John 17). From this unity and its expression in Christ's preaching (esp. the Beatitudes) the ethics of justice follows. In a way similar to the early Marx, in *Das Unmittelbare* Kutter is highly critical of "abstract" reasoning (esp. Hegel) as a sign of alienation, while he uses the early work of Schelling for the philosophical analysis of alienation and of the immediate as "identity" (e.g., 7, 17f., 61, 276). Kutter also makes frequent reference to Lotze.

9. References in the following text are to Hoskyn's English translation of Barth's *Romans*.

10. Barth drew negative support for his statement about the foundation of faith from the philosophical argument of his brother, Heinrich, that God has priority before the philosophical thought of God [cf. the late Schelling, chap. 2.4.2]. McCormack, 218–26. See *Romans*, 4. He drew support also from the negative results of biblical criticism. See his exchange with Adolf Harnack in Martin Rumscheidt, ed., *Adolf von Harnack*, 85–106.

11. *Romans*, 212: "Finitum non capax infiniti." See Heppe, *Reformed Dogmatics*, 416, 432, 437. See also the "wholly other" in Rudolf Otto, chap. 4.7.

degree of truth in this world rather than in the kingdom of God.[12] In the revelation in Christ, the kingdom of God does not commingle with world, but—as "a new world"—it touches this world as a "tangent touches a circle, that is, without touching it" (30). The New Testament witnesses to a truth and reality that is "otherworldly" (e.g., 126), beyond this world. One who believes in the gospel steps "in the air" (Overbeck's image), where there is no "this-worldly" ground to stand on (e.g., 94, 98, 230). There is a "barrier," a "boundary," a "death line" that radically separates what is of God from what is of humanity and its world (e.g., 49, 120, 286). Yet God is this world's creator and its lord.

The sin of humanity is that it lives as if there were no God; even when it thinks it worships God, in its sinfulness it has forgotten God and is actually atheistic, a judgment directed against the contemporary church (332ff., 378, 392). "Religion" is essentially behavior and thought subtly manipulated by sinful humanity to secure, not deny, sinful life in this world (e.g., 236f.). Religious and metaphysical concepts in religious usage are but clever tools of this manipulation, such as when one speaks of the "infinite" and actually means only the obverse of the finite (290, 303). For Barth, revelation has nothing to do with religion but is God's own act, "vertical from above" (e.g., 30). On the cross of Christ God suffers humanity's sin, and in the miracle of the resurrection God proclaims God's lordship. God speaks "No!" to humanity's all-pervasive sin, but "Yes!" to God as truly God and to humanity as the creature of God's love and grace (e.g., 38, 188ff., 204ff.). The impact of this Word of God in the believer is such that the Word itself creates the condition for its acceptance (as in Kierkegaard) and lets the truth about sin and the grace of justification be perceived (37f.).[13] From Overbeck Barth takes his criticism of the "rivalries of competing theologies" and the recognition of the judgment of the "No!" on the individualist self-interest involved in theology as it ordinarily exists (372–74).

In order to be true to the witness of the New Testament and to avoid the compromises of cultural worldliness, theology must subordinate itself to Scripture,

12. See Barth's essay on Overbeck in *Theology and Church*, 1st German ed. 1928, trans. Louise Pettibone Smith (London: SCM, 1962).

13. Barth's Catholic critic, Hans Urs von Balthasar, *Karl Barth, Darstellung und Deutung seiner Theologie*, 2nd ed. (Cologne: Jakob Hegner, 1962), 77, thinks that Barth's hidden presupposition in the 2nd ed. of Romans is from Idealism, namely, the original "identity" or oneness of the opposites in God. Barth does use the word "identity" (329) for the reconciliation of God and humanity in Christ. He probably has the expression from Kutter, and he probably means it analogically or metaphorically, insofar as God always remains, in the union we have with God in Christ, absolutely other (162). On p. 403 Balthasar refers with approval to an article by Ludwig Lambinet, "Zur Analogia-Entis-Problematik in Karl Barth's Theologie," *Catholica* (Paderborn: Verlag des Winfried Bundes) 6 (1937): 89–107. The article compares statements in the work of the later Schelling to statements in Barth. There are interesting parallels, but Lambinet does not assert, as he should not, direct influence. The claim that *Romans* presupposes the dialectic of Idealism had also been made by the Catholic theologian Erich Przywara, e.g., *Ringen der Gegenwart*, 2 vols. (Augsburg: Benno Fisler, 1929), 2:686f.; cf. 548–65, 688–95. See the discussion of Balthasar in McCormack. The English abridged translation of Balthasar's work by John Drury, *The Theology of Karl Barth* (New York: Holt, Reinhart & Winston, 1971), should be used only with some caution.

not because it is an abstract ruling authority, but because as a whole Scripture is "placed under the 'krisis' [sc. crisis] of the Spirit of Christ." This is "the true subject matter" (17). The New Testament itself is not Word of God but refers beyond itself to the true Word. This referring beyond itself is the mystery of its Spirit-filled witness to revelation. As we view Scripture, it is as if we were looking out of a window and seeing persons on the ground looking at something above the roof that we cannot see.[14] No human language can directly express the truth that is God, because humanity has no direct perception of God. Theology can only speak indirectly of God: dialectically, metaphorically, ever pointing beyond itself to the truth it cannot definitively and rationally grasp and knows only through revelation. Apart from the revealed Word, God "speaks" only in eternal silence (98).

In *Romans* an unmistakable boundary separates the eternal God from all things created and finite, an image that recalls Neo-Kantianism and Kant himself, whom Barth in fact praises for recognizing the barrier between humanity and the God it cannot know by use of its reason (386, cf. 45, 271, 294, 432). Secular culture should recognize the limitation of scientific knowledge in its questions about ultimate reality (531).[15] Philosophical metaphysics cannot cross the boundary. Only God can cross it, and God crosses it only to redeem what is lost. In *Romans* Barth often calls the truth of God or God's act in revelation the "impossible possibility" (e.g., 42, 338, 380f.). Humanity in its sin and atheism could not possibly have anticipated this act, this crossing of the boundary "vertically from above."

But *Romans* speaks also of a human potential (possibility) for the right relationship to God (faith), a potential, however, that is not recognized or perceived by human being apart from revelation (e.g., 37). In order for it to be perceived, it must be actualized by the act of God in Christ. This is an important point with which Barth will later disagree. Essentially the same relationship of potential to actual is present in Idealism, Kierkegaard, Schleiermacher, and the mediation theology. Both in Kierkegaard's and in Tholuck's analysis of human existence, for example, despair prepares human being for faith [chaps. 2.6; 3.1]. According to Barth in *Romans,* sinful existence, existence apart from the truth, leads to doubt and despair (45). "Religion," Barth says, "is the possibility of the removal of every ground of confidence except the confidence in God alone. Piety is the possibility of the removal of the last traces of a firm foundation upon which we can erect a system of thought. The judgment of history is that those devoted to its investigation are driven to a final deprivation: they become dumb before God"

14. Barth, *The Word of God and the Word of Man,* trans. Douglas Horton (London: Hodder & Stoughton, 1935), 62f. (from a 1920 essay).
15. In the *Church Dogmatics,* III/2:113–15, Barth speaks with reserved approval of Karl Jaspers's philosophical category of "limit situations" in human existence beyond which human thought cannot go. Jaspers refers to what is beyond the limits as an unknown "other," which he relates to Kant's boundary. See Jaspers, *Kant,* trans. Ralph Manheim (New York: Harcourt, Brace & World, 1957), 18, 88, 146; *Karl Jaspers: Basic Philosophical Writings,* ed. and trans. Edith Ehrlich, Leonard H. Ehrlich, George B. Pepper (Athens: Ohio University Press, 1986), 97. Jaspers was Barth's postwar colleague in philosophy at Basel.

(88). "Does religion not look beyond itself and beyond its own reality to that by which humanity is established [*begründet*, grounded]?" In *Romans* the answer is yes (127, cf. 250).[16]

Barth's change of mind about this is one important marker that distinguishes the *Church Dogmatics* from his earlier work. The question was whether or not human life in some sense is prepared for faith by natural experience, such as despair. In the mediation theology and for Kierkegaard, it is, if the right circumstances of personal life permit (often such preparation is lost in thoughtless existence). Kierkegaard also says the "condition" that makes faith possible is given only by revelation itself. Nevertheless, for Kierkegaard there are prior existential conditions that open the way for faith, conditions that Kierkegaard skillfully expounds in his analysis of existence in his pseudonymous writings.[17] In the *Church Dogmatics* (e.g., I/1:130; II/1:5) Barth begins only with the Word of God, and thus with a procedure that is consciously not Kierkegaardian and one that has now broken the last link with mediation theology. He is also aware of having broken from the historic Augustinian tradition of the human condition prior to faith that also intended a certain preparation for faith in the instability of natural life.[18] For Barth, one may no longer begin dogmatics with an analysis of human experience apart from revelation. Such a dogmatics begins with existence "under the law" as the condition for speaking about existence "under grace." The truth is that before grace is received, there is no search for meaning in life that is "answered" by grace. If there is a question that is answered by grace, then the question itself is created by grace, by the Word of God.[19] This is foundational for Barth's rejection of "natural theology," that is, of an anthropology that defines the human condition as in some way containing a potential for accepting the gospel.[20]

But there is also continuity between Barth's earlier and later work. "Dialectic" theology is continued in the doctrine that God and God's Word limit and stand

---

16. Cf. *Romans*, 37, 117f., 129. Sinful life ends in profound confusion (ibid., 68). In *Die christliche Dogmatik im Entwurf* (Munich: Christian Kaiser, 1927), 68–70, Barth says that if human being is not "at home" with God, it wanders in constant self-contradiction.

17. See Kierkegaard in chap. 2.6. Eberhard Jüngel remarks that Kierkegaard's existential analysis is like the concave that fits the convex of revelation, i.e., like two interlocking puzzle pieces: *Barth-Studien* (Zurich: Benzinger, 1982), 171; on Barth and Kierkegaard, 173–79. See also Egon Brinkschmidt, *Sören Kierkegaard und Karl Barth* (Neukirchen: Neukirchener Verlag, 1971).

18. McCormack, 390; Dorrien, *The Barthian Revolt*, 96f.; Jüngel, *God's Being Is in Becoming*, 63. On the Augustinian tradition, see, e.g., the section earlier in this book on Tholuck, chap. 3.1, note 9.

19. *Church Dogmatics*, IV/1:§60; Busch, *Great Passion*, 152ff., esp. 153: according to some dogmatics, life under the law prior to gospel "causes one to despair . . . thus making one ready to hear the gospel."

20. See Barth's comments on ridding his work completely of existential elements and of "philosophical anthropology," in *How I Changed My Mind* (Edinburgh: St. Andrews, 1969), 42f., and in *Church Dogmatics* I/1:xiii, 125–27; cf. I/2:259; III/2:399f. See also Busch, *Great Passion*, 45, 70–72. Busch (p. 26) points out that one reason for the rejection of natural theology is that it allows (or creates) the suspicion that the Word of God is just another human conception of God among others. In this case Feuerbach's explanation of religion as human projection becomes cogent. Cf. *Romans*, 236, and Barth's introduction to Feuerbach's *Essence of Christianity* [chap. 2.5.2]; cf. II/1:467. See further the section on Emil Brunner, chap. 6.2.

over against all comprehension of God within human being's own religious experience or thought. Another important continuity is the concept of "parable" or "analogy" (both words translate Barth's German word *Gleichnis*). In *Romans* merely human religion, although it is misdirected, is nevertheless a paradoxical "parallel" and "parable" of Christian truth (254). According to *Romans* parable is also faith's own mode of speaking of God. Human beings "are not competent, even if they are gifted with tongues of fire, to speak of God otherwise than in a parable." "The paradox of the final, despairing inadequacy of human speech as a medium for expressing the truth is a parable of the absolute miracle of the Holy Spirit" (333; cf. other instances: 96, 114, 161, 338, 462). The absolute difference between God's truth and human language is such that the human language of faith can speak of God only parabolically or analogously. Otherwise it must be silent.

In the 1920s Barth became involved in a theological dialogue with the Roman Catholic theologian Erich Przywara. The dialogue centered in the Catholic doctrine of "analogy" or, in Przywara's formulation, "analogy of being." (An example of what is meant is the intelligence of human being as analogous or similar to the mind of God.) The doctrine of analogy, formulated by the Fourth Lateran Council of 1215, states that "one cannot conceive of the similarity [between God and creature] without conceiving of the greater dissimilarity between them."[21] According to Przywara this doctrine means that the whole of creation is a "parable or analogy [*Gleichnis*] that refers beyond itself to a God who is above analogy," so that what is created is "upwardly open" to God as its "mysterious 'meaning.'" For this reason the human creature relates as "potential obedience" to God's free creative will. This does not mean, he insists, that the analogy gives science a way to grasp God in a kind of "world formula." God is always "completely different" from the similarity with creation. Nevertheless God is also "in us" in the sense of the created analogous similarity of our being to God's being. God is therefore both "in and above us," a phrase that Przywara uses to summarize the doctrine. It "speaks an originally Catholic Yes of God to the whole of creation"; it is "the great and constant consecration of the world."[22]

Barth could not accept this doctrine, for it seemed to be what he in *Romans* had opposed, namely, mediation theology. Przywara's "analogy of being" seemed to be another form of mediation: God and world were both defined as "being," which implied a kind of identity of God and world.[23] In opposing Przywara, Barth referred to the traditional argument that God is not an object for thought. God is unconditioned, entirely dissimilar to the being of things in the world and

21. "Non potest similitudo notari, quin inter eos maior dissimilitudo sit notanda" (from Przywara, see below).

22. Przywara, *Religionsphilosophie katholischer Theologie* (Munich: R. Oldenbourg, 1926), 22–24, 63; cf. 57. With regard to the following discussion, it should be noted that the Catholic defenders of "analogy of being" do not think Barth's doctrine of analogy overcomes it. See Balthasar, *Karl Barth*, 106, 175–81; Thomas F. O'Meara, *Erich Przywara, S.J.* (Notre Dame, IN: University of Notre Dame Press, 2002), 73–83.

23. Barth later thought his criticism was exaggerated. See Eberhard Jüngel, *God as the Mystery of the World*, 282–85 [see chap. 8.5].

in this sense not "being" but "nonbeing," as was implicit in the "wholly other" God of *Romans*. Barth also objected that the doctrine of "potential obedience" could lead to an entirely wrong "acceptance of fate"—the acceptance of a situation in the world because it was thought to contain such potential.[24] The supposed potential could lead the church to avoid speaking a prophetic word of judgment. The objection was itself prophetic in view of the coming of Nazism and the churches' response to it [chap. 1.4].

But if God is entirely dissimilar to humanity or creation, how can one speak of God at all? In *Romans* the solution had already been indicated: the language of faith is parable or analogy. This Barth will now develop, although not as the "analogy of being" but as an analogy mediated by Christ, the "analogy of faith." Only in Christ are all things placed in true relationship to God, and only so can we see them as analogies of the things of God. Barth will now also, like Przywara, concentrate far more on God's Yes than he had before.[25]

6.1.2 *Church Dogmatics*

A central concern of Barth in the *Church Dogmatics* is that the doctrine of God must be derived solely from revelation. The use of any other source would presuppose that certain truths can be taken from some aspect of natural human life, such as philosophical metaphysics. But revelation does not give the kind of knowledge of God that, for example, a flower gives of the science of botany. Rather, in revelation God reveals God as the hidden God whose eternal being is incomprehensible, utterly beyond human thought (I/1:320).[26] The Word of God is "divine act." It is "free, as free as God Himself, for indeed God Himself is in the act. God is the Lord. There is no one and nothing . . . to condition Him or to be in a nexus with Him. . . . We understand the Word of God very badly in distinction from the unconditional freedom in which it is spoken" (I/1:157, cf. 371; II/1:580). God is "free from all conditioning by that which is distinct from Himself." But God makes God "being for" humanity and therefore "conditioned" being: "God must not only be unconditioned but, in the absoluteness in

---

24. From Barth's 1929 essay "Fate and Idea in Theology," in H. Martin Rumscheidt, ed., *The Way of Theology in Karl Barth* (Allison Park, PA: Pickwick Publications, 1986), 41–47. See McCormack, 386f.

25. See, e.g., *Church Dogmatics*, III/1:368ff. Przywara was among several theologians who criticized the negative character of *Romans* (see McCormack, 320). He put it rather strongly: Barth, like Luther, sees the world as "the work of the devil" that must "remain left to its gradual suicide" (*Ringen der Gegenwart. Gesammelte Aufsätze*, 2 vols. (Augsburg: Benno Filser, 1929), 2:552). In effect this says that Barth (with Luther) is guilty of the Marcionite heresy. An eminent Protestant professor of New Testament, Adolf Jülicher, accused Barth of the same thing: Robinson, ed., *The Beginnings of Dialectical Theology*, 78. [On Marcion, see the section on Harnack, chap 4 4 above.] (Cf. *Romans*, 13.) Later, in the time of the *Church Dogmatics*, Barth himself said that *Romans* contained "an almost catastrophic opposition of God and the world, God and humanity, God and the church." From Barth's essay in *Ex auditu verbi: Festschrift für G. C. Berkouwer* (Kampen, Holland: Kok, 1965), 29, as quoted by McCormack, 244.

26. Cf. note 11: "finitum non capax infiniti," the finite cannot contain the infinite.

which He sets up this fellowship [with human being], He can and will also be conditioned." To be conditioned is to have determination and definition, and human being can only know what has determination and definition. God freely conditions God as love, as "Creator, Reconciler and Redeemer," the God of Holy Scripture, "the triune God known to us in His revelation" (II/1:303).[27]

The "economic Trinity," or the work of the Trinity for human being in the history of creation, revelation, and redemption, is completely analogous to the "immanent Trinity" or God's triune being (I/1:299, 306). Therefore, in the "immanent" Trinity above creation, God not only eternally loves the Son, but also "elects" the human person Jesus, and with the human person Jesus God elects humanity (II/2:§§32–33).[28] For all humanity, which God always sees in Christ, Christ is the one and only truth. He is the truth of the Old Testament and its revelatory covenants as well as of the New. There is no creation, covenant, revelation, or doctrine that does not center in Christ.[29] All of created life exists through the grace of God's election of humanity in Christ. This is the truth in which all things exist and without which they would not exist. Sin essentially means denial or disregard of the truth that all things exist through the grace of God. Without this all-deciding and all-pervasive truth, existence is untruth, "nothingness" (III/3:§50). But Christ and his truth are ever near to sinful existence and through the power of the Holy Spirit they become real in faith.[30]

Revelation makes what is human the analogous means of God's self-communication.[31] The terms "father" and "son" are not "natural" analogies to God's Trinitarian being, but they "become" such analogies by God's action in Christ. In all "analogies of faith" God is the agent who creates the analogies through the act of revelation, which in Christ encompasses all creation. In Christ God speaks the Word of grace, God's Yes, to creation, and through this Yes all things are seen in faith and for faith in the light of Christ. Creation becomes a transparent witness, a "correspondence" to or mirroring of the truth that is revealed in Christ, for in him creation is revealed in its truth.[32] Not "God in us" is the basis of the analogy, but "God in Christ." Only in the reality of revelation

---

27. Cf. Barth, *The Humanity of God* (n.p.: John Knox, 1960, 71; Jüngel, *God's Being Is in Becoming*, 30ff.

28. See E. Jüngel on Barth's doctrine of the Trinity in *God's Being Is in Becoming*, trans. John Webster (Grand Rapids: Eerdmans, 2001), 27–29, 84–95. Barth's interpretation affirms the traditional doctrine of the "perichoresis" of the three modes of being of the Trinity. While they remain distinct, they "mutually penetrate and condition one another so completely that one is always in the other two and the other two in the one." I/1:370; cf. 396.

29. Secondary literature that provides a guide to the Christology and doctrine of the Trinity in the *Church Dogmatics* includes Jüngel, *God's Being Is in Becoming*; George Hunsinger, *Disruptive Grace*, chaps. 6 and 8; Eberhard Busch, *Great Passion*, 43–47, 82–127, 227f.

30. On Christ and the Holy Spirit, see, e.g., III/2:455; IV/1:158, 223f.; and Hunsinger, *How to Read Karl Barth*, 152ff.

31. Cf. Romans 12:6; cf. *Church Dogmatics*, IV/2:166; further I/1:173, 299, 320ff., 436f.; I/2:471; II/1:55ff. Jüngel, *Karl Barth*, 42ff.; Busch, *Great Passion*, 112–27; cf. McCormack, 327f.

32. III/3:49ff. See Barth's book on Anselm, 117 (see note 35); see further III/2:322–24; III/1:185, 380. See E. Jüngel's essay on Barth's concept of analogy in *Barth-Studien*, 210–32.

is creation "a sign of the covenant, a true sacrament" (III/1:234; III/3:51). In Christ the eternal God is "wholly other" in "nearness" to us (IV/1:186); the analogies show that God is intimately related to human life. The attitude of theology (as of all Christian life) is prayer that invokes and is thankful for the gifts of grace (e.g., I/1:12–24). Those who truly hear the Word respond in obedience analogous to Christ's obedience to God. And the church's faithful theological reflection and language are analogous ("similarity in dissimilarity") to the Word of revelation.[33]

Barth's understanding of the analogy of faith is related to certain insights he gained through his work on Anselm, published in 1931. After *Romans* he studied the dogmatics of the pre-Enlightenment period: the Reformers, the theologians of Protestant Orthodoxy (as mediated especially by Heppe's *Reformed Dogmatics* [chap. 1.2]), but also major Catholic theologians and especially Anselm (1033–1109). Barth said his book on Anselm contained the key to the "process of thought" in the *Church Dogmatics*.[34] We turn now to Barth's work on Anselm's book, *Fides Quaerens Intellectum* (Faith Seeking Understanding).[35]

Barth frequently uses Latin terms in Anselm that are the root of the English word "creed": the *Credo* for what is believed, and *credere,* the act of believing. Faith for Anselm is based on Scripture and the great creeds of the church. The Credo, and therefore also the church, precedes *intelligere,* understanding. It is the objective confession of the church into which the Christian is baptized, and as such it is the "fact" that "limits" theology to a specific subject matter and is its presupposition (26–28). But faith differs from understanding "only in degree, not in kind"; that is, faith—far from being irrational—contains its own sense or reason, it is "an embryonic intelligere" (40).[36] Christ, the object of faith, is the author of truth and can only proclaim the truth. Faith in Christ therefore "makes the science of theology possible and gives it its basis" (22–26).[37] Theology's task is to understand the content of faith by using its own words and thought, although its words and thought cannot directly express what the Credo expresses. Theological expressions are "only by similarity [analogy] appropriate." Theological statements are "scientific," by which Barth means "science" in the broad sense

---

33. II/2:§33; IV/1; IV/3/2:533; I/1:241.

34. From the preface of Barth's book on Anselm (see note 35). On Barth's development in the period after *Romans,* see McCormack, 291ff.

35. *Fides Quaerens Intellectum,* trans. Ian W. Robertson (Cleveland: Meridian, 1962). The following references in the text are to this translation.

36. Barth employs two philosophical terms that he often uses in the *Church Dogmatics.* "Ontic ratio" expresses the reason within faith itself; "noetic ratio" expresses the secondary reasoning of theology that seeks understanding.

37. Theology is not about the business of agreement with other sciences but only about understanding its own unique object or subject matter: I/1:§1; cf. II/1:§§25–27. See also Barth, *Evangelical Theology: An Introduction,* trans. Grover Foley (New York: Holt, Reinhart & Winston, 1963), 49: "Theology is science seeking the knowledge of the Word of God spoken in God's work—science learning in the school of Holy Scripture, which witnesses to the Word of God; science laboring in the quest for truth . . . In this way alone does theology fulfill its definition as the human logic of the divine Logos. In every other respect theology is really without support. While, seen from the point of view of an outsider, it hovers in mid-air, it depends actually upon God's living Word."

of the German word *Wissenschaft*, namely, as the theologian's understanding of the subject matter, the content of faith. Theological statements "can be made with only scientific certainty, [a certainty] which, on account of its relativity, has to be distinguished from the certainty of faith" (29f., 80, 117). Insofar as there is progress in theology, it is attributed to grace, that is, "the wisdom of God who well knows what it is good for us to perceive at any given time." But because it is relative, theology is also "vulnerable"; it cannot demonstrate God's approval of what it says and thinks. It does however have a criterion of admissibility, namely, agreement with Scripture. Scripture is "the determining norm" for theology (32f.). But Scripture and the Credo are "wrapped in mystery that requires understanding beyond mere reading" (42). As theology is dependent on grace, understanding must be sought in prayer (36ff.). And the "anxiety" of the theologian in her or his vulnerability, which is part of theological seeking, is justified through grace (62). Theology is "trust in the objective ratio that both enlightens and is enlightened" (71).

For Anselm the understanding achieved by his quest is a joyful event as a kind of proof of God and a paradigm of the work of all theology, but not as a straightforward demonstration of God. The proof is that God is "that beyond which nothing greater can be thought." Anselm considered it as valid for secular thought as for theology.[38] Barth surmises that Anselm envisioned the secular unbeliever too within the church, seeing him or her in the light of truth. The sinner is not held guilty for his or her sinfulness, but always already "claimed for God," the truth. And here, says Barth, "we must move on past the listener's tragic non credo [I do not believe] to our task with a sense of humor" (68ff.).

Anselm's proof is "merely speculative," "simply per similitudinem" and "per analogiam," and it "stands of course under the shadow of the incomprehensibility of God" (Anselm, 80, 117). Theology is "speculative," although its speculation is an "empty shell" without the truth that only God can give it (ibid.). This means that theology uses the language of speculation, philosophy, for purposes of interpretation, but it does not give philosophy authority over the Credo; that is, it uses philosophy only to understand revelation in Christ. *Intelligere* is formed—analogously, *per similitudinem*—in the language of the theologian's time and place but it does not replace the Credo.[39] Theology must prayerfully begin and end with creed and Bible within the community of faithful witness, the church—hence the title of Barth's chief work, *Church Dogmatics*. The Credo is not only the confession that Christ is Lord, as in the Barmen Declaration and in *Romans*, but includes the ecumenical creeds and confessions of the early Catholic church, above all the Nicene (Nicene-Constantinopolitan) and Chalcedonian—both of which employ

---

38. Barth apparently does not consider the relationship between Anselm's "that beyond which nothing greater can be thought" and the designation of God in the nineteenth century as the "unconditioned," a term derived from the medieval tradition of the *via negativa* [chap. 2.2.1].

39. See, e.g., *Church Dogmatics*, I/1:345; I/2:728f.; II/1:45, 233f.

the philosophical language of Greek metaphysics.[40] The Christology and exposition of the Trinity in the *Church Dogmatics* are in conformity with these creeds of the church. For this reason the work is often called "neo-orthodox." But theology does not simply repeat the creeds. The analogies or parables of faith make living theological language possible, language that "corresponds" to the God who has taken human reality into God's eternal power.[41]

Barth's doctrine of Scripture also accords with the primacy of *credere* before *intelligere*. Like all literature, Scripture must be taken seriously according to its own intention, which is to witness to Christ.[42] A central problem of modern biblical criticism had long been the credibility of what appear to be legendary elements in Scripture. "Saga or legend," Barth writes, "can only denote the more or less intrusive part of the story-teller . . . in the story told" (I/1:327). Elements of saga or legend "in the history of divine grace," however, must be regarded "as true and not false legend in the relevant sense," and therefore we must "treat this history too as credible in its distinctive form." "Once this is grasped, it obviously makes no odds [sc. is not a problem] that in the construction of these accounts the active imagination of the biblical authors, as is only to be expected, lived with images and conceptions which were stamped by the outlook and mythology of their day and which we can no longer accept, but which it was not the purpose of the texts in question to impart or to force upon us." These images and conceptions must be poetically translated in terms of the images and conceptions of our own "mythology" (III/3:374f.).[43] The Bible "is full of this kind of history." But there are crucially important differences. While the creation stories in Genesis are "pure saga" (III/1:80–82), the New Testament miracle stories are about real divine-human events. The different accounts of Christ's resurrection appearances tell of real events "couched in the imaginary, poetic style of historical saga" and "describe an event that is beyond the reach of historical research and depiction" (III/2:452). The resurrection of Christ "bursts through the framework of

40. I/1–2; I/1:§11.2; 2. The shift in Barth's thought from severe critique of the church to traditional church orthodoxy in *Romans* or, as Barth's *Church Dogmatics* is usually called, "neo-orthodoxy," is also signaled by his high valuation of the ecclesiology of the conservative-confessional nineteenth-century Lutheran theologian August Vilmar [chap 1.2]. Already in his publication of 1927, *Die christliche Dogmatik*, p. vi, Barth counts Vilmar among those with whom he "in decisive points feels theologically at home." See Barth's essay on Vilmar in *Protestant Theology in the Nineteenth Century*. But Vilmar is mentioned only rarely in the *Church Dogmatics*, once critically in Barth's remarks against the view that the sacrament has priority before the Word (I/1:71). Another sign is the shift away from the emphasis in *Romans* on the nearness of the kingdom, e.g., II/1:634.

41. On the Christ event as "language gain," see E. Jüngel, *God's Being Is in Becoming*, 22f.; Jüngel develops a Barthian theory of theological language in *God as the Mystery of the World*, §18. See Jüngel in chap. 8.5.

42. E.g., IV/1:287ff; cf. I/1:325f.; on exegesis and hermeneutics: I/2:§§19–21. See George Hunsinger's chapter on Barth's hermeneutics in *Disruptive Grace*, and Hunsinger on miracle in *How to Read Karl Barth*, 189ff.

43. Cf. I/1:327f. Barth is aware of the "hermeneutical circle" of interpretation that tries to comprehend the difference between the way a person of the New Testament understood the world and the way a contemporary person understands it. [Cf. Schleiermacher, chap. 2.7.1.]

historical relation," that is, the story, the telling of it (III/1:78f.). The stories are therefore a kind of analogy of what they depict. The "content" of the resurrection stories, Barth says, is that "when they [the disciples] had lost Him through death, they were sought and found by Him as the Resurrected" (III/2:453). This is the historic significance of the resurrection stories expressed conceptually in and for our time, and each of the New Testament miracles is a parable that requires such understanding. But none can be dissolved into the ideas through which we understand or interpret them (IV/2:212ff., 228ff.). If the resurrection stories were only about ideas or concepts, the events themselves would be indifferent, and theoretically one could dispense with them.[44] All the New Testament miracles are for Barth real events couched in the language of legend and saga, and they all reflect the one great divine wonder, the gift of Christ (e.g., I/2:85ff.; IV/2:215ff.). They stand in analogous relationship to a divine reality that conceals even as it reveals itself; they signify a mystery that bursts the limits of ordinary understanding, knowledge, and history. "God is known only by God; God can be known only by God. At this very point, faith itself, we know God in utter dependence, in pure discipleship and gratitude" (II/1:183).

6.1.3 Ethics

Ethical decision and action stand in relationship to the living presence of truth in Christ. Christian ethics, which Barth does not separate from dogmatics, is grounded in God's "command" as God's living address of grace to persons in concrete situations. The "law" (of "law and gospel") is the "form" of Christian freedom in decision and action. The grace or gospel of election grants the hearing of the command and the freedom and will to be obedient. The commands are generalized in the specific biblical commandments of covenant law, but covenant law is not an abstract universal statue to be followed literally as something we know in advance and only have to apply. Rather, in each concrete situation we must discern and decide what constitutes Christian obedience.[45] And because we are sinful, God claims us ever anew through the address of God's command in the particular, concrete situations of life.[46] Barth does not dismiss ethical guidelines; for example, he can argue for a "respect for life" that is much like Albert Schweitzer's "reverence for life" (III/4:344–74).[47] But ethical decision may not be based on abstract ethical princi-

---

44. This is what, e.g., D. F. Strauss and the "left wing" interpretation of Hegel intended [chap. 2.5.1].

45. See II/2: chap. 8; III/4:§§52–56; and the essay "The Gift of Freedom: Foundation of Theological Ethics," in *Humanity of God*, 69–96. See Busch's discussion of the foundation of Barth's ethics in *Great Passion*, 152–75; cf. *Romans*, 475–526. See Eberhard Jüngel, *Theological Essays*, 1:154–72. [See Jüngel, chap. 8.5.] Barth's position on specific issues (e.g., abortion) in III/4 is summarized by Bromiley, *Introduction to the Theology of Karl Barth*, 167ff.

46. E.g., I/2:81ff. On sin as concrete, a matter of the immediately real here and now: IV/1:§60; IV/2:§65; IV/3:§70.

47. Cf. "special ethics," III/4:3–31, esp. 31. Barth does not oppose ethical "theory," "guide," or "conditional imperatives" [otherwise there would be no ethics] (*The Humanity of God*, 85f.).

ples, whether derived from natural law or from Christian revelation, because they exclude both the concrete character of the command and the freedom of Christian discernment.[48] Therefore, Christian ethics cannot be made into a political or economic program, especially not in an age in which church and society are no longer wedded together. "No appeal can be made to the Word or Spirit of God in the running of its [sc. the state's] affairs." There can be no Christian state that corresponds directly to the Christian church.[49] God may produce "parables of His own good will and actions" in cultural life, but "culture testifies clearly in history and in the present to the fact that man is not good but rather a downright monster."[50] The dialectic of nature and grace cannot be covered over in a so-called Christian state.

The gospel has political consequences because it has to do with the concrete reality of God's righteousness in God's commands. For Barth the possession of atomic weapons was a sin; he insisted that the issue was a matter of Christian confession itself.[51] The church, he said, "must stand for social justice." In making its choice of possibilities "it will always choose the movement from which it can expect the greatest measure of social justice (leaving all other considerations on one side)." Nevertheless Barth says quite firmly, "With all its strength it will be on the side of those who refuse to have anything to do with the regimentation, controlling, and censoring of public opinion."[52] As is stated in the fifth thesis of the Barmen Declaration, the state provides for law and peace in a world that still awaits redemption. The church has the responsibility to discern and expose the state's need for redemption. But the state is also an "allegory" or "analogy" of the kingdom of God, which is "the mystery of its own center."[53] Here again Barth points to the truth of Christ as the all-encompassing foundation of all that exists, when it is seen by faith in the light of Christ.

The church is the community of those who have heard the Word, confess their sins and accept justification, and enter into a life of obedience and courageous witness to the world. Since church and society are no longer joined as in previous centuries, Barth challenges the church to make the responsible decision for adult baptism (IV/4:179–200). But this may be understood only in the context of God's election of all humanity in Christ, which makes the "obstinately joyful proclamation" possible, in spite of monstrous sinfulness, that "the human spirit

48. Barth, *Against the Stream: Shorter Post-War Writings 1946–52*, trans. Stanley Godman and E. M. Delacour (London: SCM, 1954), 114; cf. 163; Busch, *Great Passion*, 173; cf. 169. On the following discussion, see Will Herberg's introductory essay in *Against the Stream*; Karl Barth and J. Hamel, *How to Serve God in a Marxist Land* (New York: Association Press, 1959); *Karl Barth and Radical Politics*; Busch, *Karl Barth*, 354–57; and Busch, *Great Passion*, 170–75.

49. *Against the Stream*, 151, 160; cf. 165.

50. *Humanity of God*, 54.

51. Busch, *Karl Barth*, 430f. Barthianism in Europe has been typically to the left politically and sometimes known as "leftist orthodoxy." See, e.g., Wolf-Dieter Marsch, *Institution im Übergang: Evangelische Kirche zwischen Tradition und Reform* (Göttingen: Vandenhoeck & Ruprecht, 1970), 109f.

52. Barth, *Church and State* (Macon, GA: Mercer University Press, 1991), 184; *Against the Stream*, 173; cf. 185; 177.

53. *Against the Stream*, 151, 188f., 169–71.

is naturally Christian."[54] This echoing of Anselm's attitude toward the unbeliever is heard again when Barth speaks of unbelievers as "virtual and prospective" Christians; insofar as the one truth, in which they too exist, is Christ, they are the objective of Christian missions (IV/2:275; cf. IV/3:516). Barth also now speaks of "true words" outside the church, which are made possible through the election of all humanity in Christ and Christ's lordship—words that are always to be measured by Scripture (IV/3:110–53).[55] While the saving perception of the truth of Christ is given only to faith, the election of humanity in Christ opens the possibility of universalism or the salvation of all, a possibility about which Barth makes no decision. "This much is certain, that we have no theological right to set any sort of limits to the loving-kindness of God which has appeared in Jesus Christ. Our theological duty is to see and understand it as being still greater than we had seen before."[56]

6.1.4 Parallels in Nineteenth-Century Theology

One reason the *Church Dogmatics* is so extensive is that Barth repeatedly engages in lengthy discussions with the theological tradition, and only in exceptional cases is he not aware of important disagreements or agreements. In spite of his rather comprehensive disagreement with theology in the nineteenth century, there are notable points of agreement, not all of which he discusses in the *Church Dogmatics*. For Isaak Dorner as for Kierkegaard, God in God's self is incomprehensible, and God becomes comprehensible only through revelation. Barth admits taking from Dorner the thought that the God of the Bible freely acts to define or condition God's self as Trinitarian being.[57] Dorner also makes a point of affirming the absolute freedom of God, and he refers to the late Schelling's concept of the absolute act to which all thought and existence owe their being, which may be called the late Schelling's version of "that than which nothing greater can be thought."[58] One may also compare the late Schelling's statement on the relationship between faith and science—namely, that belief proves itself through discovering how "that in which

54. Cf. *Humanity of God*, 60; cf. 59: "The so-called 'outsiders' are really only 'insiders' who have not yet understood and apprehended themselves as such."

55. This does not mean there is "Christianity outside the church," as in Rothe [chap. 3.2; cf. "anonymous Christianity," chap. 8.4.4]. In a late essay, "Philosophie und Theologie," Barth again underscores the distinction between starting "from above" with revelation, as in theology, and "from below" with anthropology and "world," as in philosophy (Heinrich Gruber, ed., *Philosophie und Christliche Existenz. Festschrift für Heinrich Barth* [Basel: Helbing & Lichtenhahn, 1960], 93–106, esp. 101f.).

56. Barth, *Humanity of God*, 60–62. See Busch, *Great Passion*, 217f. Cf. Barth, *Church Dogmatics*, IV/1:483.

57. See Barth, II/1:§29ff., e.g., 493. Barth's source is Dorner's *Divine Immutability*, trans. Robert R. Williams and Claude Welch [see chap. 3.3]. That God conditions God is also in Kähler [chap. 5.1].

58. Cf. Schelling, *Werke*, 14:27: revelation is that "quo majus nil fieri potest, than which utterly nothing greater can happen." Its content is the person of Christ (ibid., 35). Cf. also ibid., 25: "God is not at all an opposite of finitude." Eberhard Jüngel, *God's Being Is in Becoming*, 29, notes the similarity of the late Schelling's and Barth's understandings of the relationship of the economic Trinity to the immanent Trinity, i.e., that in both cases the Trinity "doubles" itself. Schelling and Barth also have a similar (Augustinian) understanding of human freedom as being in the truth of revelation, in

belief believes was also made plausible to reason and the strictest science" (*Werke*, 10:183)—to Barth's and Anselm's understanding of the task of *intelligere* as one of comprehending the reason in the *Credo*. Furthermore, for Barth and also for the late Schelling [chap. 2.4.2], there is no true reality outside of Christ or revelation.

Barth acknowledged that Dorner's understanding of the work of theology in relationship to faith was similar to his own: theology understands the content of faith.[59] But Dorner shares with the mediation theology what Barth rejects: the double beginning point of theology, in anthropology and in Christian faith. For Barth, therefore, Dorner's theology fails to be a true theology, for theology may begin only with the freedom of God who reveals God's self in God's act. Yet again, for Barth, once this point is secure, theology may and must use philosophy to interpret (*intelligere*) the meaning of the Credo in contemporary language.[60] In his exposition of the doctrine of the Trinity one finds the triad thesis-antithesis-synthesis, in formulations that are reminiscent of Hegel. For example, in a discussion of the Trinity Barth can say: "[God] is the speaker without whom there is no word or meaning, the word which is the word of the speaker, and the meaning which is the meaning both of the speaker and his word" (I/1:364). The triad is one of subject, the object (or "other") produced by the subject, and their unity. In another place he says, "God is both the One and the Other [the Son]" in the unity of love (IV/2:757). Barth is of course not in agreement with Hegel's "Absolute Idealism," and one must also take into account Barth's knowledge of the interpretative triads in Augustine's doctrine of the Trinity.[61]

---

contrast to the autonomous freedom of arbitrary choice. Barth does not mention that evil is unreal in Schelling's *On Human Freedom*, although he knows that this tradition stems from Augustine (e.g., III/3:318), a tradition with which Barth is in essential agreement.

59. Barth, *Protestant Theology in the Nineteenth Century*, 565. [Cf. Martin Kähler, chap. 5.1.] Barth also acknowledges the same concept of theology in Johann Tobias Beck (ibid., 604ff.). Beck, however, mixes philosophical theories into his presentation of revelation and faith, so that the Credo does not stand apart from the interpretation [chap. 1.2].

60. An example of Barth's dialectical attitude toward philosophical terms is his discussion of the "infinity" of God: as a philosophical concept it is the obverse of finitude (limitedness) and in no way escapes the confines of the human and human sinfulness. It may be experienced as a godless revolutionary force or as a terrible threat that causes one to retreat back into a godless "normalcy." [Cf. the "unconditioned" in chap. 2.2.1.] As a human concept it is "the creaturely infinite." Yet for Barth, God is nevertheless infinite: beyond the limitation of space and time. But to say this theologically the concept must be thought (analogically) from the point of view of God's sovereign freedom. II/1:464–68; cf. 303f.; IV/1:159.

61. According to Barth, I/1:338, Schelling's and Hegel's formulations of thesis-antithesis-synthesis "would be quite unthinkable except against the background of Christian dogmatics, even if they were not just new variations on Augustine's proof of the Trinity." See *Saint Augustine: The Trinity*, trans. Stephen Mckenna (Washington: Catholic University of America, 1963), e.g., 207, on the love that unites Father and Son. Concerning Hegel's influence, Barth once remarked that he has "a certain weakness for Hegel and am always fond of doing a bit of 'Hegeling'" (Busch, *Karl Barth*, 387). He occasionally uses Hegel's word *Aufhebung*, which Hegel uses to define the "lifting" of religion into absolute knowledge [Chap. 2.3]. The title of a subsection of the *Church Dogmatics*, I/1:§17, is "The Revelation of God as the *Aufhebung* of Religion" (the ET of this text has "Abolition" for *Aufhebung*). See Barth's essay on Hegel in *Protestant Theology in the Nineteenth Century*. On Hegelian elements in Barth, see Helmut Thielicke, *Modern Faith and Thought*, 399–409, and Eberhard Jüngel, *God's Being Is in Becoming*, xixf., 127–29.

6.2 EMIL BRUNNER

6.2.1 The Debate with Karl Barth

Emil Brunner (1889–1966) was also Swiss and a member of the early group of dialectic theologians associated with Barth in the 1920s. In 1926 he became professor of theology in Zurich. He too was influenced by the Blumhardts and Hermann Kutter. In the 1920s his theology largely parallels Barth's *Romans,* whereby Brunner always had special appreciation for Kierkegaard. In his christological work from the year 1927, *The Mediator,* he writes: "The revelation in Christ is . . . absolutely decisive, for in it the non-historical, the eternal, breaks through into time at one point, and in so doing makes it a place of decision."[62] *The Mediator* argues in support of the doctrine of the divine person of Christ in the Reformers and the ancient church, in opposition to the Ritschlian concentration on the work of Christ.[63] Characteristic of all of Brunner's theology is his concept of God as personal "Thou" who addresses human being in the Word.[64] His conflict with Barth had to do with the human potential for receiving grace, a theory he began developing in the late 1920s.

In 1934, the year of the Barmen Declaration, Brunner published a short work entitled *Nature and Grace: On the Conversation with Karl Barth.* Barth answered in the same year with *No! Answer to Emil Brunner.* These were later published together in English under the title *Natural Theology.*[65] Barth had already publicly disagreed with what Brunner had been saying about a human potential for receiving grace,[66] and Brunner was responding to this disagreement in *Nature and Grace.* Brunner connected his theory with the definition of a new theological discipline that he called "eristics." It had to do with addressing the human potential for faith in order to move it toward faith, and it was closely connected with ethics. In *The Divine Imperative,* published in 1932, Brunner defined eristics as a "discussion between the Christian and non-Christian knowledge of God and of the Good." Brunner distinguished it from apologetic theology, which in his view sacrificed essential aspects of revelation for the sake of a compromise with culture.[67]

---

62. *The Mediator,* trans. Olive Wyon from the 2nd ed. of 1932 (Philadelphia: Westminster, 1947), 308. On Brunner, see Charles W. Kegley, ed., *The Theology of Emil Brunner* (New York: Macmillan, 1962); Gary Dorrien, *The Barthian Revolt in Modern Theology;* Heinrich Leipold, *Missionarische Theologie. Emil Brunners Weg zur theologischen Anthropologie* (Göttingen: Vandenhoeck & Ruprecht, 1974).

63. Against Ritschl and Harnack, e.g., *The Mediator,* 249; on Calvin: ibid., 343; cf. Calvin, *Institutes,* 2.12–14.

64. *The Mediator,* chap. 7, esp. p. 209.

65. Barth and Brunner, *Natural Theology* (London: Geoffrey Bles, Centenary Press, 1946). In defense of Brunner, see Edward A. Dowey, *The Knowledge of God in Calvin's Theology* (New York: Columbia University Press, 1952), 64f., 138–40, esp. 247ff. On the debate, see also Dorrien, *Barthian Revolt,* 116–30; John W. Hart, *Karl Barth vs. Emil Brunner* (New York: Peter Lang, 2001).

66. Barth, *Church Dogmatics* I/1:27ff., 238f. See McCormack, *Karl Barth's Critically Realistic Dialectical Theology,* 403–14, 416–20.

67. *The Divine Imperative,* trans. Olive Wyon (Philadelphia: Westminster, 1947), 61 (eristics = "deed word"). The German title of *The Divine Imperative* is *Das Gebot und die Ordnungen* (The Command and the Orders). Page references in the following text are to this edition.

The Divine Imperative is a work on ethics written partly in answer to Troeltsch's judgment that Christian ethics does not effectively influence cultural or secular life (594, 613)[cf. chap. 4.6]. For Brunner, Christian ethics cannot be based on principles, insofar as this would be legalistic. Rather, unconditional obedience to the "command of God," the "basis and norm of the Good," means being free to do "what God wills at any particular moment" (82f., 111f., 196f.). There are, however, two kinds of command and two forms of grace, although both belong to the same divine will and grace. One has to do with natural law as the work of the Creator in the world, while the other has to do with the work of the Redeemer. In obedience to the Creator "we must accept the world, adjust ourselves to it, obey its concrete demands, before we can begin to reform it" (126, cf. 127ff.). For in Christ God has judged, forgiven, and accepted the world, and the Christian is not called to deny or condemn its existence. One lives in Christian freedom within the world's "natural orders." They form the natural situation of persons that one tries to lead to Christ (129f., 214ff.). "What is decisive always takes place in the realm of personal relations, and not in the 'political sphere,' save where we are concerned with preserving the whole order from a general breakdown" (233).

The natural orders are given by God's grace with the intent of preserving and nourishing natural human life and preparing it for faith. "When conscious self-determination and faith awaken, man has already been molded both by nature and by history, he has already been absorbed into the intricate web of human life with its manifold claims; duties of all kinds chain him to a certain way of living." This web is composed of the orders of marriage, family, community, economic life, and the state, all of which partly consist of natural law and are partly formed historically by social custom and habit. Their true meaning and therefore their right use is known only in Christian faith, where they are transformed by the love commandment into true practice, but they can be perceived to a degree of truth by natural reason.[68] Christians must work with nonbelievers in upholding the orders and, where possible, increasing their humane effects in all areas of social life. Where, however, Christians find it ethically impossible to cooperate with unbelievers, they must refuse.[69] There is a false "autonomy" in the economic "disorder" of both capitalism and communism. Christians should work for a better economic order, but since any new political-economic order will be sinful, the attitude of the Christian toward it will always be critical, always on the way to a better order (426–39).

The state is "the order of a folk [*Volk*]." "Folk" roots in family ties, but it is more a product of history than a racial-ethnic identity. While the state must practice justice and recognize human rights (450f.), inequality belongs to creation. But there is a difference between natural inequality and sinful existing social forms of inequality (407f.). Brunner does not say how this can be resolved, and what

---

68. Brunner joins here with a long tradition of Christian understanding of natural law or reason. Cf. Luther [chap. 1.4 note 74], Schleiermacher, Ritschl and Wilhelm Herrmann. One should also recognize a connection with Kierkegaard's concept of the ethical-universal.

69. *The Divine Imperative*, 140ff., 208ff., 220–33, 249–60.

form the state should take in the present is also a clouded issue. He recommends a combination of expert authority with a means of building community. Autocracy by itself leads to abuse of power, democracy by itself to mob rule. Democracy arises from a false optimistic view of human nature [cf. chap. 1.4]. "Real community is based on inequality" (466f.). The result for Brunner is a conservative attitude toward the state, although the Christian must oppose state absolutism (462). The horror of modern war, in which no state can really be a victor, requires Christian opposition to war, although states must be able to defend themselves (469ff., 697f.). While the ideologies of both fascism and communism are irreconcilable with Christian faith, Christians may be fascists or communists "from sympathy with their practical political objectives." But in any case "every policy and political tendency stands under the judgment of Jesus Christ" (481).

Brunner assumes a middle position in ethics between Barth and Friedrich Gogarten, who, like other German theologians of the time, understood the orders of German folk life as orders of natural law [chap. 1.4]. "In Barth Creation comes off badly compared with Redemption, and in Gogarten Redemption comes off badly compared with Creation" (615). He "cannot blame" Paul Althaus and Emanuel Hirsch "for trying to argue that the individual nation is willed by God," but he thinks this is misguided (682f., cf. 698). Hirsch was at the time a German Christian and Althaus supported the movement [chap. 1.4]. Brunner strongly disagrees with their nationalism but agrees with them where he can, especially with regard to what constitutes the orders (e.g., Gogarten, 603; Althaus, 641, 646). Brunner is evidently interested in maintaining communication with these theologians, at a time when Barth is not. This has consequences for the Barth-Brunner debate.

The Divine Imperative also gives an interpretation of the doctrines of sin, grace, and the image of God, doctrines that connect sinful human being in the natural orders with conversion to Christianity. It begins with a point made previously by Wilhelm Herrmann: natural, sinful human being cannot avoid the moral question about decision, freedom, and responsibility in relationship to other persons. It also cannot solve the essential problem that confronts it in this question, namely, the evil of egotistic autonomy, whose true solution is found in revelation in Christ.[70] God has created natural humanity in the image of God, "designed for freedom in God." This design is indelible in human being, although it is completely corrupted by sin. By means of it natural, sinful human being maintains the capacity of being in a genuine relationship of love to the neighbor and to God as "Thou" instead of impersonal "It" (62, 302ff.).[71] Human being is created "with an inherent tendency" toward God and "therefore with the capacity for knowing" God. It has "a share in the knowledge of God's will and life"

---

70. Ibid., 17–33. Hans Grass points out the parallel to Herrmann in his article on Brunner in Martin Grechschat, ed., *Theologen des Protestantismus im 19. und 20. Jahrhundert*, 2:350–66.

71. For the relationships of "I," "Thou," and "It," Brunner is dependent on the work of Ferdinand Ebner and Martin Buber. See *The Divine Imperative*, 590; *The Mediator*, 208f.; see further Hart, *Barth vs. Brunner*, 39f.

because it is created "*in* the Word of God as the being . . . whose peculiarity is that he is responsible to God." But as a result of sin human being is sick with the "sickness unto death" that Kierkegaard describes (153f.). It finally falls into despair with questions that have no answers (146f.). Yet it is still responsible and in the consciousness of its guilt still related to God. All this means that a potential for Christian faith remains within it (505–10).

In *Nature and Grace* Brunner defines more carefully his interpretation of the doctrine of humanity as the image of God. "Formally," he says, human being remains this image, while "materially" the image is obliterated by the fall of sin. "Materially" natural sinful human being is in no way the image of God; formally this same human being is still a subject with reason, language, and conscience or the awareness of responsibility. It exists within God-given orders of grace that maintain life, as in *The Divine Imperative*.[72] The formal image of God in humanity is the "*point of connection*" or "*point of contact*" for the revelation in Christ. Without language humanity could not understand revelation, and without responsibility it could not understand sin. Materially only God can create faith; formally human being is able to hear the Word. In order for God to encounter human being in Christ, a subject that can be encountered must be presupposed; this too belongs to the formal image.[73] The church should be attentive to those who hear its proclamation and to the personal conditions they bring to hearing it. Only the Holy Spirit opens hearts for the Word, but in pastoral work among intellectuals and in instruction of youth, pastors must seek the right "point of connection," and this is the work of eristics.[74]

In his response to *Nature and Grace,* Barth begins by stating his conviction that Brunner's theories of natural orders and eristics are opening the way for "a new mediation theology."[75] The only "natural order" of life-maintaining grace that Barth can recognize is that life still exists. And why call existence grace? It would be better called an "antechamber of hell." Where is any mention of *Volk* in the Reformation doctrine of *sola scriptura*? In what does theology say marriage consists as a natural order of creation? One would receive better answers about "natural" marriage from biology or sociology.[76] In short, Barth denies that Brunner's "orders of creation" are given by grace. They do not compare with the covenants of the Old Testament, which are given by grace. With regard to Brunner's use of Kierkegaard, Barth concedes that he too, in places in *Romans* and in other writings of that period, had spoken of despair in a way similar to Brunner, but that is now past. Brunner may wish to call his use of Kierkegaardian despair a "capacity for revelation," but Scripture and the creeds speak only of human "incapacity." When we truly hear the Word, it is "the realization of a divine

---

72. *Natural Theology,* 22–31.
73. Ibid., 31–35.
74. Ibid., 58f.
75. *Natural Theology,* 68, 72. The ET of *Natural Theology* translates *Vermittlungstheologie* (mediation theology) as "theology of compromise."
76. Ibid., 83f., 86.

possibility, not one that is inherent in our human nature."[77] As for the unbelievers, intellectuals, and youth that Brunner mentions, one speaks best with
them, Barth says, "when one treats them quietly and simply (remembering that
Christ has died and risen also for them), as if their rejection of 'Christianity' was
not to be taken seriously. It is only then that they can understand you, since they
really see you where you maintain that you are standing as an evangelical theologian: on the ground of justification by faith alone." In preaching, this means
allowing "my language to be formed and shaped and adapted as much as possible by what the text (of Scripture) seems to be saying."[78]

Barth makes pointed reference—also by citing Przywara—to the use of
Kierkegaard's analysis in the doctrine of potential for faith in recent Catholic theology, and he makes an oblique reference to the use of Kierkegaard in Martin
Heidegger, who at the time (beginning in 1933) was known to be in complicity
with Nazism.[79] In his introduction Barth had mentioned—and this cannot have
been of lesser significance for Barth—that Brunner's Nature and Grace had been
positively received by theologians associated with the German Christians who
supported Nazism [chap. 1.4].[80] The debate with Brunner occurs in the same
year in which the formation of the Confessing Church and the Barmen Declaration took place.

In a following work, Man in Revolt (1937), Brunner defends his interpretation of Kierkegaard but sharpens certain distinctions. Kierkegaard's analysis of
natural human existence has to do with "structures of existence" that make it possible "to perceive the true connection between humanity and faith." Only Christian faith recognizes existential despair; natural humanity constantly tries to

77. Ibid., 115–17; cf. McCormack, 410. Brunner appealed in Nature and Grace to Calvin's doctrine of the natural knowledge of God (Institutes, bk. 1). Barth responds that it was not a source of
actual knowledge of God for Calvin (ibid., 102, 104–9). It is a "possibility of real knowledge,"
although "not a possibility to be realized by us" but only by God (106).

78. Ibid., 127. On the attitude toward nonbelief, cf. Barth's Anselm interpretation in chap. 6.1.2.

79. Natural Theology, 116; cf. 96–99, 103. For Przywara (see chap. 6.1.1), Kierkegaard's philosophy of existence is a description of the state of human life in original sin, waiting for redemption,
and ready to be momentarily lifted into the "all-effective" power (Allwirksamkeit) of love. It therefore
describes Przywara's "God in us" (Przywara, Analogia Entis, 2nd ed., 1st ed. 1932 [Einsiedeln:
Johannes Verlag, 1962], 216). Przywara also says that Heidegger's "Existence-Phenomenology" is an
extension of Kierkegaard's "dialectic of existence" (ibid., 109). See Heidegger and Nazism in chap.
6.3 on Rudolf Bultmann.

80. Emmanuel Hirsch [chap. 1.4, note 76] uses Kierkegaard in his advocacy of German traditional values. For Hirsch, Kierkegaard's "Religiousness A" (Kierkegaard's "ethical" religion) prepares
human being for Christian faith or "Religiousness B," with which A is inseparably linked. "General"
or "prevenient grace" forms the concrete historical situation in which A comes to be and has its existence, that is, the national life of Germany, which is therefore also the presupposition and continuing historical context of B. National life is the general grace of the Creator, of creation. Since
Christianity has had an important role in forming the historical life of the nation, it is already part
of A (Emmanuel Hirsch, Schöpfung und Sünde [Tübingen: Mohr Siebeck, 1931], 13f., 31–38, 44–46,
99f. Kierkegaard himself does not discuss Religiousness A in connection with nation, folk, or orders
of creation [chap. 2.6]. Related to Hirsch's interpretation of Kierkegaard is his theory that creation
and sin are "one and the same" as a relationship of identity in opposition (33). The thought is evidently derived from Idealism. Brunner strongly rejects it: Divine Imperative, 608, 618, 683, but oddly
he has nothing to say about Hirsch's interpretation of Kierkegaard.

escape it. Kierkegaard writes about despair as a Christian, not from a neutral point of view. Brunner admits, however, that Kierkegaard's analysis of existence can also be understood in a secular way without reference to faith, as in the existentialism of Martin Heidegger.[81] In his post–World War II works Brunner defends eristics, his understanding of created natural law and the orders with reference not only to creation as God's divine work, which sin does not destroy, but also to the unity of truth in the one Logos, through whom all things were made and in which all truth, in science as in faith, has its one source. For Brunner the unity of truth occurs only in faith.[82] He continues to say that aspects of natural life, such as language and the understanding of what "person" means, are natural presuppositions of revelation.[83] A theory such as Kant's concept of radical evil demonstrates how an "unprejudiced analysis of evil" may come "very near to the Christian truth." But Kierkegaard brings the truth of the original sin of all humanity in alienation from God into clear view.[84]

6.2.2 Brunner's Dogmatics

According to Brunner's most popular work, *Truth as Encounter*, personal experience of the encounter with Christ and the grace of justification given in the encounter are the center of New Testament proclamation. The dogmatic sections of the New Testament are secondary to the encounter, but they are integrally related to it: they say who Christ is and what his work does. The later creeds and confessions of the church are of a different kind. They are objective, distant, intellectualistic expositions of "articles of faith." All doctrines and creeds refer us to the unique reality of the encounter with Christ. They are wrongly interpreted when,

---

81. *Man in Revolt*, trans. Olive Wyon (Philadelphia: Westminster, 1947), on Kierkegaard: 544. The original title is *Der Mensch im Widerspruch* (Human Being in Contradiction). *The Divine Imperative*, which was published in Berlin, was later banned by the Nazi government, but apparently not before *Man in Revolt* was published in Berlin in 1937. It is a Christian anthropology (in defense against Barth) with emphasis on the vestiges of the image of God in humanity and the contradiction of this image in sinful life. It rejects the absolute state and faults a people that wills it (294f.). But the book walks a fine line between racial difference, "revulsion," and superiority, and the admonition that racial divisions play no role in Christian faith (330–35). According to a later work, published in Zurich in 1943, justice, which is completely different from love, "is the supreme and ultimate standard in the ethics of institutions" (Brunner, *Justice and the Social Order*, trans. Mary Hottinger [New York: Harper & Brothers, 1945], 20, 125–30).

82. Brunner's thought is identical with Barth's when he says that the philosophical idea of the Absolute "is the final modification in abstract terms of the idea of the world," but that, if theology understands this idea only "a means of clarification of the revealed nature of God's Being, then it is not only useful but indispensable." *The Christian Doctrine of God. Dogmatics: Vol. 1*, trans. Olive Wyon (Philadelphia: Westminster, 1950), 143f.; cf. 145–50, 242–47.

83. Brunner, *The Christian Doctrine of Creation and Redemption. Dogmatics: Vol. 2*, trans. Olive Wyon (London: Butterworth, 1952), 18f., 24–45.

84. Ibid., 95, 117, 126f. (where Brunner quotes Augustine: the human heart is restless until it rests in God). In a work published in Zurich in 1941, *Revelation and Reason*, trans. Olive Wyon (Philadelphia: Westminster, 1946), 422f., Brunner makes a distinction of degree between the existential distress of natural humanity and the open confession of "despair about himself" that occurs only at the point of its being overcome in Christ (as in Kierkegaard).

instead of beginning with the encounter with Christ, faith is asked to adapt itself to them through subjective appropriation. For Brunner this is a historic mistake of the church, repeated ever again, sometimes with focus on the objective (as in Barth's *Church Dogmatics*), sometimes with focus on the subjective, as in Schleiermacher. In the encounter with Christ, however, the true origin of faith, the objective-subjective dichotomy is overcome [cf. Dorner, chap. 3.3]. God gives God's self in Christ to the believer; the human response is trust.[85] In the third volume of his dogmatics Brunner writes: "This identity of God's self-communication and man's self-understanding . . . is Christian faith."[86]

Brunner's approach to biblical criticism is coherent with his doctrine of truth as encounter. Criticism should be pursued freely, partly because it enlightens us about biblical history, partly because "it destroys nothing of the truth of God." The encounter to which Scripture witnesses is beyond the range or reach of objective historical science.[87] The Christian believes in the resurrection of Jesus "because through the whole witness of the Scriptures He attests Himself to us as the Christ and the living Lord." The truth of the biblical accounts of the resurrection lies in the encounter with the risen Christ "as a personal spiritual reality." The stories of the empty tomb are events that even unbelievers could have witnessed, which is not true of the New Testament accounts of personal encounters with the risen Christ. For Paul the stories of the empty tomb are evidently not important.[88] As for the miracles of Christ's life and ministry, Brunner interprets them as glorifications of Christ and manifestations of his divinity. "There are no absolute, fool-proof criteria . . . by which we can distinguish a legend from a credible miracle story. Here the subjectivity of the judgment of faith is given a great deal of play . . . however . . . no one becomes a Christian by believing all the recorded miracles. But we may well assume that no one can be a Christian who does not believe in the one great miracle, which is Jesus Christ Himself."[89]

In the third and final volume of his dogmatics, Brunner recapitulates the major themes of his theology with a focus on the doctrine of the church. The life of the contemporary church is dependent on the encounter with the truth in Christ, not on objective creeds, dogmas, sacraments, and offices, all of which, in

---

85. *Truth as Encounter* (Philadelphia: Westminster, 1964), 65ff., 81f., 108f., 132f., 160. (Original edition: *Wahrheit als Begegnung*, 1938.) See also *Revelation and Reason*, 145–47, 371f. In Brunner's understanding of trust, one notes again the similarity to Wilhelm Herrmann, as Hans Grass points out: *Protestantische Theologen des 19. Jahrhunderts*, 2:360. Cf. also Ritschl.

86. *The Christian Doctrine of the Church, Faith and the Consummation. Dogmatics: Vol. 3*, trans. David Cairns (Philadelphia: Westminster, 1962), 11, 228.

87. *Revelation and Reason*, 292f. Cf. Schleiermacher, Kierkegaard, Wilhelm Herrmann, and Martin Kähler.

88. *Doctrine of Creation*, 366–70.

89. Ibid., 163–70; *Revelation and Reason*, 294–309. The virgin birth story is legend: *Doctrine of Creation*, 352. Brunner approves of Bultmann's existential interpretation of the New Testament but criticizes his demythologizing program. In agreement with Bultmann, he quotes Luther (*Werke*, Weimar Ausgabe, 38:271) to the effect that while other doctrines do not touch us immediately, justification by faith touches us constantly. Brunner, *Doctrine of Creation and Redemption*, 267.

false dependency, foster a narrow intellectualism in the theological specialist. In such false dependency, the contemporary church has lost the vitality of personal faith held before us in the New Testament. Modern humanity has responded by leaving the church. Barth's theology (at Barmen) was highly important in the Nazi period when the church needed a wall to protect it against a hostile state and environment, but it becomes irrelevant when confronted with the indifference of the "post-Christian masses." What is now required is not objective dogma and being "preached at," but dialogue.[90] Unbelief is false autonomy, a not-being-founded in love, which results in a struggle for dominance and a caprice in human life limited finally only by the moral law within human being.[91] The answer to unbelief is Christ, whose Word is met in faith with trust and love. Trust, not belief about something, is true faith. "Doctrine is an It-word about something, which does not touch me in my existence, but concerns my understanding only." Belief in the Bible is equally doctrinaire and intellectualistic. In the traditional creeds "a speculative ontology took the place of the existential soteriology based on saving history." The encounter with Christ is the "experience of the intrinsic authority of the Word of God."[92] Faith is not knowledge in the ordinary sense. It is not objective, and therefore not a science, but a matter of personal communication in the immediate presence of God's love, of I and Thou.[93]

"Missionary theology," into which, as Brunner says, eristics finally issues, "is an intellectual presentation of the Gospel of Jesus Christ, which starts from the spiritual situation of the hearer and is addressed to it." It is "wholly concerned with . . . his need, his helplessness, his skepticism and his longing." It "unveils the 'cor inquietum' [restless heart], and shows why it is 'inquietum'; . . . its aim is to show that it is only the miracle of revelation in Jesus Christ which can meet man's need, because this distress is caused by man's distance from God and indeed consists in this alienation." The success of this theology, which should have the form of a conversation with the unbeliever, always lies in the Holy Spirit, but this does not lessen the urgent need for missionary theology to strive to produce "the fruit of human teaching," Brunner's shining example of such fruitful, successful teaching remains Kierkegaard. "Kierkegaard is incomparably the greatest Apologist or 'eristic' thinker of the Christian Faith within the sphere of Protestantism. The pioneer task which he began still waits to be carried further; indeed, this work has scarcely begun."[94]

90. *Doctrine of the Church*, 16, 93–102, 213. Brunner sees modernism progressing more slowly in the American church, in part because the competitive-voluntary church system requires that it be more aware of practical concerns. The Americans need the charisma of European theology's ability "to grasp conceptually the gospel in its uniqueness," while the Europeans need the charisma of American church practice. The American danger is reduction of the gospel in the interests of popularity. The European danger is intellectualism (Ibid., 103).

91. Ibid., 145–50, 257f.

92. Ibid., 176, 188, 232.

93. Ibid., 259ff.; Brunner, *Doctrine of God*, 61–66.

94. *Doctrine of God*, 102f.; on Kierkegaard: 100. Cf. the Holy Spirit and success in *The Divine Imperative*, 284ff.

6.3 RUDOLF BULTMANN

Rudolf Bultmann (1884–1976), professor of New Testament at Marburg, studied under Wilhelm Herrmann, who was particularly important for him, and for a time under Adolf Harnack.[95] As a New Testament scholar he was also a student of the most important historical critics of the time. In the Nazi period he was a member of the Pastors' Emergency League and associated with the Confessing Church. He coauthored the judgment of the Marburg theological faculty against the Aryan paragraph that banned Jews from church office [chap. 1.4].[96] In his early years he was instrumental in the development of form criticism, from which came his first famous work, *History of the Synoptic Tradition,* in 1921.[97] In the 1920s he became an advocate of dialectic theology, although in his own distinctive way. Bultmann was never a systematic theologian.[98] Besides his scholarship in New Testament interpretation, his major work was in theological hermeneutics, which he deals with primarily in a series of essays, most of which are gathered in four volumes entitled *Glauben und Verstehen* (Faith and Understanding). Two of these (with minor omissions) have been translated.[99]

As a dialectic theologian Bultmann's concern was, like Barth's, to separate faith from "religion" as something merely human, something that belongs to the fur-

---

95. See Bultmann's "autobiographical reflections" in *Existence and Faith,* trans. Schubert M. Ogden (Cleveland: World Publishing, 1960), 283ff. A complete bibliography of Bultmann's works is in Charles W. Kegley, *The Theology of Rudolf Bultmann* (New York: Harper, 1966). The most authoritative interpretation is by Bultmann's student Walter Schmithals, *An Introduction to the Theology of Rudolf Bultmann,* trans. John Bowden (London: SCM Press, 1967). See also James F. Kay, *Christus Praesens: A Reconsideration of Rudolf Bultmann's Christology* (Grand Rapids: Eerdmans, 1994); James D. Smart, *The Divided Mind of Modern Theology: Karl Barth and Rudolf Bultmann 1908–1933* (Philadelphia: Westminster, 1967).

96. See Walther Früst, ed., *"Dialektische Theologie" in Scheidung und Bewährung 1933–1936* (Munich: Christian Kaiser, 1966), 79f.; cf. 13–15. However in another document he conceded the right of the state, outside of the church, to consider Jews a "guest-folk" (ibid., 90f., 95). "Guest-folk" was a term used by the Nazis for the Jews: see Gerlach, *And the Witnesses Were Silent,* 184 [see chap 1.4]. He remained professor in Marburg throughout the Nazi period.

97. ET John Marsh (San Franciso: Harper & Row, 1963). The significance of the work lies in its determination of layers of tradition in the Synoptic Gospels, the oldest being sayings and parables of Jesus. Bultmann considers the Gospel of John a completely different work. His interpretative work on the New Testament is comprehended in *Theology of the New Testament,* trans. Kendrick Grobel, 2 vols. (New York: Charles Scribner's Sons, 1951, 1955).

98. Systematic theologians associated with his work are Gerhard Ebeling (see chap. 6.4) and Friedrich Gogarten. On the latter, see Larry Shiner, *The Secularization of History* (Nashville: Abingdon Press, 1966). [See also chap. 1.4.]

99. *Glauben und Verstehen,* 4 vols. (Tübingen: Mohr Siebeck, 1st eds. 1933, 1952, 1960, 1965). ET vol. 1: *Faith and Understanding,* trans. Louise Pettibone Smith (London: SCM, 1969). ET vol. 2: *Essays: Philosophical and Theological,* trans. G. C. Greig (New York: Macmillan, 1955). The most important later essays are published in Bultmann, *New Testament and Mythology and Other Basic Writings,* trans. Schubert M. Ogden (Philadelphia: Fortress, 1984). Essays from different periods are in Bultmann, *Existence and Faith.* An important collection mainly from these sources is in Roger A. Johnson, ed., *Rudolf Bultmann* (London: Collins, 1987). Much of the important content of the essays is contained in Bultmann's lectures on "theological encyclopedia": *What Is Theology?* trans. Roy A. Harrisville (Minneapolis: Fortress, 1997). See also James M. Robinson, ed., *Beginnings of Dialectic Theology.*

niture of the world, so to speak, and in doing so to clear the way for the Word of God to be heard anew. Like Brunner, however, Bultmann says that human being, as sinful under the law, possesses the "possibility of coming to God," a possibility that is "actualized" only by revelation, and only revelation discloses the true state of the questionableness and despair of sinful life (*Faith and Understanding*, 316f., 50f.).[100] Sin and false religion stem from the human need to "secure" one's life and faith. Securing one's life is justification by one's own works, what Paul calls "boasting" and "putting confidence in the flesh."[101] Repeatedly Bultmann says that authentic Christian faith requires us to leave all "worldly" security and to rely on God's promise alone, that only in this way are doubt and anxious care for one's life overcome (e.g., 50, 143f.). In the crisis of faith one must decide, and decide again and again, to risk understanding one's life through the justification of Christ's cross and resurrection and so to receive one's future from God (142f., 276).[102] As in Barth's ethics, Christian ethical decisions are made for Bultmann in the concrete moment in which one encounters God and the neighbor in love, so that there is no possibility of an immediate connection of the ethics of encounter with a political program.[103] Beyond this, Bultmann does not discuss ethics, other than in the interpretation of New Testament texts. In important ways Bultmann diverged significantly from Barth, and with time they came to see each other as opponents rather than as coworkers.

A major concern of Bultmann's is the problem of expressing the gospel in the language of contemporary humanity [cf. Brunner]. It was with this interest that his work at Marburg with the philosopher Martin Heidegger (1889–1976) became important. Bultmann and Heidegger formed a community of interdisciplinary discourse in which recent theology (e.g., Barth and Overbeck) was read and discussed.[104] This period saw the emergence of both Bultmann's dialectic theology and Heidegger's *Being and Time*, published in 1927. In the following year Heidegger moved to the University of Freiburg, ending the period of conversation. According to Bultmann, not only were key terms in Heidegger's existential analysis in *Being and Time* derived from Kierkegaard; they also formed a philosophical parallel to the understanding of natural human being in Paul's letters. In

---

100. Page references in the following text are to *Faith and Understanding* (see note 99). The question about God in natural human life reflects Augustine's classical statement that "the heart is restless until it rests in God." Cf. *New Testament and Mythology*, 106; cf. 26, 110.

101. *New Testament and Mythology*, 16f., 28. (See, e.g., Phil. 3:3–4; Rom. 3:27; 1 Cor. 1:29.)

102. "Man before God always has empty hands. He who gives up, he who loses every security shall find security" [Matt. 10:39]. Bultmann, *Jesus Christ and Mythology* (New York: Scribner's, 1958), 84. Cf. *New Testament and Mythology*, 122: "They alone find security who let all security go."

103. *New Testament and Mythology*, 13, 141ff.; *Glauben und Verstehen*, 3:195; cf. *Faith and Understanding*, 142.

104. Hans-Georg Gadamer, *Heideggers Wege* (Tübingen: Mohr Siebeck, 1983), 29; Theodore Kisiel, *The Genesis of Heidegger's Being and Time* (Berkeley: University of California Press, 1993), 218, 282; cf. 452; Schmithals, 14ff. See also the preface to Heidegger's 1927 essay, "Phenomenology and Theology," in *The Piety of Thinking: Essays by Martin Heidegger*, trans. James G. Hart and John C. Maraldo (Bloomington: Indiana University Press, 1976), 4. In this essay Heidegger's view of theology is much like that of Bultmann.

Bultmann's view, Heidegger's existential analysis was dependent on Christian tradition. Bultmann later summarized the commonality in the understanding of human being in Paul, Heidegger, and his own theology: Humans are "beings existing historically in care for ourselves on the basis of anxiety, even in the moment of decision between our past and the future, whether we will lose ourselves in the world of what is available . . . or whether we will attain our authenticity by surrendering all securities and being unreservedly free for the future."[105] These concepts can be used for understanding the gospel message in the modern world because they are concepts that speak to and about the existence of modern humanity in a way this humanity understands. Such "*existential interpretation*" is required if the gospel is to be intelligible in the contemporary world. But Bultmann is also critical of Heidegger. For Bultmann, as for Kierkegaard, authentic human existence is understood and attained only through faith in Christ. Heidegger, Bultmann says, remains within the sinful "security" of the possibilities and power of his own self [*Eigenmächtigkeit*]. In assuming only the reality of death as the future of human being, Heidegger claims but does not actually find freedom for truly authentic existence.[106]

Bultmann has high regard for Wilhelm Herrmann's understanding of faith (esp.132–44) [Herrmann, chap. 4.3]. He agrees with Herrmann's critique of metaphysics; he quotes with approval a passage in which Herrmann says that when human being tries, apart from revelation, to grasp God, it only grasps itself or some self-made abstraction (52).[107] Talk "about" God makes God into an

105. *New Testament and Mythology,* 23; cf. *Faith and Understanding,* 327. (Both texts also mention Karl Jaspers's existential philosophy as an appropriation of Kierkegaard.) Cf. Schmithals, 63ff. Here it is not a matter of whether or not Bultmann rightly represents Heidegger (or in what ways he may be dependent on Heidegger) but only of how he presents Heidegger's analysis of existence in the framework of his understanding of faith. For Bultmann "care" (*Sorge*) and "anxiety" (*Angst*) are treated primarily as elements of sinful existence that are overcome by the encounter with God in Christ, although the sinner remains sinner and therefore falls ever again into care and anxiety. The interpretation is continuous with Kierkegaard's understanding of these concepts. For Heidegger the terms name unchanging structures of human existence: *Being and Time,* trans. John Macquarrie and Edward Robinson (New York: Harper & Row, 1962), 84, 228–44. See also Bultmann's "Autobiographical Reflections" in *Existence and Faith,* 286; Michael Wyschogrod, *Kierkegaard and Heidegger* (New York: Humanities Press, 1954); Michael Weston, *Kierkegaard and Modern Continental Philosophy* (London: Routledge, 1994), 33–57.

106. *New Testament and Mythology,* 28; cf. 117. (The translator translates *Eigenmächtigkeit* as "highhandedness." The German term literally means "own [*eigen*] powerful [*mächtig*] ness [*keit*].") (On "being-unto-death" in Heidegger, see *Being and Time,* 354–56.) In the same place Bultmann uses the striking word *frevelhaft,* a word meaning "sacrilegious, criminal, and outrageous," to characterize Heidegger's *eigenmächtige* assertion of authenticity. Bultmann published this in 1941. In 1933 he had already distanced himself from Heidegger because of Heidegger's brief but fateful association with Nazism as rector of the University of Freiburg (Schmithals, 15). Through a romantic view of German folkness Heidegger had apparently found hope in Nazism (and its anti-Semitism) for overcoming the dehumanization of modern industrial society. In any case, what his actions achieved was the very opposite, as he later realized. After the war he lost his position as professor but was soon reinstated, thanks especially to Karl Jaspers. See the biography by Rüdiger Safranski, *Martin Heidegger,* trans. Ewald Osers (Cambridge: Harvard University Press, 1998).

107. Herrmann, *Schriften zur Grundlegung der Theologie,* 1:187. See esp. Bultmann, *What Is Theology?* 62–70, where he rejects the concept of the unconditioned as metaphysical. In a later

object that is not God (53). Bultmann agrees with Herrmann that faith is a decision brought about by the encounter with God in Christ and that faith is characterized above all by trust in God and is by no means a "work" (132–36, cf. 140)[cf. Brunner]. For Bultmann, as for Herrmann, historical criticism clears the way for an encounter with God that is "unshakable and inwardly compelling" (29f., 31, 123). Biblical criticism only removes false supports for faith; it has nothing positive to contribute to it. God is accessible to us only through revelation (31–33, 263–65). Bultmann disagrees, however, with Herrmann about what constitutes revelation: it is not the "personal life of Jesus" but the Word of God, which Bultmann defines with Paul as Word of the cross and resurrection of Jesus. He argues that the "impression of the person of Jesus" is something only Jesus' contemporaries could experience and that, most importantly, the New Testament itself pays no such attention to Jesus' person (137, 267f.). One must distinguish between the historical Jesus—the Word who "became flesh"—and the "kerygmatic Christ," the crucified and risen Christ of New Testament proclamation through whom salvation is given.[108] As Paul says (2 Cor. 5:16), we no longer know Jesus "according to the flesh" (4). The Jesus of history is inextricably bound up with historical research. For the church to rely on this would mean "dependence on professors" (30).[109] For Bultmann, Christ proclaimed in the church is Christ present, as present to the modern hearer as the crucified and resurrected Christ was to the early church [cf. Kierkegaard].

As for Herrmann, truthfulness for Bultmann requires that theology clearly say that the biblical view of the world [*Weltbild*, literally "world-picture" or "world-formation"] is not our view of the world. Modern humanity does not understand itself as living in a world in which God is in heaven above, hell is below, and supernatural spirits intervene in human life. It reads the Bible with the eyes of its own understanding of the world, whatever its attitude, positive or negative, toward the biblical worldview may be. Bultmann calls the modern worldview, which includes modern humanity's understanding of itself, modern humanity's "*pre-understanding*," the understanding it brings to its reading of the Bible before it attempts to interpret biblical texts.[110] There is a wide gulf between modern humanity's "*self-understanding*" and the worldview of the Bible. But the Christ of the kerygma, of the church's proclamation, is radically present and alive with Holy Spirit, for in it the eternal God enters time and encounters the hearer of the Word, and the encounter determines absolutely the Christian's personal life or history.

---

publication, however, he uses the concept in reference to God as experienced in the encounter of faith: *Glauben und Verstehen*, 4:125; cf. 108, 112; see also Bultmann's essay in Robert Funk, ed., *Translating Theology into the Modern Age* (New York: Harper & Row, 1965), 90–94.

108. *New Testament and Mythology*, 42.

109. Cf. Troeltsch's view that the church depends on historical research to secure the personal being of Jesus and his teaching [chap. 4.6].

110. [Cf. Schleiermacher, chap. 2.7.1.] Bultmann states this most clearly in the opening paragraph of his famous 1941 essay "New Testament and Mythology," in *New Testament and Mythology*, 1; cf. 72–74, 82–87.

Here again is a theme from Herrmann: the story of one's personal experience with God is entirely different from scientific, critical history. "I love you," Bultmann says, cannot be said by science, and forgiveness cannot be demonstrated objectively.[111] Scientific statements are "general [*allgemeine*] truths" that ignore a person's specific life situation (54) and therefore miss the mystery of what "limits" and is "beyond" human existence.[112] For Bultmann as for Herrmann the gospel is characteristically addressed to the individual. Proclamation of the kerygma is an "eschatological occurrence" in which, "as personal address, the event Jesus Christ becomes present ever anew—an event affecting me in my own unique existence."[113] Where, however, the kerygma is not truly heard, it is just another piece of objective information. If preaching simply recites kerygmatic formulas and makes flat statements (however passionately) about their effect as creating faith, it too remains within the sphere of objectivity and therefore requires a "work" of belief. In the communication of Word of God as encounter, preaching should penetrate the walls of modern objectivity, walls that block out the kerygma, by making effective use of "existential interpretation" [cf. Brunner's eristics].[114]

The "event" of the kerygma of Christ's cross and resurrection in the present is the sudden dawning of a light in which one recognizes sin and sees that one's sin is judged and forgiven, that the past of "care" is overcome, that the future no longer has to do with our anxious efforts to secure it but is received from God, and that in every moment of life with others we may act in love (254f.). True hearing of the Word means, in the very hearing itself, that we freely decide to understand ourselves as justified sinners before God, which is the meaning of obedience. We understand ourselves in a radically different way than we had before (254f., 276).[115] It is "eschatological existence," because in living radically before God we live, as Paul lived, at the end of the world. For the "world" no longer has power over us as the reality in which anxious care moves us to secure

111. Ibid., 101. See also Bultmann's essay in Robert Funk, ed., *Translating Theology into the Modern Age*, 91.

112. *New Testament and Mythology*, 9f.; *Essays*, 14. "When reason has followed its road to the end, the point of crisis is reached and man is brought to the great question mark over his own existence" (*Faith and Understanding*, 46).

113. *New Testament and Mythology*, 163.

114. E.g., ibid., 51–55. An important criticism of Bultmann's theology is that it dualistically assumes two realities, one "temporal" available to science, and the other "eschatological" available to faith. Bultmann answers by saying that God is creator and lord of all reality. Natural occurrences can be seen scientifically within the continuum of natural historical processes, but for faith they occur as acts of God: they are "sublated" or "lifted" [*aufgehoben*] into faith's understanding of itself and the world (*New Testament and Mythology*, 162; cf. 158, 112). Bultmann also says unbelieving existence is "sublated" or "lifted" (*aufgehoben*) in believing existence, "being preserved even as it is overcome" (Ibid., 57). Bultmann makes rather frequent use of the Hegelian word *Vorstellung* (representation) to characterize mythical conceptuality: *New Testament and Mythology*, 100; *Faith and Understanding*, 265, 276, 280.

115. Esp. *New Testament and Mythology*, 16–20, 33–35; *History and Eschatology*, 150–55. Love as characteristic of the behavior of the Christian is "indirect" proclamation that, like God's direct address, is a question to its unbelieving recipient (*Faith and Understanding*, 141f.). See also the essay "The Crisis of Belief," in Bultmann, *Essays*, 1–21.

our lives. We are both in time and "above time," spiritually in eternity with Christ. We are in the world "as if not."[116]

The means of sinfully "securing" life are at all times basically the same, whether in accumulating wealth or in pious religious life: one looks at oneself, the world, and God "from the outside" as a careful observer and calculates what is needed and how to go about attaining it (e.g., 58, 138, 276). This happens first of all because human understanding of the world is limited and there are irrational elements in the world that one does not control. Religion, as it naturally arises in human life, has always existed in relationship to these mysterious powers. It naturally makes God and self into objects and tries to manage the attainment of security in an insecure world. Christian religion too develops means to secure its faith in God, all of which distract or lead away from the call of God in Christ. The call is addressed immediately, directly to the person, without the intervention of the observer perspective. Like all false supports of faith, the observer perspective is subject to the insecurity of doubt (50, cf. 39). When one looks for support to the miracle stories of the New Testament, the same sin of the self-securing outside observer is involved (255f.). With God there is no "outside" but only eternal presence, and the moment of God's address is always now, as in Kierkegaard. "Those who believe in God . . . need to know that they have nothing in hand on the basis of which they could believe, that they are poised, so to speak, in midair [Overbeck] and cannot ask for any proof of the truth of the word that addresses them. For the ground and the object of faith are identical. They alone find security who let all security go."[117]

There is another parallel to Kierkegaard. In the pseudonymous *Philosophical Fragments* Kierkegaard wrote "about" faith from a perspective outside of living faith. Bultmann says that theology can fulfill its task of setting forth the true nature of faith in opposition to all misunderstandings only by reflecting objectively on the meaning of faith and the misunderstandings of faith. Therefore, theology must assume an objective perspective outside of the personal existential dimension of faith, and this objective perspective is "unbelief." But the theologian does this—steps outside of the immediate presence of God—as a justified sinner before God, ever in the awareness of the difference between faith and theology. "Theology is . . . the reflective, methodical unfolding of the word of God and of the self-understanding disclosed through this word and given in faith."[118] The objective, outside perspective also characterizes historical-critical research in the Bible. The "historical Jesus" is the Jesus of this perspective.[119]

116. On this paragraph, see *New Testament and Mythology*, 15–19, 33–42; Bultmann, *History and Eschatology: The Presence of Eternity* (New York: Harper & Brothers, 1957), 36f., 43, 146–53 (on eternity with Christ).

117. *New Testament and Mythology*, 122.

118. Ibid., 54–58; cf. further the essay "Theology as Science," ibid., 46–66; *Theology of the New Testament*, 1:190; *Faith and Understanding*, 120. In *Theology of the New Testament*, 2:244, Bultmann relates this understanding of theology to F. C. Baur's understanding of the relationship between faith and knowledge, but he rejects Baur's Hegelianism and Baur's dissolution of the kerygma into conceptual thought. (Cf. theology and faith in the late Schelling, Dorner, and Barth.)

119. *New Testament and Mythology*, 32ff.; cf. *History and Eschatology*, 116–22.

Bultmann thinks that he can also identify "outside" perspectives in the New Testament itself, namely, in his program of "*demythologizing,*" which he carries out for the purpose of clarifying the church's proclamation. The key to recognizing "outside" perspectives in the New Testament is the kerygma itself: there is no "guarantee" (security) for faith other than the claim of God in cross and resurrection (64f.). But this is no guarantee as one normally understands a guarantee. "As Herrmann already taught us, the fact that faith cannot be proved is precisely its strength." Guarantees and proofs are objective, whether they are formulated as myth, as in antiquity, or as science. "Myth" for Bultmann is first of all only the antiquated world-picture of the New Testament. But secondly it provides a kind of objective proof, an imagined security, based on objective conceptions about God acting powerfully in the world, for example, to destroy devils or crush enemies. "Mythological thinking objectifies divine action and projects it onto the plane of worldly occurrences."[120] Especially apocalyptic imagery in the New Testament is the product of its objectifying mythological worldview. There is in the New Testament a mythological development that begins with Jesus as the promised Messiah and ends with Jesus as the divine preexistent Son of God who will come again to judge the world [cf. Baur, chap. 3.5]. Myth, however, is not to be discarded but understood in light of the kerygma, for it always has a deeper intention than what meets the eye. "The motive for criticizing myth . . . is present in myth itself, insofar as its real intention is to talk about a transcendent power to which both we and the world are subject." The problem is that this intention "is hampered and obscured by the objectifying character of its [myth's] assertions."[121] The real intention, to use Harnack's terms, is the kernel in the husk of the myth. For example, in a Christmas sermon Bultmann interprets the story of the virgin birth as a mythical statement about the kerygmatic significance of Christ.[122] For Bultmann, demythologizing is "the parallel to the Pauline-Lutheran doctrine of justification through faith alone without the works of the law." To require acceptance of a mythical "world-picture" foreign to the modern worldview would amount to a legalistic work, including the case of the person who accepts it willingly. Demythologizing, like existential interpretation, dispenses with false supports of faith in order to rely on grace alone.[123]

Bultmann is known for saying that the resurrection "is not an historical event," that the stories of the empty tomb are myths, and that all that historical science can truthfully determine about Easter is the belief of the first Christians in Christ's resurrection [cf. Baur, chap. 3.5]. For Bultmann, faith does not come from miracle reports but from hearing the Word.[124] "God's act is hidden from all eyes other than the eyes of faith." "Faith as freedom from ourselves and open-

120. *New Testament and Mythology,* 111, 114.

121. Ibid., 10; cf. 8ff., 161, 105; cf. *Faith and Understanding,* 142.

122. *Existence and Faith,* 278–82; cf. *Faith and Understanding,* 52, 121f. Cf. the interpretation of "saga and legend" in Barth [chap. 6.1.2].

123. *New Testament and Mythology,* 122. Cf. *Jesus Christ and Mythology,* 84: "Demythologizing is the radical application of the doctrine of justification by faith to the sphere of knowledge and thought."

124. *New Testament and Mythology,* 32–40.

ness to the future is possible only as faith in the love of God."[125] Bultmann makes faith utterly without any "outside" support. The Word alone works true faith. But then he also says: "The Christian hopes precisely where there is no hope (Romans 4:18), namely, in God who raises the dead and calls into existence the things that are not (Rom. 4:17, cf. 2 Cor. 1:9)."[126] "The final proof of the Christian attitude would be . . . to go forward to meet it [death] undismayed in the assured conviction that 'neither death nor life, nor angels nor principalities . . . will be able to separate us from the love of God'" (Rom. 8:38f.).[127] The theologian and the preacher must speak not simply of trusting in God but also about what is beyond death.[128] "Historical events" are objective and subject to historical research. The kerygma of Christ's cross and resurrection is not.

Bultmann's demythologizing program drew a large response from the theological world, much of which is contained or summarized in the publication *Kerygma and Myth*.[129] His separation of the "Jesus of history" from the "Christ of faith," the division of history into objective and eschatological (existential), as well as demythologizing and existential interpretation, were all common topics of debate.[130] "Dekerygmatizing" was a related development; at times it has been confused with Bultmann's program of demythologizing. Its main representatives were Schubert Ogden in the United States and Karl Jaspers and Fritz Buri in Europe [cf. Buri, chap. 4.10]. They argued that Bultmann arbitrarily terminated demythologizing at the critical point: he did not demythologize the supernatural act of God in Christ's cross and resurrection. They called for demythologizing the kerygma of cross and resurrection, for "dekerygmatizing."[131] Bultmann had

125. Ibid., 31; cf. 111ff.

126. *Existence and Faith*, 85.

127. Bultmann, *This World and the Beyond: Marburg Sermons*, trans. Harold Knight (New York: Charles Scribner's Sons, 1960), 79.

128. Schmithals, 320f.

129. *Kerygma and Myth*, trans. Reginald Fuller, 2 vols. in one (London: SPCK, 1972). This translation comprises selections from, and some cases summaries of, the arguments in the first four volumes of the German publication *Kerygma und Mythos* (1948ff.). Bultmann was attacked by orthodox Lutheran theologians, as, e.g., in a parody of the Apostles' Creed "à la Bultmann" by Hermann Sasse, quoted in *Kerygma and Myth*, 2:6, where "not" is inserted before most of the verbs.

130. Emil Brunner, *Christian Doctrine of the Church*, 212–17; *Christian Doctrine of Creation*, 263–70. See Karl Barth's critique in *Kerygma and Myth*, 2:83–132; cf. 29ff., 306–35; *Church Dogmatics*, III/2:437–54; *Karl Barth—Rudolf Bultmann Letters 1922–1966*, trans. Geoffrey W. Bromiley (Grand Rapids: Eerdmans, 1981), esp. 98–101. A well-known response to Barth by Christian Hartlich and Walter Sachs is that Barth's concept of miracle in the New Testament, as both real and as legend and saga, does not reflect the moral honesty of serious criticism. Hans Werner Bartsch, ed., *Kerygma und Mythos*, vol. 2 (Hamburg: Herbert Reich, 1952), 113–25; cf. *Kerygma and Myth*, 2:129; see Van Harvey, *The Historian and the Believer: The Morality of Historical Knowledge and Christian Belief* (London: SCM, 1967), 153–59.

131. Bultmann's debate with the philosopher Karl Jaspers (1883–1969) is in *Kerygma and Myth*, 2:133–215. Fritz Buri's critique is summarized in the same volume, 63–65; cf. 306f. See Schubert Ogden, *Christ without Myth* (New York: Harper & Row, 1961); Buri is discussed pp. 105–111. Ogden's theological orientation (he was professor of theology at Southern Methodist University) is related to Whiteheadian process philosophy. Jesus is the "decisive manifestation of divine love" in history, and faith is essentially authentic existence.

anticipated this criticism in his 1941 essay "New Testament and Theology" and considered it answered.[132]

Among Bultmann's students, the question of the relationship between the historical Jesus and the kerygmatic Christ received the most attention. While Bultmann thinks we can know nothing of Jesus' person because the Synoptic Gospels do not tell us about this, he does think we can know Jesus' teaching, even if in the Synoptic Gospels it is seen through the lens of the early church. *Jesus and the Word*, published in 1926, is written as an encounter with Jesus as teacher and preacher.[133] Jesus preaches God's saving action in the forgiveness of sins and calls for decision; those who hear him are addressed by God through his preaching. But Bultmann says this encounter with the historical Jesus is not what the Synoptic Gospels actually intend to communicate. What they proclaim is, as in Paul, the kerygmatic Christ of Easter. What he had done in *Jesus and the Word* was in effect to extrapolate Jesus from the Synoptic Gospels as a figure of history. In *Jesus and the Word* Jesus remains a figure of the past.

A group of Bultmann's students challenged the distinction between the historical Jesus and the Christ of the kerygma. They argued that the teaching of the historical Jesus in the Synoptic Gospels is essentially the same authoritative Word of God that is in Paul's proclamation of the crucified and resurrected Christ. This, they said, is especially so in view of Jesus' claim to authority (Mosaic law says . . . "but I say unto you" Matt. 5; cf. 7:29).[134]

6.4 GERHARD EBELING

The systematic theologian of this group of Bultmann's students was Gerhard Ebeling (1912–2001). Ebeling, a German who once studied with Bonhoeffer at the seminary of the Confessing Church at Finkenwalde [chaps. 1.4, 6.5.4], was Brunner's successor on the theological faculty in Zurich.[135] In his popular series of lectures *The Nature of Faith* the relationship to Bultmann is evident. All the major themes of Bultmann's theology are present, including the difference between the historian and the believer in the understanding of the resurrection of Christ.[136] However, for Ebeling we can only understand the kerygmatic Christ

---

132. *New Testament and Mythology,* 21ff.

133. *Jesus and the Word,* trans. Louise Pettibone Smith and Erminie Huntress Lantero (New York: Scribner's, 1958).

134. Schmithals, 202–19. James M. Robinson, *A New Quest of the Historical Jesus* (London: SCM, 1959); Günther Bornkamm, *Jesus of Nazareth,* trans. Irene and Fraser McLuskey with James M. Robinson (New York: Harper & Brothers, 1960); Gerhard Ebeling, *Theology and Proclamation,* trans. John Riches (Philadelphia: Fortress, 1966).

135. Ebeling's chief works are *Dogmatik des christlichen Glaubens,* 3 vols. (Tübingen: Mohr Siebeck, 1979, 1982), and *Wort und Glaube,* 3 vols. (Tübingen: Mohr Siebeck, 1960, 1969, 1975), ET vol. 1: *Word and Faith* (Philadelphia: Fortress, 1963). On Bonhoeffer, see *Word and Faith,* 98–161, 282–87.

136. *The Nature of Faith,* trans. Ronald Gregor Smith (Philadelphia: Fortress, 1961). Page references in the following text are to this work.

by first understanding the faith of Jesus, who teaches what faith is or means. For Ebeling as for Herrmann, Jesus is the "ground" of the faith of Christians who believe in and through him. What the historical Jesus teaches about faith and especially what he means by the word "God" are inseparably connected with the kerygmatic Christ of the cross and resurrection. Without his teaching, which cannot be separated from his person, the first Christians would not have known the "who" and the "what" that constituted the meaning of cross and resurrection. And this connection must be demonstrated by historical research within the whole process of New Testament interpretation.

Another exception to Bultmann in the *Nature of Faith* is reminiscent of Wilhelm Herrmann, namely, the "verification" of faith in experience (76, cf. 131). Bultmann himself speaks of faith as freedom from anxious care; it has the fruits of the Spirit mentioned in Galatians 5:22.[137] All these have to do with experience. As we have seen, however, Bultmann denies that faith may seek and find support in experience. Because the justified sinner remains sinner, faith must again and again hear the Word and decide for it, so that faith depends entirely on hearing and deciding for the Word. Ebeling speaks of "successes of faith" that can be "positively offered as an experiential proof of faith," namely, "the experiences of freedom, peace, joy, power to love and to be patient" (170). Salvation includes these fruits of the Spirit as healing experiences; they are prefigured in the healing miracles of Jesus and brought about through faith's participation in the "power," the "omnipotence" of God [in Word and Spirit].[138] Ebeling cautions that such verifications are always jeopardized by oppositions to faith, and that doubt and despair can displace them altogether so that one has only God's promise to rely on (170ff.). Nevertheless verification belongs to faith.

Ebeling's interest in the "success" of faith is also, as he acknowledges, an interest of Brunner's.[139] As Brunner had said (and as Ebeling discusses in the first chapter of the *Nature of Faith*), success is sought in the communication of faith to a post-Christian world (9–18, 22). But this presents a problem that is characteristic of modernity. Modern humanity has so thoroughly "fallen victim" to existence under the law—the law of self-security, as Bultmann had said—that it exists in comfortable distance from the truly serious questions of life. Because it does not experience radical questionableness, it has no sense of the relevance of the gospel and salvation. "This is the real core of our theological task." Again with similarity to the way Herrmann related conscience to faith, Ebeling says, "It is essential that we should follow the urgent dictates of conscience as a guide for the proper interpretation of theology."[140] By these dictates he means faith's penetrating questions and answers about who modern human being is and how it

---

137. *New Testament and Mythology*, 20.
138. *Word and Faith*, 241, 245; cf. 195ff.
139. *Wort und Glaube*, 3:388–404; cf. *Word and Faith*, 336f.
140. Ebeling, *Theology and Proclamation*, 80f.; *Nature of Faith*, 82; see also Ebeling, *Introduction to a Theological Theory of Language*, trans. R. A. Wilson (Philadelphia: Fortress, 1973), 192ff. See John C. Staten, *Conscience and the Reality of God* (New York: Mouton de Gruyter, 1988).

understands itself. For example, the obverse of modern secularism is radical "historicalness": for modern humanity everything is historical and hence relative. Nothing binds it to the past and nothing historical is sacred.[141] Such is modern humanity's natural life. Since this same natural life is the very reality from which the theologian has been liberated, the theologian's task is to communicate this liberation to and for this humanity. What is liberating is the encounter with God's Word in the conscience. As effective Word it discloses both God and the truth to humanity about all reality: about personal existence, its world, and its being before God. Preaching this Word effectively is the task of the church, a task that theology helps to clarify.[142]

Through the influence of the later Heidegger's work on language and in extension of Bultmann's theory of interpretation, Ebeling became a major voice in theological hermeneutics.[143] For Ebeling, meaning in the human world is so entirely a matter of language that one may say that human being exists in language. According to Scripture, Word of God is the medium of creation, and the second person of the Trinity is the Word that became flesh. For Ebeling the "image of God" means human "liguisticality," humanity's being in language. This is where the potential for faith is located. Through language humanity and world are related to God, the "mystery of reality."[144] Through language God is a hidden presence in unbelief itself, as the "questionableness" of human existence shows. The authority of the church's proclamation "lies in the fact that it . . . calls things by their true names, summons them forth from concealment, brings them out of darkness to light." This is faith's most fundamental verification.[145] When preaching is effective, "Word event" occurs. In the light of this event the truth of the human situation (the "law" of natural modern existence) is revealed, the forgiveness of sins becomes reality, and human life is opened to the future of God's grace.[146]

141. *Word and Faith*, 367–71.

142. Ibid., 196–98, 372, 407–23. "Compared with preaching, is the danger of being out of touch with reality not many times greater in theology?" (ibid., 198). Ebeling's concept of conscience, as decision about oneself in relationship to God and world, is largely based on Bultmann's concept of self-understanding. See, e.g., ibid., 411. See John C. Staten, *Conscience and the Reality of God*.

143. See James M. Robinson and John B. Cobb Jr., eds., *New Frontiers in Theology*, vol. 2: *The New Hermeneutic* (New York: Harper & Row, 1964). Ebeling's hermeneutical thought is related to the philosophical hermeneutics of Hans-Georg Gadamer's work *Truth and Method*. Gadamer was a student of Bultmann and Heidegger in the 1920s in Marburg. His hermeneutics is developed on the basis of Heidegger's philosophy and work on language [cf. chap. 8.4.1]. His hermeneutical concept, the "fusion of horizons"—the interpreter's "horizon" of understanding with that of the text interpreted—reflects Bultmann's concept of the encounter of the interpreter's "pre-understanding" with texts from the past. History is a synthesis of the past and a present in constant movement toward the future. Gadamer, *Truth and Method*, 149f., 273f., 337f., 463–78.

144. Ebeling, *God and Word* (Philadelphia: Fortress, 1967), 31.

145. Ibid., 360; *God and Word*, 8, 27–32, 41–45; *Word and Faith*, 324f., 327; *Wort und Glaube*, 2:38, 92–98. Here Ebeling also shows his relationship to (and dependence on) Bonhoeffer [chap. 6.5.5].

146. His kinship with Bultmann is recognizable in what he says about the future and death: "It is essential for faith that it expect, in this darkness [of death], light, joy, and peace, without being able to form in the least an idea of what this might be" (*Dogmatik*, 3:506).

6.5 DIETRICH BONHOEFFER

Dietrich Bonhoeffer (1906–45) was executed at the age of thirty-nine by the Nazi government shortly before the end of World War II.[147] Most of his student years were spent at the university in his home city of Berlin, where he studied under among others Adolf Harnack and the "modern positive" theologian and historian, Reinhold Seeberg (1859–1935).[148] The strongest influence in his student years was his work in Luther. He was soon also influenced by Karl Barth and the dialectic theology, although not without criticism.[149] There is a clear affinity between Barth's and Bonhoeffer's theologies of the church, Christology, and ethics. They were agreed on the task of the Confessing Church and resistance against the Nazi state. In 1933, when Hitler came to power, Bonhoeffer was barely twenty-seven years old; from then on, his life was determined by his leadership in the Prussian wing of the Confessing Church and in the war years by his participation in a plot to overthrow the Nazi government. In the following we focus on Bonhoeffer's six best-known works.[150]

6.5.1 *Sanctorum Communio*

Sanctorum Communio (Communion of the Saints) was written as Bonhoeffer's first dissertation for the theological faculty of the University of Berlin in

147. Eberhard Bethge, *Dietrich Bonhoeffer, A Biography*, Revised Edition (Minneapolis: Fortress, 2000). A grandson of the theologian Karl Hase, Bonhoeffer was born into the academic upper middle class in Berlin. In 1930 he became a lecturer (*Privatdozent*) on the theological faculty of the university at Berlin. In 1931/32 he was a visiting scholar at Union Theological Seminary in New York and spent time there again in 1939. In 1933 he served for a year as pastor of the German-speaking church in London and was after this active in international ecumenical gatherings on behalf of the Confessing Church. In 1935 he was named director of a Confessing Church seminary in Finkenwalde in eastern Germany; the seminary was closed by order of the government in 1937. In 1940 he joined the conspiracy to overthrow the Nazi government led by the head of the government office for counterintelligence, Admiral Canaris. Bonhoeffer was appointed as an agent of this office in Munich, which facilitated his travel out of the country to make contact with the Western Allies on behalf of the conspiracy. He was arrested in April 1943 on suspicion of subversion and remained in prison until his execution. Nothing could be proven against him until after the conspirators' failed attempt on Hitler's life in July 1944, when investigators found his name among the papers of Canaris. He was hanged on April 9, 1945.

148. On Ritschlian influences on Bonhoeffer, see Bethge, 70; cf. 74, 86, 88.

149. Andreas Pangritz, *Karl Barth in the Theology of Dietrich Bonhoeffer*, trans. Barbara and Martin Rumscheidt (Grand Rapids: Eerdmans, 2000); Dorrien, *The Barthian Revolt in Modern Theology*, 149–57.

150. The standard edition of Bonhoeffer's works is *Dietrich Bonhoeffer Werke*, ed. Eberhard Bethge et al. (Munich and Gütersloh: Christian Kaiser/Gütersloher Verlagshaus, 1986–89). Where currently available, I use the English translations of this edition: *Dietrich Bonhoeffer Works*, general ed. Wayne Whitson Floyd Jr. (Minneapolis: Fortress, 1996ff.). Until the translations are complete, the volume of Bonhoeffer's early works entitled *No Rusty Swords* remains important: trans. Edwin H. Robertson and John Bowden (London: Collins, 1965). Some important works on Bonhoeffer are Ernst Feil, *The Theology of Dietrich Bonhoeffer*, trans. Martin Rumscheidt (Philadelphia: Fortress, 1985); Larry L. Rasmussen, *Dietrich Bonhoeffer, Reality and Resistance* (Nashville: Abingdon, 1972); Heinrich Ott, *Reality and Faith: The Theological Legacy of Dietrich Bonhoeffer*; Edwin Robertson, *The Shame and the Sacrifice* (New York: Macmillan, 1988); John W. de Gruchy, ed., *The Cambridge Companion to Dietrich Bonhoeffer* (Cambridge: Cambridge University Press, 1999).

1927.[151] Its purpose is "to understand the structure of the given reality of the church of Christ, as revealed in Christ, from the perspective of social philosophy and sociology" (33). The overriding theme, however, is Bonhoeffer's theological interpretation of the church. Important concepts taken from sociology are the distinction between *Gesellschaft* (society) and *Gemeinschaft* (community) (89), and the concept of the "collective person" (77, 118–21).[152] *Gesellschaft* is "a multiplicity of atomistic wills" (253). The church is a "genuine community" and an "ethical collective person" (260, 118–21). It is "not derived from individual wills" but "exists only through Christ" and "is sustained by the Spirit" (158, 160). "Community with God exists only through Christ, but Christ is present only in his church-community, and therefore a community with God exists only in the church. Every individualistic concept of the church breaks down because of this fact" (158). For these reasons theology begins with the doctrine of the church (134).

"Christ existing as church-community" is the most important formulation of the book. The church-community is "the present Christ himself, and this is why 'being in Christ' and being in the church-community are the same thing" (190, cf. 199).[153] Christ's "vicarious representative action" (155) in bearing sins and granting forgiveness is a present reality "actualized" by the Holy Spirit in the love within the church community (144). The church-community lives in this reality. This true church and the sinful "empirical" (organized) church as it visibly exists are not the same. Nor is the true church a "core community" within or separate from the empirical church (213ff., 245).[154] The true or "essential" church of "Christ existing as church-community" must be believed as Christ himself is believed. It is invisible, attaining visibility only in the eschaton, "and yet it already has its actual beginning in the present" (200, 216).[155] Christ is the "divine unity" of the church and the "peace that passes understanding," which is not the same thing as "human unanimity of spirit." In the empirical church "Jew and Greek clash" (192).

The visible, empirical church is the "bearer and instrument" of the Holy Spirit; "it has certain visible forms that the Holy Spirit produced and implanted into it." The Holy Spirit "is the guarantor of the efficacy of these forms," that is,

151. Page references in the following text are to *Dietrich Bonhoeffer Works*, vol. 1: *Sanctorum Communio*, trans. Reinhard Krauss and Nancy Lukens.

152. Bonhoeffer was perhaps introduced to this concept by the member of the Berlin theological faculty for whom he wrote the dissertation, Reinhold Seeberg (Bethge, 69). For Seeberg the "collective I" or "we-being" was interpreted in terms of culture and race, so that it led into the affirmation of the German Christian movement and the Nazi state. Seeberg identified the Jews with "individualistic" democracy. See Friedrich Mildenberger, *Geschichte der deutschen evangelischen Theologie im 19. und 20. Jahrhundert*, 155–58. [See also chap. 1.4.]

153. Bonhoeffer's main biblical texts (ibid., 199) are 1 Cor. 12:12; 6:15; 1:13; Gal. 3:28; Col. 3:10; Eph. 1:23.

154. Attempts to "purify" the visible church, as for example in pietism, are misguided by the wish for a visible kingdom of God (ibid., 222).

155. Bonhoeffer (ibid., 199f.) refers to the "communio sanctorum" as the body of Christ in which all are one, in Barth's *Romans*, 443. Barth is cited again by Bonhoeffer (250) in support of the statement that the church "rests upon the Word," although for Bonhoeffer the theology begins with "Christ existing as church-community." See the Afterword, 293, where the editor demonstrates that Bonhoeffer's view of the church is dependent on Lutheran scholarship in Berlin.

of preaching and the celebration of the sacraments (216). The visible, historical church is the *Volkskirche* (folk-church), whose members have the "latent potential" to become "real" members of the church. The visible church is the "objective spirit" of the true or essential church (216) and is used by the Holy Spirit as its "medium" (233). Therefore the historical, visible form of the church of the people is "to be counted among the church's greatest strengths" (221f.). The local parish church is "a piece of the world organized exclusively by the sanctorum communio." In all its imperfection it guarantees the relative unity of doctrine and "includes Jew and Greek, slave and free." "As such it stands not only in the world, but also against the world" with moral will and courage (231). "The history of the church is the hidden center of world history" (211).

6.5.2 *Act and Being*

Bonhoeffer's second Berlin dissertation was written in 1929/30 for qualification as a privatdozent (lecturer) on the theological faculty.[156] In *Act and Being* Bonhoeffer develops a theory of transcendence that is fully nonmetaphysical. This is consistent with all his theological writing. (He nowhere enters into speculation about the Trinity.) It is to be remembered that the rejection of metaphysics is a characteristic of Ritschlian theology. In fact in a manuscript from 1933 Bonhoeffer opposes the reality of "the Kingdom of God among us" to the *Hinterweltler,* a pejorative term that means "behind-the-world persons." (He also uses the adjective and adverbial form, *hinterweltlerisch.*)[157] Ritschl rejected metaphysics as a mistaken assertion of a reality "behind" the world [chap. 4.2]. Bonhoeffer is also opposed to "inwardness." The word occurs frequently in the nineteenth century as a term that indicates inner disposition, personal religiosity, the opposite of following laws, rules, and dogmas. Bonhoeffer associates "inwardness" with theological individualism that speculates about God beyond the world, as opposed to theology that begins with life in the community and Christ's presence in it.[158] "Inwardness" is also unimportant for Ritschl, and when Ritschl speaks of the individual, he does so only with reference to the individual as a member of church and society. Like Barth, however, Bonhoeffer clearly rejected Ritschl's thesis that Christ is known only by his benefits.[159]

In *Act and Being,* "act" is punctual and discontinuous; "being" is continuous. Act takes place in consciousness and is of two kinds, direct and reflective. In a direct act, consciousness is directed outward, away from itself; in reflection, consciousness

---

156. Page references in the following text are to *Dietrich Bonhoeffer Works,* vol. 2, *Act and Being,* trans. Martin Rumscheidt.

157. *Dietrich Bonhoeffer Werke,* 12:264‑69, 273, 276. "Von den Hinterweltlern" is the title of a section in Nietzsche's *Also sprach Zarathustra: Friedrich Nietzsche, Werke in drei Bände,* ed. Karl Schlechta, 3 vols. (Munich: Carl Hanser, 1966), 2:297. It has to do with the fiction of a world "beyond [*jenseits*]" this world.

158. Ibid., 155, 184; *Werke,* 14:544. See also *Ethics,* 62 (see note 181).

159. Bonhoeffer, *Christ the Center,* 37 (see note 170); Pangritz, *Karl Barth,* 113.

remains with itself and can become its own object by reflecting on itself. But reflection cannot "find" the direct act, because the direct act is "displaced" by the act of reflection. "This distinction will prove to be of crucial importance for theology" (28f.). In reflection's inability to "find" the direct act, one recognizes the belief of Kant and the early Idealists that the act of thinking is always beyond or transcends one's ability to objectify it [chap. 2.2.2]. When Bonhoeffer names "act" "the infinitely extensive," meaning it has no bounds but extends forever, one thinks of the active ego in Fichte.

"Being" is "the infinitely intensive"(29). Now mentioning Kant, Bonhoeffer says that the act of thinking about an object (outside consciousness) relates "to something transcendent which is not at its disposal." It cannot fully grasp or possess the object or being. This means that in both "act" and "being," the self has to do with what is not at its disposal. The self is "suspended between two poles that transcend it."[160] One pole is the object (being). In Kant's concept of the "boundary" given by the "thing in itself," all objects are always something more, something other than what we objectively perceive or can know about them. The other pole is thinking.[161] As Kant had said, thinking is always beyond or transcends a person's ability to make it an object of thought (34f.). Thinking is "on the brink of the non-objective," a "boundary" of human understanding, an "unconditional" that transcends human being (36–38). Human being is encompassed by nonobjective boundaries both in its thinking and in what it thinks, that is, in its objects.

Philosophy is tempted to ignore these boundaries and to "raise itself to the position of lord over what is non-objective." When it does, it is "imprisoned in itself." It "lays violent hands on the unconditional" and becomes Idealism. The "I" is the creator, "going out of and returning to itself" (38–40, 91). For Bonhoeffer, Hegel and Fichte (42f.) are the paradigms of all such false philosophy. Using Luther's phrase, Bonhoeffer says that Idealism's "return to itself" is "ratio in se ipsam incurvata": reason curved into itself (41).[162] As opposed to Idealism, Kant's boundaries leave room for the true Creator; yet there is in Kant "a deep unclarity," insofar as for Kant reason limits itself, whereas in fact (natural) reason recognizes no boundaries. It cannot, for it is the expression of human sinfulness that makes itself the creator. Natural human being is also "curved into itself," as is "natural religion." "If revelation is to come to human being, they must be

160. Here and frequently in *Act and Being* Bonhoeffer refers to human being as *Dasein*, which he apparently takes from Heidegger's *Being and Time* (the word is explained on p. 32 of *Being and Time*), a work he discusses in *Act and Being*, 69–72, 96–98. The word literally means "there being" and has to do with an inherent reference to "Being" in "human being."

161. In speaking of the thinking ego, Bonhoeffer uses Kant's term, "transcendental unity of apperception" [chap. 2.1.1, cf. 2.2.2].

162. In a later section Bonhoeffer discusses "ontology" as a form of philosophy that, like Idealism, dissolves the reality of existence into "essence," that is, into ideas (64). Bonhoeffer uses the phrase "pulling God down to its level," i.e., the level of the theologian who has not escaped the ego, the "I" (66). This same figure of speech occurs in Overbeck [chap. 5.2].

changed entirely" (58). For Bonhoeffer as for Karl Barth, revelation has nothing to do with a human potentiality for revelation (134).[163]

According to Bonhoeffer, however, some theologians, notably Karl Barth [sc. the Barth of the 1920s] and Rudolf Bultmann (83ff.), base theology one-sidedly on act, while especially Catholic theologians base theology one-sidedly on being (31). Both are partially true. God is pure nonobjective act and as such not at the disposal of human reflection, for otherwise philosophy would order God together with the phenomena of the world. God would be something "for the I" and, like all phenomena of cognition, "formed by cognition," "taken into the I" (44, 54, 91). However, considered only as nonobjective act, not only is God "utterly free, unconditioned," but revelation itself is only act, never something that has real existence or being in the world." For this reason, in a theology like Barth's, no historical moment can be "capax infiniti" [receptive of the infinite] (82–84).[164]

Opposite the theology of "act" is theology that interprets revelation in terms of being. In such theology revelation appears in three forms: as doctrine, as psychic experience, and as institution. According to Bonhoeffer they all avoid the encounter with God in Christ and hence also the "offense" of cross and judgment (103f.). The result is that the "I" remains "by itself." When the believing "I" submits itself to this revelation, the submission is actually a means of the "I" to have revelation "in its own power" (108). It worships, but it itself enthrones what it worships. Both in doctrine and in psychic or internal experience, the revealed God is understandable as something that can be classified within the "human system" of the all-powerful "I." Bonhoeffer names two kinds of revelation as institution: the church in Catholicism, and the verbally inspired Bible in Protestant Orthodoxy. In both God is "bound immediately and at the disposal of human beings" (103–5).

Again, act and being are the "two poles" of transcendence in human life; one is the transcendence of thinking (act), and the other is the "genuine" objectivity of the object (being) that transcends "the clutches of cognition." In sinful existence the first pole, the "I," understands itself in effect (if not in conscious awareness) as the creator and judge of all things. It "takes all that exists" into its power (105). Sinful existence is false existence. Human being "does not understand itself until the I has been encountered and overwhelmed in its existence by an other" (44f.). It must be "touched" at "that 'boundary' that is no longer located in or can be established by human beings, but which is Christ himself" (82). This is the crucial point in *Act and Being*.

---

163. According to *Sanctorum Communio*, there are natural "basic social relations" that are, while broken by sin, analogous to the church that in revelation are "lifted" (*Aufhebung*) into the reality of Christ and made fully new (144, 166). But Christian love is not a human possibility and is realized only in Christ and through the work of the Holy Spirit. Apart from Christ, all love is self-love (168).

164. That the finite cannot receive (or contain) the infinite (an inheritance from scholastic thought) had been defended in Reformed theology (the so-called "extra Calvinisticum") and is included in Barth's *Romans* [chap. 6.1.1]. See the discussion in the Afterword by the editor of *Act and Being*, 178.

When we encounter Christ, the "I" no longer takes the world into its power, but is itself "lifted" [*aufgehoben*] into the transcendent being of revelation, which is Christ in community (109f.).[165] This "lifting" is the synthesis of thesis (act) and antithesis (being) that has been Bonhoeffer's goal from the beginning (33, cf. 120). The act of the "I" is "lifted" into the being of Christ existing as community: it is now the act of faith and being in Christ.[166] In existence in the community, Christ becomes the one who "acts": not the sinner's "I," but in faith Christ is the "subject" of the community acting through its members. And the church is the "being of the community of persons that is constituted and formed by the person of Christ, and in which individuals already find themselves in their new existence" (112f.). "Only through Christ does my neighbor meet me as one who claims me in an absolute way from a position outside my existence. Only here is reality utterly pure decision" [about how one will think and act](127). In acknowledging the claim of the community of Christ, the "I" freely decides to gives up its autonomy and yet remains free in this decision (128, cf. 71).[167] Sin and death are not eradicated, but they are borne by the community of faith, "and so instead of sin and death I see forgiveness and life" (123).

Revelation is not, as it were, "contained" in the community (as in an institution) but always comes to it "from the outside" of the community, from beyond the boundary, from Christ. In this sense, revelation is always "coming" and the life of the community is characterized by its relationship to the future, which is ultimately the second coming of Christ (112). The past characterizes the world under the domination of the sinful "I." The past world is always already formed by reasoned judgments, the "coherence of reason." Revelation gives human existence a new understanding of time, insofar as the present of the Christian community is determined not by the past but by the future (111). "Being is God's being person" (115), namely, in Christ. By this remarkably brief statement Bonhoeffer defines all being, when seen from the perspective of faith, as being in Christ and as present existence determined by the future. "It is only in faith that being discloses itself" (123).[168] Estranged from Christ, the world is enclosed in the "I" and therefore in the past. Enclosed in the past, "life is reflection," and as reflection it refuses "immediate acceptance of what is to come." The model of faith is the child, for the child "sees itself in the power of what 'future things' will bring, and for that reason can live only in the present" (157–59).

"If existence is in the truth only in the act of being encountered by God, then it faces falling into untruth at every turn" (96), that is, when the encounter passes and

---

165. The translator prefers "suspend" as the translation of *aufgehoben* (from *Aufhebung*). Bultmann makes frequent use of another Hegelian word, *Vorstellung* ("picture, representation"), when he is speaking of the mythical world-picture of the New Testament. [See Hegel, chap. 2.3.]

166. The editor of *Act and Being* (164) notes that the distinction between act and being in nineteenth-century philosophy originated in Schelling's *System of Transcendental Idealism* [chap. 2.2.2]; cf. *On Human Freedom* [chap. 2.4.1].

167. Being determined and being free are one and the same in the Augustinian tradition of freedom in Christ. See, e.g., Barth [chap. 6.1.2].

168. This thought is developed especially by Heinrich Ott [chap. 8.4.3].

reflection begins. For reflection—as the act of the "infinitely extensive" self—knows no "rest." It always questions knowledge (37f.). It finds its true limitation in the faith that is anchored in the being of Christ in community. Bonhoeffer also makes the following distinction: While faith is "directly" related to Christ and does not reflect on itself (esp. 154f.),[169] theology is reflective. Theology steps outside of the immediate relationship of faith to Christ and has to do with the past; it is the "memory" of the church-community [cf. Bultmann]. Is theology, Bonhoeffer asks, therefore "profane"? No, he answers, because it understands itself as rooted in faith; it is science in the service of faith (130f., cf. 85ff.). The preacher, who is a person in the service of the community and occupies its highest office, must also be a theologian, but the preacher's task is to allow Christ, not the theologian, to speak (129–32).

6.5.3 *Christ the Center*

This work is based on notes by students who attended Bonhoeffer's lectures at the University of Berlin in 1933.[170] *Christology* or, as it is known in America, *Christ the Center* begins with statements about Christ in *Act and Being*. It is not Christ's work that is crucial, as some theologians have said [cf. Ritschl], but his person. The right question is "*Who* is this?" Christ confronts the "human logos" (the "I") from the "outside" with what this logos cannot truly comprehend within the possibilities of its understanding. In the encounter with the "other," Christ, human being discovers the "boundaries" of its existence and with these the reality of transcendence within existence itself. "So the question of transcendence is the question of existence, and the question of existence is the question of transcendence. In theological terms: it is only from God that man knows who he is" (28–31). As the boundary of human existence, Christ stands between "the old I" (the sinful Adam) and "the new I" that should be, "a boundary that I am unable to cross." Christ is "between the I and the I, the I and God." "Thus Christ is at one and the same time my boundary and my rediscovered center" (60).[171] "In the fallen world the center is also the boundary." As the one standing between what human being is and what it should be, Christ is judge. But Christ is also human being's justification and the beginning of the new existence (61).[172] Through Christ, history is led to its boundary, and Christ is also history's center (62f.). In similar fashion the church, Christ existing as community, is the boundary and center of the state (63). Christ is also the center between God and nature. Nature as it now is, is "enslaved under the guilt of man" and suffers from loss of meaning (64f.).[173] Nature's redemption is already present in the sacraments,

---

169. Here Bonhoeffer attacks the Karl Barth of the 1920s for confusing faith and theology (reflection), insofar as reflection inevitably brings doubt into faith.

170. Page references in the following text are to Bonhoeffer, *Christ the Center*, trans. Edwin H. Robertson (San Francisco: Harper & Row, 1978).

171. Cf. Christ as the "center" in Schelling's *On Human Freedom* [chap. 2.4.1].

172. Christ is therefore both "no" and "yes"; cf. Karl Barth.

173. Rom. 8; cf. Schelling's depiction of the death of nature [chap. 2.2.6].

which are the "embodied Word." God addresses the elements of water, bread, and wine by name, and they become the "corporeal forms of the sacrament." As the preached word reaches human reason and understanding, so the sacrament reaches human nature (52f.).

"God in timeless eternity is not God; Jesus limited by time is not Jesus": "God is God" only in Jesus (45). In its christological formulations the ancient church was wrong to try to conceive of two substances or entities, divine and human. The reality is rather personal, having to do with the "who," not the "how," of Christ—a correction Bonhoeffer finds in the Chalcedonian formula that the one man Jesus Christ is fully God (101–4). He echoes the criticism of many previous theologians in saying that historical criticism reaches only inconclusive results. He affirms with Kierkegaard the paradox that the historical Christ is contemporary, present reality (72–75). As in Christ's historical appearance, so also in the church-community Christ takes the form of humiliation, the "likeness of sinful flesh" (Rom. 8:3). "His sarx [flesh] is our sarx" (107; 58f.). As Bonhoeffer had rejected "psychic experience" in *Act and Being,* so also now he rejects forms of piety "that avoid the encounter that transforms the person into the new being in church-community," particularly reliance on belief in miracles [cf. Bultmann] and moral piety that bases itself on Jesus' moral life (109f.).

6.5.4 *The Cost of Discipleship*

Completed in 1937, shortly before the seminary at Finkenwalde was closed, and soon after published (in Munich by Christian Kaiser), *Discipleship* or *The Cost of Discipleship,* as it is known in America, is Bonhoeffer's statement on the condition of the contemporary church and what is required of it.[174] But it is also a continuation of his theology of the church and of Christ, who is now not only the "center" but also the "mediator." God and all things in existence are mediated to and for the believer through Christ, so that there is nothing outside of Christ to which one might have an "immediate" relationship (93f.).[175]

Discipleship means especially taking the Sermon on the Mount (including its pacifism) seriously, as real possibility, even as one remains in need of forgiveness. (An exposition of the sermon occupies the extensive second part of the book.) The doctrine of justification is only effective and meaningful when one is drawn into discipleship, the way of following Christ, in a life under the Sermon on the Mount. Otherwise the grace of justification is "cheap grace" (43ff.); in fact it is no grace at all but "another word for damnation" (67). "Only the believers obey, and only the obedient believe" (63). Obedience also means being conformed to the image of Christ (281f.). The "simple obedience" required of the believer is not the believer's work but grace (83). But the "first step"—such as the one Peter

---

174. Page references in the following text are to *Dietrich Bonhoeffer Works,* vol. 4: *Discipleship,* trans. Barbara Green and Reinhard Krauss.
175. Cf. Feil, *Theology of Bonhoeffer,* 79f.

took when he left his nets—is an "external deed," a work of personal freedom that is preliminary to conversion; only this creates the situation in which faith becomes possible. It is commanded and one must do it (64–67).

A striking feature of *Discipleship* in contrast especially to *Sanctorum Communio* is Bonhoeffer's attitude toward the *Volkskirche,* the "church of the people," the "national church"—in other words, the established church.[176] In *Sanctorum Communio* he strongly affirmed it, but in *Discipleship* no longer. His only use of the expression *Volkskirche* is to describe the people of Israel out of which Jesus calls the disciples; and the relationship between them and the people of the *Volkskirche* is one of "enmity." A considerable part of the first chapter is devoted to a history of the increasing secularization of the church and with it the church's increasing identification with "cheap grace" (46ff.).[177] Luther rightly understood the relationship of grace and obedience, but this was forgotten (49ff.). "What do the three thousand Saxons whose bodies Charlemagne killed compare with the millions of souls being killed today? . . . Cheap grace was very unmerciful to our Protestant Church. . . . The glowing wick was mercilessly extinguished" (54). In a concluding chapter on the "visible church" Bonhoeffer gives his doctrine of the offices of the church, again in continuity with his previous work, but now obviously in contrast to the established church. The church is "spiritual," founded only by Christ's Word and the Holy Spirit. Its office bearers are, in accord with New Testament texts, appointed by God through the church-community (245f.).[178]

In *Discipleship* Bonhoeffer is obviously describing his vision of the Confessing Church as a church called out of a *Volkskirche* that was losing itself, in his view, either in blatant German Christian heresy, in orthodox quietism, or in some combination of these. Some critics associated *Discipleship* with monastic piety. The impression was underscored in 1939 by Bonhoeffer's next publication, *Life Together,* a theological account of the life of the spiritual community.[179] Later, in 1944, Bonhoeffer wrote in a letter to his friend Bethge: "I thought I could acquire faith by trying to live a holy life, or something like that. I suppose I wrote *The Cost of Discipleship* as the end of that path. Today I can see the dangers of

---

176. On the meaning of "established church," see above, chap. 1.2 note 35.

177. Like Overbeck [chap. 5.2], Bonhoeffer (*Discipleship,* 46f.) interprets early monasticism as a movement of protest against the secularization (*Verweltlichung*) of the church. Bonhoeffer's advocacy of a purely spiritual, obedient church in opposition to the church of "worldly" compromises and cheap grace may remind one also of Overbeck's (and Barth's) criticism of contemporary Christianity. In a lecture at Berlin in 1931/32 Bonhoeffer cites Overbeck's criticism: *Dietrich Bonhoeffer Werke,* 11:188. Cf. Barth, *Romans,* 430.

178. Bonhoeffer will elaborate on this concept of church office in his *Ethics* (396f.) [see chap. 6.5.5] with reference to the theology of the church of August Vilmar [see chap. 1.2]. Vilmar also conceives of a church in the Holy Spirit whose offices are apostolic, yet in the form of a highly authoritarian, essentially Catholic system of church order. Bonhoeffer has to do only with the former, the church in the Holy Spirit, which also is characteristic of Karl Barth's positive evaluation of Vilmar [chap. 6.1.2].

179. *Dietrich Bonhoeffer Works,* vol. 5: *Life Together and Prayerbook of the Bible,* trans. Daniel W. Bloesch and James H. Burtness.

that book, although I still stand by what I wrote."[180] He did not say what the dangers were.

6.5.5 *Ethics*

Ethics is based on a series of manuscripts written in the years 1940–43, when Bonhoeffer's arrest ended his work on the project.[181] *Ethics* is similar to the ethics of Karl Barth in that the whole of reality is understood as being in Christ, and the access to this truth is given only in faith in Christ (75). Like Barth, Bonhoeffer addresses the unbeliever as a person ultimately within this truth [chap. 6.1.3]. But his interpretation of Christian ethics is not identical with Barth's.

Christ is the "middle" between God and the world and the "center of all that happens." In Christ the "mystery of the world" is disclosed. "The abyss [*Abgrund*] of the love of God embraces even the most abysmal godlessness of the world" (83, cf. 58).[182] "Good is life as it is in reality, that is, in its origin, essence and goal" (253). "Christian" and "worldly" are not opposed to each other "like two eternally hostile principles. Instead the action of the Christian springs from the unity between God and the world and the unity of life that have been created in Christ" (253). The way of disclosure of the sin of the world and the truth of Christ begins with Christ, as does all that has to do with truth. The truth means both yes and no, both justification and judgment (261f.). Both are included in the fact that God has entered into intimate unity with all of humanity, and indeed in such a way that that "righteous" judgment by human beings is displaced. "While we distinguish between pious and godless, good and evil, noble and base, God loves real people without distinction. . . . God stands beside the real human being and the real world against all their accusers. So God becomes accused along with human beings and the world, and thus the judges become the accused" (84).[183] In order that sinful persons become what they in truth are, they must be "conformed" to the form of Christ. Conformed to the form of the crucified, they die before God because of sin (94). Conformed to the form of the risen one, they "live in the midst of death"; they are "righteousness in the midst of sin" and "new in the midst

---

180. *Letters and Papers from Prison*, 369 (see note 188). An example of rejection of the work because of its closeness to monastic obedience is quoted in Bethge's biography (617f.; cf. 459f.): a letter to Bonhoeffer from a former Finkenwalde student, Gerhard Krause.

181. Page references in the following text are to *Dietrich Bonhoeffer Works*, vol. 6: *Ethics*, trans. Reinhard Krauss, Charles C. West, and Douglas W. Stott. I have in good part followed Feil's outline in his discussion of *Ethics* in *Theology of Bonhoeffer*, 138–52.

182. See *Abgrund* in chap. 2.1.1. It is the same concept as the encompassing transcendent in *Act and Being*.

183. There is a "hopeless godlessness dressed up in religious-Christian finery," and a "promising godlessness that expresses itself in antireligious and antichurch terms." "This is the protest against pious godlessness insofar as it has spoiled the churches. It thus preserves, in a sure though negative way, the heritage of a genuine faith in God and a genuine church. Luther's saying belongs here, that God would rather hear the curses of the godless than the hallelujahs of the pious" (*Ethics*, 124). According to the editors, the reference is to Luther's "Lectures on Romans," *Luther's Works*, ed. Jaroslav Pelikan, 55 vols. (St. Louis: Concordia, 1955ff.), 25:390.

of the old." Although the new life in Christ is still "hidden in Christ with God" (Col. 3:2), the new life is already "glimmering" (95). Those who participate in this new life are the "small flock" of the true church (96).

"Whatever in the fallen world is found to be human and good belongs on the side of Jesus Christ." This encompasses also those who are not conformed to Christ. Bonhoeffer's illustrations are the older brother in the story of the prodigal son (Luke 15) and the rich young man who kept the commandments (Mark 10). Today, Bonhoeffer says, unbelievers who practice ethical goodness may have had a previous "bond to the ultimate," and Christian behavior toward them would be to claim them "as Christians" and patiently to help them "to move toward confessing Christ" (169f.). This discussion comes at the end of a chapter entitled "Ultimate and Penultimate Things." The "ultimate" or "last" is the truth of Christ. The "penultimate" ("next to the last," the things that go before the "ultimate") means a sinful but relatively good form of life that is a "preparing the way for the Lord": feeding the hungry, giving the homeless shelter, providing justice to those deprived of human rights, community to the lonely, order to the undisciplined, freedom to the slave (163). These are not preconditions for becoming Christian, for only Christ "will bring fulfillment to being-human and being-good." But a hindrance "is placed in the way of receiving Christ" where the "given orders" of life are destroyed (164f.). The penultimate is natural human life understood as what it should be: "The natural is that which, after the fall, is directed to the coming of Jesus Christ." It is "that form of life preserved by God for the fallen world that is directed toward justification, salvation and renewal in Christ" (173f.). The task at hand is "to strengthen the penultimate" (169) [Cf. Brunner, chap. 6.2.1].[184] This is the case even though the dissolution and destruction of the penultimate are, according to Luke 21:16, signs of the approaching end of the world (177).

The good order of the penultimate or the "orders" are what Bonhoeffer calls divinely given "mandates": church, marriage and family, culture, and government. There is an obvious similarity to the orders of creation in Brunner's ethics. But for Bonhoeffer the mandates are not based on creation but on the "command of God" as given through Christ (388–408). They include the church, which is not an order of creation.

Christian ethics is founded not on rules but on Christ as the one who bore human sin (231).[185] The Sermon on the Mount is an expression of the "joy of

---

184. Bonhoeffer says that the "last deed of the penultimate, of preparing the way," is actively going to church (as Bonhoeffer envisioned it) where God gives the Word (166). With this he connects the penultimate of the *Ethics* with what *Discipleship* called the "first step" that human being must take, on his or her own responsibility, to prepare the way for conversion. It is an area of Christian responsibility.

185. Bonhoeffer can make statements rejecting "ethical principles" that sound identical to statements in Karl Barth, e.g., they are abstract, timeless, placeless, and hence lack concrete warrant (371) [chap. 6.1.3]. Yet for Bonhoeffer the "mandates" do have to do with principles, e.g., justice is a principle of government. See Neville Horton Smith's translation of the *Ethics* (New York: Touchstone, 1995), 335, 348. This translation includes material not included in the new edition of *Ethics* in Bonhoeffer's *Works*.

the reconciliation of God and the world." It is truth, although not in the literal sense of principles for application to sinful life, principles that would mean the abolition of property, military service, and so forth (236f.). The love of God proclaimed by the sermon transcends the penultimate and yet it is the ultimate meaning of the penultimate. Christ represents the place where the world should be, the place where ultimate and penultimate are reconciled. The sermon is therefore always valid, also in political life (243), in which the Christian acts on behalf of the world in "vicarious representative responsibility" (238). As Christ stands for humanity in the reconciliation of ultimate and penultimate, so now the church acts as an imperfect but responsible representative of Christ in the world. "Christian life is the dawn of the ultimate in me. . . . But it is also always life in the penultimate, waiting for the ultimate" (168). Ultimate and penultimate are both in tension and in coherence with one another. They cohere to the extent, for example, that Bonhoeffer rejects theories that define political action essentially as self-assertion and relegate the Sermon on the Mount politically to utopian idealism (239f.).[186] In the concrete, he says, one must rely on one's conscience in Christ and make the decision to assume responsibility for acting in a given situation (278–80). This may involve breaking the law in order to affirm it (297)—a foreshadowing of Bonhoeffer's participation in the attempt on Hitler's life. And it may be, as Bonhoeffer had said in another place, that the church "not only has to help the victims [of injustice] but must fall [throw itself] in the spokes of the wheel itself."[187]

6.5.6 *Letters and Papers from Prison*

Letters and Papers from Prison is based on written material that could be smuggled out of the prison in Berlin where Bonhoeffer spent most of his internment.[188] His thought takes a new turn in the spring of 1944, after he had been in prison for a year (esp. 279ff.). This is when he begins to write about "religionless" Christianity, "non-religious interpretation" of Scripture, and humanity "come of age." (The German expression is *mündig*, which literally means "able to speak for oneself"; it designates the legal age at which one is no longer under the authority of parents.)[189] Bonhoeffer's discussions of these topics are relatively brief and unsystematic. One can, however, recognize continuities with his earlier thought. The revelation of Jesus Christ is the "center of life" (312, 337). "Transcendence" has the same meaning Bonhoeffer had given the word in *Act and*

186. Cf. Wilhelm Herrmann's contrast of Christian ethics with the actions of the state, chap. 4.3.

187. *Dietrich Bonhoeffer Werke*, 12:353, from a 1933 essay "The Church before the Question of the Jews." The same expression with a minor change is in a manuscript from 1942: Ibid., 16:551. Cf. the wheel image in Albert Schweitzer and the earlier instances in Strauss and Ritschl [note to Schweitzer, chap. 4.9].

188. Page references in the following text are to Bonhoeffer, *Letters and Papers from Prison*, ed. Eberhard Bethge (New York: Touchstone, 1997).

189. Bonhoeffer sketches a history of human autonomy that underscores the significance of the Renaissance and the Enlightenment for modern humanity (ibid., 229f., 325ff., 359ff.).

Being: it is not a metaphysical reference to what is beyond the world but the presence of God "in the midst of reality" and in one's relationship to the neighbor. Metaphysical concepts make God an extension of the world (282, 341, cf. 376, 381f.). In his earlier work Bonhoeffer had faulted religious individualism, including "inwardness," for its metaphysical speculation about God [chap. 6.5.2]. In *Letters and Papers* he continues this criticism (279f., 286).

In order to validate religion, theology exploits the concept of God as being beyond the boundary of the world or of human perception and ability. (This is a different boundary from the ones meant in *Act and Being*.) Whether this boundary is conceived scientifically or existentially, it always has to do with human weakness and inability. God at or beyond the boundary of world knowledge is a "stop-gap" to reassure believers of God's place in the world of science. But the boundaries of knowledge are being steadily pushed back by modern science, so that God's place too recedes (311).[190] Moreover, in the modern world neither science, art, nor ethics has any need to refer to God as a "working hypothesis." In these areas God is neither necessary nor mentioned (325f.). When theology tries to evoke God in this situation, it is, Bonhoeffer says, like the old Greek theatrical device of the "deus ex machina" (282, 341): the god who, without having had any previous role in a drama, is suddenly made to appear on stage by means of a mechanical device to bring resolution to a problem.[191] Theology has used the same device—as Feuerbach recognized (360)—to exploit human existential weakness. "Religiosity" makes human being look in its "distress" to the power of God as a "deus ex machina" (361; Kierkegaard is mentioned: 374). Theology exploits human vulnerability by "sniffing" after sins, thinking that the "essential nature" of human being is what is most intimate and private, the "inner life."[192] Indignantly he raises protest against a theology that thinks it is "precisely in these secret human places that God is to have his domain!" The God of the Bible confronts sinners rather in their strength (341f., 344f.).

The church should also address human life in its strength, the only place where a humanity "come of age" can be effectively addressed (327, cf. 282). But the church will not have great success, at least not in the imaginable future. The future church, he says, will be a far smaller church, one that emerges from the conflicts of the time with its bare life.[193] But Bonhoeffer is confident that in a distant time there will emerge a powerful new Christian language, "the language

190. Cf. D. F. Strauss on the receding place of religion in the modern world [chap. 2.5.1]. Bonhoeffer also says (341) that theology's scientific-apologetic efforts in opposition to Darwinism have been in vain.

191. The use of the image in philosophy has ancient precedent: Aristotle charges a philosopher with arbitrarily using an argument deus ex machina to solve a problem: *Metaphysics*, bk. 1, chap. 4, 985ª.

192. Bonhoeffer uses the phrase "from prayer to his sexual life" (*Letters and Papers*, 344; cf. 345, 381, 383). In *Ethics*, 305, he writes "the most profound and most personal joys and pains must also be kept from being revealed in words." Cf. the chapter on prayer in *Life Together*.

193. The most striking use of a biblical text in Bonhoeffer's *Letters and Papers* is one he also applies to the church (*Letters and Papers*, 297), Jer. 45:5: "And do you seek great things for yourself? Seek them not; for I am bringing evil upon all flesh, but I will give you your life as a prize of war in all places to which you may go." Cf. ibid., 105, 219, 279, 370.

of a new righteousness and truth, proclaiming God's peace with men and the coming of his kingdom" (300). Until then, there will be a "secret discipline" of worship separated from the world based on the "difference between penultimate and ultimate" (281). Through the secret discipline the "mysteries of the Christian faith are protected against profanation" (286). Such protection is needed in the autonomous, enlightened, scientific world come of age, whose sins characteristically stem from the arrogance of human strength (369, 383, cf. 298f.).[194] In this world it is the present and living Christ who is weak and suffering, and the church is called to share in his weakness and suffering in the midst of the world, in the human community (348f., 360f.).

All of this is recognizably the work of the same theologian who wrote *Act and Being* and the *Ethics*. The church of the secret discipline is none other than the spiritual church of *Discipleship*, which Bonhoeffer now sees in complete separation from the state.[195]

In *Letters and Papers* Bonhoeffer praises Bultmann's 1941 essay "New Testament and Mythology" for its "intellectual honesty," especially in initiating discussion about a "non-religious" interpretation of the New Testament, but he does not endorse demythologizing (285).[196] He criticizes Karl Barth for ignoring nonreligious interpretation in favor of "a positivist doctrine of revelation" (328).[197] Every dogma that Barth discusses is for Barth "an equally significant and necessary part of the whole, which must simply be swallowed as a whole or not at all. That isn't biblical. There are degrees of knowledge and degrees of significance." The final effect of Barth's theology is a "law of faith." Moreover, the world "is in some degree made to depend on itself and left to its own devices, and that's the mistake" (286). "For the religionless working man . . . nothing is gained here" (280). Bonhoeffer remarks in a late letter to his friend Bethge (August 1944), "We must move out again into to the open air of intellectual discussion with the world." He is "still aware of the debt I owe to liberal theology" (378). Perhaps he means by this his openness to the penultimate, to accepting the reality of autonomous humanity in the modern world.[198] In the *Ethics* Bonhoeffer had written about unbelieving ethical persons who should be claimed as Christians. It is an extension of this thought when, in *Letters and Papers* (373, 380, 394), he speaks of "unconscious Christians" in the contemporary world [cf. Richard Rothe in chap. 3].

194. See Bonhoeffer's confession on behalf of the church in *Ethics*, 138–41.

195. In *Letters and Papers*, 382. Cf. Neville Horton Smith's translation of the *Ethics*, 341–48.

196. Bonhoeffer does not agree that either God and miracle or kerygma and myth can be separated, but he affirms Bultmann's direction toward a "non-religious interpretation" of God and miracle (285, 328f.). Letters dated in 1942 evaluating the significance of Bultmann's essay "New Testament and Mythology" are in *Dietrich Bonhoeffer Werke*, 16:248, 344, 358.

197. See Pangritz, 77–87 (on Bultmann: 78–82); Ott, *Reality and Faith*, 1:120–42 (on nonreligious interpretation: 142–66).

198. This has an effect on Bonhoeffer's dogmatics, insofar as he—with reference to Harnack—wanted to keep open the discussion about the propriety of the Apostles' Creed in the contemporary church. See Pangritz, *Karl Barth*, 112f.

Chapter 7

Postliberal American Theologians

7.1 PAUL TILLICH

Paul Tillich (1886–1965)[1] served two years in the pastorate and four as a chaplain in the German army during World War I before becoming a lecturer in theology at the University of Berlin in 1919.[2] His last position before moving permanently to the United States in 1933 was as professor of philosophy with specialty in philosophy of religion at the University of Frankfurt. The reason for his leaving Germany was political; the Nazi government removed him from his position because he was an active member of the Socialist Party, whose members

---

1. What makes the theologians discussed in this chapter "postliberal" is the influence of dialectic theology, although not to a degree that would warrant removing "liberal" as a characteristic term.
2. Tillich's theological autobiography is *On the Boundary*, 1st ed. 1936 (New York: Charles Scribner's Sons, 1966); the authoritative biography is Wilhelm and Marion Pauck, *Paul Tillich: His Life and Thought*, vol. 1: *Life* (New York: Harper & Row, 1976); see also Wilhelm Pauck, *From Luther to Tillich* (San Francisco: Harper & Row, 1984), 152–209. Information in the following paragraph is from these sources unless otherwise noted. Important interpretations of Tillich's thought are James Luther Adams, *Paul Tillich's Philosophy of Culture, Science and Religion* (New York: Harper & Row, 1965); Adrian Thatcher, *The Ontology of Paul Tillich* (Oxford: Oxford University Press, 1978); Langdon Gilkey, *Gilkey on Tillich* (New York: Crossroad, 1990).

were accused of antigovernment agitation and communist subversion. He was taken into the faculty at Union Theological Seminary; later he moved to Harvard and after that to the University of Chicago.

Tillich is an unusual theologian in the number and kinds of significant influences on his work. As a student at Halle he studied under the aging Martin Kähler. He knew Schleiermacher's works. In a time of Ritschlian domination in theology he became a student of Schelling and German Idealism, writing two prewar works on Schelling.[3] He brought the philosophy of nature together with his appreciation of Nietzsche and Romantic poets and with dialogue with artists. He knew Greek philosophy. He read Kierkegaard and Sigmund Freud before the war. After the war Rudolf Otto became a major influence, as did Karl Marx when Tillich turned his attention to reform movements and became a "religious socialist." Although he never studied under Ernst Troeltsch, he considered him an important teacher. Then came Karl Barth's *Romans* and Heidegger's *Being and Time,* which like Bultmann he understood as existentialist philosophy. One of Tillich's last works in German was a major study of Hegel in a series of lectures at the University of Frankfurt.[4]

In the preface of *The Protestant Era* he writes: "The task of theology is mediation, mediation between the eternal criterion of truth as it is manifest in the picture of Jesus as the Christ and the changing experiences of individuals and groups, their varying questions and their categories of perceiving reality."[5] Tillich's theology is a revival of the basic pattern of nineteenth-century mediation theology, both in its eclectic method and in returning to its sources in German Idealism. Here we concentrate on Tillich's most important work, his three-volume *Systematic Theology.*[6] We begin with Tillich's concept of "being-itself."

"The being of God is being-itself." Being-itself is "unconditional" and the "ground" of all created beings.[7] As the ground of all beings, being-itself is their possibility and the "power of being" in all creation, that is, its source of life and meaning. It is the "identity" of subject (thought) and object, for in it all such dis-

---

3. Both have appeared in English at the same publisher in the same year: *The Construction of the History of Religion in Schelling's Positive Philosophy,* and *Mysticism and Guilt-Consciousness in Schelling's Philosophical Development,* both trans. Victor Nuovo (Lewisburg, PA: Bucknell University Press, 1974). What Tillich appropriated from Schelling was mainly the philosophy of nature and the ontology of the being of God in *On Human Freedom,* with which he combines concepts from Hegel's ontology. He does not accept the late Schelling's doctrine of God (in the philosophy of revelation), nor does he accept the late Schelling's interpretation of the New Testament as the expression of revelation in its complete concretion. In *On the Boundary,* 51, Tillich writes that Schelling saw but "soon covered up again" the "chasm" or the abyss of being. Tillich does, however, in a general way, adopt the late Schelling's interpretation of mythology as an ascending history under the influence of the Logos.

4. Recently published in German: *Vorlesung über Hegel,* ed. Erdmann Sturm (Berlin: Walter de Gruyter, 1995).

5. *The Protestant Era* (Chicago: University of Chicago Press, 1957), ix.

6. *Systematic Theology,* 3 vols. (Chicago: University of Chicago, 1951, 1957, 1963). Volume and page references in the following text are to this work. In the following, the parallels with Schelling or Hegel are rather too frequent to be identified in each case. [Cf. chaps. 2.2.2, 2.3, 2.4.1.]

7. The God of traditional theism is only a being among other beings and in the modern world no longer credible. Ibid., 1:235, 245.

tinctions or conditions disappear and flow into one another (235ff.). Therefore God or being-itself is an impenetrable mystery, and all language about God is at best symbolic or by analogy from human experience. It is "divine life" [cf. Troeltsch]. The most appropriate philosophical description of God is given in the Trinitarian terms "power" (ground, energy, vitality), "Logos," and "Spirit." Logos is the principle of order and meaning; Spirit is the unity or synthesis of power and Logos (1:156, 250f.). In religion God is known as person, the highest human concept of conscious being, in analogy to human personhood. But as the mystery of the unconditioned, God or being-itself is above the distinctions or conditions that make personhood what it is. Yet God is the power and possibility of personhood, and for this reason God is rightly symbolized as person (1:244f.). The mystery of unconditioned being-itself is always greater than its philosophical description and greater than religious knowledge. Being-itself is an "abyss" [*Abgrund*, chap. 2.2.1] in which all such distinctions disappear. With Rudolf Otto, Tillich describes the experience of the divine presence in all religion as the holy "nouminous." The abyss as divine is the "mysterium tremendum"; the abyss as "ground of being" is the "mysterium fascinosum" (1:215f.).[8]

Creation has two distinct levels, "existence" and "essence." In religion, the essential being of humanity is Adam as unfallen human being. For Tillich essential humanity has never existed. Adam is a myth, but a myth about a higher truth, about human essence. In its beginning human being exists in the childhood of "dreaming innocence," from which it awakens as it becomes aware of the estrangement that existence always involves, as for example in the experience of sexuality. Estrangement or alienation indicates that existence is not entirely a product of the power of being, in which there is only identity or unity. The power that produces existence must therefore be mixed with a negative, "nonbeing" (1:186–210).[9]

The result of estrangement in human existence is anxiety, which always includes anxiety about death and drives humanity to search for ultimate meaning. "Ultimate" or "unconditional concern" is that to which every human being's ultimate question about meaning is directed (1:11f.).[10] Finally this can only be

8. Cf. Tillich, *Dynamics of Faith* (New York: Perennial, 2001), 14–18.

9. On dreaming innocence see Kierkegaard, *Concept of Anxiety*, 41ff. Hegel is the main source for Tillich's concept of nonbeing [cf. chap. 2.3]. In the *Phenomenology of Spirit* otherness is the temporal and transitory appearance of Spirit, and as such it is "nonbeing." There are other notable elements of Hegel in Tillich's thought, for example, life moves dialectically "through self-affirmation, going out of itself and returning to itself" (1:234). See also Tillich's early work, *System of the Sciences*, trans. Paul Wiebe (Lewisburg, PA: Bucknell University Press, 1981), 37: the foundation of the system of the sciences is the three elements, "(1) the pure act of thought, (2) that which is intended by this act, and (3) the actual process in which thought comes to conscious existence—in other words the triad of thought, being and spirit." Tillich mentions Fichte [chap. 2.2.2] in connection with this triad (thesis, synthesis, antithesis). He could also have mentioned Hegel.

10. Human concern as "unconditional" is intentionally connected to God as "the unconditioned." Without the presence of "something unconditioned" in the human self and the world, there could be, Tillich says, no question about God, nor could an answer be received (1:206). This relates to the original identity of subject and object in the ground of being (see above). As Dorner and others had said in the previous century, Tillich says the infinite God is not limited by finitude (1:252). The "divine life" participates in finitude as the ground of finitude (1:245).

being-itself; but in a provisional sense it can be the gods of other religions or a "quasi-religious" idol, such as the Nazi state. But God, being-itself, does not abandon human existence to nonbeing: to estrangement, anxiety, and death, that is, to being a question without an answer. The "heritage" of nonbeing is anxiety, but there is a counter heritage in human life that is rooted in being-itself: courage. Courage partakes of the power and possibilities of being-itself, which enables one to accept unavoidable anxiety and to deal with the concrete tasks one faces (1:64, 253; cf. 198, 209f.).[11]

There is another sense in which natural human life is not abandoned by God. The Logos leads humanity forward, preparing it through preliminary "revelations," to the "fullness of time," the "Kairos," when the preparation requires and issues into the full revelation of the Logos in Christ [cf. Schelling, chap. 2.4]. What is revealed is the Logos as the "New Being" of reconciliation and love. In Christ, whose person is the New Being, the ultimate concern of all humanity finds its true answer. The New Being overcomes death in eternal life. This does not mean reabsorption back into the abyss of the unconditioned, but the expression of God's love for creation, so that in the New Being the whole person participates in eternal life (3:409–14).[12]

The Christ who is the New Being is not the Jesus of historical research but the "picture" of Christ given in the New Testament, as Tillich says in following his teacher Martin Kähler [chap. 5.1]. He is, however, quite unlike Kähler in important respects. For Tillich, historical-critical method can make important historical determinations about Jesus and the New Testament that affect the "picture" of Jesus, and its main benefit is the "de-literalizing" of what are usually taken to be historical facts in the biblical stories. Still, this method is only objective, and as such it is never "Spiritual," that is, it never brings subject (the believer) and object (the New Being) together in the unity required for faith and the healing of human existence that is salvation (2:101–18, 167). Once the New Testament is deliteralized, one may realize that the "picture" of Christ, the stories and myths about him, are in reality transparent symbols of the New Being. (All true symbols, as opposed to mere signs, "participate in the reality" they symbolize (1:239).) True faith is not a matter of literally believing stories and dogmas but of participation in the new reality called into being in Christ (2:150–68). The New Being in the person of Christ himself is not a "transmutation" of the divine into a human being, but the manifestation of God "as a saving participant in the human predicament" (2:95). It is similar to Schleiermacher's concept of the presence of God in Jesus' "God-consciousness" (cf. 2:150; cf. 121ff.).

In the New Being reason too is transformed, for its ultimate origin is the Logos. In isolation from the Logos, reason falls either into self-sufficient "autonomy" or into subjection to "heteronomous" authority. In the New Being reason is

---

11. See Tillich, *The Courage to Be* (New Haven, CT: Yale University Press, 1952).
12. Tillich calls this "essentialization" (3:400, 413) with reference to the late Schelling (*Werke*, 14:206–22).

"theonomous," united with its own depth in the ground of being and therefore in right relationship to human life and to nature. There is, however, no complete or perfect theonomy under the conditions of human existence (1:84f., 147–50; cf. 79f.). In theology itself there are similar pitfalls: to forget the ground of being is to fall to a "rationalist deism" that "transforms revelation into information"; to forget the activity of the Logos in human life is to fall to an "irrationalist theism" that "transforms revelation into heteronomous subjection" (1:157).[13]

The "Protestant principle" is a concept that pervades all levels of Tillich's work.[14] It is historically represented by the Reformation and Protestantism, but it is often also betrayed by Protestantism. According to Tillich a finite phenomenon is "demonic" when the claim is made that it is the object of ultimate concern or requires unconditional devotion. Only the unconditional, being-itself, is ultimate (1:224–27). This is the Protestant principle: the recognition of the difference between the true ultimate and the demonic.[15] One example is given by the situation of doubt. Christian confessions and dogmas, which should refer beyond themselves to the new Being, are made up of historical elements that are finite expressions of human existence. If they are made requirements of belief simply as they are stated, they become demonic (e.g., 3:174–77).[16] When they lose their symbolic power of referring to the life of the New Being, they become subject to doubt.

Doubt can arise in other ways, such as when a Christian becomes familiar with another religion or with the historical criticism of the Bible (1:241f.). In fact, for an enlightened age it is normal that religious myths are recognized as myths. Tillich calls these "broken myths": their finitude is recognized, but insofar as they retain their symbolic power of referring to the New Being, they remain meaningful. This is an important aspect of Tillich's Protestant principle: there is no Christian myth that is not "broken," because of myth's finite, historical, non-ultimate nature (e.g., 1:151f.).[17] Tillich calls this relationship to the church's

---

13. In *System of the Sciences,* 206–7, Tillich discusses the degeneration of theology and revelation into autonomy and heteronomy. In the modern period God ceased to be the transcendent theonomous spiritual unity of the Middle Ages. Autonomy treated God and revelation as objects in the science of religion, while heteronomy established the same objects as absolute authorities requiring the subjection of reason. [Cf. Heidegger, chap. 8.4.1, and Jüngel, chap. 8.5.] Subjection to heteronomous authority is the substance of Tillich's complaint against Karl Barth in *Systematic Theology,* 1:4f., 36; 3:285. See also the discussion of Barth in Tillich's *History of Christian Thought* (New York: Simon & Schuster, 1968), 535ff.

14. In this concept Tillich rather unites the late Schelling's "Pauline Principle" [chap. 2.4.2] and the early Hegel's concept of the "principle of Protestantism" as a subjective personal relationship to the infinite. Hegel, *Faith and Knowledge,* 57 [see chap. 2.3].

15. See esp. Tillich, *Protestant Era,* 162f.

16. Cf. Tillich, *Dynamics of Faith,* 33, 112f. [Cf. Brunner on the church's creeds and confessions, chap. 6.2.2.]

17. Ibid., 18–25, 58–62. The brokenness carries with it the possibility that the symbols may become meaningless [cf. religion in Lange in chap. 4.1]. In *Systematic Theology,* 1:25, Tillich says that the theologian's commitment to experience could drive her or him "beyond the theological circle," which suggests beyond Christian faith. But in 2:119f., he clearly says that the New Being in Christ is the final revelation; there is no greater truth. See also *Protestant Era,* xviii, where Tillich answers the

mythical and dogmatic symbols "dialectical," insofar as it involves a yes and a no to the symbols, both belief and doubt (1:10, 25).

The New Being is the answer to the question of doubter, for the justification of the sinner includes the justification of the doubter, and the New Being's promise is that it can be expressed in such a way as to meet and answer the concrete question of the doubter. The New Being is "essential" being that lives from the eternal life of God, not from what is transitory and vanishing. It requires that things falsely judged to be ultimate be revealed as demonic. And as essential being it holds the promise that any given form of human existence can be transformed into the form of Christ.

The deeds and words (including the moral teaching) of Jesus as recorded in the New Testament are evaluated in two ways: as historically limited to their time and as symbolic of the universal truth that transcends them. According to Tillich, Jesus "sacrifices" his particular, historical self to his (essential) being as the Christ (1:133–53). Although Tillich does not use this word in his English publications, what he means by this sacrificing of the particular to the essential is expressed in Hegel's term *Aufhebung*, the "lifting" of Jesus' particular appearance into the absolute universality of the New Being.[18] The New Being is for Tillich as much the truth of philosophy as it is of theology, and also for this reason it is similar to the *Aufhebung* that occurs in Hegel's process of Spirit. In other ways Tillich is like Hegel. Sin, for example, is the power of estrangement from God and from one's essential being, and to be estranged from the one is to be estranged from the other (3:225). The Hegelian word is "otherness," alienated being for itself. In other Tillichian terms a Hegelian root may be involved. The presence of the New Being is "Spiritual Presence," a reality in which human life both individually and in community is transformed [lifted, *aufgehoben*] into a life of love and reconciliation in the New Being (3, chap. 2). The New Being encompasses the world and is its truth, and the human world is in process toward it. The world religions show themselves as the "latent" church where communities exist in them in which ultimate concern, faith, and love are progressing toward the recognition of Christ, although they may resist the preaching and actions of the Christian churches (2:152–54).[19]

The promise of the New Being to answer the ultimate question of human existence, in whatever situation it finds itself, is actualized in the power of "Spiritual Presence" by the theologian who lives in the same time and situation as those to and for whom she or he speaks. The theologian strives to understand the grace

---

question about how Christianity can continue to exist given the ever-critical negations of the Protestant principle. "The answer is this: In the power of the New Being that is manifest in Jesus as the Christ. Here the Protestant protest comes to an end. Here is the bedrock on which it stands and which is not subjected to its criticism. Here is the sacramental foundation of Protestantism, the Protestant principle, and of the Protestant reality."

18. Cf. Tillich, *History of Christian Thought*, 430. [On Hegel's word, see chap. 2.3.]

19. Cf. the "anonymous Christian" in chap. 8.4.4 below. In his final lecture Tillich pleads for theology's attention to world religions and the history of religions, in opposition to the absolutism of Barthian neo-orthodoxy and to nonreligious secularism (Tillich, *The Future of Religions*, ed. Jerald C. Brauer [New York: Harper & Row, 1966], 80–94).

she or he has been given in order to answer the existential questions of the human world in which the theologian lives. Tillich calls this the "method of correlation," of the answer to the question (1:3–8)[cf. Bultmann, chap. 6.3]. Theology is a circle in which each part or aspect of the New Being presupposes the other parts, so that there is no one specific starting point (1:11), and entrance into the circle is whatever the correlation requires. The New Being is not confined to any one sphere of religious worship or practice. As the existential question about ultimate meaning involves all areas of life, so does the New Being (e.g., 3:243). Correlation itself is an event of grace; revelation "invades" and "overpowers" the theologian, thus integrating itself in the situation that the theologian shares with her or his period of history (1:53f.). The "medium" of reception is the theologian's experience, in which the content of revelation is always already involved in interpretation for the present (1:46). When Tillich defines theology as "the methodical explanation of the contents of the Christian faith," this means correlation from the very beginning (1:28, 32).[20]

Christian ethics is "theonomous" ethics, ethics under the impact of the Spiritual Presence of the New Being, which lifts consciousness into what human being essentially is. Essentially it is determined by the love of the New Being as "agape." But this consciousness lives within the fragmentary conditions of existence and its elements of estrangement, not in pure essence. For help it must look to the wisdom of the past expressed in "abstract ethical norms." These general rules, just because they are abstract, have no immediate connection to the concrete situations of life. In these situations theonomous ethics must distinguish, and is able through Spiritual Presence to do so, a right course of action between "impoverishing asceticism" on the one hand and "disrupting libertinism" on the other (3:266–75). One of Tillich's most important (and most modern) thoughts comes from Freudian psychology and has to do with the recognition of the creativity and demonic aspects of "eros" on the one hand, and the "psychodynamics of repression" in "Protestant moralism" on the other (3:240f.).[21]

Tillich's practical theology is directly related to his understanding of ethics. In certain of his shorter works he employs a Christian interpretation of psychoanalysis to speak to persons who experience personal despair and confusion.[22] A second practical area in which he made an important contribution is social ethics. Tillich does not address the situation of the state as such, in keeping with the rule—which he follows in his life in America—that theology "should remain in the situation of ultimate concern" and not leave it "to play a role in preliminary concerns." However, theology recognizes that ultimate concern is expressed in the

20. Cf. the related statements of the late Schelling, Dorner, Ritschl, and Barth on the reception of revelation as a content that is expounded in theology.

21. Cf. moral legalism as suppression of love: 1:90f., 200, 279–82; 2:51–55; 3:240f. Cf. also *Love, Power, and Justice* (New York: Oxford University Press, 1960), 78–90; Wilhelm and Marion Pauck, *Paul Tillich*, 86–93.

22. *The Eternal Now* (New York: Charles Scribner's Sons, 1963), and *The New Being* (New York: Charles Scribner's Sons, 1955).

"preliminary concerns" not only of society and politics but also in art and music, and it must speak to these dimensions of reality (1:12f.).[23] His short work *Love, Power, and Justice* outlines a Christian social ethics in which he states principles of justice that should apply at all times and everywhere. They include human equality and dignity but perhaps most importantly the principle of adequacy, which means that the form of justice applied to a situation must be conceived with the purpose of producing creative results.[24] Essays in *The Protestant Era* make use of the concept of *kairos,* not in the sense of the fullness of time in which Christ was incarnated, but as a concept derived from the New Being, which, because it is love, must involve justice. Here kairos is the specific historical situation in which the time is ripe for action and the requirement of action is apparent. Not to act in a kairos situation is to fall to the demonic aspects of political and economic privilege.[25]

7.2 REINHOLD NIEBUHR

Reinhold Niebuhr (1892–1971) was reared in Missouri in the church in which his father was a pastor, the German Evangelical Synod, an offshoot of the United Church in Germany.[26] He served for thirteen years as a pastor in Detroit, where he became an outspoken advocate for social justice in issues involving labor and racial discrimination. Fluent in German, he studied German theology as much as American theology. He joined the faculty of Union Theological Seminary in New York City in 1928. Theologically he was influenced by his church upbringing, as a student at Yale by liberal theology, including American equivalents of Ritschlianism and the history of religions school in biblical criticism, and by his reading of William James. During his pastorate he was influenced by Marx and Troeltsch, and in the late 1920s and 1930s by the dialectical theology of Emil Brunner. Richard Fox has called him a Jamesian, while Wilhelm Pauck wrote that Niebuhr was from first to last a Troeltschian.[27] Toward the end of his career

23. He addresses art in *Theology of Culture* (New York: Oxford University Press, 1964).

24. *Love, Power, and Justice,* 57–66, 75f.

25. See esp. *Protestant Era,* 27, chaps. 3, 10, and 11. On Tillich's social ethics, see esp. Ronald H. Stone, *Paul Tillich's Radical Social Ethics* (Lanham, MD: University Press of America, 1986).

26. Biographical works on Niebuhr's life and thought are Charles C. Brown, *Niebuhr and His Age,* New Edition (Harrisburg: Trinity Press International, 2002); Ronald H. Stone, *Professor Reinhold Niebuhr* (Louisville, KY: Westminster John Knox, 1992); Richard Wrightman Fox, *Reinhold Niebuhr* (San Francisco: Harper & Row, 1987). Important interpretations are Langdon Gilkey, *On Niebuhr* (Chicago: University of Chicago Press, 2001); Robin W. Lovin, *Reinhold Niebuhr and Christian Realism* (Cambridge: Cambridge University Press, 1995); Gary Dorrien, *Soul in Society: The Making and Renewal of Social Christianity* (Minneapolis: Fortress, 1995); Gabriel Fackre, *The Promise of Reinhold Niebuhr,* Revised Edition (Lanham, MD: University Press of America, 1994); Stanley Hauerwas, *With the Grain of the Universe,* 113–40.

27. Fox, *Reinhold Niebuhr,* 84; cf. Hauerwas, *With the Grain of the Universe,* 96ff.; Wilhelm Pauck, *From Luther to Tillich,* 106. On Troeltsch and Niebuhr, see also Stone, *Professor Reinhold Niebuhr,* 48f., 106.

Niebuhr himself said that his theology was more indebted to Emil Brunner than to anyone else, a judgment that seems validated by Niebuhr's magnum opus, *The Nature and Destiny of Man*.[28] What he shares with Troetsch is above all his concern for the ethical influence of Christianity in social and political life, which was also Brunner's concern [chap. 6.2.1]. He also shares with Troeltsch [chap. 4.6] the concept of human being as "nature" and "spirit." With Troeltsch and James [chap. 4.8] he shares, besides a pragmatic attitude toward politics, a conviction of the relativity of historical forms of religion in relationship to transcendent reality, although for Niebuhr this reality is clearly the God of Christianity. And he agrees with Troeltsch in much of his analysis of the social forms of the church in history. While he was critical of Brunner's political theories, Brunner was probably the first inspiration for Niebuhr's study and growing appreciation of Kierkegaard and Augustine.[29] He adopted Brunner's concept of the "point of contact" for revelation in natural human life. It was above all through Brunner that Niebuhr found the way to integrate his earlier liberal thought with a more orthodox theology of revelation, with the result that Niebuhr's theology is a blend of both and distinctly his own.

Niebuhr's influence extended broadly and deeply into American social and political life.[30] His first major work, *Moral Man and Immoral Society*,[31] published in 1932, demonstrated the thesis for which he became famous, namely, that social groups, especially advantaged social classes, behave from the perspective of self-interest more than individuals normally do, and that the more powerful a group is, the more developed is its moral self-justification, and the greater is its abuse of power. The thesis is obviously related to Marx's concepts of class interest and ideology [chap. 2.5.3], although the book was also critical of Marxism. It was, however, only in Niebuhr's later thought that he realized how fully his thesis applied in the critique of Marxism and of communist Russia. For Niebuhr it is also true that social groups, especially Christian groups, usually do have good ethical intentions, although these are most often subordinated to self-interest. The task of Christian "realism" is to make recognizable both the good and the bad, above all the problem of immoral power, in the dynamics of social life. Niebuhr was convinced that only the perspective of Christian faith makes true realism possible.[32]

28. In Niebuhr's personal response in Charles W. Kegley, ed., *Reinhold Niebuhr* (New York: Pilgrim Press, 1984), 507.

29. See Brown, 37f., 54, 60ff. Niebuhr was sharply critical of Brunner's political conservatism in *The Divine Imperative*: Niebuhr, *An Interpretation of Christian Ethics*, 1st ed. 1935 (New York: Meridian, 1956), 141. See also Niebuhr's essay on Brunner in Charles W. Kegley, ed., *The Theology of Emil Brunner*, 268–71, which criticizes Brunner's concept of inequality. [See Brunner in chap. 6.2.1 above.]

30. See Brown, *Niebuhr and His Age*, and Ronald H. Stone, *Reinhold Niebuhr, Prophet to Politicians* (Lanham, MD: University Press of America, 1981).

31. *Moral Man and Immoral Society* (Louisville, KY: Westminster John Knox, 2002).

32. See, e.g., the critique of Christian America in *The Children of Light and the Children of Darkness* (New York: Charles Scribner's Sons, 1944); *The Irony of American History* (New York: Charles Scribner's Sons, 1952); and *Pious and Secular America* (New York: Charles Scribner's Sons, 1958).

The Nature and Destiny of Man is Niebuhr's most important theological work; its two volumes were first published in 1941 and 1943.[33] It begins with the statement that human being is a combination of nature and spirit. As spirit, human being has the freedom to stand outside of its world and itself, that is, it can make both objects of its thought, and within limits it can use natural things to create human social order (1:3f., 26f.). But because its freedom transcends the finitude of the world and of itself, it cannot find the meaning of either nature or human existence in the finite world. Any meaning derived from finite existence shares the limitations of finitude. Human being's transcendent spirit must look beyond itself and the finite world for meaning (1:156ff.). This truth is "general revelation," given with human existence itself, but it is only a question inherent in human life, not an answer. One possible answer is mysticism: the meaning of life is found in "an unconditioned ground of existence." But in mysticism the finite is lost in this ground (1:14ff.).

Niebuhr sees three elements in "general revelation" that direct human being toward God: a sense of the ultimate source of being and awareness of dependence on it, a sense of moral obligation and personal unworthiness, and a longing for forgiveness. But without special revelation, revelation in Christ, human being has no understanding of these elements (1:131ff.). Its inclination is to misuse its transcendent freedom in regarding itself as the center of the universe and to transmute its "partial and finite self" and its "partial and finite values into the infinite good." Therein lies its sin, its rebellion against God (1:122, 124f., 179). With reference to Kierkegaard [chap. 2.6], Niebuhr defines the human self as a synthesis of the limited and unlimited, both of which are corrupted by sin. "In the externalization of the self one escapes the self endlessly and in the temporalization of the self one endlessly returns to the self."[34] In its transcendence it sees before it not only limitless possibilities but also the perils and chance they involve, which causes insecurity and anxiety (1:178ff., 251ff.). Again with reference to Kierkegaard, Niebuhr defines anxiety as the "dizziness" of human freedom in its relationship to the infinite and to finitude (1:252).[35] Anxiety is the state of temptation to sin (1:182).

Sinful existence tries to secure existence by a "will to power" that overreaches human being's finite limits. From the relative success of securing existence comes pride (1:188ff.), which in its collective form is injustice. "The group is more arrogant, hypocritical, self-centered and more ruthless in the pursuit of its ends than the individual" (1:208). Cultural, moral, and religious values formed by sinful humanity are created out of finitude and can only be historically relative (1:146);

---

33. *The Nature and Destiny of Man*, 2 vols. (Louisville, KY: Westminster John Knox, 1996). Page references in the following text are to this edition of the work. Cf. Niebuhr, *Faith and History* (New York: Charles Scribner's Sons, 1949).

34. Cf. Kierkegaard, *The Sickness unto Death*, 30. "Temporalization": time allows only return to self, not escape from it.

35. Cf. Kierkegaard, *The Concept of Anxiety*, 61. [See Kierkegaard in chap. 2.6; cf. Schelling, chap. 2.4.1].

the pride of nations is to make unconditional claims for their conditioned values (1:208). Pride generally leads human being to forget the limits of creatureliness (1:56, 137). In pride ambition seizes upon the unlimited possibilities it sees in human transcendence, while at the same time it sublimates and obscures its prideful egotism by "ideological" pretensions in religion, philosophy, and morality that in fact support its claim to power (1:194–200). "The ultimate sin is the religious sin of making the self-deification implied in moral pride explicit," which can also happen in Christianity (1:200f.). As the Hebrew prophets, beginning with Amos, prophesied against the pride of the chosen people (2:23ff.), so also must the sin of the Christian churches and its consequences be exposed (2: chap. 8).

God's love is a transcendent reality above history and yet it touches history, so that both human existence and through it world life are affected by this transforming love. Self-centered existence is never left to itself but forced to move forward toward truth. This results from human being's freedom or transcendence, which moves it to search for a greater meaning of life than it knows. A second factor is the "structure" of human existence in the moral law of spiritual obligation, which is reflected in the law of the Old Testament and which leaves all human being with an uneasy conscience about its self-centered actions. Both are evidence of the "point of contact" between sinful humanity and the truth that comes through revelation (2:117; cf. 64) [cf. Brunner]. Other evidences of the point of contact are sinful humanity's ideas about a messiah or savior. There are ideal images of a savior in pre-Christian religions and especially among God's chosen people, the Hebrews [cf. mythology in chap. 2.4.2]. Yet these ideals are bound with finite conceptions of salvation, so that when the true Messiah comes, even the chosen people reject him because he does not fit the right image. Pre-Christian traditions with a strong mystical sense of eternity reject Christ because he is a finite being (2: chap. 1). But behind both forms of rejection is the anxiety of sinful self-centered human being that seeks to secure its life. Nothing can overcome sin but God's taking it into himself in the cross of Christ, suffering its consequences, and granting forgiveness to those who believe (2:46, 56f.). To come to faith means to be convicted of sin, that is, to despair of one's false securities and pride and to come to contrition, out of which faith is born (2:56f., 61). Once faith is won, it is validated by opening an understanding of nature, human life, history, and God that gives the final meaning to life and direction to human behavior (2:15, 61, 63, 67).[36]

Christ is both the perfect human and the revelation of the eternal God, and in Christ the two aspects of human existence, transcendence and finitude, are in complete harmony. To believe this is a matter of faith, which only God can work in us (2:52, 64). Niebuhr strongly rejects metaphysics in the doctrine of the person of Christ. "All definitions of Christ which affirm both his divinity and humanity in the sense that they ascribe both finite and historically conditioned

---

36. Cf. Niebuhr, *Faith and History*, chap. 10: "The Validation of the Christian View of Life and History."

and eternal and unconditioned qualities to his nature must verge on logical non-sense" (2:60). Niebuhr repeats the point: "Since the essence of the divine consists in its unconditioned character, and since the essence of the human lies in its conditioned and contingent nature, it is not logically possible to assert both qualities of the same person" (2:70). Such doctrines also have no ethical value (2:61, 74). All statements about Christ's divinity can only be symbolic, since they have to do with what is unconditional. Yet his divinity is real, he is the miraculous revelation of God (2: chap. 3).[37] Christ lives the truth of the words of Matthew 16:25: Whoever loses his or her life will find it, which have their fulfillment only in the resurrection. It is truth that transcends history; in fact it contradicts every supposed truism of sinful historical human existence (2:68ff.). But in it the love of God is revealed. Love, agape, is not only the nature of God but also the transcendent truth of human life in community (2:70ff.). Christ's perfect and sacrificial love is the "norm of human nature" but it transcends history and cannot be attained within it.

In history the highest good is mutual love and an ethics of true benevolent reciprocity. But "mutuality is not a possible achievement if it is made the intention and goal of any action." It needs the support of Christians who follow Christ in being willing to practice the sacrifice required by love, which eliminates the thought and fear of good actions not being reciprocated (2:68f., 82). Realistic Christian ethics has to do with the relative good in concrete situations, something for which the Christian must work. It requires, for example, that criminal justice always be informed by love (2:86). Since Christian humanity is not purged of sin, the cross is a constant reminder of the difference "between sinful self-assertion and the divine agape" (2:89). Yet the Holy Spirit is with Christians informing all they think and do (2: chap. 4). It always opposes the sin of pride (2: chap. 5) and the fanaticism of intolerance (2: chap. 8). The Christian hope expressed in the symbol of the resurrection is valid and will not be destroyed. It is best expressed in Paul's words in 1 Corinthians 15 (2:289, 294–98).

The ninth chapter of *The Nature and Destiny of Man* addresses the problem of justice in society and the Christian's attitude toward government. Democracy has for Niebuhr no abstract definition. In the American experience it is the pragmatic product of "a tortuous process" of "stumbling upon the proper techniques for avoiding both anarchy and tyranny" (268). These techniques were still being "stumbled upon" throughout Niebuhr's life, above all in the civil rights movement. The correction of the two extremes of anarchy and tyranny involves, on the one hand, just and equal representation of all the people and, on the other, the expertise of professional leaders[38]—the same elements that Max Weber and Emil Brunner sought to bring together for a Germany that was only beginning its own stumbling, tortuous, and catastrophic process of discovery [chaps. 1.4, 6.2.1].

37. See Paul Lehmann's article on Niebuhr's Christology in Kegley, ed., *Theology of Reinhold Niebuhr*, 328–56.
38. According to Niebuhr, democracy "requires an aristocracy of knowledgeable and wise leaders in every realm of policy" (quoted by Brown, *Niebuhr and His Age*, 192; cf. 194).

7.3 H. RICHARD NIEBUHR

H. Richard Niebuhr (1894–1962), professor of theology at Yale, was more influential in American theological education than either his older brother, Reinhold,
or Tillich. His work *The Purpose of the Church and Its Ministry: Reflections on the
Aims of Theological Education*[39] was used in the education of almost an entire
generation of Protestant ministers. He was a theologian for the church. Like his
brother he was initially a student of Troeltsch's works.[40] His first major publication, *The Social Sources of Denominationalism,* in 1929, applied Troeltsch's
method of sociological analysis in *Social Teachings of the Christian Churches* to the
churches in America. His conclusion was that social factors dominated church
life in America: "The evil of denominationalism lies in . . . the failure of the
churches to transcend the social conditions which fashion them into caste-
organizations, to sublimate their loyalties to standards and institutions only
remotely relevant if not contrary to the Christian ideal."[41] In a later work, *The
Kingdom of God in America,* Niebuhr's judgment was more positive. In the preface he states that the analysis of the previous book had not explained "the Christian movement which produced these churches" nor "the unity which our faith
possesses." "While it could deal with the religion which was dependent on culture it left unexplained the faith which is independent . . . and which molds culture instead of being molded by it." The task now was to "account for the force
of the stream itself," the stream of Christian faith.[42] Niebuhr's intention is to
demonstrate, especially in the Great Awakenings, not only the inner unity of
Christianity in America but also its transforming effect on American culture, as
it moved in various ways toward the kingdom of God. He did not abandon his
critical edge. In this book he fired his famous broadside at the "naive optimism"
of liberal theology: "A God without wrath brought men without sin into a kingdom without judgment through the ministrations of a Christ without a cross."[43]

In a third major historical work, *Christ and Culture,* Niebuhr develops
Troeltsch's analysis of sect-, church-, and mixed-type Christian communities into
a scheme of five types of the relationship of Christ and culture: Christ against
culture, the Christ of culture, Christ above culture, Christ and culture in paradoxical relationship, and Christ the transformer of culture. The last had become
the focus of his theology, the "conversion" type that works to transform culture.
It does this, not in an attitude of naive optimism, but in belief in possibilities that

---

39. *The Purpose of the Church and Its Ministry* (New York: Harper & Brothers, 1956).
40. On Niebuhr, see Paul Ramsey, ed., *Faith and Ethics: The Theology of H. Richard Niebuhr* (New
York: Harper & Brothers, 1957); Ronald F. Thiemann, ed., *The Legacy of H. Richard Niebuhr* (Minneapolis: Fortress, 1991); Douglas F. Ottati, *Meaning and Method in H. Richard Niebuhr's Theology*
(Washington, DC: University Press of America, 1982).
41. *The Social Sources of Denominationalism* (Cleveland: World Publishing, 1957), 21.
42. *The Kingdom of God in America* (Chicago: Willett, Clark & Co., 1937), vii–viii.
43. Ibid., 193. Niebuhr does not identify whom he means, other than to say he does not mean
the social gospel theologians Walter Rauschenbusch and Washington Gladden.

are the result of "a dramatic interaction" between God and human being.[44] All these books were to have a formative effect on the writing of American religious history.[45]

Niebuhr's main theological work is *The Meaning of Revelation*, first published in 1941. In the preface he says theological readers will recognize in the work that Troeltsch and Karl Barth have been his theological teachers. He has, he says, "combined" them.[46] In doing so he produces a unique theology quite different from either. One does clearly recognize the influence of Troeltsch: a major category is the relativism of historical existence and therefore also of the relativity of perspectives among Christians (10). One also recognizes the influence of the distinction between *Historie* and *Geschichte* in Niebuhr's categories of "external" and "internal history."[47] "External history" is purely scientific history; it is seen from the perspective of the outside observer [cf. Bultmann, chap. 6.3]. "Internal" history is personally meaningful, history in which one is a participant (67ff.; cf. 152). It is for "internal" history that Barth is significant, although he is not mentioned in the text of the book, namely, in Niebuhr's concept of revelation. Revelation is "that part of our inner history which illuminates the rest of it and which is itself intelligible" (93). In its light one recognizes the life and death of Christ as a "parable" in which all of personal life and of history itself can be and is interpreted (124). The content of revelation is not Jesus but God, "our author, our judge and our only savior" (152). Revelation is an event of such significance that our understanding of the whole of reality—past, present, and future, which is now the kingdom of God—is transformed. Faith's historical perspective is relative and limited, but it exists in relationship to the God who is "unlimited" and "eternal" and who gives the "underlying unity" to the whole history of faith, a unity that transcends the limitations of finite perception (86f., 22).

Revelation is given to "natural" human being in its state of sinful corruption; its intent is "conversion" and "transformation." It is "the fulfillment and radical reconstruction of our natural knowledge about deity through the revelation of one whom Jesus Christ called 'Father.'" It is "the continuous conversion of our religious ideas" and a "permanent revolution in our religious life" (182). Revelation is an event that "happens over and over again when we remember the illuminating center of our history" (177, 138).

The theme of transformation or conversion pervades another major work, *Radical Monotheism and Western Culture*, published in 1960. Culture, Niebuhr

---

44. *Christ and Culture*, 1st ed. 1951 (New York: Harper & Brothers, 1956), 194.

45. See the essays by Harry Stout and William R. Hutchison in *The Legacy of H. Richard Niebuhr*, 83–106.

46. *The Meaning of Revelation* (New York: Macmillan, 1960), x. Page numbers in the following text refer to this edition, unless otherwise noted. See also the section "Toward a Definition of Christ," in *Christ and Culture*, 11–29.

47. Martin Kähler [chap. 5.1] applies the term *Geschichte* only to New Testament history, while Wilhelm Herrmann [chap. 4.3] speaks more broadly of personally experienced history.

says, is heathen in its natural state. Natural cultures are of two basic types: "henotheistic," professing "loyalty to one god among many," and "polytheistic," professing "belief in many gods."[48] The terms apply to culture in the modern world. The one that applies best to American society is henotheism (27). It is "that social faith which makes a finite society, whether cultural or religious, the object of trust as well as loyalty, and which tends to subvert even officially monotheistic institutions, such as the churches" (10). The obedience to social laws, such as those of nationalism, is supported by conscience as "the internalized voice of society."[49] The "god" is society itself (26f.). Polytheism emerges when the dominant henotheism breaks down, something Niebuhr sees in existentialism and in contemporary forms of Epicureanism, the philosophy of the pursuit of pleasure (28f.). In Western history radical monotheism, belief in the God of Israel and of Jesus, is usually mixed with the other two types (31). Radical monotheism is belief in the "One," the "principle of being" and of being's origin (32f.). "Radical monotheism dethrones all absolutes short of the principle of being itself" (37) [cf. Tillich's Protestant principle]. In the Christian history of the Western world, cultural henotheism is constantly and indelibly challenged and in process of being transformed by "radical faith" in God (69). Niebuhr sees such an effect in the American liberties of religion and equal rights, but he also notes that these are easily interpreted henotheistically (70–77). Christian ethics is essentially a transformational or conversionist ethics. It presupposes the natural, or what is naturally given in morality and ethics within the historical relativities of human existence. These are distorted by sin, especially as pervasive distrust of human beings and God, but they are in their root products of the ongoing work of the Creator.[50]

In a posthumously published work, *Faith on Earth*, Niebuhr addresses problems of faith in the present world, again with attention to the problem of pervasive distrust and to the beginning and building of trust through Christ. "By his resurrection from the dead, by his establishment as the ruler of life, by the power of his resurrection as Paul has it, it is established that the Transcendent One is indeed what Jesus Christ in his faithfulness and trust acknowledged him to be, and it is equally established that the faithful servant is acknowledged by Reality itself. The Father reveals himself as Father in the resurrection of the Son; the Son is revealed as Son by his life and resurrection." This is not the statement of a triumphal theology, but only an assurance that "the two great problems of existence are solved in principle," namely, the distrust involved in thinking that the "Power whence all things come" is not good, and that the good is not powerful but always defeated "by loveless,

48. *Radical Monotheism and Western Culture* (New York: Harper & Brothers, 1960), 24. Page numbers in the following text refer to this edition.

49. Cf. conscience in Kant [chap. 2.1.2], where, merely by itself, it is not above the corruption of human nature. See also Heidegger's concept of the "they" that dictates ordinary opinion (*das Man*), *Being and Time*, 163–68.

50. Niebuhr, *The Responsible Self* (New York: Harper & Row, 1963), esp. 131; cf. 158 on Barth's ethics; see also James Gustafson's introduction to this work. [Cf. Schleiermacher's ethics, chap. 2.7.1.]

thoughtless power."[51] Faith is interpersonal. "The community of faith which rises into view as the great possibility with the restoration of faith in the Creator by Jesus Christ is the community of every self with God and all God's creatures."[52]

7.4 MARTIN LUTHER KING JR. AND THE BEGINNINGS OF LIBERATION THEOLOGY

Martin Luther King Jr. (1929–68) was a Baptist pastor and, until he was murdered, the leader of the civil rights movement in the United States in the late 1950s and 1960s. King was a practical theologian who spoke with great effect the language of Christian laity for the benefit of theologian and laity alike. His works and actions, in focusing on the problem of equal rights for African Americans, are addressed to all Americans. Here we concentrate on his relationship to the theological tradition and turn especially to his own listing of the notable intellectual influences on his thought in his first book, *Stride toward Freedom*.[53] Reinhold Niebuhr's social criticism, especially in *Moral Man and Immoral Society*, was important for King's understanding of the sociological structure and behavior of powerful groups in relation to oppressed groups. King also says, however, that for him Niebuhr's view of humanity was too pessimistic.[54] Walter Rauschenbusch [chap. 4.5] reinforced his belief that a more just and loving Christian society was possible and should be a realistic goal of Christian hope and ethical action.[55] King's teacher at Boston University, where he received the PhD degree, L. Harold DeWolf (1905–86), emphasizes the role of personalism for the development of King's theology. The roots of Boston personalism lie in its founder, Borden Parker Bowne, who, as noted previously [chap. 1.3], was a personal student of Hermann Lotze [chap. 4.1].[56] The main elements in personalism's liberal theology, elements also learned by King, were the personhood of God as the basis of all reality; the formation all human beings in God's image with a corresponding emphasis on ethics; the universe as God's work, so that science (including biblical criticism) and faith are ultimately reconcilable; and the immanence of God in the world,

---

51. *Faith on Earth,* ed. Richard R. Niebuhr (New Haven, CT: Yale University Press, 1989), 100.
52. Ibid., 109.
53. *Stride toward Freedom* (New York: Harper & Brothers, 1958), 90–107. On King's life and work, see *The Autobiography of Martin Luther King, Jr.,* ed. Clayborne Carson (New York: Warner Books, 1998); David L. Lewis, *King: A Critical Biography* (New York: Praeger, 1970).
54. *Stride toward Freedom,* 97–100; cf. King, *Where Do We Go from Here? Chaos or Community,* in *A Testament of Hope: The Essential Writings of Martin Luther King, Jr.,* ed. James Melvin Washington (San Francisco: Harper & Row 1986), 602. See also Ronald Stone, *Professor Reinhold Niebuhr,* 110, 234–37.
55. Ibid., 91f., where King mentions especially Rauschenbusch's *Christianity and the Social Crisis.* [See Rauschenbusch, chap. 4.5.]
56. Bowne, *Studies in Christianity* (Boston and New York: Houghton Mifflin Co., 1909). On Bowne's theology, see Paul Deats and Carol Robb, eds., *The Boston Personalist Tradition in Philosophy, Social Ethics and Theology* (Macon, GA: Mercer University Press, 1986), 55–80. See also Gary Dorrien, *The Making of American Liberal Theology: Idealism, Realism, and Modernity,* chap. 5.

immediately interacting with each human being.[57] Hegel's dialectical historical process and its path of human suffering was also an influence on King.[58]

King's thought is, however, more than anything else a product of the African American Christian experience, an experience that included the theme of liberation from the beginning, in slavery. His main point is God's great purpose for the United States in the African American quest for justice and equality.[59] King envisioned a new world for everyone.[60] He believed, taught, and preached that justice and equality for all would make the whole society more humane and more Christian. He knew the heralds of justice must not only speak but also act, and in doing so risk martyrdom, as was proven in the violent racist reaction against him, his family, and the black community. The influence of Niebuhr is evident in the direct action realism of King's 1963 "Letter from a Birmingham Jail," in which he writes on behalf of African Americans: "We know through painful experience that freedom is never voluntarily given by the oppressor; it must be demanded by the oppressed."[61] Niebuhr's thought should however be regarded as a confirmation and reinforcement of the lessons of African American experience, not as King's primary source. The same seems to be characteristic of much of King's use of academic theological resources; they clarified and helped to give expression to the prophetic spirit in the African American church: belief in the God of exodus, the thrust toward liberation, and profound Christian hope. Rauschenbusch's vision of a new society in *Christianity and the Social Crisis,* for example, surely reinforced the passionate hope for justice, peace, and reconciliation for all Americans that King eloquently expressed in his famous "I Have a Dream" speech.[62] In learning from Mahatma Gandhi (1869–1948) and his nonviolent method of gaining freedom from oppression in India, King found a method for applying Jesus' ethics of love and his proclamation of the kingdom of God in a program of direct action.[63]

---

57. L. Harold DeWolf, "Martin Luther King, Jr., as Theologian," in David J. Garrow, ed., *Martin Luther King, Jr. and the Civil Rights Movement,* 3 vols. (Brooklyn: Carlson Publishing, 1989), 1:257–67; Rufus Burrow Jr., *Personalism: A Critical Introduction* (St. Louis: Chalice, 1999), esp. 218–25; King, *Stride toward Freedom,* 100f. See also *The Boston Personalist Tradition.* In *Stride toward Freedom,* 106f., King affirms that "the universe is on the side of justice" and that " there is a creative force in this universe that works to bring the disconnected aspects of reality into a harmonious whole."

58. *Stride toward Freedom,* 100f. Cf. Theodor Adorno on Hegel's dialectic in the notes to the section on Hegel in chap. 2.3.

59. See, e.g., Paul R. Garber, "King Was a Black Theologian," in *Martin Luther King, Jr. and the Civil Rights Movement,* 2:395–411, and David Garrow, "The Intellectual Development of Martin Luther King, Jr.: Influences and Commentaries," in *Martin Luther King, Jr. and the Civil Rights Movement,* 437–52, as well as other essays in this collection. See also Page Smith, *Rediscovering Christianity: A History of Modern Democracy and the Christian Ethic* (New York: St. Martin's Press, 1994), 196–200.

60. See, e.g., King, *Where Do We Go from Here?* in *A Testament of Hope: The Essential Writings,* 617–33.

61. *A Testament of Hope: The Essential Writings,* 292. One finds the same realism in the published collection of King's sermons, *Strength to Love,* in *A Testament of Hope,* part V.

62. Ibid., 217–20.

63. On Gandhi: *Stride toward Freedom,* 101ff. On the influence of Rauschenbusch, Niebuhr, and Gandhi, see also Kenneth L. Smith and Ira G. Zepp Jr., *Search for the Beloved Community* (Valley Forge, PA: Judson, 1974).

Seen in retrospect, King's work appears as a first step in a new development in theology that emerged shortly after his death: liberation theology. Whether as black liberation theology, Latin American liberation theology, or as feminist or womanist liberation theology, the person speaking is a member of the oppressed group and speaks very specifically to its situation. The situation is presented in relationship to the dominant oppressive culture in connection with which the particular history occurs. Indeed liberation theology shows this culture in sharp relief, contributing important insights into its history and sociology. It has also found in the theological tradition helpful sources for explicating its insights. In *Black Theology and Black Power*, James H. Cone mentions Karl Barth's reaction to a liberal theology wedded to the culture of the time and Barth's resulting transition to a "thoroughgoing theocentric" theology of "complete trust in God," a theology that knows "no human righteousness can be equated with divine righteousness." Nazism caused Barth "to launch a devastating attack on natural theology," an attack Cone in principle agrees with. According to Cone, natural theology in America exists in the form of a comfortable interweaving of theology, the Bible, and the power structures of society.[64] The only American theology that has really heard the message of the gospel, the message that Barth heard in his situation, is black theology, one of whose aims is to bring to an end "the influence of white seminaries with their middle class white ideas about God, Christ and the Church."[65] Liberation theology is implicitly and explicitly revolutionary.

The first major work of the Roman Catholic Latin American theologian Gustavo Gutiérrez, *A Theology of Liberation*, written on behalf of the large majority of oppressed poor in Latin America, includes an important use of Bonhoeffer's *Letters and Papers*. Secularization, he writes, is "a breaking away from the tutelage of religion," in this case the tutelage of the dominant conservative Latin American church, which maintains itself by supporting the social status quo. Secularization is the affirmation of "the existence of creation as distinct from the creator" as "the proper sphere" of human being. Bonhoeffer's "world come of age" does not, he says, mean a dualism of natural and supernatural but a new possibility, a new awareness of the "infinite openness of the human spirit to God." It is in accord with Catholic natural theology—Gutiérrez frequently cites documents and theologians of the Second Vatican Council—when he adds that "the orientation toward God" is a "constitutive element of the human spirit." Affirmation of the world means affirmation of and orientation toward humanity and its earthly needs, above all of the poor and oppressed, instead of toward the religious sphere of the church.[66]

---

64. *Black Theology and Black Power*, 1st ed. 1969 (San Franciso: HarperSanFrancisco, 1989), 86f., 148; cf. 82ff. See also the references to Barth in Cone's next work, *A Black Theology of Liberation,* 1st ed. 1970 (Maryknoll, NY: Orbis, 1990), esp. 48f.

65. *Black Theology and Black Power*, 131. Instead of responding to problems in American society, theological students go to Europe and look there "for the newest word worth theologizing about." "Little wonder that American theology is predominantly 'footnotes on the Germans'" (ibid., 85).

66. Gutiérrez, *A Theology of Liberation*, trans. and ed. Caridad Inda and John Eagleson (Maryknoll, NY: Orbis, 1973), 66–70.

In a representative work of early feminist theology, *Human Liberation in a Feminist Perspective*, Letty Russell addresses the problem of how one can appropriate Christian history that has supported and continues to support the oppression of women ("unexamined myths operate as fate").[67] She finds an answer by reflecting on history itself. With reference to Gerhard Ebeling [chap. 6.4], she writes that in modern existence all of reality has become "historicized," aware of the temporal nature of all traditions. In the modern world "people are set free to shape themselves and their destiny in different ways, and it is just because of this that [all] liberation theology takes on such an important meaning in today's world. . . . Liberation theologies are trying to seek out the meaning of the Christian tradition so that it speaks the good news of liberation." In developing a method for a meaningful interpretation of the tradition, Russell distinguishes between *Historie* and *Geschichte* [cf. Martin Kähler, Wilhelm Herrmann, and H. R. Niebuhr]. *Historie* is factual history that can be determined by critical methods; it is emancipating insofar as it perceives myths in the tradition. *Geschichte* is history that is meaningful for the community of faith as it remembers its origins, and it can be reinterpreted through living involvement.[68]

---

67. *Human Liberation in a Feminist Perspective: A Theology* (Philadelphia: Westminster, 1974), 88.
68. Ibid., 82–88.

Chapter 8

German Theologians Emerging in the 1960s

The theologians considered in this chapter came to prominence in the 1960s.[1] In the previous decade they had been the students of Barthian and Bultmannian theologians. Four of the five are German and were reared under Nazism; one is Swiss. Particularly the first two, Dorothee Sölle and Jürgen Moltmann, and to a lesser degree Wolfhart Pannenberg, reflect the influence of a newly emerging social criticism, especially that of the Jewish philosopher Ernst Bloch (1885–1977), who escaped East Germany in 1957; in 1961 he was appointed professor of philosophy at Tübingen. Under the impression of the failure of past religion and philosophy, as evidenced by the ruin of war, the Holocaust, and the terror of Soviet communism, Bloch, who was essentially Marxist, developed a philosophy of life that looked to the future. In 1959 he published his most influential work, *The Principle of Hope*, in which he makes substantial use of the biblical eschatology of

---

1. Sölle, Moltmann, and Jüngel gave personal accounts of development since their youth (but with little or nothing said about life under Nazism) in Jürgen Moltmann, ed., *How I Have Changed*, trans. John Bowden (Harrisburg, PA: Trinity Press International, 1997), 3–28; cf. 95–130. In this publication, two related Roman Catholic theologians also give such accounts: Johann Baptist Metz (born 1928), the student of Karl Rahner associated with Moltmann, and Hans Küng (also born 1928), who was barred from teaching priests because of his criticism of papal infallibility.

both biblical testaments. He develops a view of history as a history of hope and an anthropology in which human being is understood as always transcending the limitations of the present toward the future, always hoping for future fulfillment, for "homecoming."[2] In rejecting Soviet communism Bloch returns to the humanism of the early Marx, to Hegel's forward-moving dialectic of history, and to Schelling's philosophy of nature.

Most of the theologians in this chapter represent a revival of Hegelian theology, although they exclude Hegel's concept of the "Absolute."[3] The influence of the later Heidegger is of importance in Heinrich Ott and to a lesser degree in the youngest of the group, Eberhard Jüngel. Our concentration here is on their early works, but we include a review of their later works.

8.1 DOROTHEE SÖLLE

More than any other theologian, Dorothee Sölle (1929–2003) represents the moral pain of a generation of youth confronted with the brutal truth about Nazi oppression and the Holocaust. After the war she turned an intensely critical eye on society and soon also on theology. She would later say that it was through the impression of truthfulness in Bultmannian teachers that she came to theology and to faith. In reflections on her past she wrote: "As a young theologian, I could not understand how people could talk about an almighty God after something like Auschwitz had happened." If God is all-powerful, then God must be devoid of love.[4] In the 1960s she became known for her leadership in the discussions and meditations of the "political night prayer" movement in Cologne, a movement that made identifying and taking action on social injustices a matter of Christian confession.[5] She qualified as a university lecturer in theology but, in spite of growing recognition, was never appointed a full member of a German theological faculty. She was appointed honorary professor in Hamburg in 1994, and 1975–1997 she was, for six weeks each year, professor of theology at Union

2. *The Principle of Hope,* trans. Neville Plaice, Stephen Plaice, and Paul Knight, 3 vols. (Cambridge: MIT, 1986); *Atheism in Christianity: The Religion of Exodus and the Kingdom,* trans. J. T. Swann (New York: Herder & Herder, 1972); *Man on His Own,* trans. E. B. Ashton (New York: Herder & Herder, 1970). The Frankfurt School of social criticism led by Theodor Adorno, Max Horkheimer, and their student Jürgen Habermas was of similar influence.

3. In Roman Catholic theology, see Hans Küng's interpretation of Hegel, originally published in 1970: *The Incarnation of God: An Introduction to Hegel's Theological Thought as Prolegomena to a Future Christology,* trans. J. R. Stephenson (New York: Crossroad, 1987).

4. *The Strength of the Weak: Toward a Christian Feminist Identity,* trans. Robert and Rita Kimber (Philadelphia: Westminster, 1984), 98, where she discusses her theological development especially as a feminist theologian; *On Earth as in Heaven: A Liberation Spirituality of Sharing,* trans. Marc Batko (Louisville, KY: Westminster/John Knox, 1993). A recent publication on her theology is Sarah K. Pinnock, ed., *The Theology of Dorothee Soelle* (Harrisburg, PA: Trinity Press International, 2003), and, more recently, *Dorothee Soelle, Essential Writings,* selected and introduced by Dianne Oliver (Maryknoll, NY: Orbis, 2006).

5. D. Sölle and Fulbert Steffensky, eds., *Politisches Nachtgebet in Köln* (Stuttgart: Kreuz Verlag, 1969), 24: prayer prepares persons to take responsibility for the world.

Theological Seminary in New York City. Sölle did not develop a systematic theology, perhaps because she lacked the faculty appointment that would have facilitated such work, but also because she chose concentration on political and social justice issues, within the context of feminist and liberation theology. In her early works, however, she laid the foundation for a systematic theology, and much later she published an introduction to theology as liberation theology. Here we concentrate on her first book, *Christ the Representative*.[6]

Sölle begins the work with the problem of personal identity in the modern technical world, a world in which all things and people are mechanically replaceable; even attempts to make oneself unique are anticipated by and are responses to the entertainment industry (41).[7] The God who once guaranteed the identity of the person, namely, as the soul made in God's image, is no longer evident or even relevant. Human being longs for irreplaceable identity, something it innately knows about in childhood memories and in loving and being loved. When one sets one's hope (or faith) in a person, one affirms that person's identity (31, 39, 46). Only such personal relations as love and hope make persons irreplaceable, and this means that we depend on others for our irreplaceability in a world in which otherwise everything and everyone are replaceable (33f.). Sölle rejects Christologies that speak only of the substitution theory of Christ's death for us, for they do so with a term of depersonalization: Christ replaces us; all is focused on him (61f., 72f., 90f.). The problem of identity in the depersonalized world requires the better concept of "representation" [*Stellvertretung*], which has two parts, responsibility and dependence. "We experience representation when we are dependent on another or others, and when we bear responsibility for another or for others." When another loves me, that one represents me, holds my identity in her or his life. When I bear responsibility for another, I hold that person's identity in my life. When either dependency or responsibility is made absolute, the result is, in the one case, reduction of personhood to immaturity and, in the other case, tyranny. Authentic personal existence and Christian existence involve both dependency and responsibility (56).

The concept of the "representative" is taken from language about Christ and the church in the New Testament and from Bonhoeffer's *Ethics*, although Sölle thinks Bonhoeffer emphasizes responsibility at the cost of dependence (92–97). From Bonhoeffer's *Letters and Papers* she takes the image of the "weakness" of God, who is no longer a "working hypothesis" for life in the world. Christ the representative of God becomes important because we live in a "post-theistic" age, in which there is no longer any immediate certainty of God, whether objective or subjective (130f., 10ff.). God is no longer an "object directly present to the consciousness" (133; cf. 140); where such objectification or "direct experience" of God still occurs in the modern world, they are private matters "with no claim

6. *Christ the Representative: An Essay in Theology after the "Death of God,"* German ed. 1965, trans. David Lewis (Philadelphia: Fortress, 1967).
7. See also *Strength of the Weak*, 165–82.

to authority" (141).[8] But this state of things is a consequence of Christ himself, through whom the world was desacralized (the gods were banished). This happened as God came into the world as a servant and identified not with powerful gods but with the poor of the world, "the least of these" of Matthew 25:40. This identification has become God's incognito in the world (129). "From a definite date onwards, from the time of the man Jesus of Nazareth," God has been progressively regarded as "a disinherited and homeless being whom one might any day meet at any street corner" (138). This does not mean that God is dissolved into human life, although God is indeed identified with and invisibly present in human life. In representing God, Christ and his church proclaim this invisible presence, this transcendence within immanence, of "the living God" until God's kingdom of love becomes visible in the world (110f., 133f.).[9] The way of love in the world is the way of identifying with the world and therefore suffering on behalf of the world, risking all for the sake of the truth that Christ lived and proclaimed.

Christ is the "teacher" who represents the pupil by believing in or loving the pupil, giving himself to the pupil, holding open the future place of the pupil, and patiently waiting for the pupil to mature into responsible being that no longer needs the teacher.[10] Therefore the teacher "provisionally" represents the pupil, an image that for Sölle corresponds to the Synoptic Jesus' proclamation of the kingdom of God (116–22). His suffering on behalf of the world (the pupil) means that he "does not come down from the cross" (151f.; cf. 124). For this reason, that is, the continuing reality of the cross, it is no longer appropriate to speak of God's "lordship, power, or any of the other kingly attributes of God" (141). Easter is not the kingly God's final triumphal victory over evil. It is rather "an anticipatory sign of hope" and "a sign of the dawn, a pledge of redemption" (125f.). Indeed Sölle sees an evil influence in the idea of the kingly God of final victory in Christ, for in Christian history it has led to the intolerant triumphal church, as seen in the history of anti-Semitism (109f.).

In identifying with the world, the representative Christ and, following him, the representative church are not simply bearers of responsibility for the world. Christians depend on each other. But they and Christ also depend on those for whom they suffer in the world to confirm their identity by recognizing and

8. On p. 141 Sölle refers to Rudolf Otto's *fascinans* and *tremendum* as no longer meaningful experiences of God.

9. Cf. Sölle's affirmation of mysticism's experience of the love of God, in *Suffering*, trans. Everett R. Kalin (Philadelphia: Fortress, 1975), 95–99; cf. 127. See further Sölle, *Death by Bread Alone: Texts and Reflections on Religious Experience*, trans. David L. Scheidt (Philadelphia: Fortress, 1978), chap. 6. See also "transcendence as radical immanence" in Sölle, *Thinking about God* (London: SCM Press, and Philadelphia: Trinity Press International, 1990), 190.

10. On previous theological concepts of the "Teacher," see Kant [chap. 2.1.2] and Kierkegaard (esp. *Philosophical Fragments*, 23–36). A striking parallel to Sölle's Christology is Kierkegaard's conception of the concealment of divinity in the suffering of the lowly person of Christ and in that of his Christian imitators (see esp. *Practice in Christianity*).

affirming the truth of Christ (123–26). The church misunderstands itself and Christ if it rests in triumphal "complacent superiority," addressing the world merely as "an object of mission." Rather, its dependence on the world means its solidarity with and patient suffering for it, giving it time, in "participation in the powerlessness of God in the world" (96f., 151f.). In dependence on Christ, faith means following Christ and the way of the cross in the world, the way of love, in the belief that this love means a hope that can never be broken (151).

Throughout the book Sölle uses the concepts "identity" and "non-identity" in speaking of God, Christ and humanity. "Identification always includes non-identity." "Identification is a relation between those who are differentiated." "The content of the gospel can be described as follows: Christ identifies himself with God in the area of non-identity" (138). The element of "non-identity" in Christ's identification with God is humanity: Christ identifies himself with human being and in this identification is also identified with God. Sölle takes the terms "identity" and "non-identity" from Hegel's lectures on the philosophy of religion [chap. 2.3]. She quotes from the lectures in the first part of the book, namely, sentences that have to do with Hegel's concept of the relationship of God (or Spirit) to finite human being in Christ. Prior to the coming of Christ, human being is "for itself" (Hegel's "otherness") in alienation from God. It is on its own, it has to make itself what it is, to give itself its identity. This it can do only through its own labor. When Christ comes, God in Christ brings ["lifts," *Aufhebung*] finite human being into unity (identity) with God. This is an act of love that does not eradicate but maintains the distinct personal identity of all those who accept Christ. Human beings are both in nonidentity with God, as being distinctly who they are, while the unity means identity with God (32–35). What changes for human being is the overcoming of alienation in the love of God.

The faith of the first Christians is the beginning of a process of "the progressive awakening of consciousness" to the truth of Christ (identity with God) in all humanity (140; cf. 133). God's identity with human being in Christ is God's "incognito," God's "weakness" in the world. Faith knows that God lives, but this is not evident in the power relationships of the world. In the concrete here and now, the truth of God must be represented and risked in the suffering love of Christ, "who does not come down from the cross," and of the church. Faith is hope for the future. The full identity with God that Christ represents is "for us still in the future, is not yet ours." Christ "provisionally" portrays this full identity in the "kingdom of God." "Provisional"—the German word is *vorläufig*, literally "running before" (anticipating)—means that the realization of faith's hope is a future reality that Christ represents for us until we can stand in this reality on our own.[11] "It is an ultimate and final provisionality" (107).

---

11. In Heidegger's *Being and Time*, 306, 349f., *vorläufig*, which is translated as "anticipatory," has to do with resolve of decision with reference to one's future personal end as death. Anticipatory is also the meaning of "prolepsis" in theology, the anticipation of the end of history (see esp. Pannenberg, chap. 8.3).

In a following work, *Political Theology*,[12] Sölle conducts an appreciative but critical review of Rudolf Bultmann's theology. She agrees with Bultmann on the need for historical criticism, which since the Enlightenment has meant emancipation from false authorities (3ff.). She also agrees with him that Christ's claim on us is absolute, and she agrees with the "orientation toward personal self-understanding" (55). She appreciates Bultmann's contribution to awareness of the hermeneutical circle, between the self-understanding of the interpreter and the text, in understanding a biblical text (15). She criticizes his exclusive concentration on the individual and his corresponding disregard for social and political aspects of self-understanding (60).

Bultmann's concept of the kerygma is "irrelevant to the real questions of life" (23), especially insofar as it calls the Christian beyond the world instead of into it (62). A "depoliticized theology" like Bultmann's becomes naively subservient to prevailing political interests (36). Dialectical theology generally, with its sharp separation of God and world, leads to "kerygmatic neo-orthodoxy" (38), that is, to a new form of propositional doctrines and an "indifferent ideological superstructure independent of situations." It is "undemythologized theology" (33). It leads away from instead of toward the truth of faith and the task of theology, just as for Bultmann myth detracts from the kerygma. The political awareness of the gospel message is for Sölle evident in the Synoptic Jesus, namely, in his preaching in favor of the poor and against the rich. Attention to his language "would enjoin us to rediscover the political relevance of the gospel" (36). Here Sölle reflects the significance of the "new quest" for the historical Jesus among Bultmann's students, and she remarks that Gerhard Ebeling, in speaking of the hermeneutical problem of formulating the kerygma to address "situations" in such a way that "the necessity of the kerygma becomes evident," comes close to what is meant by political theology (25f.). She has a similar appreciation for Tillich.[13]

In his treatment of sin, Bultmann's focus on personal individual history in the conviction and forgiveness of sin, which Sölle says is typical in the church, does not recognize the saturation of the individual with ideas absorbed from the social world and the accommodation to social-political conditions (48f., 89). Sin is primarily social, so that both sin and forgiveness must be reinterpreted (93–98, with reference to Matt. 5:23–26). What seems harmless to ordinary consciousness is its collaboration with social and political forms of reality that involve "a structurally founded, usually anonymous injustice" (88). For those who have some

---

12. *Political Theology*, German ed. 1971, trans. John Shelley (Philadelphia: Fortress, 1974). Page references in the following text are to the English edition.

13. Ibid., xix: "A political theology could be developed far more directly from the early writings of Paul Tillich, who understood religious socialism as the 'radical application of the prophetic-Protestant principle to religion and Christianity.'" The quotation is taken from Tillich, *Political Expectation*, ed. James L. Adams (New York: Harper & Row, 1971), 54. A critical essay by Sölle on Tillich is in *Paul Tillich: Studien zu einer Theologie der Moderne*, ed. Hermann Fischer (Frankfurt: Athenäum, 1989), 281–300.

awareness of this, the inevitable capitulation to the "superior power of the structures" of sin leads to a "despair of weakness," a term Sölle takes from Kierkegaard (95). In her next work, *Suffering*, she scores the "theological sadism" of attitudes toward sin and suffering that breed apathy toward the suffering of the poor and oppressed. "It is axiomatic for me that the only humanely conceivable goal is the abolition of circumstances under which people are forced to suffer, whether through poverty or tyranny." "God is not in heaven; he is hanging on the cross."[14]

In the first chapter of her later work, *Thinking about God: An Introduction to Theology*, Sölle explains the task of systematic theology as an ongoing circle between faith and action on the one hand and theology and reflection on the other.[15] In the following chapter, H. Richard Niebuhr's five types of the relationship between Christ and culture [chap. 7.3] are used to frame a discussion of the situation of theology and church today. She compares the understanding of faith and sin in orthodoxy, liberal theology, and radical theology. Orthodoxy has lost its original paradigm of the contrast between Christ and culture and has become blind to its "cultural provisos," so that it "lacks any suspicion that it might be an ideology" (in Marx's sense) (12). Liberal theology, as a consequence of its cooperation with culture, falls into the inability to distinguish between Christ and the values of culture (15f.). Radical theology means a shift of the familiar paradigms in faith and theology. "For about twenty years there has been a theology which is not done by people who are white, relatively well-to-do and almost exclusively male: the theology of liberation" (18). The remainder of the work discusses the meaning of this change of paradigm for theology, faith, and the church.

8.2 JÜRGEN MOLTMANN

Jürgen Moltmann (born 1926) was until his retirement a professor of theology associated with the Reformed tradition at Tübingen. During World War II he served in the military and spent considerable time in British captivity, where he first became a student of theology. He was most influenced by Karl Barth, by his Barthian teachers in Germany, and by Ernst Bloch.[16] He has strongly supported liberation theology. The main direction of his thought has been the integration

---

14. *Suffering*, 2, 148; cf. 162–78. "Christian masochism" and "theological sadism's tradition of despising humanity" are "perversions of love" that turn the concept of sin into a deeply problematic way of relating both to oneself and to others, especially those who suffer misery (ibid., 2). The section on "theological sadism" features words of Calvin on the guilt of personal sin and acceptance of suffering as God's discipline (ibid., 22ff.).

15. *Thinking about God: An Introduction to Theology*, trans. John Bowden (Philadelphia: Trinity Press International, 1990), 1–6. Page numbers in this paragraph are in reference to this book.

16. On the influence of Barth and Bloch on Moltmann's early theology, see M. Douglas Meeks, *Origins of the Theology of Hope* (Philadelphia: Fortress, 1974); on Moltmann's later theology, see Joy Ann McDougall, *Pilgrimage of Love* (Oxford: Oxford University Press, 2005); Geiko Müller-Fahrenholz, *The Kingdom and the Power: The Theology of Jürgen Moltmann* (Minneapolis: Fortress, 2001).

of liberation theology in the theological tradition and its mediation with Western ecclesial, social, and political culture.[17]

Moltmann published his first major work, *Theology of Hope: On the Ground and Implications of a Christian Eschatology*, in 1964.[18] Eschatology is the doctrine of Christian hope: hope for the future of the resurrected Christ as hope for the world, the promise of Easter (16–18). In the resurrection of Christ, God promises "a new world of all-embracing life, of righteousness and truth, and with this promise he constantly calls this world into question." All that exists is "submitted to the crisis of the promised future." "Where the new begins, the old becomes manifest. Where the new is promised, the old becomes transient and surpassable. . . . Thus 'history' arises in the light of its end." Death and sin have become "transient" in God's promise of the future raising of the dead (164). Sinful reality now exists in the crisis of this future. In Christian hope there can be "no compromise" with evil, death, suffering, offence, humiliation, for one lives in protest "against reality as it is" (21). "Peace with God means conflict with the world, for the goal of the promised world stabs inexorably into the flesh of every unfulfilled present" (17). To live in Christian hope is to know the transforming, world-changing power of that act of love now and to act accordingly in and for the community of human beings. Christian hope must "transform thought and action" (33). The church is sent in mission to the whole world, to give it hope, to "transform the present because it is open to the universal future of the kingdom" (327–35).

The cross of Christ symbolizes the conflict of Christ's whole life with a reality that negates what God in the resurrection affirms. The disciples experience the cross as this negating reality, as an "absolute nihil also embracing God." The resurrection is a complete contradiction of this experience and something faith must hold firmly in mind. The "dialectic of cross and resurrection" cannot be obscured by attempts to lessen the harsh significance of the cross for faith (198–200). The radical newness of the raising of the dead at Easter is so great that it has no analogy anywhere in history, and what verifies it as true is still future, the promise of God (180, 197). The raising of the dead is a "creatio ex nihilo," a miraculous act of God's love (31f.). One cannot know what exactly happened at Easter, but it is clear that the earliest Christians use this expression, "resurrection of the dead," as the basis of their hope. It definitely "explodes modern concepts of reality"; the theologian "battles" with modern views of history "for the reality of the resurrection of Jesus" (182). In the light of resurrection eschatology, the Christian historian recognizes that there is nothing stable in history, a history that, because of constant change, is constantly being rewritten

---

17. In his short work *Theology Today*, trans. John Bowden (London: SCM, 1988), the second of the book's two parts is entitled "Mediating Theology Today." In its introduction Moltmann writes, pp. 53f.: "Historical mediation must both work to achieve the true preservation of the identity of the Christian message and see that it is relevant to the present."

18. *Theology of Hope*, trans. James Leitch (New York: Harper & Row, 1967). Page references in the following text are to this work unless otherwise noted.

(240). Modernity itself means crisis; traditions have been broken down and have become objects of criticism (230ff.; cf. 294). There is awareness that human being is directed to the future for meaning.

A significant obstacle to Christian eschatology and hope exists within theology itself: the pervasive influence of Greek antiquity. Theology dominated by Greek thought is not about the future but the present: revelation is an "epiphany" of God's "eternal presence." Its concentration is on the world as it is. The Reformation broke with this influence, but Protestant orthodoxy reintroduced it (44, 35). Moltmann finds it dominant in Kierkegaard's "moment" (29), in the early Barth of *Romans* (as eternal present reality God contradicts the world), and in Bultmann's kerygmatic theology (the kerygma is a timeless reality) (39f., 45f.). There are other consequences. In understanding the kerygma as above history, Bultmann tries to "go around science," to evade the conflict with it. This, Moltmann says, does not take modern atheism seriously enough.[19] He agrees with Pannenberg (with reference also to Barth and Bonhoeffer) that the theologian must testify to and present "the lordship of Christ all the way to the very heart of secular reality." "The theologian is not concerned merely to supply a different interpretation of the world, of history and of human nature [than modern science], but to transform them in expectation of a divine transformation." Moltmann disagrees with Pannenberg's interpretation of biblical apocalyptic thought, namely, that it gives a limited conception of the end of history [see chap. 8.3]. For Moltmann the end of history is beyond our conceptual grasp; furthermore apocalyptic does not adequately portray the mission of the church to the world (83f.). Christians live, rather, by the hope that God will be faithful, as Israel did in the Old Testament and as did the early Christian community (30, 42).[20]

In Moltmann's next work, a collection of essays with the title *The Crucified God*, the themes of kenosis, Christ's "emptying himself" (Phil. 2:7), and finding one's life in losing it (Matt. 16:25) are interpreted as guides for Christian ethics. In situations of conflict, Christians "abandon the traditions, institutions and opinions, accepted by faith, in which they previously found their identity," in

19. Moltmann defines unbelief essentially as hopelessness, with no real future, which results in resignation, inertia, sadness, frustration. The general forms of hopelessness are "despair" and "presumption." Presumption is "the premature, self-willed anticipation" of fulfillment; despair is the same thing as anticipation of nonfulfillment. Moltmann's example of presumption is Karl Marx (ibid., 22–24).

20. According to Moltmann, Pannenberg replaces Greek cosmology, the metaphysical theory of the unity of world, with an "eschatological unity," a theory of all reality and history that is equally Greek. Pannenberg's theory of history is like Hegel's: it is resolved in an eternal concept (*Theology of Hope*, 78f.). See also Moltmann's critique of Pannenberg in *The Way of Jesus Christ: Christology in Messianic Dimensions*, trans. Margaret Kohl (London: SCM, 1990), 235–45. Cf. Moltmann, *The Coming of God: Christian Eschatology*, trans. Margaret Kohl (Minneapolis: Fortress, 1996), 10: like Albert Schweitzer's concept of Jesus' failed expectation of the kingdom, apocalyptic theology "forces eschatology into history," i.e., it is made part of history. It does not see that eschatology is "a transformation of time itself." For Moltmann, theology can only anticipate the goal of history by approaching in mystical silence to God, who "dwells in inaccessible light" (1 Tim. 6:16) (Moltmann, *Experiences of God* [Philadelphia: Westminster, 1980], as quoted by Müller-Fahrenholz, 150f.).

order to identify, as Jesus did, "with the godless and those abandoned by God." This they do in trust in their identity with Christ hidden in God (Col. 3:3) (15–18). Such Christian behavior is the effect of the Spirit that goes forth from "the crucified God." Traditional theological metaphysics maintained that God is "impassible" or cannot suffer, for this gave security to a finite world threatened with nothingness (214). It is right to say that God does not suffer as do creatures (229), but the crucifixion of Christ teaches us that God does suffer.

Moltmann's interpretation of the suffering God is developed in a section entitled "Trinitarian Theology of the Cross" (235–49). In the crucifixion the Father grieves the loss of his Son, just as the Son grieves the loss of the Father. The fatherhood of the Father itself is lost when the Son dies, so that the Father suffers death (243). And yet they are "most inwardly one" in their "surrender," for both surrender themselves, lose themselves, for love, and in love they remain what they always are: "God is love," and, while the love of God suffers, it does not die. What goes forth from this mutual loss in the crucifixion is love, the Spirit that is greater than death and that in the resurrection of Christ raises the dead and justifies godless humanity (244). "It is the unconditioned and therefore boundless love which proceeds from the grief of the Father and the dying of the Son and reaches forsaken men in order to create in them the possibility and the force of new life" (245). God is "unconditional love" that "takes all contradiction into itself." And it is "full of hope" (248). Now, in the crucifixion and resurrection, "all disaster, forsakenness by God, absolute death, the infinite curse of damnation and sinking into nothingness is in God himself, is community with this God, eternal salvation, infinite joy, indestructible election and divine life" (246). All creation is in God. The "theology of the cross" sees the whole cosmos "in the eschatological history of God" (218).

One recognizes a familiar pattern in Moltmann's metaphysics of love—Moltmann himself gives the reference to it (253ff.)—namely, Hegel's speculative dialectic of Spirit. In Hegel's interpretation of Christ's resurrection, Spirit shows that is greater than death, that its truth overcomes the most extreme alienation. All "otherness" is united with the Absolute. For Moltmann, over all reality is the eternal God as unqualified, unconditional love. Unlike Hegel, however, for Moltmann, love's ultimate victory culminates in a real and concrete future, the raising of the dead.[21]

Moltmann's next major work, *The Church in the Power of the Spirit*, first published in 1975, is an ecclesiology in the light of liberation theology.[22] The overriding theme of the book is that the church is found where Christ is, not vice versa. The apostolic church is "Christ's representative." "That is why the exalted Lord is also to be present in the church's testimony through the Spirit. He iden-

---

21. Cf. Moltmann's criticism of Hegel's interpretation of history as governed by the concept of the Absolute, in *The Coming of God*, 326–30; cf. 218–26. For Moltmann (as for Barth), theology "is free to take up metaphysics" as a theological task (*The Crucified God*, 218).

22. *The Church in the Power of the Spirit: A Contribution to Messianic Ecclesiology*, trans. Margaret Kohl (New York: Harper & Row, 1977). Cf. Müller-Fahrenholz, *Kingdom and the Power*, 84–100.

tifies himself with the apostolic word and joins the human world of his witness with the eschatological word" (123). His presence in baptism, the Lord's Supper, and the apostolate "is a Real Presence in the Spirit" (123–25). Christ is present among those with whom he identifies in the cross, namely, those who suffer the injustices of power (Matt. 25:40). So also the church must identify itself with those who suffer injustice (97, 126). The church is the "exodus community" that hears and follows the message of the messianic Christ of liberation and joy to the poor (76ff., 220ff.). It is opposed to the powers of exploitation, oppression, exclusion, and violence in economic, political, and cultural life (163ff.).[23] The "exodus community" is not an authoritative hierarchical church, nor is it divided along racial or class lines. It is a church of the priesthood of all believers, a priesthood that must become also the sovereignty of all believers, a fellowship (106, 224f., 314ff.). In missions it does not seek to assert absolute authority over against other religions but to be in relationship with them for the purpose of awakening hope, love, trust, and responsibility for the world (152f.).[24]

Moltmann's following publications develop traditional doctrines in dialogue with the theological tradition and often also with Jewish scholarship. In *The Trinity and the Kingdom*, a doctrine is developed that is already previewed in *The Church in the Power of the Spirit*, namely, the interpretation of the "economic" Trinity in history and the church as the image of the "immanent" Trinity in God.[25] The Trinity is not a "monarchic" God but a God of relationships, and so also the history of God with humanity has to do with relationships, not hierarchical authority. In Christianity persons are through the Creator servants of the Lord, through the Son children of the Father, and through the Spirit friends of God in personal and communal freedom.[26] The "perichoresis" or indwelling of the persons of the Trinity in one another is the love that unites them.[27] The Trinity in human history is the "social Trinity"; authoritarian structures are broken down in favor of democratic forms, mutuality, dialogue, and consensus. The Trinitarian love of God in the world, as in Christ, extends to all humanity and creation, suffering with and for them, to lead them to the goal of the kingdom.[28]

---

23. In *The Crucified God*, 20, 67, Moltmann acknowledges continuity with Richard Rothe's ethics of the Christian formation of social and political life. (Indeed his projections of the ideal of a democratic, liberated world, as what should be in historical development, bear a certain similarity to Rothe's "normal" as opposed to "sinful" history.) But Moltmann is critical of Rothe's dissolution of the church into the state as a form of "millenarianism" (i.e., apocalyptic) (Moltmann, *The Coming of God*, 166, note 79 [pp. 362f.]). [See Rothe, chap. 3.2.]

24. The second half of *Church in the Power of the Spirit* develops the biblical doctrine of the church as the exodus community, which includes celebration and joy in the Spirit. It also deals with practical questions having to do with emerging liberation and justice communities that stand in peripheral relationship to the established churches. It ends with a chapter on the traditional marks of the church.

25. *Church in the Power of the Spirit*, 54f.; *The Trinity and the Kingdom*, trans. Margaret Kohl (New York: Harper & Row, 1981), chap. 5. [Cf. Barth, Pannenberg, and Jüngel.] On the following text, cf. Müller-Fahrenholz, *Kingdom and the Power*, 137–52.

26. *The Trinity and the Kingdom*, 219ff.

27. *The Trinity and the Kingdom*, 174f. Cf. Jüngel, chap. 8.5.

28. Ibid., 202, 57–60. See also the work by Moltmann's student Miroslav Volf, *After Our Likeness: The Church as the Image of the Trinity* (Grand Rapids: Eerdmans, 1998).

In *The Way of Jesus Christ* Moltmann develops the theology of *The Crucified God* in a comprehensive Christology. In *The Coming of God* he interprets the Christian doctrine of the "last things" and the eschatology of the *Theology of Hope,* also with regard to the "messianism" and "millenarianism" of traditional Western Christian culture and the catastrophes of the twentieth century. In *God in Creation* he delivers a sharp criticism of the modern technical destruction of nature in regard to traditional Christian doctrine and to philosophical criticism of economic systems that disregard the intimate connection of nature and human bodily life.[29] In *The Spirit of Life* Moltmann again contrasts his interpretation with the eschatology of Karl Barth, which is "not linked with the future of the new creation of all things; it is related to God's eternity, over against the temporality of human beings. Consequently the Holy Spirit reveals nothing to human beings which they could see, hear, smell or taste. . . . By setting up this antithesis between revelation and experience, Barth merely replaced the theological immanentism which he complained about [in mediation theology] by a theological transcendentalism. But the real phenomenon [of Spirit] is to be found . . . in God's immanence in human experience, and in the transcendence of human beings in God. Because God's Spirit is present in human beings, the human spirit is self-transcendentally aligned towards God. . . . The new approach now develops eschatology as the horizon of expectation for the historical experience of the divine Spirit. The Holy Spirit . . . is the power that raises the dead, the power of the new creation of all things, and faith is the beginning of the rebirth of human beings to new life. . . . The Holy Spirit is called 'holy' because it sanctifies life and renews the face of the earth."[30]

8.3 WOLFHART PANNENBERG

Wolfhart Pannenberg (born 1928) was until his retirement professor of theology at the newly created Protestant theological faculty in Munich. Like Moltmann he served in the military during World War II.[31] Afterward he studied with leading biblical theologians, notably with the Old Testament scholar Gerhard von Rad and a related circle of scholars, and with Karl Barth. From the beginning of his academic career he participated in a new movement in biblical theology in the 1950s: the exploration of the significance of apocalyptic thought in the intertestamental and New Testament periods. As a young teacher in the early 1960s he was a colleague of Moltmann's at the *Predigerseminar* (preacher seminar) for young pastors in Wuppertal. Their theologies are in certain respects

---

29. *God in Creation: A New Theology of Creation and the Spirit of God,* trans. Margaret Kohl (San Francisco: Harper & Row, 1985).

30. *The Spirit of Life,* trans. Margaret Kohl (Minneapolis: Fortress, 1992), 7f. Cf. *The Coming of God,* 13–19. In *Theology of Hope,* 57, 87, Moltmann had said that in the *Church Dogmatics* Barth moves toward but does not realize a concept of revelation eschatology.

31. A biographical sketch is in E. Frank Tupper, *The Theology of Wolfhart Pannenberg* (Philadelphia: Westminster, 1973), 21ff.

rather closely related. Like Moltmann, Pannenberg laid the foundation in publications of the 1960s for his later works, the most significant of which is a comprehensive three-volume *Systematic Theology*.[32]

Basic for Pannenberg's theology is the understanding of the gospel as a message of faith in the God whose coming kingdom will transform the world. The way for Jesus' message is prepared by the eschatology of the Old Testament, including Jewish apocalyptic thought both prior to and in Jesus' own time. The gospel of the coming kingdom embraces the whole of world history, a history whose meaning is revealed "proleptically" (in anticipation) in Jesus, his death, and his resurrection. It will be revealed fully and for all persons only at the end, in the final judgment and raising of dead in the kingdom of God. A second basic concept is the anthropological structure of transcendence: human being transcends itself and its present state of life in a way that is directed toward the future. This transcendence toward the future implies human being's quest for the coming God. God is the power of the future that draws human being toward the future, freeing it from bondage to the past. Pannenberg has therefore the "double starting point"—one biblical, one anthropological—that Karl Barth so strongly objected to in nineteenth-century mediation theology. Also characteristic of mediation theology is Pannenberg's conviction of the unity of truth that ultimately unites faith, science, and philosophy, a concept that supports and promotes interaction with science and philosophy.

8.3.1 Theology of Universal History

In an important essay from the year 1962 entitled "What Is Truth?" Pannenberg defines the Hebrew understanding of truth as the truth of the God who acts in history, who is always faithful to God's promises, who is always the same, and who therefore justifies the confidence that this same truth will show itself in the future. But this is not a truth that is stated directly; it is a reality too great for direct or immediate communication. It rather unfolds its meaning in history, and in such a way that the fulfillment of God's promise at definite times in history is always beyond or greater than what was prophesied or expected. Old Testament faith does not doubt that God will be faithful to God's promises, and therefore it is open toward the future.[33] According to Jewish apocalyptic thought, which

32. *Systematic Theology*, trans. Geoffrey W. Bromiley, 3 vols. (Grand Rapids: Eerdmans, 1989, 1993, 1998). Other translated works (not cited below) are *Christianity in a Secularized World*, trans. John Bowden (New York: Crossroad, 1989; *Ethics*, trans. Keith Crim (Philadelphia: Westminster, 1981); *Faith and Reality*, trans. John Maxwell (Philadelphia: Westminster, 1977). See also James M. Robinson and John B. Cobb Jr., eds., *New Frontiers in Theology*, vol. 3: *Theology as History* (New York: Harper & Row, 1967); and Robert W. Funk, ed., *History and Hermeneutic* (New York: Harper & Row, 1967).

33. Pannenberg, *Basic Questions in Theology*, trans. George Kehm, 2 vols. (Philadelphia: Westminster, 1983), 2:2f., 6–11; Wolfhart Pannenberg, ed., *Revelation as History*, trans. David Granskou (New York: Macmillan, 1968), chap. 4. In this essay from 1961, Pannenberg sketches his theses on biblical interpretation.

continues this tradition, God is fully revealed only at the end of history. Jesus and the early church belong to this same tradition, and this tradition is an important content of Christian revelation. In a later period the church combined the tradition with a different concept of truth in Greek thought, especially truth as that which remains constant behind the flux of sense experiences. Such syncretism is for Pannenberg a sign of Christianity's "assimilative power" in interaction with the evolving cultures of history, in pursuit of the unity of truth in the whole of reality [cf. Harnack, chap. 4.4].[34] But for Pannenberg the biblical understanding of truth is always dominant.

Pannenberg's interpretation of Jesus and New Testament eschatology is given comprehensively in his book *Jesus—God and Man,* first published in 1964.[35] According to Pannenberg, Jesus' world of thought was formed by the Jewish apocalyptic expectation of the transformation of the world at the end of history [cf. Schweitzer, chap. 4.9]. The figure that represents this expectation for Jesus is the "Son of Man" in Luke 12:8 and Mark 8:38, where no time limit is given for the coming of the Son of Man to judge the world. This is an indication that the delay of the expected end of the world was not a problem for the early church, and it should not be a problem for the church today (58f., 107). For the earliest church the end of history had in fact already begun in the raising of Jesus from the dead. According to the church's apocalyptic expectation (and that of Jewish apocalyptic), the raising of the dead was the characteristic event of the end of history. The resurrection of Jesus was understood as the "prolepsis" or anticipation of the final raising of the dead at the end of history, a sure sign of God's promise to fulfill apocalyptic-prophetic expectation (66–68, 106).[36]

It is of crucial importance that the resurrection of Jesus was a factual event, even though it is impossible to know, in any scientific way, how this happened; this too is a mystery that is too great for immediate human knowledge. The New Testament's expression, raising of the dead, is a metaphor taken from awakening from sleep. Paul's words about a "spiritual body" in 1 Corinthians 15 are also the statement of a mystery that our understanding cannot penetrate [cf. Barth, chap. 6.1.2]. But there can be no doubt that for those who witnessed the resurrection, the common element in expressing it was the raising of the dead (74–83, 92f.). The verification of the resurrection does not and cannot rest on historical assertions by church authority. For New Testament faith, the verification of Jesus' resurrection, in the visible rule of God, will take place in the raising of the dead at

34. *Basic Questions,* 2:1–6, 87. Pannenberg's theory is far removed from Harnack's "essence" of Christianity in Harnack's theory of Christian-Hellenistic syncretism.

35. *Jesus—God and Man,* 2nd ed., trans. Lewis L. Wilkins and Duane A. Priebe (Philadelphia: Westminster, 1977). The page numbers in the following text are from this work. On Jesus' resurrection and its significance, see also Pannenberg, *The Apostles' Creed* (Philadelphia: Westminster, 1972), 96–127.

36. Pannenberg's student Lothar Kugelmann has published a history of the concept of prolepsis or anticipation in modern theology: *Antizipation* (Göttingen: Vandenhoeck & Ruprecht, 1986).

the end of history.[37] "Until then we must speak favorably in thoroughly legitimate, but still only metaphorical and symbolic, form about Jesus' resurrection and the significance inherent in it" (397).

The Easter faith of the first Christians can be explained reasonably only by the real event of the resurrection; the skeptical view that it was a hallucination of strong belief cannot withstand criticism (95)[cf. Strauss, chap. 2.5.1]. Pannenberg supports his understanding of the miracle with reference to contemporary science. Echoing Schleiermacher [chap. 2.7.2], he says that modern science is aware that it does not entirely comprehend the laws of nature, that not all events are completely determined by natural laws, and that in natural law one has to do with probability, not possibility (98).[38] The resurrection of Jesus is of his whole person. Contemporary science's understanding of the indissoluble unity of human being has effectively dissolved belief in the immortality of the soul, so that the raising of the whole person, however this happens, is more in accord with science than belief in an immortal soul (86f.).

In Christology one must establish Christ's relationship to God by beginning "from below" with Jesus, its real beginning, not "from above" with traditional doctrines about his divinity (115ff.).[39] Here again the key event is the resurrection. Other events in Jesus' life, such as the baptism, are only anticipations of the unity with God in the Easter event (137f.). Jesus is fully human, and it is only in his resurrection that God identifies him as the Son of God and confirms his earthly life as life in complete dedication to God. With reference to Hegel as well as relevant biblical texts, Pannenberg describes Jesus as overcoming the otherness of human isolation from God through being one with God in love, so that Jesus exists only in this love and not on his own apart from it (335–39). The Holy Spirit unites Jesus and God as it unites the church and God (169–77). In the Spirit the dichotomy of "subject" and "object" is overcome in relational union (175). The unity of the Trinity is the Spirit as love, in which Father and Son —again with reference to Hegel—are "in" one another (182f.). And it is with

---

37. Cf. *Systematic Theology,* 2:352–63. See the discussion "Faith and Historical Knowledge," *Systematic Theology,* 3:144–61. Here Pannenberg writes (154) that it is a mistake to make "the historical knowledge presupposed in Christian trust" in God "a matter of faith," so that it evades all criticism. "If we do that, faith falls victim to the perversion of being its own basis and is robbed of any sense of having a ground in history preceding itself. Since the age of the mediating of all historical knowledge by authority ended, we can have the sense of a historical basis for faith only by accepting the involved relativity of historico-exegetical knowledge and being ready constantly to examine the historical foundations of faith and to revise contemporary presentations where necessary. . . . Faith's own sense of truth must leave room for the fact that our knowledge of its object is relative and provisional." Christians can be confident that the truth of revelation will emerge "from the results of critical exegesis and reconstruction of the history of Jesus if revelation really did take place in that history." Further (161) we cannot avoid the relativity or provisional character of our conceptions or thoughts of faith, but we can expect that the promise and object of our trust will prove to be trustworthy, as Jesus believed.

38. See also *Systematic Theology,* 2:40ff.

39. Cf. Ibid., 2:282ff.

reference to Hegel that Pannenberg explains (in a provisional way that also must be clarified at the end of the world) the incarnation as God's ability to become an "other" while remaining identical with God's self (319–21).[40]

The relationship of Jesus and God is to be understood completely through the resurrection. Not only has Jesus been raised from the dead, but he also gives life to the dead (Rom. 4:18 and 8:11), and in him one sees "the end that stands before us and all things" (129). God and Christ are in such indissoluble unity that God cannot be thought of apart from or without Jesus. "God was always one with Jesus, even before his earthly birth. Jesus is from all eternity the representative of God in the creation. Were it otherwise, Jesus would not be in person the one revelation of the eternal God" (153). In Israel's eschatological-apocalyptic understanding of truth, the final act of truth reveals the truth of all things. All things await the time when what they truly are will be revealed; "their eschatological summation through Jesus is identical with their creation through Jesus." Only in their relation to him do they receive their place in the context of the whole creation. In this way "the creation of all things is mediated through Jesus" (391).

8.3.2 Anthropology and Metaphysics

The "ontological structure of man's being" is transcendence, an assertion that Pannenberg makes with reference especially to Troeltsch and Ernst Bloch.[41] Troeltsch's attempt "to establish that religious life is a necessary element in the structure of man's existence" within the relativities of history has continuing relevance. This religious element should not be conceived in such a way that it controls or limits revelation [cf. Barth, chap. 6.1.1]. But it is through natural religious life that human being is aware of what is beyond the finitude of existence. Human being can have "a well-founded hope for the fulfillment of existence" only in connection with the "mysterious ground of all reality," which is the final truth. It belongs to the religious "structure" of human being to reach out beyond its finitude in "expectation" of the "infinite mystery" that is present in the finite world. It hopes for the fulfillment of its existence from this infinite mystery. The movement of religious humanity is an "uncloseable path" toward the future in all religions. Every religious comprehension of the infinite mystery is necessarily finite, yet "the infinite mystery does appear" in the finite, in the history of the various religions. Christian faith believes that only in Christ does this occur as the revelation of God and, even so, in such a way that full revelation of the mystery is only anticipated. Moreover, according to belief in the unity of all truth, Chris-

---

40. On the Trinity, see Pannenberg, *Systematic Theology*, 1:300–336, where he also discusses his agreement and disagreement with Barth's doctrine of the Trinity. For Pannenberg, the economic Trinity of God's presence in the history of Christ and his work is "provisionally" the basis of the doctrine of the immanent Trinity of God in God's self (ibid., 335).

41. The words in quotation marks are from *Basic Questions*, 2:191.

tian revelation must be tested by comparison with the other religions and in connection with the understanding of the whole of reality.[42]

No assertion of larger meaning in life can be made without "a foreconception of the final future" of the totality of life. All reasoning about life's meaning is therefore eschatological. "The eschatological structure of reason opens up room for faith's talk about an eschatological future." Faith and reason ultimately aim at the same goal.[43] Like theology, science and philosophy make assertions about human life, the world, and history. In belief in the unity of truth, theology must "participate in the whole range of philosophical discussion." If there is only one truth about one and the same thing, then theology must work on the assumption that theology and science are ultimately reconcilable. Indeed, since God is the origin of all reality, theology must itself be a universal science.[44]

This does not mean that theology seeks to establish or discover concepts that are universally valid everywhere and for all time. History involves changes that require the revision of assertions of meaning. "The decisive factor . . . is that the structure of meaning proposed by Christianity is open to a future . . . which alone will provide a basis for the totality of its structures of meaning. This makes possible a constant revision of the Christian understanding of existence in every detail." In this way also Christianity is free from authoritarian structures that bind it to the past.[45] Pannenberg's model for such a theology is Hegel's dialectic of history, which rightly intends but fails to be a history of the whole of reality. Hegel's "Absolute," the "concept" that is itself the whole truth, loses all sight of a real future. But what Hegel realized in the dialectic is that reason has a history and that in historical process truth reveals itself. Hegel saw that this process—like the biblical concept of history—moves forward in ever-new syntheses of meaning whose final goal, the truth of the whole of reality, is anticipated in Christ and in faith in him.[46]

In *Theology and the Philosophy of Science,* one of whose purposes is to justify the place of theology among the sciences of the university, Pannenberg discusses the relationship of faith's perceptions of truth to the most challenging contemporary theories of science. He does not deny but affirms the processes they

42. Ibid., 2:98, 101–4, 106f., 118, 191; cf. 1:131ff. See also the essay in appreciation of Ernst Bloch, "The God of Hope," ibid., 134–249. In this essay Pannenberg's quotations from Bloch's *Das Princip Hoffnung* are found in the (later published) English translation, *The Principle of Hope,* 3:1193–1203. See also Pannenberg, *Systematic Theology,* 1: chap. 3, and 2:228f.

43. *Basic Questions,* 62–64; cf. 25, 47, 233; cf. Pannenberg, *The Idea of God and Human Freedom,* trans. R. A. Wilson (Philadelphia: Westminster, 1973), 120, 132f.

44. *Idea of God and Human Freedom,* 121, 128. One example of Pannenberg's dialogue with science is his concession to Fichte that the concept of person, as derived from human life and applied to God, apparently makes God finite [see chap. 2.2.3]. But, he says, the modern concept of person actually originated in religion in reference to what is not at our disposal and is holy, as the history of religions can demonstrate (*Basic Questions,* 2:227ff.).

45. Ibid., 142. Cf. Schleiermacher's hermeneutic [chap. 2.7.1].

46. *Basic Questions,* 2:21–23, 60, and the chapter "The Significance of Christianity in the Philosophy of Hegel," in *Idea of God and Human Freedom,* 152–77. See also Pannenberg, *Grundfragen systematischer Theologie,* 2 vols. (Göttingen: Vandenhoeck & Ruprecht, 1967, 1980), 2:258f.; cf. 263f.

employ in making truth claims, and he aims at a future real resolution of differences. The beginning section of the work gives a history of theology as science.[47] He faults the dialectical theology (Barth and Bultmann) and its successors for quitting the task of engagement with secular science, an engagement required by the quest for truth in the totality of reality.[48] In earlier publications he had agreed with Hegel (and Ritschl) that religion that withdraws from interaction with the secular world, such as pietism, must be rejected.[49] Theology is a rigorous science, and a condition for the recognition of any theological hypothesis is adequacy "to the stage reached in theological discussion."[50] "A plurality of theological constructions" is justified because of the provisional nature of all theology and the relativity of personal and situational perspectives. Criticism shows, however, that some theologies are not as competent as others.[51]

In a later work, *Metaphysics and the Idea of God*, Pannenberg tries to answer a question that is implicit in his constant reference of faith to the God of the future, namely, how God can be present for faith.[52] He uses concepts from his earlier work: the relationship of the finite to the infinite and of the part to the whole, and the totality of reality as a whole seen retrospectively from its eschatological end. The whole of finite reality, he says, is not God, but God is the ground of this reality and its unity. "Finite" means what is bordered by a boundary, and the very thought of "finite" or "boundary" implies reference to what is beyond the boundary, the infinite. Pannenberg refers to a work of the Neoplatonic philosopher Plotinus (AD 205–70), namely, *Enneads*, book III, section 7 (§§11f.), "On Eternity and Time." What Pannenberg takes from Plotinus is the concept of reality as an ideal whole that has fallen into time, which divides the ideal whole into successive moments of time. These are moments of becoming the whole, which for Pannenberg implies a point when time reaches or becomes wholeness, and this is evidently how Pannenberg wishes to understand Plotinus. For Plotinus, however, what is in time never reaches or becomes the whole, but always remains separated in an endless series of successive parts.[53] What is important for Pannenberg is that the whole is both present reality and a definite future.

47. *Theology and the Philosophy of Science*, trans. Francis McDonagh (Philadelphia: Westminster, 1976), Introduction. Cf. *Systematic Theology*, 1: chap. 1.

48. *Theology and the Philosophy of Science*; on Bultmann and Ebeling, 169–75, 278–85; on Barth, 265–76. Pannenberg sets out his own position in chap. 5. See also Pannenberg's earlier critique of dialectic theology: *Basic Questions*, 2:65, 67, 123, 192, 199. Bonhoeffer's late works restrict theology's interaction with the world to ethics. *Idea of God and Human Freedom*, 192.

49. *Idea of God and Human Freedom*, 177 (Hegel); *Basic Questions*, 2:34, 53. Pannenberg faults Richard Rothe [chap. 3.2] and his influence for the separation of the message of the historical truth of revelation from the inspiration of the Spirit, which for Pannenberg is a characteristic of "subjectivist" faith. See, e.g., *Basic Questions*, 2:38–42; *Systematic Theology*, 1:224–26.

50. *Theology and the Philosophy of Science*, 345.

51. Ibid., 158f.

52. *Metaphysics and the Idea of God*, trans. Philip Clayton (Grand Rapids: Eerdmans, 1990), 1ff., 97.

53. Ibid., 77. See *Plotinus*, trans. A. H. Armstrong, 6 vols. (Cambridge: Loeb Classical Library, Harvard University Press, 1967), 3:342f. Pannenberg refers for support to the commentary of Werner Beierwaltes, *Plotin über Ewigkeit und Zeit* (Frankfurt: Vittorio Klostermann, 1981), 272f.; cf. 65ff., but Beierwaltes says only that in Plotinus's concept of time the whole is a never-ending future because

God is not the totality of the whole but the "unifying unity" of the whole. But as the infinite, God cannot be completely different from the finite, because such difference would have to be defined by a boundary. Since what defines the finite is its boundaries, the difference would make God finite.[54] "In the reflection on the most comprehensive whole of all finite reality, each particular finite thing in its concrete individual definiteness is mediated with God. For this reason religion as a vivid and deeper apprehension of reality consists, as Schleiermacher saw, in the becoming conscious of the infinite and whole in the individual and finite, a whole out of which each individual thing is, as it were, carved by means of its definition and its determination" [cf. Schleiermacher, chap. 2.2.4].[55] As already seen above, Pannenberg faulted Hegel for having no real future, no end of history in his philosophy, and this particular reference to Schleiermacher also has no real end in view. The eschatological future that Pannenberg envisions has no other basis than his understanding of biblical apocalyptic. Joining this with philosophical concepts of the infinite is evidently an act of theological mediation.

8.4 THE LATER HEIDEGGER AND THEOLOGY

8.4.1 Being and Language in the Later Heidegger

In previous chapters we noted the influence of Martin Heidegger's existential analysis of human being in the theology of Bultmann [chap. 6.3] and to a lesser degree in that of Tillich [chap. 7.1], and we have spoken of the influence of the later Heidegger on Gerhard Ebeling, to whom we return later in this chapter. Traces of influence have appeared in other theologians as well.

In his first major work, *Being and Time,* Heidegger asks, "What makes it ontologically possible for entities [beings] to be encountered within-the-world and objectified as so encountered?"[56] The question has to do with the recognition of beings as what they are, a tree, for example. Ordinarily beings or things have meaning that we assume without thinking about it. Certain experiences, however, especially anxiety, evoke a sense of distance from the meaning of things. Meaning seems insecure, no longer anchored in ordinary self-evidence. In reflection on this

---

it cannot be attained in time. See also A. H. Armstrong, *Plotinian and Christian Studies* (London: Variorum Reprints, 1979), 21:115. Cf. Pannenberg, *Systematic Theology,* 1:403f. Pannenberg's understanding of the whole bears a certain similarity to Kant's theory of God outside of time, perceiving the whole of temporal reality [cf. chap. 2.2.2].

54. *Metaphysics and the Idea of God,* 142f.

55. Ibid., 146. Cf. Pannenberg, *Idea of God and Human Freedom,* 204f.

56. *Being and Time,* 366. On Heidegger's philosophy, see William J. Richardson, *Heidegger: Through Phenomenology to Thought* (The Hague: Martinus Nijhoff, 1963); Wolfgang Stegmüller, *Main Currents in Contemporary German, British and American Philosophy* (Dordrecht, Holland: D. Reidel, 1969), 133–80. See also Jeff Owen Prudhomme, *God and Being: Heidegger's Relation to Theology* (Atlantic Highlands, NJ: Humanities Press, 1997).

experience, Heidegger says the meaning of things and their connectedness in the world is in fact not self-evident but mysteriously given.[57] Animals do not or only minimally share in this givenness of meaning; only human beings are the recipients. Heidegger shows that it is expressed in statements about what "is," as in the phrase "this is a tree." Reflection on the givenness of the meaningful world is reflection on what "is," on "being." The word for "being" in German is *sein* (the infinitive "to be"), from which comes the noun, *das Sein*. A traditional philosophical term for anything that "is" (e.g., a tree) is *Seiendes* (a noun formed from the participle *seiend*). For Heidegger *Sein* and *Seiendes* are not the same, although they cannot be separated, as in the sentence, "this is (*sein*) a tree (*Seiendes*)." *Seiendes* means a being, and *sein* discloses it as being what it is. Without our thinking about it, the "is" or *das Sein* (Being) always already tells us what things "are." Since this happens in language, language "speaks"; it "discloses" or "illumines," "enlightens" the meaning of things in the world. The human relationship to this speaking is to speak in "correspondence" with it, to speak the language of Being, of the meaning of things.

The language of Being is the "horizon" within which things are recognized as what they "are" and cohere with one another meaningfully in the world. Within every human horizon of meaning there is an aspect of universal disclosure of meaning: a tree, the sky, a jug for water or wine. But in important ways different cultures and even different periods in a given history speak of what "is" differently. How does this happen? To locate a "cause" within the world of beings does not answer the question, because in this case one is already operating within a specific horizon of meaning: modern science.[58] When Darwin makes natural selection the explanation of life, he thinks within the framework of the modern scientific understanding of what "is" true—namely, as objective, analyzable, and usable. Other times in Western history did not, and other cultures do not. For Heidegger this points thinking not to cause-and-effect analyses but to the mystery of Being.

According to Heidegger, in the beginnings of Western history, in Greek language and thought, truth meant the "unconcealment" of things, what let them be seen as what they are. With Plato, however, something new happens in the understanding of truth, as represented by his image of the cave. In the cave and facing its back wall, one sees only shadows of the reality outside the cave. Outside the cave, one sees the things as they truly are. For Plato, truth is the right or correct perception of the things, namely, as true ideas that are unchanging and timeless. In the Middle Ages this changes to become the rule that thought must adequately represent things as they are, whether in the world or above the world in heaven.[59] In the early modern period the famous statement of René Descartes (1596–1650),

---

57. *Being and Time*, 228–35; cf. 321f., 393f., 407. Cf. anxiety in Kierkegaard and in Schelling's *On Human Freedom*.

58. *Being and Time*, 23–28, 32–34; 67–90; *An Introduction to Metaphysics*, trans. Ralph Manheim (Garden City, NY: Anchor, 1961), 45f., 70; "Letter on Humanism," in Heidegger, *Pathmarks*, ed. William McNeill (Cambridge: Cambridge University Press, 1998), 239–76.

59. "Plato's Doctrine of the Truth," in Martin Heidegger, *Pathmarks*, 155–82, esp. 167f.

"I think; therefore I am," represents the beginning of modern science; the "I" secures certitude by a method anchored in the subjective self, the "I." It uses its sciences or reasoning to secure, prove, or demonstrate the truth of anything, including God (metaphysics). God becomes a being among others, an object of thought, whether God's existence is believed or denied.[60] What happens in history from Plato to the present is an unfolding of Plato's concept of truth, but not as a logical development, as in Hegel. Hegel's method of ascertaining truth is essentially like that of Descartes. He reviews the thought of previous philosophy and "lifts" it [Aufhebung] into his own thought, making it steps in the logic of "absolute knowing," absolute truth. For Heidegger, this is the culminating thought of all modern metaphysics and science: the truth of everything is scientific, and the subjective self is the real power behind it. In the twentieth century this power is the will that wills itself and, as a part of this, what it wills to be true. It uses technology to secure what it wills, and it lives in perpetual conflict with the will of other individuals and groups. The development of the meaning of truth since Plato increasingly obscures the mystery of Being. To catch sight of it, Hegel, for example, would have to "step back" from his philosophy to the point where the philosopher becomes a "thinker" who "thinks" the primal givenness of meaning.[61]

There are no "results" of this thinking, as there are in science, but only the personal meditative following of the openings to thought about what "is" that Being provides. Such openings are given particularly in poetry. In his late work Heidegger explores the etymology of certain words and meanings in order to open modern thought to a horizon that includes the awareness of Being. There is a reverent aspect to this, as, for example, in his thought on the meaning of "thing." For human being a thing— a jug, a tree—gathers a world together: earth and sky, "mortals" and "the gods," the dimension of divinity.[62] The "gods" or "God" that come to be in history, by whatever power, do so within the givenness of the meaning of Being. In thinking Being itself there are no scientific certainties but only, to use Heidegger's metaphor, a "way," so that the thoughts that thinking (in corresponding) "speaks" are only "markers along the way" [Wegmarken].[63]

Scholarship has demonstrated that Schleiermacher's description of religion in the Speeches—as the primitive experience of subject-object unity within the unity of the universe or the infinite—was an important early influence in the development of Heidegger's concept of Being.[64] For Heidegger, however, the nature of

---

60. Heidegger, Nietzsche, vol. 4, Nihilism, trans. Frank A. Capuzzi and David Farrell Krell (San Francisco: Harper & Row, 1982), 96–118; "Letter on Humanism."

61. Heidegger, Identity and Difference, 42–74; cf. Being and Time, 480–86. On the will to will, see the "Letter on Humanism" and esp. the essay, "Überwindung der Metaphysik," in Vorträge und Aufsätze, 1:63–91. In the history of meaning or of Being, statements of what "is" in modern science are also given by Being, so thinking this meaning and its history is part of thinking the mystery of Being.

62. See Heidegger's essay, "Building Dwelling Thinking," in Basic Writings, ed. David Farrell Krell (New York: Harper & Row, 1977), 320–39. Cf. "The Origin of the Work of Art," in ibid., 143–89.

63. So the title of Heidegger's collection of essays, Pathmarks, in German Wegmarken.

64. See Theodore Kisiel, The Genesis of Heidegger's Being and Time (Berkeley: University of California Press, 1993), 89–93.

Being is time, not the eternal presence of the infinite universe. As Being gives meaning, Being conditions humanity and the human world temporally, giving existence its determinations in the wholeness of world. Transcendence for Heidegger is not the opening of the finite to the infinite and unconditioned, but to Being as time, as meaning: Being comes in time or with time—and in a certain sense it gives time itself—through language as the meaning of being in the world.[65] One could say that insofar as Being cannot be conceived in or by itself, it seems to have the aspect of the unconditional, but to try to imagine what Being is "before" time would only repeat the metaphysics of subjective reason.[66]

The question about how, if at all, Heidegger is relevant for theology has received widely varying and contradictory answers. The most important objection in both philosophy and theology is that his thought on Being is fatalistic and irrational, insofar as thought corresponds only to the givenness of Being.[67] For those who follow Heidegger this is an exaggeration and a misunderstanding of his method.[68] One of the most important positive responses in theology has been that of Gerhard Ebeling. According to Ebeling, who spoke for his generation of Bultmannian scholars, theology should, in a limited and qualified sense, appropriate Heidegger's philosophical thought on Being and language and his criticism of modern subjectivist reason. The qualification was that for theology in the tradition of Luther, all philosophy relates to theology only as "law" to "gospel." Philosophy has only to do with the law as with "natural" human existence and its reason. But what is "natural" in the modern world is necessarily important for understanding what gospel means in the modern world, as Ebeling demonstrates in his theology. Gospel is the word of liberation from the law [chap. 6.4].[69]

There was another important way of appropriating Heidegger's thought, the way of Karl Rahner and Heinrich Ott, which interprets Heidegger's "Being" as

65. Heidegger, *Vom Wesen des Grundes* (Frankfurt: Vittorio Kostermann, 1973), 20ff., 43–54.

66. "We have left behind us the presumption of all unconditioned." The attempt to "explain" Being misses Being altogether (*Vorträge und Aufsätze*, 2:52f., in the essay "Das Ding" [The Thing]). Here (p. 53) Heidegger focuses attention on the German words: *be-dingen*, (to condition, literally "to thing") and *un-be-dingt* (unconditioned, "un-thinged"). [Cf. chap. 2.2.1.] Human beings are *die Bedingten* (the conditioned, "the thinged"). The sense lies in Heidegger's understanding of the simplicity of a thing as the bearer of meaning. In his late work, Heidegger criticizes the (metaphysical) "god of philosophy" as a god to whom one can neither pray nor sacrifice, "neither fall on one's knees in awe nor play music and dance before" (*Identity and Difference*, 72). See also the "Letter on Humanism," *Pathways*, 266f.

67. See also Jürgen Habermas, "The Undermining of Western Rationalism through the Critique of Metaphysics: Martin Heidegger," in *The Philosophical Discourse of Modernity*, 131–60. See also Habermas's discussion of Heidegger and Derrida, ibid., 161–84. Habermas's concern for the subordination of reason is related to Hegel's critique of Schleiermacher [chap. 2.7.2, at the end], but it is related mainly to the destruction of reason in the Romantic ideas that intellectually supported Nazism. For Christian theology, this reason is "natural" reason, to which the tradition of dialectic theology stands in an ambiguous relationship.

68. See, e.g., William J. Richardson, "Heidegger and God—and Professor Jonas," in *Thought. Fordham University Quarterly* 11; no. 156 (1965): 13–40.

69. Ebeling, "Verantworten des Glaubens in Begegnung mit dem Denken M. Heideggers," in *Wort und Glaube*, 2:92–98. See also Ernst Fuchs, in H.-G. Gadmer, *Truth and Method*, 463, 476ff.

the light of the God of Christianity. The images of disclosure as "illumination," "lighting," and "enlightenment" are found in distant antiquity in both philosophical and religious tradition. In Plato's *Republic* the "Good" is like the light of the sun, illuminating all things.[70] In both biblical testaments God is spoken of as light and as the source of light (e.g., Pss. 36:9; 43:3). And in previous chapters of the present work there are several instances of God, Word, or Holy Spirit as "light." Since Schleiermacher and early Idealism—and long before in the *via negativa* of patristic and medieval thought—theologians have understood authentic thought and language about God as nonobjective or nonscientific. For Schleiermacher and Idealism, metaphysics, represented by the concept of a "first cause," was considered an improper method of speaking of God or the Absolute. For these reasons the later Heidegger's thought on Being as "lighting" was not inherently alien to theology.

8.4.2 Karl Rahner

Karl Rahner (1904–84) was a Roman Catholic professor of theology at Innsbruck and Munich and a widely recognized if controversial interpreter of the documents of the Second Vatican Council. He had been a favored student of Heidegger in the 1930s; as a Jesuit he had to have his dissertation on Thomas Aquinas approved by a certified Catholic scholar—who failed it as being too Heideggerian.[71] In his second book, *Hearer of the Word*, published in 1941, Heidegger's concept of the Being of beings, which Rahner describes as "luminosity," is evidently employed for a new interpretation of the theological metaphysics of Thomas Aquinas.[72] Here we only briefly review one area of Rahner's work, which covers practically all areas of Roman Catholic life and doctrine.[73]

Basic to Rahner's theology is the mystery of God and of God's presence in the world. As revealed in Christ, God is the ground, origin, and goal of all human experience, and in life itself—in the "luminosity" of Being—God is always communicating with every person.[74] According to *Hearer of the Word*, God is the highest and infinite being, utterly incomparable with any finite being or with

70. *The Republic of Plato*, trans. Cornford, 219f. [see chap. 2.2.2].

71. On Rahner's life and work, see Herbert Vorgrimler, *Understanding Karl Rahner* (New York: Crossroad, 1986).

72. Thomist theologians friendly to Rahner have insisted that the "ontological difference" between beings and Being in Rahner is essentially Thomist, and Rahner himself, who wrote no commentaries on Heidegger, also points the reader in this direction. On Rahner, Thomas, and Heidegger, see Thomas Sheehan, *Karl Rahner: The Philosophical Foundations* (Athens: Ohio University Press, 1987), 150–55; see further John D. Caputo, *Heidegger and Aquinas* (New York: Fordham University Press, 1982). See also Rahner's dissertation on Thomas (which was accepted at Innsbruck for the doctorate): *Spirit in the World*, trans. William Dyck (New York: Herder & Herder, 1968).

73. See Leo J. O'Donovan, ed., *A World of Grace. An Introduction to the Themes and Foundations of Karl Rahner's Theology* (New York: Crossroad, 1981).

74. *Theological Investigations*, 23 vols. (Baltimore: Helicon Press, 1961ff.), 6:244f. See also the important essay, "The Mystery of God in Catholic Theology," ibid., 4:48ff.

Heidegger's "Being." Although God constantly communicates with human being, without revelation in Christ, God remains unknown.[75] The reason is that human perception or human existence in the luminosity of Being is limited by its temporality and therefore incomplete. God's being is complete; it is pure luminosity. Although God's being is hidden for finite human perception, it is the ultimate source of the light of Being that illumines the world for human being, the source of meaning.[76] As for Heidegger, it is "Being" that allows "beings" (things) to be recognized and known as what they are.[77]

Heidegger's concept of human transcendence toward Being is recognizable in what Rahner calls human being's *Vorgriff*, which literally means reaching before or ahead. In ordinary human existence *Vorgriff* reaches beyond finite things, always already transcending the things themselves toward Being, that is, the meaning that originates in the absolute luminosity of God. Because Being's ultimate source is God, and insofar as Being is the medium of meaning, the *Vorgriff* is the medium or condition of the possibility of hearing God's Word, the historical event of Christ.[78] Human *Vorgriff* defines, so to speak, what it means to have human ears, whether they hear the Word or not. As for Heidegger, human being's transcendence toward Being, because it is temporal, is a feature of human being's historical existence. God communicates with human being historically, both in the temporality of human existence and perception and in the historical revelation of Christ.

8.4.3 Heinrich Ott

Heinrich Ott (born 1929), a native of Basel, Switzerland, was until his retirement professor of theology at the university in Basel. For a time he served as an elected member of the Swiss Parliament, where he was involved in the politics of peace in national and international conflict resolution. Ott is best known for his interpretation of Heidegger for theology in his *Denken und Sein* (Thinking and Being)[79] and for his two-volume *Wirklichkeit und Glaube* (Reality and Faith), which is his

75. In the German edition of *Hearer of the Word*, revised with Rahner's approval by his student Johannes Baptist Metz, the problem of "being" and "Being" as appropriate language for God is addressed: *Hörer des Wortes* (Munich: Herderbücherei, 1963), 58 (cf. 61).

76. God is "inaccessible light" (1 Tim. 6:16), "infinite," "inexpressible," "incomprehensible," "absolute reality" (Rahner, *Theological Investigations*, 5:6, 146–49). Cf. in Pannenberg the concepts of the "whole" in God and the temporal and partial in human perception [chap. 8.3.2].

77. See also the definition of "being," in K. Rahner and Herbert Vorgimler, eds., *Theological Dictionary*, trans. Richard Strachan (New York: Herder & Herder, 1965), 53f. Cf. the article "Proof of the Existence of God," in ibid., 381–83.

78. *Hearer of the Word*, trans. Joseph Donceel, ed. Andrew Tallon (New York: Continuum, 1994). Luminosity: 23–44; *Vorgriff* and revelation: esp. 45–64, 68–70, 121–36, 152. *Vorgriff* is a concept in Heidegger's *Being and Time*, 191. See also Pannenberg's affirmative but qualified use of Rahner's concept, *Basic Questions*, 2:102ff.

79. *Denken und Sein* (Zurich: Evangelischer Verlag, 1959) was (and remains) perhaps the single most important work on Heidegger's relevance for theology. It sparked a wide-ranging debate that included Heidegger himself. James M. Robinson reviews the debate in *New Frontiers*, vol. 1, *The Later Heidegger and Theology* (New York: Harper & Row, 1963), 30–76. See also H.-G. Gadamer, *Truth and Method*, 476ff.

definitive work, especially the second, untranslated volume.[80] His two popular works are *Theology and Preaching*, arranged according to the first eleven articles of the Heidelberg Catechism,[81] and *Die Antwort des Glaubens* (The Answer of Faith), a systematic theology similarly arranged as fifty questions and answers.[82]

Even before his university studies Ott was a student of Karl Barth's *Church Dogmatics*. Barth's understanding of the "wholly other" God, of all creation within the truth and reality of Christ, whose lordship is given witness in all the New Testament without exception and proclaimed in the Christian community—these are indelible elements in Ott's theology. Like Barth he opposes Bultmann's demythologizing distinction between aspects of the New Testament that are kerygmatic and aspects that are mythological.[83] Bonhoeffer was another early influence on Ott. Basic themes in Bonhoeffer adopted by Ott—namely, Christ as the "center" of life and God's presence in all reality—were clearly related to interpretations in Barth (B 164, 167ff.). When Ott says that only in Christ is it possible to understand what human being is (B 392ff., 424ff.), one hears both Barth and Bonhoeffer. Ott came, however, to think that Bonhoeffer and not Barth was right about the "non-religious interpretation" of the New Testament in the task of speaking to modern secular humanity. He agreed with Bultmann's concept of "existential interpretation" of the New Testament, but again without demythologizing (B 142ff.). He learned from Martin Buber that human being is structurally dialogic, made for community and dialogue about reality and God with other human beings (e.g., P 78f.).[84] Two final influences were of great significance: Martin Heidegger (e.g., P 97ff., 127ff.) and Karl Rahner, with whom he carried on extensive conversations.[85]

"Horizon," a concept taken from Heidegger, is for Ott a term of key hermeneutical importance. Faith and the witness of Christ in the New Testament, both of which are centered in the revelation of Christ, are "the exclusive horizon of theology" (S 98). The light of Christ illumines or lightens everything within the horizon that encompasses the world. It suffers loss or is darkened by human sin, but in itself it knows nothing "secular" or "natural" beside it. Like "Being"

---

80. Page numbers in the following text are to these works by Ott: **B**: *Reality and Faith*, vol. 1, *The Theological Legacy of Dietrich Bonhoeffer*, 1st German ed. 1966 (Philadelphia: Fortress Press, 1972); **P**: *Wirklichkeit und Glaube*, vol. II, *Der persönliche Gott* (Göttingen: Vandenhoeck & Ruprecht, 1969); **S**: "What Is Systematic Theology?" in James M. Robinson and John B. Cobb Jr., *New Frontiers in Theology*, vol. 1, *The Later Heidegger and Theology*, 77–111. The address was originally given in 1960. On Ott's theology, see Colin B. O'Connell, *A Study of Heinrich Ott's Theological Development: His Hermeneutical and Ontological Programme* (New York: Peter Lang, 1991), which includes a list of Ott's publications.

81. *Theology and Preaching*, trans. Harold Knight (Philadelphia: Westminster, 1965). Another translated piece is the short work written for a series on dogmatic topics, *God*, trans. Iaian and Ute Nicol (Richmond: John Knox, 1974).

82. *Die Antwort des Glaubens*, 3rd revised ed. (Berlin: Kreuz Verlag, 1981). In this work Ott works with a team of theologians who give summaries of recent theology on each of the questions.

83. Ott's first major work was *Geschichte und Heilsgeschichte in der Theologie Rudolf Bultmanns* (Tübingen: Mohr Siebeck, 1955).

84. [Cf. dialogue in Brunner, chap. 6.2.2.]

85. See Ott in Vorgrimler, *Understanding Karl Rahner*, 120.

for Heidegger, for Christian faith "everything of which God's Word [in the New Testament] speaks" is a "concrete determination" of reality "given by God's illumination, which fills the entire horizon" (P 220).[86] "When the Word of God goes forth, the 'lighting' [*Lichtung*, illumination] of 'God is' occurs, the 'I Am' of God. . . . God announces God's presence. This is the basic event of the Word. . . . The only possibility of speaking meaningfully of God is as [the] 'lighting' and [the] determination [*Bestimmung*] of our horizon as a whole" (P 222).[87] The "wholeness" of the truth of revelation is expressed in Martin Kähler's concept of the New Testament's "picture" of Christ, which contains all expressions or determinations of the Word (B 410, 447).[88] God, the "encompassing" itself, transcends all effort to comprehend God and would not be known save for the "encounter" with God in the Word.[89] All language of faith, including theology, takes place within the horizon of God's illuminating presence in Christ. Theology (as for Barth) is a form of prayer (P 297–329, S 92).

Time is encompassed by God and is directed to God. Eschatology culminates in Christ, in whom the reality of God is revealed.[90] But meaning is understood only in one's own history and language; the Word comes to us temporally, in history. It is addressed to us personally as we live in time, in our world and in our personal situations and communities. Like Being's disclosure of the meaning of beings in Heidegger, the Word is the revelation of the meaning of all things. "Situations illuminate in the light of the Good News, they show themselves from themselves. They become, so to speak, truly the phenomena that they really are."[91] Their truth is the illuminating presence of Christ, who is "the way, the truth and the life" (John 14:6; D 393). In Christ the meaning of the Trinity is

---

86. Cf. J. T. Beck [chap. 1.2], and the late Schelling's saying that in Christianity there is no reality outside of Christ [chap. 2.4.2]. Faith is then grounded in the Word not only as the revelation of God but also as the recognition of the world in its truth or in the dimension of truth. The hearing of the Word is "disclosure," which occurs partially in time and fully only in the eschatological future.

87. Ott develops these thoughts in his later books, *Das Reden vom Unsagbaren* (Berlin: Kreuz, 1978) and in *Apologetik*, e.g., 185f. According to this work, in which he returns to a discussion of method in theology, in the act of faith there is no "subject" standing over against an "object," but "light" in which all things are seen anew and decision is made for faith (59).

88. Cf. *God*, 74f.; *Apologetik des Glaubens*, 174f. [See Kähler, chap. 5.1.]

89. According to *Apologetik des Glaubens* (§§16–19), Anselm's "name" of God, "that than which nothing greater can be thought," sets a "limit" to human thought [cf. chap. 6.1.2]. One cannot speak "about" God as if God were an object but only out of the encounter with God. Anselm's name of God is in the tradition of "negative theology," of the *docta ignorantia* in Nicolas of Cusa [cf. chap. 2.1]. *Apologetik*, 71, 82f., 122. See also *God*, esp. 99–105. An important text is Acts 17:27f. (cf. Eph. 4:6): in God "we live and move and have our being" (P 285).

90. See Ott's discussion of eschatology in Fritz Buri, Jan Milic Lochmann, and Heinrich Ott, *Dogmatik im Dialog* (Gütersloh: Gerd Mohn, 1973), 207–10.

91. *Apologetik*, 50. The last part of this work (§34) outlines the application of method of phenomenological analysis in the philosophy of Edmund Husserl (1859–1938) to faith and revelation. In Husserl's analysis, the aspects of temporal experience in consciousness are not separate, discrete parts, but always integrated with one another. Ott sees the possibility of a phenomenological exploration and confirmation of the integrated "perichoresis" of faith and life. On Husserl, see H.-G. Gadamer, *Truth and Method*, 479, and Wolfgang Stegmüller, *Contemporary Trends in German, British and American Philosophy*, 63–100.

revealed: the Father, who rightly claims us in the here and now; the Son, who is God's gift of grace to us in the present; the Holy Spirit, who "makes us free" in placing us in relationship to God (P 354). For Ott as for Barth, the possibility we have to trust God does not go before the reality of God, but the reality goes before, making the "possibility a function of the reality" (P 347, 349).[92]

In existence in the truth certain "structures" of all human existence come to light: (1) the "between" of human beings in which all communication takes place and has reality (P §11).[93] The Christian community makes explicit that human life is not made up of isolated individuals but of communities. In the "between" of God and human being that characterizes the horizon of faith, all reality is personal reality in communion with God. (2) The truth of God's "perichoresis," the "indwelling" of the persons of the Trinity in one another, is reflected in the interpersonal relations of the human community. In truth all things of creation are "in" and not separate from one another (P §12). (3) The "nearness" of God to human being is reflected in the "nearness" of human beings to one another in the "between" and the "perichoresis" or human community (P §13). The horizon in which we exist also includes the "perichoresis" of our past, present, and future, including the eschatological future of the kingdom of God.[94] This integration of past, present, and future does not happen all at once, but progressively, given through time, in the maturing experience of faith as it ever again and with increasing depth understands all things in the light of the Word (P 131ff., 246f., 276). Moreover the whole truth of the present horizon of faith cannot possibly be expressed in one person's experience or insight. Only within the temporal horizon of faith and in and through dialogue with others is truth expressed and understood.[95] This is also true in theology, which in the past has been susceptible to the *rabies theologorum,* the "madness of theologians" fighting one another.[96]

The evil of refusing the reality of God imposes meaninglessness and suffering on oneself and others with whom one is related in the "between," in "perichoresis" and in "nearness." The threatening darkness also involves the *Anfechtung*

---

92. In *Apologetik des Glaubens,* 207, Ott agrees with Barth in the Barth-Brunner debate about the presuppositions in natural humanity for faith [chap. 6.1–2]. "All communication of God rests on pure grace alone." If Brunner's position is modified, so that it speaks not of presuppositions but of "structures" of human being used by God to "make possible" the response of faith, then Ott has no difficulty with it.

93. See Buber's *Between Man and Man,* trans. Ronald Gregor Smith (New York: Macmillan, 1965).

94. Cf. Barth, *Church Dogmatics,* II/1:639f.; III/2:463f.; IV/3:295f.; cf. E. Jüngel, *Karl Barth, a Theological Legacy,* 44.

95. Cf. Schleiermacher's hermeneutics in chap. 2.7.1.

96. Ott, *Apologetik,* 2. Ott probably takes *rabies theologorum* from Barth, who "is not afraid" of it when he is forced to "sharply contradict" other theologians. *Humanity of God,* 95. [Cf. the conflict of theologians in Overbeck, chap. 5.2, and Barth, chap. 6.1.1.] Ebeling (for one) accused Barth's polemic of not discussing subjects fairly: *Word and Faith,* 202. Ott (ibid.) urges dialogue in theology that transcends defending positions and yet maintains polemical argumentation as necessary. An example of dialogic method is given by the lectures *Dogmatik im Dialog,* which Ott held together with the liberal theologian, Buri, and the Barthian Lochmann.

(Luther) of faith, the temptation not to believe.[97] The church's proclamation begins with the light of Christ, the gospel of forgiveness and freedom, for it is in this light that one recognizes sin. Ott agrees with Bonhoeffer in refusing to focus on sin as human weakness. In the modern world grave sins are those of human strength and mainly of social injustice. Human beings discover the "tragic nature" of natural human life on their own. What they need is the gospel that in forgiveness liberates, that opens a new future.[98]

Ott ends his book *Der persönliche Gott* with reference to the Word that confronts the Christian with the mystery of God, the horizon that exceeds one's ability to grasp it, "so that, astonished and shaken, we confess 'He is the Lord (John 21:7), it is God!' . . . in the face of this inexpressible mystery, our theological 'formula' of human existence as 'being encompassed' is only a poor marker on the path"—the path of the thinking of faith (P 386).

8.4.4 Anonymous Christianity?

Ott expressed his essential agreement with Karl Rahner—and with the brief statements of Bonhoeffer about "unconscious faith"—on the subject of "anonymous Christianity," or as Ott usually says, "anonymous faith." We have seen certain parallels in previous history. Richard Rothe [chap. 3.2] and Tillich [chap. 7.1] could suggest the reality of some form of Christian belief existing outside of the explicit confession of Christ. In nineteenth-century mediation theology one commonly finds an ontological continuity of potential and actual in the relationship of humanity to God. In Kierkegaard's pseudonymous writings the unbelieving reader is led in ever-greater insight forward toward the confession of Christian faith.

Karl Rahner began addressing the subject of "anonymous Christianity" in the early 1960s in connection with evaluations of human life outside the confession of Christ in documents of Vatican II.[99] In a short work from this period entitled "Anonymous Christians," Rahner says that human being is in itself a "tendency toward God." It is a being "of unlimited openness for the limitless being of God."

97. In *Theology and Preaching*, 103, original sin is characterized as "transcendental." Like Kant's a priori categories, it is the "condition of the possibility" of all human actions, none of which therefore escapes the consequence of "total depravity" (following the Heidelberg Catechism). According to *Antwort des Glaubens*, 212–18, sin destroys the meaning of existence. It arises in the situation of the question about meaning that is at the core of natural human existence and that only God can answer. According to the same work (226f.), the theoretical question of the origin of evil cannot be answered. The question is different in the experience of one's own evil, whereby what is wanted is not a theoretical explanation but deliverance from meaninglessness. The whole question is a reminder that thought has no access to the origins of theology's subject matter. What we do know is that "God has sunk God's self into the meaninglessness of suffering and of evil and is now present in it." In Christ's resurrection we know "God has the power to create a new beginning out of the nothingness of absolute meaninglessness."

98. *Das Reden vom Unsagbaren*, 166–87. The task of preaching is to speak the Word that discloses, illumines the truth of all things. *Theology and Preaching*, esp. 128, 155f.

99. See esp. Rahner, *Theological Investigations*, 6:397f. Page numbers in the following paragraph refer to this volume. Rahner's first important essay on the subject was "Dogmatic Notes on 'Ecclesiological Piety,'" ibid., 5:336–65. See also his defense of "anonymous Christianity," ibid., 14:280–94.

This openness goes "beyond every individual thing that can be known and grasped, [it is] that openness which is always already opened by the creative call of infinite mystery which is and must be the ultimate and the first, the all-inclusive and the fathomless ground of all that can be grasped, of all that is real and all that is possible." Because of this "tendency toward God," natural human being lives in a certain "expectancy" of hearing more than the silence of God (392). The expectancy is fulfilled in Christ, who may for different reasons be resisted and rejected. But even in rejection there may be a presence of "anonymous Christianity." In experiencing the limitless openness toward God in human transcendence, [natural] human being "experiences the offer of grace," so that "the express revelation of the word in Christ" does not come as "entirely strange" but as "the explication of what we already are by grace and what we experience at least incoherently in the limitlessness of our transcendence." The "anonymous Christian" is only that unbeliever who does not close himself or herself to "the holy mystery of God in deed and in truth." This is no substitute for the confession of Christian faith, in which alone, as Augustine says, rest and peace are found (395). But it is an existence influenced of the reality of God.

An important aspect of Rahner's conception of the anonymous Christian is his understanding of modern atheist humanity, an understanding he expounds both for the sake of Christians who live in the midst of modern atheist humanity (396) and in the interest of the dialogue with this humanity (e.g., 14f., 20). "I see the approach of times in which Christianity will no longer be a matter of course . . . but ultimately it cannot really trouble me. Why not? Because I see everywhere a nameless Christianity, and because I do not see my own explicit Christianity as one option among others [but as the only truth] . . . I see nothing other in my Christianity than the explicit recognition and home-coming of everything in the way of truth and love which exists or could exist anywhere else." Christianity is "the universal message" that "gathers up (*aufhebt*) and thus preserves everything else."[100] This is the horizon in which the truth of all things appears, and so also nonbelief is disclosed in its truth.

Ott's motivation to speak of "anonymous faith" is, like Rahner's, given by the reality of the presence of God and the universality of God's claim on all human beings, and by the church's relationship to its atheist-secular neighbor.[101] In *Das Reden vom Unsagbaren* (Speaking of the Ineffable) Ott explores the nature of human being in the light of Christ: human being has a "depth dimension" that it does not consciously control and that ordinarily escapes its attention. It is in this dimension that the mystery of the work of the Holy Spirit takes place.[102] Every human being is a questioner confronted with making decisions in a reality in

---

100. *Theological Investigations*, 5:9f.; cf. 359ff.

101. In *Apologetik*, 136f., the concept of anonymous faith is significant for the church's dialogue with other religions.

102. *Das Reden vom Unsagbaren*, 141–43. The Spirit proceeds from Father and Son, who through perichoresis are indwelling in the Spirit. See "Holy Spirit" in *Antwort des Glaubens*, 143–45. Here Ott quotes Acts 2:17 (Joel 2:28): in the end times the Spirit will be poured out on all flesh.

which Christ is Lord.[103] But for the secular atheist or agnostic no statements about the mystery of God are persuasive, nor is such a person aware of being "borne by a mystery." The point of the concept of anonymous faith is not that the atheist must be conscious of the mystery of God, but that faith sees the atheist in this light. If, however, there is a movement of anonymous faith in the atheist, it occurs only in the existential dimension as something the Christian neither sees nor controls. The indications of its presence are in behavior, in ethical personhood. It is for Ott generally true that "whether the question about God . . . is important or not can finally only be decided in the question about ethics."[104] The case of the believing nonbeliever is typified by the parable of the Good Samaritan, which illustrates the "nearness" of God to the Samaritan. The parable is related to Jesus' words in Matthew 25:40: "What you have done to the least of these . . . you have done to me." The "call" of the near God occurs in every relationship to the neighbor in all places and everywhere.[105] Where it is heard, it opens the future to new encounters, to the awareness of the neighbor as person, of the "between," the "nearness," and the "perichoresis" of all human life (P 280–96). In another place Ott defines "anonymous faith" as the existential answer of human being to the ever-present call of God in relationship to one's neighbor (as in the parable), to one's death (as trustful acceptance of the encompassing mystery), and to the future (as openness to new encounters with the neighbor and the encompassing mystery, to new illumination).[106] According to Ott this is not "natural theology," because reality is christological. Here "natural theology and revelation theology meet."[107]

A recent example of interest in anonymous Christianity is found in the conclusion of a short work by a leading Christian layman in Germany, Robert Leicht (born 1944), former editor of the eminent German weekly *Die Zeit,* member of the Council of the Evangelical Church in Germany, and president of the Evangelical Academy in Berlin. The work is *Ihr seid das Salz der Erde!* (You are the Salt of the Earth!). It originally appeared as a series in *Die Zeit* and was intended for a largely secular reading audience. In discussing the last of the Beatitudes, Leicht writes, with reference to Bonhoeffer's "unconscious Christians," that there is behavior that witnesses to the truth without the verbal assertion (confession) of the truth: it is "truth confirmed [*beglaubigt*] existentially." Leicht's examples are non-Christians who made decisions of self-sacrifice in aiding Jews and resisting Nazi tyranny.[108]

Theological discussion about "anonymous faith" or "anonymous Christianity" in the 1960s and afterward produced very different answers. For Wolfhart

---

103. *Antwort,* 339ff.
104. *Das Reden vom Unsagbaren,* 155; *Apologetik,* 37f., cf. 78: There is greater human dignity in the principled [*vornehmen*] agnostic humanist than in the Christian fanatic.
105. Cf. the "summons" of Transcendence in Fritz Buri [chap. 4.10].
106. *Antwort des Glaubens,* 339–41.
107. *Apologetik,* 74.
108. *Ihr seid das Salz der Erde! 2000 Jahre Christen im Widerspruch* (Gütersloh: Gütersloher Verlagshaus, 1999), 79.

Pannenberg there is a presence of truth in other religions and in philosophy, but this does not mean "anonymous Christianity" or "faith."[109] For Jürgen Moltmann eschatological theology must oppose a theology of "eternal presence." He applauds the outreach to the secular world that "autonomous Christianity" intends but rejects it as "the old claim of the church to rule the world." It is not legitimate, for example, to call "believing and righteous Jews 'anonymous Christians.'" Furthermore, the act of righteousness on behalf of "the least of these" (Matt. 25:40) should be to bring the poor and oppressed "out of the anonymity into which they have been driven."[110] In *Christ the Representative* (135), Dorothee Sölle writes: "There is in the world an anonymous Christianity, ignorant that it is Christian . . . , yet serving his [sc. Christ's] cause representationally and provisionally. The task of the organized Church in relation to this anonymous or 'latent' [Tillich] Church is the education of the consciousness." Representing Barthian theology, Eberhard Jüngel accepts that the truth of reality is Christ, but rejects anonymous Christianity as but another variation of natural theology. There is no aspect of faith that is or can be anonymous; faith and the church's public confessional proclamation of Christ are necessarily joined together.[111]

8.5 EBERHARD JÜNGEL

Eberhard Jüngel (born 1934) was until retirement professor of theology and philosophy of religion at Tübingen.[112] He was schooled in communist East Germany, where he found freedom only in the church. His first teachers were associated with Bultmann: Ernst Fuchs (1903–83) and Gerhard Ebeling [chap. 6.4]; and he has remained in dialogue with the biblical criticism of the Bultmann

109. See Pannenberg [chap. 8.3.2]. See also *Systematic Theology,* 3:499f., where Pannenberg refers affirmatively to patristic Logos theology in speaking of Christianity's relationship to other religions. See also his positive discussion of Rahner in Hans Walter Wolff, ed., *Probleme biblischer Theologie,* esp. 361–66. In *Modern Faith and Thought,* 415, Helmut Thielicke mentions anonymous Christianity in his discussion of Richard Rothe. He points out that it has certain precedents in patristic Logos theology. [Cf. Logos theology in chap. 2.4.2.]

110. Moltmann, *Theology Today* (London: SCM, 1988), 76f.

111. Jüngel, *God's Being Is in Becoming,* 137f.; *Theological Essays,* 1:173–88 [see below].

112. On Jüngel, see Paul J. DeHart, *Beyond the Necessary: Trinitarian Faith and Philosophy in the Thought of Eberhard Jüngel* (Atlanta: Scholars Press, 1999); Roland Daniel Zimany, *Vehicle for God: The Metaphorical Theology of Eberhard Jüngel* (Macon, GA: Mercer University Press, 1994), and John B. Webster, *Eberhard Jüngel: An Introduction to His Theology* (Cambridge: Cambridge University Press, 1986). See further Webster's introductions to works he has translated: Jüngel, *Theological Essays,* trans. John Webster, 2 vols. (Edinburgh: T. & T. Clark, 1989, 1995); *God's Being Is in Becoming: The Trinitarian Being of God in the Theology of Karl Barth,* trans. John Webster (Grand Rapids: Eerdmans, 2001). See also John Webster, ed., *The Possibilities of Theology: Studies in the Theology of Eberhard Jüngel in His Sixtieth Year* (Edinburgh: T. & T. Clark, 1994), which includes a list of Jüngel's publications. Further translated books by Jüngel (other than those quoted and cited below) are *Karl Barth: A Theological Legacy,* trans. Garrett E. Paul [see Barth, chap. 6.1]; *The Freedom of a Christian,* trans. Roy A. Harrisville (Minneapolis: Augsburg, 1988); *Christ, Justice and Peace: Toward a Theology of the State,* trans. D. Bruce Hamill and Alan J. Torrance (Edinburgh: T. & T. Clark, 1992).

school.[113] Jüngel opposes the theologies of hope insofar as they focus on social conditions that can be changed by human work. He does not oppose Christian action for justice in political life; rather in his view the proper business of Christian theology has to do not with human work but with God's work of new creation.[114] In his understanding of language and of the history of Christian thought Jüngel was influenced by the later Heidegger, and he also incorporated aspects of Schelling's and Hegel's thought into his theology. But Jüngel is most importantly a Barthian theologian who on practically every point is in agreement with Barth's *Church Dogmatics*. He does not, however, simply repeat Barth but interprets his thought in his own way, thereby demonstrating the progressive vitality of Barthian theology.[115]

Jüngel's most important publication, and the one we shall concentrate on here, is *God as the Mystery of the World: On the Foundation of the Theology of the Crucified One in the Dispute between Theism and Atheism*.[116] He begins with the problem of the "dubiousness" of talk about God in the modern age, a problem that must be taken seriously and without "mourning." "Such aporias (situations of doubt or dubiousness), if they are really thought through, are still an appropriate way to intensify not only the awareness of the problem but also the possibilities for the further development of a science" (4). The initial focus of Jüngel's reflection is modern humanity's difficulty with the thought of God. In the modern age, "man has made himself the measure of all things" (14). Bonhoeffer was right: for the modern world God is not necessary (17f., 57f.). Jüngel approaches the problem from the perspective of Heidegger's analysis of modern "subjectivist" thinking.[117] It was, Jüngel says, the philosopher René Descartes who first introduced modern subjectivism ("I think; therefore I am") into philosophical thought, and in this way established the basis of modern science. The subjective self was made the source of scientific certainty. Descartes thought God was still necessary in order to make certain the existence of the world, but in this case too the self set the criterion by which God was held to be necessary. With time and the progress of modern science and philosophy, God became "only a formal condition of thought" with no real meaning and was eventually abandoned (19f., 148f.). But this development involved a new experience of anxiety. Human being exists by nature in uncertainty, threatened by the nothingness that accompanies all that is in time, that is, by death or perishing. Modern humanity's situation is one of requiring that truth be certain while being itself deeply uncertain.

---

113. See esp. his first book, *Paulus und Jesus* (Tübingen: Mohr Siebeck, 1964). On Fuchs, see Gadamer, *Truth and Method*, 477f.

114. Jüngel, *Theological Essays*, 1:114f.; cf. Webster, *Eberhard Jüngel*, 99. See his critique of Dorothee Sölle's *Christ the Representative*, in *Unterwegs zur Sache* (Munich: Christian Kaiser, 1972), 107.

115. The forerunner of the work by Jüngel considered in this chapter is his interpretation of Barth: *God's Being Is in Becoming* [see chap. 6.1.2].

116. *God as the Mystery of the World*, trans. Darrell L. Guder (Grand Rapids: Eerdmans, 1983). Page numbers in the following text refer to this work.

117. See Jüngel's tribute to Heidegger (with regard to the overcoming of metaphysics): ibid., 153. See also H. Thielicke, *Evangelical Faith*, 2:30–218. On Descartes, see Barth's discussion, *Church Dogmatics*, III/1:350–63.

Christian faith interprets temporal, historical life differently, namely, in belief in the God who not only gives life but also preserves it from nothingness (30ff.). The God of Christian faith is not the God who is conceived as necessary based on some conclusion of human reason. God is known only by revelation, and there is no way of thought that leads from natural human reason to God (158).[118] Rather, as formulated by Jüngel, "God comes from God." From the viewpoint of modern scientific reason and philosophy, God is "groundless." There is no condition or reason that requires God to be. God "stands under no conditions of any kind." "God is unconditioned [*unbedingt*]."[119] To preserve this thought theologically is to preserve the mystery of God (389f.). But God's freedom is the freedom of self-determination, of conditioning or defining God's self, as revealed in Christ (35f.).[120] To this self-determination belongs God's will to be in relationship to human being and to enter into human history (37f., cf. 376–79).

The modern phrase "death of God" expresses modern humanity's emancipation from the need for God, a fact represented, for example, by Kant's question, "Whence is God?" a question whose unanswerability sinks reason itself into nothingness (40ff.) [chap. 2.1.1]. Hegel showed that at an earlier time "infinity" expressed Protestantism's belief in the greatness of God over against every finite expression of God, but in the Enlightenment it became simply an abstract concept and an "abyss of nothingness in which all being is engulfed" (74).[121] This vanishing God of modern thought is the God of metaphysics and of "theism," the "God over us" (48). According to Jüngel, Hegel is helpful for the interpretation of this situation, specifically, Hegel's concept of the "death of God" as the divine "other" above human history. "Atheism as the negation of theism is a critical moment of Christian theology which should be brought to bear in the concept of God" (97). For Jüngel the God who dies is "the omnipotent one who controls everything, the one beyond," the "superterrestrial ruler" (102). Indeed Karl Barth went so far as to say, "If there is a devil, he is identical with a supreme being which posits and wills itself, which exists in solitary glory and is therefore 'absolute'" (197).[122] Theology,

---

118. See, e.g., Jüngel's disagreement with Pannenberg, *God as the Mystery of the World*, 44.

119. The German text for these quotations is in Jüngel, *Gott als Geheimnis der Welt*, 2nd ed. (Tübingen: Mohr Siebeck, 1977), 44.

120. In speaking of God's freedom to self-determination, Jüngel refers to Martin Kähler [chap. 5.1] but he could also have referred to Dorner [chap. 3.3] and, as Jüngel certainly knows, to Barth [chap. 6.1.2]. Jüngel returns to these themes at the end of the book, where he says that God is the unconditioned who freely determines or conditions God's self and freely communicates this self-determination in Christ. He refers to John 1:18f., 6:46f., and 1 Tim. 6:13–16 as texts that combine God's "invisibility" with revelation in Christ (377). In revelation, there is no beginning with any thought other than the God who comes from God. Not only being or anything that exists, but also the nothing itself comes about because of God. So God is the "first cause" of the world, but this is only the case in faith's reasoning reflection on the God of revelation and faith, not for autonomous reason (381). [See Barth's use of philosophy in chap. 6.1.2.]

121. Jüngel's reference is to Hegel's early work *Faith and Reason*, 60f. Cf. further on Hegel in *God as the Mystery of the World*, 90–97, 373. See DeHart, *Beyond the Necessary*, 81–89.

122. Barth, *Church Dogmatics*, IV/1:422. Barth's point is that God is Trinitarian, has always elected the Son and in the Son humanity. Cf. *God as the Mystery of the World*, 382; Eberhard Busch, *The Great Passion*, 125.

Jüngel says, must "destroy" God as "*supra nos*" (above us) in order to think God in the way he has revealed himself in Jesus (187, 373).[123]

In the revelation in Christ, God is the acting subject, so that "God comes from God" (158). Where it is heard, the Word of God is an event that "interrupts" human life, bringing God near and drawing human life into the reality of the Word (165). Theology is thought or reason "thinking" or reflecting on this event, on "God and faith together" (158–63, 228f.). It "corresponds" to the speaking of God in God's Word (227).[124] In this event one is placed both before God and in a new relationship to oneself and reality, so that "the entire world" as one has known it becomes the "old" world. In faith one has a new relationship not only to one's present but also to the past, which is represented by the cross of Christ, and to the future, represented by his resurrection and parousia (174f.). Faith is both trust in God and "forsaking oneself," which includes forsaking one's modernist "self-grounding," the attempt to make oneself the measure of truth and to secure one's life through one's own reasoning. The word of Jesus in Mark 8:35, that whoever loses his or her life will gain it, "is a statement about certainty in God" and a promise that constitutes human being in its truth (180–82; cf. 196).

The "death of God" does not mean simply doing away with theism. Hegel rightly points theology toward a definition of God that "enables and allows the divine essence to be thought of as a being in history. For without negation [death] there is no history!" (101). What Jüngel means is that because Christ is a being in history and suffers negation, God is in history and suffers negation. All historical life is temporal, "perishable" [*vergänglich*]. In Christ God has subjected God's self to "perishability" (197). But mortality is not only a negative concept. "That which is ontologically positive about perishability is the possibility" (213), and "possibility is the capability of becoming" (215). Only in temporal life, in its being born and perishing, is there the coming to be of what is possible. The great threat of perishability is nothingness. Nothingness is "undetermined [*unbestimmt*]," it has no definition. It is the abyss into which, according to Kant's image, the question about the origin of God disappears. It "annihilates" all that exists. But in Christ's perishing it is God who assumes or takes on nothingness, and in so doing God "gives nothingness a place within being," "within the divine life." God gives the nothing a "determination [*Bestimmung*]," a definition, a role to play in God's being in and with Christ and the world (219), namely, that of producing a wholly new possibility in history.[125]

The absorption of nothingness into God's being has therefore positive meaning. The possibilities of temporal human life before Christ were limited by its sin-

---

123. The "destruction" of metaphysics is a concept of Heidegger's in *Being and Time*, 41–49.

124. See Jüngel's essay "Humanity in Correspondence to God," *Theological Essays*, 1:124–53. [See "correspondence" in Heidegger, chap. 8.4.1.]

125. God's acceptance of finitude in the death and resurrection of Christ is "an act of divine self-determination [*Selbst-Bestimmung*]." *God as the Mystery of the World*, 219. "The victory over death . . . is the transformation of death through its reception into that life which is called 'eternal life.' . . . What happens here is that turning around of death into life which is the very essence of love" (ibid., 364).

ful condition. Now, however, the role nothingness plays in the coming to be of the possible is "empowered" [*potenziert*] in a fully new way, for now the power of negation, the nothing, and therefore also the possibilities are under God's lordship (cf. 33, 219).[126] The new possibilities of Christian life are so radically new that they exceed and contradict any measure of them according to the world as it presently exists. They are no longer those of the "actual" or, as Paul says, "old" world of sinfulness.[127] Rather the Christian experiences a change of consciousness and a new freedom through the Word that has made her or him a participant in the eschatological reality of the coming future of God. The possibilities of Christian life are new, alive, and expressions of Christian freedom (309ff.; cf. 164, 374f.).[128] They are not developed out of human potential but are given as a gift of grace from outside the self by God.

Following his teachers Ernst Fuchs and Gerhard Ebeling, Jüngel names these possibilities "events" of language. They are related to Advent: they open fully new perspectives for faith's existence, and they are what make the "old" world "old." The parables of Jesus, which are narrative metaphorical analogies, are paradigmatic for these events, indicating the way all human talk of God must be formulated (289, 303). The language of faith uses words from the "actuality" of the "old" world, but it does so in the realization that these words can never directly express the new reality of faith. The newness of faith's reality and freedom, in which God comes utterly near (182), interrupts the normal course of words in order for faith to "say more than the actuality of the world is able to say." This mode of speech can only be metaphorical and narrative. Therefore all of faith's talk of God must be metaphorical, full of what is always new in time: the coming God. For Jüngel as for Karl Barth, these analogies are analogies of faith created in and through Christ (301ff.).[129] The gospel is "correspondence" to God, and the Jesus of the kerygma is himself (as Barth had also said) a "parable" or

126. See *Gott als Geheimnis der Welt,* 298, and Jüngel's essay "The World as Possibility and Actuality. The Ontology of the Doctrine of Justification," *Theological Essays,* 1:95–123, esp. 99, 107f., 112f. Cf. the late Schelling, *Werke,* 14:205: In Christ's death the evil "ground" is conquered, which means its old possibilities are annulled for faith in favor of the new, free "possibility of becoming children of God (John 1:12)." [Cf. chap. 2.4.2.]

127. As for Barth, for Jüngel sin is the power of nothingness in human life. It contradicts the being of creation, drawing it into destruction. It removes God from the "struggle between being and nonbeing" on the assumption that human being can deal with nothingness itself (*God as the Mystery of the World,* 225). [Cf. Schelling, chap. 2.4.1.]

128. Cf. "World as Possibility and Actuality," in *Theological Essays,* 1:119f., with special regard for the doctrine of justification. Cf. "The Emergence of the New," in *Theological Essays,* 2:35–38.

129. Jüngel, "Metaphorical Truth," in *Theological Essays,* 1:17; cf. 16–24, 60–65; cf. "World as Actuality and Possibility," in *Theological Essays,* 1:120f. See Zimany, *Vehicle for God,* 49–64; Joseph Palakeel, *The Use of Analogy in Theological Discourse* (Rome: Editrice Pontificia Università Gregoriana, 1995), 163–224. With this perspective of proper language about God, Jüngel opposes a historical investigation of the life of Jesus that "absolutizes its findings" and becomes a "metaphysics of salvific facts." *Paulus und Jesus,* 2, 4; see Webster, *Eberhard Jüngel,* 30. Jüngel also says theology must "speak the language of the world." Early Christianity rightly spoke the language of Greek metaphysics of its time: the problem lay in the temptation to fall under the dictatorship of metaphysics. As has been noted above, like Barth, Jüngel approves of the use of philosophy, if one does not allow it to control revelation (*God as the Mystery of the World,* 39).

"analogy" [*Gleichnis*] of God (288f.), for again what God is cannot be directly expressed in human language. But it is God who establishes the "correspondence" to God in Jesus and the Word of God. In all aspects of the gospel "God comes from God" (300f.). God's identification with Jesus in his life, cross and resurrection is "the humanity of God," the title of the last part of *God as the Mystery of the World* (299–396).

The doctrine of "God as the mystery of the world" is the doctrine of the Trinity. For Jüngel as for Karl Barth, the "immanent" Trinity of God in God's eternal being is the same as the "economic" Trinity of God's being in history, that is, in and through the person of Jesus Christ (369f.). And as for Barth (and Pannenberg), the doctrine of the Trinity can be derived only from the "self-definition" of God in Christ, particularly in his death and resurrection (343–73). Jüngel interprets the Trinity under three basic headings: "God comes from God," "God comes to God," and "God comes as God." His thought that "God comes from God" is a major point in Barth, although Barth does not state it in this way. We found this thought originally in the late Schelling [chap. 2.4.2], and Jüngel's formulations remind one of Schelling's demonstration of God as the origin of both thought and being. God is not merely the "unconditioned," which is only a negative statement; "God comes from God" is a "positive" statement. Being is not prior to God but comes from God; and if being comes from God, nothingness also must come from God. Therefore the only way to account for God at all is the formula that "God comes from God" and defines God as God.[130] The God before being is "God the Father" (381).

Jüngel's next formulation, "God comes to God" in the love of the Father for the Son, is also in continuity with Barth. "God encounters himself out of his origin in such a way that he becomes his own partner [the Son]. God is also his own goal" (382; cf. 346). "He is also the eternally begotten Son . . . the same [as the Father] yet as the goal of himself distinct from the origin of himself—'repetition of eternity in eternity.'" All things are made through him, "toward whom all things are" (383). As the Father loves the Son in eternity, so the Father also loves those who are created through the Son. This becomes known only in Christ, for in coming to him, God comes to humanity, revealing who God is (383). In the resurrection of Jesus, death is turned into life, "which is the very essence of love." Death is received "into the eternal life of God" (364).

Jüngel's third formulation is that "God comes as God." God is always God; there are no gaps, so to speak, in God's eternal life. "Even in perishing [in the death of Christ] he does not alienate himself." Death does not stop God coming

---

130. Jüngel quotes the late Schelling's distinction between "what" something is (its concept) and "that" it is (its existence). He agrees that the positive "that" has primacy before the concept or before reason. *Gott als Geheimnis der Welt*, 259f.; cf. ET, 192, where the Latin word *quod*, the "that" (*das Dass*), is mistranslated. See also Jüngel's *God as the Mystery of the World*, 101: thought cannot think beyond itself, therefore it cannot think God. This is essentially the late Schelling's critique of Hegel [chap. 2.4.2]. DeHart recognizes the late Schelling as an important influence on Jüngel, *Beyond the Necessary*, 89–92.

"from God to God." "God's being as such is in coming," so that "God is his own future" (387f.). This is visible in the death and resurrection of Christ, in which God "comes" to God as the Son in the resurrection. But in Christ the eternal love and life of Father and Son have entered history, so that for faith all of history must be understood anew, as determined by this eternal relationship. Eternity is repeated "in time" (383). In the Holy Spirit, God is both the present and the ever-new "coming" God. "This coming has been thought in its completion only when it is grasped as source, arrival and future. . . . In the unity of origin and goal, God is the one who is coming." The "bond of love" that unites Father and Son "moves those who are bound eternally toward something new." "To believe in God the Holy Spirit means to acknowledge Jesus Christ as our future" (388f.). "Perishing is taken up in becoming," in the advent of the new possibilities of God's coming kingdom.[131]

The pattern of these relationships has certain similarities to Hegel's philosophy of religion. For Hegel, the truth of history (as the history of Spirit) is the movement from the origin of the process of Spirit, the Father, to its fulfillment in the Son who is in unity with the Father yet differentiated from the Father. The unity is the process, and past, present, and future are moments of absolute Spirit. The negative of all finite human perishing is taken into the eternal "Idea" [chap. 2.3]. Jüngel acknowledges the relationship to Hegel and sees this pattern already present in Barth's doctrine of God.[132]

The affirmation of history and temporarily in Christ is the affirmation of the finite, the "limits" and "boundaries" of human life. "To be without boundaries would mean to be hopeless. Whoever wants everything all at once, and thus desires to be unlimited and boundariless, desires as one who has himself, possesses himself, and thus is a totally hopeless being. In the posture of the revolutionary Titan, he negates the mystery of God who is coming" (394). Limits and boundaries in human life are conditions given by God. Jüngel refers the reader to two of his earlier essays: "Lob der Grenze" (Praise of Limit/Boundary) and "Grenzen des Menschseins" (Limits/Boundaries of Human Being). In the first, Jüngel defines human being as the creature of God who (sinfully) exceeds the boundaries of its created being, who then sets its own boundaries and who in the exercise of a false freedom is destructive of nature.[133] The second essay discusses

---

131. The quotation is from Jüngel, *God's Being Is in Becoming*, 122; cf.103: in Christ humanity is "given a share in the being of God that asserts itself against death." As in Barth's *Church Dogmatics* and with similarity also to Bultmann's eschatology, eschatology for Jüngel is a matter of the "turning point of history" in which the end of the "old" world is announced and life in the newness of the coming God begins (301, 379).

132. Cf. ibid., xixf., 127–29, 28, where Jüngel discusses Hegelianism in Barth's doctrine of God [see chap. 6.1.2 note 28]. See also p. 28: God's being in the economic Trinity is the "repetition of God," with reference to Barth, *Church Dogmatics*, I/1:299.

133. "Lob der Grenze," Jüngel, *Entsprechungen: Gott-Wahrheit-Mensch* (Munich: Christian Kaiser, 1980), 372–77. The essay was first published in 1973. Jüngel's characterization of sin as the willing disregard of the good boundaries of human life is similar to Schelling's doctrine of the fall [chap. 2.4.1]. Cf. Schelling, *Werke*, 13:350f., and Kierkegaard [chap. 2.6].

the finitude assumed by God in Christ and the salvation of human beings as finite, definite, historical personalities.[134] In his previously published book *Death: The Riddle and the Mystery*, Jüngel also affirms human finitude. Finite human life, he says, is limited by "temporal boundaries"; it is defined and hence given limits by its relationships to other human beings and to the world around it. All these relationships are lost in death, as is one's finite, defined personal identity. In salvation through Christ, however, it is the finite, definite person who is saved and, in the future, raised from the dead, as the definite historical person of Christ was raised from the dead.[135]

For Jüngel as for Barth, theology must remain in truthful relationship to its source, the revealed Word of God. He exceeds Barth in his attention to the freedom of theology to take up the challenges presented to it by science and philosophy, and to do so for the sake of the church. Christian "enlightenment of the world" is also about enlightening the mind of the church.[136] But freedom means conflict, and theology cannot avoid it. Theologians know they bear responsibility for the future, and they have different perceptions about what needs to be said and done in the crises and needs of time. "Right theology is always conflicted theology."[137] "Each theologian is personally grasped by the truth to which he or she must respond. . . . In this respect theology always also bears the individual characteristics of a life story. . . . If the truth is at all experienced as liberation, as John 8:32 promises, then one's own unique experience co-determines the whole of the theological enterprise."[138] Jüngel does not mean to open theology to subjectivism. He rather means that faith's unity with its object in the love of the Holy Spirit (318–30, 374f.) has this personal dimension.

134. Jüngel, "Grenzen des Menschseins," in Hans Walter Wolff, ed., *Probleme biblischer Theologie* (Munich: Christian Kaiser, 1971), 199–203.

135. Jüngel, *Death: The Riddle and the Mystery*, trans. Iain and Ute Nicol (Philadelphia: Westminster, 1974), esp. 115–20. Cf. Schelling: God brings the truth into "the most finite [*endlichste*] form" in Christ and Christianity [chap. 2.4.2]. In another essay Jüngel quotes the late Schelling: human life after death is the "essence" of the "whole person" in its definite conditionedness (Schelling, *Werke*, 14:207f.). Jüngel, *Entsprechungen*, 342. [Cf. Tillich, chap. 7.1 note 12.] See also Webster, *Eberhard Jüngel*, 86–91, and Jüngel's essay, "Even the Beautiful Must Die," *Theological Essays*, 2:59–81.

136. Schelling speaks of the need of the laity for enlightenment by means of a theological interpretation of the science and philosophy of the time. Theology should show the "possibility" of what faith believes (*Werke*, 10:405).

137. "Die Freiheit der Theologie," from the year 1967, in *Entsprechungen*, 24; cf. 11–36.

138. From the essay "My Theology," in *Theological Essays*, 2:3.

Index of Names

Althaus, Paul, 20n71, 190
Anselm, 90n228, 181–82, 186–87, 266n89
Aquinas, Thomas. *See* Thomas Aquinas
Aristotle, 43, 44n34, 59n95, 65n114,
219n191
Augustine/Augustinian tradition, 63n109,
66n121, 80n183, 104, 136, 177, 186n58,
187, 193n84, 197n100, 212n167, 229, 269

Bach, Johann Sebastian, 152
Balthasar, Hans Urs von, 175n13
Barth, Karl, vii, 11n38, 20, 22, 90n228, 155,
168, 172–87, 188–97, 203n130, 207,
208n155, 209, 211, 213n169, 215n178,
216, 217n185, 220, 222, 225n13, 227n20,
234, 238, 249, 252–53, 256n40, 258,
265–67, 272–73, 275–78
Baur, Ferdinand Christian, 11, 73n148, 103,
107n26, 115, 118–22, 126, 129n34,
201n118
Beck, Johann Tobias, 11, 173, 187n59
Bethge, Eberhard, 215, 220
Bismarck, Otto von, 5, 13–14, 16, 123,
130n40
Bloch, Ernst, 77n175, 241, 247, 256, 257n42
Blumhardt, Christoph, 11n37, 173
Blumhardt, Johann Christoph, 11n37, 173
Bonaventura, 65–66n118
Bonhoeffer, Dietrich, viii, 19n65, 23,
206n145, 207–20, 238, 243, 258n48, 265,
268, 270, 272
Bousset, Wilhelm, 16n55, 18n64, 141n77
Bowne, Bordon Parker, 18, 236
Brown, William Adams, 18
Brunner, Emil, 188–95, 197, 204–05, 217,
228–29, 232, 267n92
Buber, Martin, 172n1, 190n71, 265
Bultmann, Rudolf, 133n51, 194n89, 196–204,
205–06, 211, 212n165, 220, 222, 246, 249,
265, 277n131
Buri, Fritz, 155–57, 203
Burkhardt, Jakob, 6n12

Bushnell, Horace, 98

Calvin, John, 192n77, 247n14
Chamberlain, Houston Stewart, 15
Clement of Alexandria, 166–67
Cohen, Hermann, 131–32
Coleridge, Samuel Taylor, 96–98
Cone, James H., 238

Descartes, René, 260–61, 272
de Wette, Martin Leberecht, 8, 94–96, 104n7,
105, 146–47
DeWolf, L. Harold, 236
Dilthey, Wilhelm, 141
Dorner, Isaak August, 67n127, 70n137,
102n3, 111–15, 186–87, 223n10, 227n20,
273n120
Dostoyevsky, Fyodor, 171

Ebeling, Gerhard, 204–06, 239, 246, 259,
262, 267n96
Emerson, Ralph Waldo, 18, 96–99, 150n118

Feuerbach, Ludwig, 70, 72, 74–75, 106, 122,
177n20, 219
Fichte, Johann Gottlieb, 40–46, 51n56,
75n162, 157, 210, 257n44
Francke, A. H., 4n5
Frederick the Great (King of Prussia), 3n3
Frederick Wilhelm III, King, 5
Freud, Sigmund, 15
Fries, Jacob Friedrich, 94–96, 97, 105, 144,
146–47, 150, 157
Fuchs, Ernst, 271, 275

Gadamer, Hans-Georg, 206n143
Gandhi, Mahatma, 237
Goethe, Johann Wolfgang von, 2, 81
Gogarten, Friedrich, 21–22, 173n4, 190,
196n98
Gunkel, Hermann, 141n77
Gutierrez, Gustavo, 238

Index of Subjects

"God" is not listed as an independent subject heading, insofar as the word regularly occurs throughout this work.

German terms: *allgemein* (see universal), *Abgrund* (see abyss), *Ahnung* (see presentiment), *Anschauung* (see intuition), *Aufhebung* (see lift), *Begriff* (see concept), *Geist* (see spirit), *Gemeinschaft* and *Gesellschaft* (see community), *Historie* and *Geschichte* (see history), *Idea* and *Idee* (see Idea and idea), *Vorstellung* (see representation), *Wissenschaft* (see science).

the Absolute, absolute, 40, 43, 45, 49, 52–60, 72, 89n225, 95, 104, 108, 142–43, 145, 151, 178, 193n82, 273. *See also* infinite; unconditioned

abstraction, abstract, 61, 63–64, 75, 77, 124, 154, 167, 174n8, 184, 227

abyss (*Abgrund*), 30–31, 40, 54n68, 216, 223–24, 273–74

academic freedom, 3

alienation, estrangement, 53–60, 76, 89, 174, 223–24, 226–27, 245

analogy, parable, 68, 92, 107–08, 143n84, 148, 178–84, 185, 211n163, 223, 234, 248, 275–76

anonymous (unconscious) Christianity, Christianity outside the church, 110, 145n92, 186n55, 220, 226n19, 268–71

anti-Semitism, 15–16, 20–22

anxiety, 62, 78n178, 79, 82n197, 182, 198, 223–24, 230–31, 259, 272

a priori, a posteriori, 29, 30
   religious apriori, 143, 147

art, 38, 50, 74, 86, 87n219, 219, 228

Awakening, 2, 9–11, 101, 103, 131, 161, 173

Barmen Declaration, 22, 192

biblical realists, 11, 173

bounds, boundary, limit, 30–37, 40–44, 45–46, 47–48, 49, 66, 67n124, 79–80, 81, 85, 94, 104, 109, 132, 151, 156, 157–58, 168, 175–76, 181, 200, 210, 211–12, 213, 219, 230, 258–59, 266n88, 277–78

certainty, 36, 38 93, 96, 106, 107, 112–14, 130, 136, 182, 243, 272, 274

Christ, Jesus, 35–36, 46, 48, 49–50, 54–56, 58, 63, 65–68, 71–73, 83, 88–93, 96, 97, 107–09, 114–15, 116–17, 120–21, 128–29, 136, 138, 140, 143–44, 148, 152–54, 162, 164–65, 180–86, 188, 199, 202–04, 208–09, 212–14, 214–18, 220, 224, 225n17, 226, 231–32, 234–35, 237, 243–46, 248–51, 255

Sermon on the Mount, 58, 73, 121, 152–53, 174n8, 214, 217

Son of God, 36, 49, 54, 121, 148, 255

"Those who lose their life . . . will find it" (Matt. 10:39 par.), 64, 197n102, 201, 232, 274

church, 35–36, 48, 50, 65, 68, 71–72, 79, 83, 87–90, 93, 97–98, 103, 109–11, 112, 121–22, 134, 138–39, 144–46, 156, 165, 166–67, 175, 181, 185, 191, 194–95, 207–09, 214–216, 219–20, 233, 238, 244–45, 248, 250–51

American, 193n90

church triumphant, 83, 244–45

Confessing Church, 22–23, 192, 196, 206, 207, 215

established church, 10n35, 208–09, 215

Lutheran, 4, 6, 88

Reformed, 4, 7, 88

Roman Catholic, 4, 12, 23, 25

sociological types, 144

Switzerland, 4

"throne and altar," 5, 13

282